Foreign Policy Issues for America

As America's first president never to have served in government or the military, Donald Trump entered the White House with an unformed foreign policy position. Yet he was confronted by a wide range of developing issues; the rise of China, Russian-United States relations, the resurgence of nationalism in Europe, U.S. Foreign Policy in Latin America, environmental challenges, terrorism, security challenges of failing states, cyber security threats, and challenges in international political economy.

This volume focuses on these sensitive foreign policy issues that determine the prospects for American decline or continued hegemony. Contributions are divided into 'regional' and 'functional' issues, exploring the nature and significance of the challenge, the previous response, and President Trump's policies and their consequences.

Topics have been selected to address political, military, economic, and social factors in global politics and the book will appeal to undergraduates and scholars of U.S. foreign policy at all levels.

Richard W. Mansbach is Professor of Political Science, Iowa State University.

James M. McCormick is Professor of Political Science, Iowa State University.

W0006920

Routledge Studies in US Foreign Policy

Edited by Inderjeet Parmar, *City University*, and John Dumbrell, *University of Durham*

This new series sets out to publish high-quality works by leading and emerging scholars critically engaging with United States Foreign Policy. The series welcomes a variety of approaches to the subject and draws on scholarship from international relations, security studies, international political economy, foreign policy analysis and contemporary international history.

Subjects covered include the role of administrations and institutions, the media, think tanks, ideologues and intellectuals, elites, transnational corporations, public opinion, and pressure groups in shaping foreign policy, US relations with individual nations, with global regions and global institutions and America's evolving strategic and military policies.

The series aims to provide a range of books – from individual research monographs and edited collections to textbooks and supplemental reading for scholars, researchers, policy analysts and students.

Eleanor Roosevelt
Palestine, Israel and Human Rights
Geraldine Kidd

US Foreign Policy in the Middle East
From American Missionaries to the Islamic State
Edited by Geoffrey Gresh and Tugrul Keskin

The United States, India and the Global Nuclear Order
Narrative Identity and Representation
Tanvi Pate

India-America Relations (1942–62)
Rooted in the Liberal International Order
Atul Bhardwaj

Ideologies of American Foreign Policy
John Callaghan, Brendon O'Connor and Mark Phythian

Alliance Decision-Making in the South China Sea
Between Allied and Alone
Joseph A. Gagliano

Foreign Policy Issues for America
The Trump Years
Edited by Richard W. Mansbach and James M. McCormick

For more information about this series, please visit: www.routledge.com/series/RSUSFP

Foreign Policy Issues for America
The Trump Years

Edited by
Richard W. Mansbach and
James M. McCormick

Routledge
Taylor & Francis Group

LONDON AND NEW YORK

First published 2019
by Routledge
2 Park Square, Milton Park, Abingdon, Oxon OX14 4RN

and by Routledge
52 Vanderbilt Avenue, New York, NY 10017

Routledge is an imprint of the Taylor & Francis Group, an informa business

British Library Cataloguing-in-Publication Data
A catalogue record for this book is available from the British Library

Library of Congress Cataloging-in-Publication Data
Names: Mansbach, Richard W., 1943– editor. | McCormick, James M., editor.
Title: Foreign policy issues for America : the Trump years / edited by Richard W. Mansbach and James M. McCormick.
Description: Abingdon, Oxon ; New York, NY : Routledge, 2019. | Series: Routledge studies in US foreign policy | Includes bibliographical references and index.
Identifiers: LCCN 2018054219 | ISBN 9780815394020 (hbk) |
    ISBN 9780815394037 (pbk) | ISBN 9781351186872 (ebk)
Subjects: LCSH: United States—Foreign relations—2017– | National security—United States. | Trump, Donald, 1946– | World politics—21st century.
Classification: LCC JZ1480 .F66 2019 | DDC 327.73—dc23
LC record available at https://lccn.loc.gov/2018054219

ISBN: 978-0-8153-9402-0 (hbk)
ISBN: 978-0-8153-9403-7 (pbk)
ISBN: 978-1-351-18687-2 (ebk)

Typeset in Galliard and Frutiger
by Apex CoVantage, LLC

Contents

List of figures and tables

Contributors

Editors

Richard W. Mansbach is a former Marshall Scholar and three-time Fulbright Scholar. He has authored, co-authored, or edited seventeen books and numerous articles and book chapters largely concerning theory in global politics. His scholarship focuses on the critical role of history and norms in understanding change and continuity in global politics and in the movement from pre-international to international and, ultimately, post-international politics in a globalizing world. Among his books, several are routinely used in major graduate programs, notably, *The Web of World Politics, In Search of Theory: Toward a New Paradigm for Global Politics, The Elusive Quest: Theory and International Politics, Polities: Authority, Identities, and Change, The Elusive Quest Continues: Theory and Global Politics*, and *Remapping Global Politics, Globalization: The Return of Borders to a Borderless World?*

James M. McCormick is Professor and Chair of the Department of Political Science at Iowa State University. He has held positions at the University of New Mexico, Ohio University, the University of Toledo, and Texas A&M University. He received his B.A. from Aquinas College and his M.A. and Ph.D. from Michigan State University. The author or editor of ten books, Dr. McCormick has published more than sixty book chapters and articles. He received the Iowa State University Foundation Award for Outstanding Research at Mid-Career in 1990, a Fulbright Senior Scholar Award to New Zealand in 1993, the Fulbright-SyCip Distinguished Lecturer Award to the Philippines in 2003, Iowa State's College of Liberal Arts and Sciences Award for Excellence in Departmental Leadership in 2004, the 2010 Iowa State University Foundation International Service Award, and the 2011 Quincy Wright Distinguished Scholar Award by the International Studies Association, Midwest. In addition, he has lectured widely on American foreign policy and international politics.

Contributors

David Carment is Professor of International Affairs, Norman Paterson School of International Affairs, Carleton University.

Yale H. Ferguson is Professor Emeritus, of Political Science, Rutgers University-Newark.

Scott Feinstein is Assistant Professor of Political Science, Iowa State University.

Mark Haichin is a Ph.D. student in the Norman Paterson School of International Affairs, Carleton University.

Jonathan Hassid is Associate Professor of Political Science, Iowa State University.

Ignacio Mamone is a Ph.D. student at the University of Pittsburgh.

Mark D. Nieman is Assistant Professor of Political Science, Iowa State University.

Lana Obradovic is Assistant Professor of Political Science at the University of Nebraska-Omaha.

Ellen B. Pirro is Senior Lecturer of Political Science, Iowa State University.

Yiagadeesen Samy is Professor of International Affairs and Director of the Norman Paterson School of International Affairs, Carleton University.

Steffen W. Schmidt is the Endowed Lucken Professor of Political Science, Iowa State University.

Amy Erica Smith is Associate Professor of Political Science, Iowa State University.

Kirsten L. Taylor is Professor of Government and International Studies, Berry College.

Bethany Vailliant is Instructor of Political Science at the University of Nebraska-Omaha.

Yu Wang is Assistant Professor of Political Science, Iowa State University.

Part I

Introduction

1 America's decline, President Donald Trump, and the global liberal order

Yale H. Ferguson and Richard W. Mansbach

INTRODUCTION

Recent years have witnessed disorder in global politics that raise questions about the direction and durability of the global liberal order that emerged after World War II. That order, based on norms of economic, social, and political interdependence, and on multilateral cooperation to meet global challenges, has its roots in the nineteenth century, when the United Kingdom (UK) acted as a global leader, fostering ideas such as free trade, the abolition of the slave trade, and political democracy across its empire and the world as a whole.

That era ended suddenly with World War I and the erosion of British power. Ensuing decades witnessed the growth of U.S. power, but, owing to U.S. isolationism, the impact of that development was not recognized until America's entry in World War II. The Great Depression fostered economic unilateralism as the great powers sought to improve their economies at one another's expense by resorting to "beggar-thy-neighbor" policies of protectionism and unilateral currency devaluations.

As World War II ended, America by then a superpower, took the lead in sponsoring international institutions to meet global challenges based on norms of cooperation – the Bretton Woods economic institutions (the International Monetary Fund, the World Bank, the General Agreement on Tariffs and Trade), the United Nations, the North Atlantic Treaty Organization, and other regional alliances. Such institutions proved pillars of globalization, facilitating the free movement of people, things, and ideas, and later a declining preoccupation with territory as information and communication technologies overcame geography and social media fostered cosmopolitan links among people worldwide. Globalization also spread liberal norms and rules such as democracy, human rights, and free trade, and America assumed responsibility for enforcing the norms of the liberal order.

Thus, much of the world came to regard the United States as a benevolent hegemon – that is, a global leader whose followers consented to that leadership because it benefitted them. After the onset of the Cold War, Washington adopted policies including the Marshall Plan for reconstructing Europe, support for European economic and political integration, and a willingness to accept a strong dollar, which reduced U.S. exports and increased its imports from allies in return for their willingness to accept Washington's leadership.

Some theorists believe that a hegemon like the UK during the nineteenth century and the U.S. during the twentieth is necessary to maintain a global liberal order. They point to

America's "decline" as a factor in growing global disorder, and describe cyclical conflicts called hegemonic wars that erupt when a hegemon is threatened by a challenger. Thus, they argue that World War I was caused by Germany's challenge to British hegemony and that the Cold War reflected a Soviet challenge to U.S. hegemony.

A resurgence of nationalist geopolitical concerns such as Russia's aggression in Ukraine, development of cyber-weapons, Chinese territorial claims, the proliferation of weapons of mass destruction (WMD), and the spread of fragile states in the developing world augur a return to a world of geopolitical national interests, Such a world, hegemonic theorists contend, raise questions about the durability of the global liberal order, which they see as resulting from America's decline. That decline, however, is *relative*, not absolute; it is not the result of reduced U.S. capabilities, but instead reflects the growing capabilities of others, especially China. Nevertheless, even a relative decline makes it difficult for Washington to control events, and hegemonic theorists predict that America's decline will undermine the practices, norms, and institutions of the liberal order in much the same way as the UK's decline destabilized the earlier liberal order.

The debate about hegemonic stability and decline is significant, not least because the liberal order encompasses the spread of democracy, deepening of political and economic interdependence, and global governance by international organizations – that liberals believe foster a peaceful and cooperative world. By contrast, an illiberal order would foster nationalism, ethnic and sectarian conflict, and preoccupation with geopolitical factors that are associated with interstate war, identity conflicts, and barriers to globalization. Globalization, argue liberals, is rendering national boundaries and national identities less important, while the reassertion of narrow national interests entails preoccupation with borders and territory at the expense of cooperation.

If America is indeed declining and hegemonic stability theory is correct, in time, there will be an absence of a single powerful but presumably benign actor able to shape global institutions and enforce the rules and norms necessary for cooperation. Even worse, President Trump's policies have accelerated the decline of the liberal order even while it grows relatively weaker and it surrenders global leadership to its illiberal hegemonic rival China. China would not protect the liberal order, or at a minimum would alter it to its advantage.

Today, as the second-largest world economy and soon the world's largest foreign investor, China is an economic superpower, a fact reflected by its ambitious plan to invest in projects across Europe, Central Asia, and Africa, and encourage trade and finance. In 2017, the U.S. economy accounted for 24 percent of the global economy, while China accounted for almost 15 percent. Between 1989 and 2016, China's economy grew by an annual average of nearly 10 percent. China's economy has been an engine for export-based growth, and Beijing seeks to transform the renminbi into a global reserve currency like the U.S. dollar. The formal opening of the Asian Infrastructure Investment Bank that Beijing founded as a rival to the World Bank also increased China's economic visibility.

China has also passed the U.S. in annual patent applications; its scientists rank second in peer-reviewed research articles, and it plans to become globally competitive by 2025 in ten advanced manufacturing sectors dominated by America including commercial aircraft, robotics, 5G mobile phone communications and computer microchips. Thus, China is becoming a science and technological superpower.

China's economic growth, however, faces challenges. After years of easy credit, China has a heavy debt burden incurred by businesses and local governments. Its state-owned corporations are experiencing strains in making a transition to market discipline, and economic inequality has grown. Thus, America will continue to have a larger economy in term of total gross domestic product (GDP) than China for several decades, and even then, Americans will be far richer as measured by per capita GDP.

Growing wealth enables China's military modernization, and its defense spending has risen rapidly. It boasts top-of-the-line military aircraft, a ballistic missile and nuclear force, anti-satellite capabilities, and sophisticated cyberwar capabilities. Such capabilities allow Beijing to pursue claims to sovereignty over virtually all the Spratly and Paracel Islands in the South China Sea and their adjacent waters, and the Senkaku Islands in the Sea of Japan. Beijing's policies have increased its presence around the world and have made it an Asian superpower. Its territorial claims are of great concern to its neighbors, and it is acquiring naval facilities around the world (see Chapter 4). Thus, Beijing opened its first overseas naval base in Djibouti, next to a U.S. naval base in the Horn of Africa, affording it access to the Middle East, and a Chinese company won a bid to operate the Port of Darwin in Australia under a 99-year lease, also near a U.S. naval facility. China ranks second behind America in defense spending and is rapidly modernizing its armed forces, but America's military budget of $716 billion remains far larger than China's and exceeds the *combined* total of the eight next largest military budgets (including China's) and will grow dramatically under Trump. *Thus, America remains by far the world's leading military power.*

Indeed, China scholar David Shambaugh (2013: 6–10)[1] describes China as a "partial power." He argues that Beijing's global influence is largely economic and that militarily, China is not (yet) able to "project power" beyond Asia. China also lacks "soft power" – the ability to attract others – because its statist development model and its positions on human rights and territorial issues make China more likely to be feared than admired. "China is a lonely power, lacking close friends and possessing no allies." However, Shambaugh acknowledges that poll data suggest that there is a widespread *perception* among "global publics" that China either *already* has or will eventually replace the U.S. "as the world's leading power."

Although the belief that China is supplanting the U.S. is widespread, in absolute terms America remains the world's only superpower. However, as Joseph Nye (2015: 14) points out, if leaders *perceive a decline* they may act in ways that produce it.[2] This was the case during the Obama years, but the Trump administration recognizes that America is confronting challengers to its hegemonic status. America's National Security Strategy released in late 2017 by the administration declares that "after being dismissed as a phenomenon of an earlier century, great power competition returned," and "China and Russia began to reassert their influence regionally and globally" (White House, 2017: 27).[3] As we shall see, however, Trump has actually surrendered U.S. leadership in several respects.

AMERICA'S PERCEIVED DECLINE: THE OBAMA YEARS

Following the Cold War, America was an unchallenged hegemon in the global system. The proliferation of nongovernmental and interstate groups advocating solutions to collective problems like global warming had fostered global civil society and enhanced prospects of global governance.

With U.S. encouragement, democracy made advances in the countries of the former Soviet bloc and the developing world. Global concern for democracy and human rights spread, and even authoritarian regimes pay lip service to these rights. This led optimists to conclude that Washington's chief foes were not "just up against the United States; they would also have to contend with the most globally organized and deeply entrenched order the world has ever seen, one that is dominated by states that are liberal, capitalist, and democratic" (Ikenberry, 2014: 89)[4] It appeared that the liberal global order had triumphed.

The Clinton administration's policies had reflected a confident hegemon – the enlargement of the North Atlantic Treaty Organization (NATO), the billions spent to save the democratic experiment in Russia, and the efforts to contain countries that threatened the global order including North Korea, Serbia, Iran, and Iraq. George W. Bush's invasion of Iraq in 2003, however, although an effort to spread democratic values, ended in disaster and contributed to President Obama's later reluctance to lead "from in front." Obama's perception of America's decline reflected an overreaction to Bush's neo-conservative triumphalism and militant unilateralism.

The Obama administration adopted a cautious foreign policy, preferring negotiations and multilateralism, and deferring to allies as though the world were *already* multipolar. When President Obama accepted a Nobel Peace Prize early in his first term, he admitted that war is sometimes necessary but should be a "just war," and was an example of "human folly." This would be the dilemma Obama would face repeatedly in subsequent years that became manifest in Europe, East Asia, and the Middle East, where countries questioned U.S. commitments and so posed threats to the post-Cold War order.

The Obama presidency coincided with the global financial crisis, and escalating partisanship in domestic politics that produced legislative deadlock. It was Obama's misfortune that he was simultaneously confronted by multiple geopolitical challenges that made a coherent strategy virtually impossible to design. Obama had to face a world that seemed to be "falling apart." His foreign challenges were among the most complex since the end of the Cold War – the European Union (EU) in disarray, turmoil in the Middle East, Iranian and North Korean efforts to become nuclear powers, China's saber-rattling in the South and East China Seas, Russia's aggression in Ukraine and its annexation of Crimea, and so on.

In a speech at West Point in 2014, President Obama declared, "Since world war two, some of our most costly mistakes came not from our restraint, but from our willingness to rush into military adventures without thinking through the consequences" (cited in *The Economist*, 2014: 23).[5] "I would betray my duty to you, and to the country we love, if I sent you into harm's way . . . because I was worried about critics who think military intervention is the only way for America to avoid looking weak" (cited in Baker, 2014).[6]

President Obama had assumed office committed to ending the "bad" war in Iraq and pacifying Afghanistan in a "good" war. He withdrew U.S. forces from Iraq in 2011 and planned to do the same in Afghanistan. In neither case did Washington achieve its objectives. U.S. forces returned to Iraq after the Islamic State (IS) occupied territory there and in Syria, yet Iraq remains the victim of sectarian violence with little to show for over a decade of U.S. intervention. Afghanistan remains threatened by a Taliban-led insurrection financed by heroin production against a government installed by Washington. Neither the War on Terror nor the invasions of Afghanistan and Iraq were part of a coherent global strategy.

Having removed most U.S. forces from Europe and cut back plans for European missile defense, the Obama administration was unprepared to respond to Russia's annexation of Crimea and heavy-handed "hybrid war" in Eastern Ukraine. The sanctions imposed by Washington and the EU and U.S. reluctance to provide Ukraine with arms were insufficient to prevent Russian "volunteers" from aiding pro-Russian Ukrainians seeking to "federal-ize" the country or secede from it. Nor did the administration react vigorously in Russia's covert intervention in America's 2016 election.

The death of Osama bin Laden was President Obama's most memorable foreign-policy triumph. Otherwise, in the Middle East, the administration's policies were largely irreso-lute. President Obama's thoughtful speech in Cairo in 2009, in which he promised "a new beginning" in U.S. relations with Islam and the Arab world and support for democracy in the Middle East more generally, encouraged those in the region who sought democracy. In 2011, the "Arab Spring" erupted across the Middle East but ended in civil wars in Syria, Iraq, Libya, and Yemen.

In Libya, the administration reluctantly contributed airpower to assist America's Euro-pean NATO allies ("leading from behind" in the words of a White House official) in protecting civilians from Muammar al-Qaddafi but did nothing to stabilize Libya after Qaddafi's overthrow when the country was convulsed by violence.

In Syria, rebels sought to overthrow President Bashar al-Assad. Having threatened to use force if Assad employed chemical weapons, Obama backed off in return for a deal brokered by Russia for destroying Syria's remaining chemical weapons. Critics argued that Obama's failure to carry out his threat undermined the credibility of U.S. commitments around the world. The administration also failed to counter large-scale Russian interven-tion in support of Assad. By the time Obama left office, Assad was in the driver's seat, aided by Russia and Iran, and without fear of U.S. intervention.

In Egypt, Washington supported an elected Islamic government of the Muslim Broth-erhood in the name of democracy after the overthrow of the long-term authoritarian but pro-American President Hosni Mubarak. However, the Obama administration said little about his successor's anti-democratic policies and even less after that government was over-thrown in a military coup led by General Abdel Fattah el-Sisi, whose government paid no attention to U.S. protests about its repressive policies. Washington's initial support for an Islamic government in Egypt incensed long-term regional allies Saudi Arabia and Turkey.

In addition, the Islamic State, originally an Iraqi terrorist group, which thrived after Obama ended the U.S. military presence in that country, seized large areas in Syria and Iraq. Although the U.S. used airpower to impede IS's advance, it refused to commit signifi-cant numbers of troops even though an internal Central Intelligence Agency (CIA) study found that aid to insurgents usually failed without the presence of American advisers on the ground. Only after IS had occupied large areas of Iraq and Syria and declared a territorial caliphate did Washington agree to help train additional anti-Assad rebels.

Elsewhere in the region, relations between Israel and the U.S. had been close during the Bush presidency but soured after Obama took office and urged Israel to stop building set-tlements in the occupied territories and show flexibility in negotiating the establishment of a Palestinian state (a two-state solution). (Former Senator George Mitchell, special Middle East envoy during the first Obama term, initiated a series of "proximity talks," separately with the Israelis and Palestinians without success.) A new round of peace negotiations begun by Secretary of State John Kerry yielded little. Obama also repeatedly clashed with Israel's prime minister, and shortly before Obama's presidency ended the U.S. abstained for the first time in a UN vote condemning Israel's continued expansion of settlements in the occupied territories.

Obama's willingness to negotiate and reach a deal with Iran in 2015 over Tehran's nuclear arms program fueled Sunni Arab and Israeli suspicion of U.S. motives. Partisan divisions in Washington over the deal climaxed in a Republican invitation to Israeli Prime Minister Benjamin Netanyahu to address Congress where he denounced the agreement. These events reflected disarray and political gridlock in Washington. Obama defended the agreement with Iran as the best that could be had short of war.

Obama's policy of restraint was reasoned and thoughtful, but led critics to question whether it risked surrendering U.S. leadership in a dangerous world. Critics noted Obama's perceived erosion of U.S. hegemony. Notwithstanding America's immense military and economic capabilities, Obama's perception of U.S. decline may have begun producing it and his caution may have tempted Russia and China to probe further to learn how far they could go. His administration retreated from America's role as the world's policeman and lacked a grand strategy like "containment" during the Cold War. For example, the Obama administration sought a "reset" with Russia that would improve bilateral relations. However, the reset proved illusory owing to numerous differences over ranging from the placement of missiles in Eastern Europe and support for democratization in Russia itself to Russian aggression in Georgia and Ukraine, its support for Syrian President Bashar al-Assad, and its deployment of cruise missiles that violated the Intermediate Nuclear Forces treaty. Obama's "Asian pivot" was a response to China's vast maritime territorial claims and consisted of a modest military buildup, reassuring allies and reasserting freedom of navigation in international waters by sending naval vessels through areas claimed by China. Thus, the Obama administration sought both to engage China, in issues such as trade and the environment, while containing Beijing in China's effort to expand territorially. The result was an unclear mix of policies.

In sum, for the liberal global order the U.S. remains the "indispensable nation" and an "indispensable nation" cannot lead "from behind." Whatever the overload of domestic and foreign problems – and despite important initiatives and progress, particularly in health-care, financial reform, and trade – the Obama administration's foreign policy leadership in the geopolitical sphere was generally weak and indecisive. America was punching well below its weight, and Trump's call to "make America great again" echoed the perception that the U.S. was in decline but that reversing it meant pursuing unilateral and national populist policies.

"MAKE AMERICA GREAT" AND AMERICA'S RETREAT FROM HEGEMONY

President Trump is a national populist who assumed office determined to reverse Obama's legacy. Populist ideology argues that elites do not represent the "real people," and traces its roots to President Andrew Jackson and, more recently, fascist demagogues like Benito Mussolini. Thus, Trump's initial reaction to violence in Charlottesville, Virginia in August 2017 equated the actions of self-professed neo-Nazis, members of the Ku Klux Klan, and other white supremacists, whom he described as "very fine people," with those demonstrating against them.

Populists like Trump's former adviser Stephen Bannon are inclined to racism, misogyny, militant ignorance, anti-environmentalism, guns, xenophobic nationalism, and isolationism. Speaking before Marine Le Pen's National Front, he declared, "Let them call you racists. Let them call you xenophobes. Let them call you nativists. Wear it as a badge of honor" (cited in Nossiter, 2018).[7] While claiming to represent the "real people," populists undermine their claim by advocating illiberal plebiscitary democracy and denunciation of institutions like courts, legislatures, government bureaucracies and the media. Even when winning elections by the narrowest of margins or in Trump's case without a popular majority, populists claim a "mandate" and run roughshod over any opposition.

To some extent, the liberal order itself is partly responsible for its erosion and the rise of populist nationalism (Inglehart, 2018).[8] Factors including slow economic growth after the Great Recession, income gaps between educated skilled workers and less educated and unskilled workers employed in manufacturing, outsourcing of jobs overseas by U.S. corporations, and migration of undocumented aliens from Mexico fueled a populist backlash in America against the liberal order.

Trump's core supporters, including "rust belt" labor who believed they were victims of unfair trade, felt ignored by elites and found their solution in an authoritarian nativist who cared little about what establishment elites thought about him. Populism reflects the politics of anger and involves a belief that foreign and domestic elites harm Americans and that Trump represents ordinary people against institutions such as the media and the courts. He also signed a tax bill that rewarded corporations and billionaires rather than his own less prosperous supporters. Indeed, many of the most ardent populist politicians, including Donald Trump, are themselves "elite" by any objective standard – wealth, education, or status.

Populists favor strengthening national borders and unilateral policies that emphasize national competition, territorial aspirations, national boundaries, and the exclusion of "outsiders." They applaud "sovereignty," a word Trump used repeatedly in a speech to the UN. Oddly, he ignored Russia's annexation of Crimea, which is among the most flagrant recent violations of sovereignty. Nationalist policies driven by unilateralism are eroding international organizations, alliances, and norms central to the liberal order involving Enlightenment belief in progress, free markets, democracy, free movement of people, and human rights. Trump's rhetoric has criticized all of these as "political correctness." For Trump, criticism from any quarter is unacceptable, conspiracy theories abound, and unflattering facts are dismissed as "false news."

Of the two candidates in the 2016 presidential election Hillary Clinton's perspectives were better known than Trump's. Having served as Secretary of State, her ideas were on the public record. Her stated objectives included pushing back against Russian President Vladimir Putin's provocations in Europe, defeating IS, enhancing relations with Israel, retaining the Iranian nuclear deal, terminating China's cyberespionage, and resisting Beijing's maritime territorial claims while cooperating with Beijing where interests overlapped – climate change and denuclearizing Korea.

Candidate Trump had no foreign-policy experience or knowledge and no consistent ideology or foreign-policy positions. Those he appointed as advisers and cabinet members have a more significant role than usual owing to the candidate's inexperience in policymaking. During the campaign, Trump voiced controversial views that run counter to U.S. support for a liberal global order. Rather than supporting internationalism and multilateralism, he emphasized isolationist and unilateralist themes (e.g., "America First") and major increases in military expenditures. Instead of supporting economic interdependence and globalization, the new president criticized multinational institutions and treaties. Rather than economic engagement with China, Europe, and Latin America, Trump was prepared to start trade wars with China and Europe and advocated policies that stressed economic self-sufficiency. Such policies threatened international economic institutions of globalization like the World Trade Organization (WTO).

Trump's populism involves rejecting the liberal order's emphasis on the unfettered movement of people and seeks to reduce illegal and legal immigration. He threatened to deport undocumented aliens, and in racist terms questioned admitting immigrants from Haiti or Africa, blind to the economic role that young migrants play for an aging population that requires taxes to pay for medical and social costs. His administration rejected a Department of Health and Human Services' study that showed how refugees provided billions of dollars more in government revenue than they cost (Davis and Gupta, 2017).[9] In December 2017, Washington withdrew from UN talks about a Global Pact on Migration, claiming it would violate U.S. sovereignty. Liberal immigration had been a source of America's soft power. "The fact that people want to come to the U.S.," writes Nye, "enhances its appeal . . . America is a magnet" (Nye, 2011: 191).[10]

Trump's nationalism also implies a rejection of multilateral efforts to solve collective dilemmas. Thus, he dismissed scientific evidence about climate change, expressing skepticism that global warming is man-made despite a report by thirteen U.S. government agencies to the contrary. He continued promoting the use of carbon-producing coal and withdrew from the Paris Climate Accord even though the 2017 defense authorization bill referred to climate change as a national security threat. After Syria endorsed the Paris Accord in November 2017, America remained alone in opposing it, allowing China's President Xi Jinping to claim leadership of global environmental reform.

President Trump terminated efforts to spread democracy or human rights and proposed slashing the budget for the National Endowment for Democracy. He criticized civil rights at home, spoke approvingly of torturing terrorism suspects, and froze funds to stabilize postwar Syria. He also expressed admiration for "strong" authoritarians like Putin, and he praised dictators including Turkey's Recep Tayyip Erdoğan, the Philippines Rodrigo Duterte, Egypt's President Sisi, and even North Korea's leader Kim Jong-un, whom he said he would be "honored" to meet. He praised China's President Xi for changing rules that limited his term in office and has encouraged other populist politicians. All of these actions eroded the liberal order.

Trump railed against Hispanic immigrants, pardoned the anti-Hispanic former Arizona sheriff Joe Arpaio, and sought to build a wall on the Mexican border for which Mexico would have to pay. He demonized Islam and sought to impose a travel ban on Muslims, praised the UK's decision to leave the EU ("Brexit"), questioned the relevance of NATO and America's traditional alliances, publicly insulted friendly leaders, and imposed tariffs on U.S. allies, all of which undermined the liberal order and U.S. hegemony. These were elements of a strident populism and rejection of globalization, and reflected impetuosity, bullying and racism.

The president discovered quickly, however, that his administration had to take account of powerful institutions like Congress, federal bureaucracies and courts, and influential interest groups in formulating foreign policy. Thus, his effort to ban the entry of Muslims from several countries into the U.S. was delayed in the courts for over six months until the Supreme Court upheld the action. However, the Court provided an exception for those who had "close" family or business relationships with someone in America. Congress, moreover, was reluctant to provide funding for Trump's proposed wall on the Mexican border, and the president repeatedly threatened to "close" the government unless Congress granted the necessary funding. Moreover, major states like California openly resisted Trump's effort to deport massive numbers of undocumented aliens and end President Obama's Deferred Action for Childhood Arrivals (DACA) program, which allows young "dreamers" who came to America illegally as children to remain. Trump briefly sought to reach a deal with congressional Democrats, then backed off, and finally demanded that Congress enact an alternative to DACA in return for restricting legal and illegal immigration. U.S. businesses that depend on migrant labor are also opposed to mass deportations or limitations on immigration.

California and other states also sought to implement the Paris Climate Accord despite Trump's opposition to it. Indeed, another reminder of the chaotic policy process in Washington was Trump's withdrawal from the Accord after his Secretary of State and National Security Adviser had suggested in 2017 that America might remain in it under certain unstated conditions.

As president, Trump has moved back and forth erratically between extremist rhetoric and more mainstream views at the urging of senior advisers. Thus, even though he had frequently declared he wanted U.S. forces out of Afghanistan, he decided to increase the number of troops there with no date set for their withdrawal. However, owing to dismissal or resignation, many initial advisers were replaced by those more attuned to Trump's impetuosity like "superhawks" John Bolton, his third National Security Adviser and Mike Pompeo, his second Secretary of State.

His tweets frequently express differences with advisers. Regarding nuclear proliferation, for example, he suggested during the campaign that Japan and South Korea should consider acquiring their own nuclear weapons, threatening to destabilize East Asia and contrary to America's anti-proliferation policy. Since then he has moved back and forth between threatening "fire and fury" if faced by North Korean threats and willingness to negotiate, while senior foreign-policy advisers assured allies that Trump was prepared to do the latter. Republican Senator Bob Corker, chairman of the Foreign Relations Committee, was sufficiently alarmed to declare that Trump was treating the presidency like "a reality show," with reckless threats that could start America "on the path to World War III" (cited in Martin and Lander, 2017).[11]

Trump ultimately terminated the nuclear agreement with Iran in May 2018 (and restored all sanctions on that country in November); an action, which the CIA Director warned would be "the height of folly." He briefly backed away from his threat to do so in 2017, but, despite no evidence that Tehran was violating the agreement, his decision not to certify that Iran was complying the agreement and his withdrawal from the deal isolated Washington from friends and foes.

Even more astonishing, after North Korea tested a powerful nuclear bomb in September 2017, the president accused South Korea's president of appeasing Kim Jong-un and threatened to leave the U.S.-South Korean bilateral trade agreement – a gift to China, which seeks to drive a wedge between Washington and Seoul. Trump also urged China to use economic pressure to persuade North Korea to cease its nuclear program, while threatening tariffs on Chinese exports if it failed to do so. Then, suddenly he agreed to negotiate directly with Kim Jong-un and to meet him in Singapore, a meeting that produced little.

During the campaign, Trump's criticism of burden sharing with NATO and Asian allies cast doubt on his willingness to uphold U.S. commitments, especially those that defended the liberal order. This doubt created profound concern among European allies about America's policy toward an aggressive Russia. Notwithstanding Trump's rhetoric, his advisers repeatedly assured allies that Washington would meet its commitments. At NATO headquarters in May 2017, the president strayed from prepared remarks to the effect that the U.S. would honor NATO's principle of common defense contained in Article 5 of the treaty, but a month later reaffirmed that principle. For its part, the EU is struggling to maintain the liberal order that Trump had abandoned.

During his campaign, Trump advocated improving relations with Russia and praised President Putin. On one occasion, he compared Russian human-rights violations favorably with U.S. policies. U.S.-Russian relations unraveled, however, after the CIA announced its judgment that Russian covert interference during the campaign was intended to help elect Trump. Nevertheless, he continued declaring that he believed Putin's denial of having done so. At this writing, investigations continue into whether Trump's campaign colluded with Russian officials or whether the president obstructed justice by impeding those investigations. Trump disregards the views of the intelligence community about Russia, thereby undermining U.S. credibility and security. Congressional mistrust of Trump climaxed with a bill that increased sanctions against Moscow, which the president could not waive without congressional approval.

In the Middle East, Trump like Obama was prepared to leave Syria's President Assad in power. He focused on defeating IS, while paying little heed to the region's ethnic and religious divisions and dithering about whether Washington would leave troops in Syria. Washington's exclusion from negotiations among Russia, Iran and Turkey for ending violence in Syria reflected America's declining influence. Syria's use of chemical weapons against its foes followed by U.S. airstrikes briefly threatened a Russian-American crisis, but chaos in Washington was again evident when America's UN ambassador in April 2018 announced sanctions against Russia for its involvement in Syria that Trump denied the next day.

Israeli leaders believed that Trump's rhetoric assured support for their unwillingness to negotiate ending Israel's occupation of the West Bank and establishing an independent Palestinian state. Regarding Israel, too, the president waffled. Meeting with Prime Minister Netanyahu, he indicated he did not care whether a single state or a two-state solution should be the outcome of negotiations. Thereafter, he suggested limiting additional Israeli settlement construction would be "helpful," but his later decision to recognize Jerusalem as Israel's capital and move America's embassy there undermined U.S. influence across the region.

America's Arab allies in the Persian Gulf because of his anti-Iranian rhetoric greeted Trump's election favorably. The president's meeting with Arab leaders, however, aggravated differences between the Saudis and the emirate of Qatar. Trump agreed with Saudi allegations that Qatar supported terrorism although the emirate hosts a major U.S. airbase, deepening the rift among America's regional friends.

Regarding trade, Trump sought to reduce trade deficits, which he considers harmful – a claim economists ridicule. A trade deficit reflects net borrowing by the U.S. government, companies and individuals less the amount they save. Trade deals do not affect the overall trade balance. Trump repeatedly expressed a preference for bilateral rather than multilateral deals, and he has invoked Section 301 of the 1974 Trade Act, which permits imposing tariffs to protect U.S. firms from "serious injury" caused by imports and unfair trade practices such as "dumping" goods below the cost of producing them. Advocating "national sovereignty" in trade, Trump repeatedly criticized the WTO.

Trump ended U.S. involvement in the Trans-Pacific Partnership, reducing U.S. influence in Asia, but a year later, he waffled indecisively about rejoining the group. Trump's tariffs have triggered trade wars with U.S. allies that he claims treat America "unfairly" and have allowed China to act as a guardian of globalization. Trump continued threatening to terminate the North American Free Trade Agreement (NAFTA), which governs trade among the U.S., Mexico, and Canada. Ending NAFTA, combined with threatened tariffs against China, would harm, among others, U.S. farmers in states such as Iowa, and Texas who had supported his election. His protectionist instincts and policies like the withdrawal from the Paris Climate Treaty have isolated America.

Sino-American relations initially eroded. Shortly after taking office Trump seemed to reject China's claim to "One China" in which Taiwan is regarded as a Chinese province, not a sovereign state. In several joint communiques, Washington had implicitly acknowledged the "One China" position while noting it would not accept the use of force to reunite Taiwan and China. Trump's comments and his phone conversation with Taiwan's president worsened Sino-American relations, as did Washington's willingness to let Taiwanese leaders visit the U.S.

American exports to China increased fivefold after China joined the WTO in 2001. However, many American firms "outsource" work to Chinese suppliers, and China became a major "offshore" destination for U.S. firms seeking to remain globally competitive. America's largest trade deficit is with China, and, seeking to reduce that deficit, Trump imposed tariffs on Chinese goods, initiating a trade war that is harming American exporters and consumers. Moreover, Chinese purchases of U.S. securities finance America's budget deficits. Were China to sell these securities, the value of the U.S. dollar and markets would plummet, and inflation would rise. Trump's policies toward China more generally have been remarkably unpredictable. Thus, having threatened a trade war with China, he pulled back briefly in May 2018 and reversed himself again shortly thereafter.

CONCLUSIONS

The post-Cold War security order is vanishing with Russia's resurgent ultra-nationalism, China's not-so-peaceful rise, and turmoil in the Middle East. Unlike Obama's policies, which reflected the liberal order in principle, Trump's policies threaten it. Although over time some of his policies came to reflect continuity, they are in the main, along with president's unpredictable behavior, surrendering U.S. leadership. Trump's "America First" policies mean that the global order will lack a benign hegemon to foster multilateral cooperation in coping with pressing global issues. Trump's rhetoric and policies have eroded U.S. leadership and the liberal order. Trump has made America a "rogue" state, undermining multinational cooperation on trade, climate change, nuclear non-proliferation, negotiating peace between Israel and the Palestinians, and letting illiberal states assume leadership in the Middle East and Asia. Moreover, his racist policies and comments regarding Latinos, Muslims, and Africans have produced a dramatic decline in U.S. soft power of which immigration is a factor.

In conclusion, the president is mercurial and repeatedly changes his mind daily, and sometimes even hourly. His propensity to act unilaterally and tweet extreme views means that neither friends nor foes can identify with any certainty what Washington wants and whether it will carry out its commitments. This was most evident in Trump's virulent attacks on NATO and the EU, and his astonishing surrender to Putin at their July 2018 summit at which Trump publicly denied the findings of his intelligence agencies that Russia had undermined America's 2016 election. (After vigorous criticisms by both Republican and Democratic politicians, he claimed a day later that he had "misspoken.") Increasingly, foes are willing to test U.S. resolve, and allies have been alienated. In some issues, America is virtually isolated. Of late, attentive publics and U.S. leaders seem to have accepted U.S. decline – or at least retrenchment to the level of a "normal" country – as a foregone conclusion. If America fails to maintain credible commitments, the absence of U.S. hegemony will be sorely missed. Moreover, changes in personnel, notably a second Secretary of State and a third National Security Adviser, raise the prospect of the dangerous use of military force to change the regimes of U.S. foes.

George W. Bush summarized the problems caused by the Trump presidency:

> We've seen nationalism distorted into nativism, forgotten the dynamism that immigration has always brought to America. We see a fading confidence in the value of free markets and international trade, forgetting that conflict, instability and poverty follow in the wake of protectionism. We've seen the return of isolationist sentiments, forgetting that American security is directly threatened by the chaos and despair of distant places.
>
> (Cited in Baker, 2017)[12]

ESSAY QUESTIONS

1) Describe and discuss the strengths and weaknesses of the United States and China relative to each other.

2) In what ways do *perceptions* of American decline and weakness matter? Provide examples of America's alleged "decline."

3) How did President Barack Obama contribute to perceptions of American decline? Do you agree with Obama's reluctance to use force? Explain your preference.

4) What are the key elements of "populism" in politics? Do you agree or not agree with the elements of populism? Explain your preference.

5) Do you think President Donald Trump's foreign policies are "making America great again?" Explain and illustrate your answer with examples.

SHORT ANSWER QUESTIONS

Define and describe the importance of the following:

Hegemonic war
The global liberal order
Article 5 of the NATO treaty
Deferred Action for Childhood Arrivals (DACA) program
The 'indispensable nation'

NOTES

1 Shambaugh, D. (2013). *China Goes Global: The partial power*. New York: Oxford University Press.
2 Nye, J. (2015). *Is the American Century Over?* Cambridge: Polity Press.
3 White House (2017). *National Security Strategy* [pdf]. Available at: www.whitehouse.gov/wp-content/uploads/2017/12/NSS-Final-12-18-2017-0905.pdf [Accessed 29 Jan 2018].
4 Ikenberry G.J. (2014). The Illusion of Geopolitics. *Foreign Affairs* 93:3 (May/June 2014), pp. 80–90.
5 *The Economist* (2014). The War on Terror, part two (May 31), pp. 23–24.
6 Baker, P. (2014). Rebutting Critics, Obama Seeks Higher Bar for Military Action [online]. *New York Times*. Available at: www.nytimes.com/2014/05/29/us/politics/rebutting-critics-obama-seeks-higher-bar-for-military-action.html [Accessed 12 Dec 2017].
7 Nossiter, A. (2018). 'Let Them Call You Racists': Bannon's pep talk to National Front [online]. *New York Times*. Available at: www.nytimes.com/2018/03/10/world/europe/steve-bannon-france-national-front.html [Accessed 10 Mar 2018].
8 Inglehart, R. (2018). The Age of Insecurity. *Foreign Affairs* 97:3, pp. 20–28.
9 Davis, J. and Gupta S. (2017). Trump Administration Rejects Study Showing Positive Impact of Refugees [online]. *New York Times*. Available at: www.nytimes.com/2017/09/18/us/politics/refugees-revenue-cost-report-trump.html [Accessed 1 May 2018].
10 Nye, J. (2011). *The Future of Power*. New York: PublicAffairs.
11 Martin, J. and Lander, M.B. (2017). Corker Says Trump's Recklessness Threatens 'World War III' [online]. *New York Times*. Available at: www.nytimes.com/2017/10/08/us/politics/trump-corker.html [Accessed 10 Oct. 2017].
12 Baker, P. (2017). Without Saying 'Trump,' Bush and Obama Deliver Implicit Rebukes [online]. *New York Times*. www.nytimes.com/2017/10/19/us/politics/george-bush-trump.html [Accessed 20 Oct 2017].

SUGGESTED READINGS

Ikenberry G.J. (2014). The Illusion of Geopolitics. *Foreign Affairs* 93:3 (May/June 2014), pp. 80–90.
Inglehart, R. (2018). The Age of Insecurity. *Foreign Affairs* 97:3, pp. 20–28.
Nye, J. (2011). *The Future of Power*. New York: PublicAffairs.
Shambaugh, D. (2013). *China Goes Global: The partial power*. New York: Oxford University Press.

2 American foreign policy making: Institutions and individuals in the Trump administration

James M. McCormick

INTRODUCTION

When President Harry Truman was asked who makes American foreign policy, he quipped: "I make foreign policy." In large part, Truman correctly described the process. Although the Constitution delegates powers to Congress and the executive branch in making foreign policy, the president has come to dominate the process, especially since World War II. Truman and his predecessor, Franklin Roosevelt, accelerated presidential dominance with the decisions they made and the actions they took. Roosevelt, for instance, unilaterally committed Washington to aid the United Kingdom (UK) in World War II before congressional action by completing the "destroyers for bases" deal as an executive (or presidential) agreement rather than as a treaty. Truman, too, made several unilateral decisions and initiated actions after the war that reflected a dominant presidential role in shaping foreign policy. These ranged from decisions at the Potsdam Conference about the future of postwar Europe, and the declaration of the Truman Doctrine for a future global role for America, to initiating the Berlin airlift and entering the Korean War – largely without congressional involvement. In these instances, the role of the president and his personal beliefs were crucial.

PRESIDENTIAL DOMINANCE IN FOREIGN POLICY

Presidents since Truman have jealously guarded their prerogatives in shaping American foreign policy. Although they have had different worldviews, each ultimately put his stamp on American actions abroad. With a military background, for instance, President Dwight Eisenhower was not only committed to reshaping the direction of American strategic policy, but was leery of the influence of a "military-industrial complex" in shaping U.S. policies. John F. Kennedy personally shaped American policy during the Cuban Missile Crisis (aided by the Executive Committee of the National Security Council), and Lyndon Johnson single-mindedly pursued America's escalation of the Vietnam War with a small coterie of advisers known as the "Tuesday Lunch Group." His successors, Richard Nixon and Gerald Ford, sought to reshape American actions abroad and foster an international structure based on détente with the USSR and China, aided by National Security Adviser and Secretary of State, Henry Kissinger. Jimmy Carter focused U.S. policy on human rights, driven by moral imperatives, and imposed sanctions on states that violated those rights. Indeed, the power of the presidency grew so dramatically in the decades after World War II that it was referred to as the "imperial presidency," especially in relation to foreign policy.

Despite congressional efforts beginning in the 1970s to challenge executive dominance, presidents from Ronald Reagan to Barack Obama continued to impose their views on foreign policy. Reagan was committed to confronting and challenging the USSR and sought to put "Marxism and Leninism on the ash-heap of history." George H.W. Bush sought to steer the global order on a stable and peaceful course as the Cold War ended. Bill Clinton initially sought to promote "free markets and free peoples" and replace the policy of containment with "democratic enlargement." George W. Bush focused on challenging the "axis of evil" and global terrorism after the tragic events of 9/11. And, Barack Obama sought to bend the "arc of history toward justice" with an agenda to end America's wars abroad, reduce the dangers of nuclear proliferation, and address climate change. Overall, presidential views have been crucial in charting the course of American foreign policy.

THE ROLE OF THE NATIONAL SECURITY BUREAUCRACY

Congress indirectly accelerated the process of executive dominance in American foreign policy. During the Truman administration, for instance, the legislative branch established institutions to assist the president and the executive branch in formulating and implementing foreign policy. The National Security Act of 1947 established the Central Intelligence Agency, the National Military Establishment (later, the Department of Defense), and the Joint Chiefs of Staff (JCS) to aid the executive branch. This legislation also established a National Security Council (NSC) which provided the president with a bureaucratic structure to bring together key foreign-policy officials – the Secretary of State, the Secretary of Defense, Chairman of the JCS, and the CIA Director, among others – to coordinate policy. Congress also aided this process by passing resolutions (e.g., the Gulf of Tonkin Resolution during the Vietnam War, the Authorization for the Use of Force after 9/11, and Iraq Resolution prior to the 2003 Iraq war) granting additional foreign-policy authority to presidents. Finally, Congress has routinely supported foreign policy initiatives by the executive in contrast to its involvement in domestic politics.

Over the decades, changes in the composition and operation of the NSC have also enhanced executive dominance. The role of the "special assistant for national security affairs," originally utilized by Truman and Eisenhower as a "policy coordinator" for the NSC, expanded during the Kennedy administration to encompass policymaking. This additional role for the National Security Adviser began with McGeorge Bundy but expanded with each new administration. During recent administrations, the National Security Adviser has become the principal formulator of foreign policy within the executive branch, reducing the roles of the Secretaries of State and Defense. The National Security Adviser is a political appointee of the president (and thus not subject to Senate confirmation), allowing the president to name an individual committed to his worldview.

Much as the role of the National Security Adviser has grown, so has the role of the NSC bureaucracy. That bureaucracy has expanded from a few individuals to hundreds during the last four administrations. Because many members of this bureaucracy are political appointees and not subject to Senate confirmation, the president can select individuals who share his views. Moreover, the organizational design of the NSC often emulates the groups within the State Department and thus, arguably, overshadows that department owing to its intellectual and physical proximity to the president.

Another change arising from the growth of the National Security Council has been the creation of the "NSC system." At least since the George H.W. Bush administration (and perhaps earlier), the executive branch has employed a hierarchical system of committees under the NSC that allows it to manage other foreign-policy bureaucracies. In general, a three-tier structure under the NSC consists of the Principals Committee (composed of the secretaries of the major foreign-policy departments), the Deputies Committee (composed of the second in command in those bureaucracies), and the policy coordination committees (interagency working groups across bureaucracies on specific issues). Policy recommendations flow upward and policy implementation flows downward. Significantly, the National Security Adviser had headed the Principals Committee and the deputy National Security Adviser the Deputies Committee during previous administrations, and thus provided more executive direction of these structures. In short, the NSC system structure allows for, and enhances, presidential control over foreign policy.

At least two important consequences result from the enlarged role of the National Security Adviser, the national security bureaucracy, and the NSC system. First, the organizational structure diminishes the impact of individual agencies like the State Department, as well as other bureaucracies, in shaping policy, since their impact is primarily through an interagency process. (To be sure, some individual cabinet members remain important such as the Secretaries of State or Defense, but their influence depends largely on their personal relationship with the president.) Second, the NSC system reduces Congress' role in shaping policy. This is especially so for congressional input on "crisis" issues that require a rapid response. Congress retains more influence on routine or long-term issues – policies toward particular countries and reviews of defense spending or foreign aid. Moreover, growing partisan polarization on foreign policy at home has further reduced the ability of Congress to affect policy by means of bipartisan legislation. Thus, presidential predominance persists.

Overall, the traditional model of foreign policymaking with presidential dominance and an enhanced NSC system has been the norm in recent administrations. The worldviews of the president and his principal advisers remain crucial for maintaining a coherent and consistent foreign policy. Furthermore, the efficient functioning of the NSC system requires that presidential appointments be in place and operating effectively shortly after a president assumes office. Deviations from this model can produce dysfunction. They not only produce domestic discord but confuse friends and foes that try to fathom the direction of U.S. policy.

THE TRUMP ADMINISTRATION

Changes in the process described above began during the George H.W. Bush presidency. Bush placed the National Security Adviser in charge of the NSC's Principals Committee for the first time and directed the deputy National Security Adviser to chair the Deputies Committee. This directive solidified control of the NSC system in the hands of the president's top foreign-policy adviser. Subsequent administrations followed this pattern. Clinton, however, expanded the NSC system by adding economic advisers as part of the Principals and Deputies Committee in order to improve coverage of economic issues. Obama made an additional change by folding the Homeland Security Council into the NSC system to coordinate counterterrorism efforts and (not coincidentally) simultaneously increase executive influence.

Although the Trump administration has followed the general outlines of this decision-making model, it has also deviated from it in crucial ways, both in terms of the individuals appointed and in its use of the NSC process.

At the individual level, the background and experience of some initial principal foreign-policy appointees did not fit the pattern of previous administrations, and the worldviews that they brought were at variance with long-standing American positions and sometimes also with one another. President Donald Trump himself had limited foreign-policy experience or knowledge. (By contrast, Trump's third National Security Adviser [John Bolton] came to that office with a particular worldview and experience in several administrations.) Trump's principal means for understanding foreign policy has been through his business experience as reflected in the transactional bargaining style depicted in his book, *The Art of the Deal*. He seeks to translate his style of negotiating business ventures into conducting foreign policy. Business transactions, however, are unlike the conduct of foreign policy with adversaries, allies, and friends seeking to achieve their own goals in an anarchic global system. Domestically, bargaining in business is ill suited to deal with a system of checks and balances across multiple participants in the U.S. political system. Consequently, Trump's ability to alter the foreign-policy directions of other states and their leaders has remained a challenge, and he has had difficulty directing foreign policy at home owing to his lack of knowledge and idiosyncratic style of governance.

Trump's constant "tweets" to convey his views on issues and share his feelings about individuals overseas and inside the administration have produced widespread concern. Indeed, several tweets insulted the leaders of key U.S. allies including those of the United Kingdom, Canada, and Australia and have contradicted and even demeaned his own advisers. By contrast, he openly admires the authoritarian style of Russia's Vladimir Putin and China's Xi Jinping and, unlike previous U.S. presidents, has largely ignored human-rights abuses or the absence of democracy. Thus, at an Association of Southeast Asian Nations (ASEAN) meeting in the Philippines in 2017, Trump did not raise the issue of human-rights violations with Philippine President Rodrigo Duterte, despite Duterte's claims of having personally murdered foes and his advocacy of thousands of extrajudicial killings of those allegedly involved in the drug trade.

Unsurprisingly, Trump's worldview is not as fully developed as that of many of his predecessors, and thus his views have often have put him at odds with long-time American foreign-policy positions. A singular theme is to put "America First," revealing his transactional style and disdain for globalization and the liberal policies followed by previous administrations. In a campaign speech, he declared:

> Americans must know that we are putting the American people first again . . . On trade, on immigration, on foreign policy – the jobs, incomes and security of the American worker will always be my first priority. No country has ever prospered that failed to put its own interests first . . . We will no longer surrender this country, or its people, to the false song of globalism.
>
> (Trump, 2016)[1]

Trump also identified several issues that his administration would address. Owing to the actions of the Obama administration, Trump argued, America's friends "are beginning to think they can't depend" on the U.S., and "our rivals no longer respect us." In addition, allies "are not paying their fair share" for defense. Presumably, Trump would seek to reinforce U.S. commitments to allies, while making them pay more for their security. He also called for increasing America's military might, restoring the health of the U.S. economy, curbing, and halting the spread of radical Islam. In his inaugural address, he repeated many of these themes, again emphasizing "America First."

Several of Trump's other comments produced concern among U.S. friends and allies. Some of his statements were also at odds with his initial foreign-policy positions and challenged long-standing commitments to U.S. allies in Asia and Europe. Thus, during the campaign, candidate Trump stated that Japan ought to get nuclear weapons to defend itself against North Korea. On other occasions, Trump called NATO "obsolete."

Although he walked back both statements and reaffirmed U.S. commitments to Japan and South Korea, he failed initially to endorse the core commitment of collective action of Article 5 of the NATO Treaty and rebuked America's allies for providing insufficient funding for defense. Far from reaffirming U.S. commitments, such comments led German Chancellor, Angela Merkel to remark sadly "the times in which we could completely rely on others are, to some extent, over," thus questioning Trump's commitment to NATO. Only two months later, at the prodding of advisers, Trump finally endorsed Article 5. Trump's policy flip-flops and his reluctance to endorse long-standing commitments illustrated the opaque nature of his worldview and damaged America's global reputation. Increasingly, allies lost confidence in American support, and they looked to U.S. actions rather than Trump's tweets to gauge the direction of U.S. foreign policy.

Some members of Trump's national security team had more experience in foreign policy than the president, but they, too, brought idiosyncratic credentials to the process. Moreover, their foreign-policy views tended to clash with the president's. This was particularly the case for his appointments to the Departments of State and Defense.

Rex Tillerson, long-time executive of ExxonMobil, was Trump's initial and surprising choice for Secretary of State. Although Tillerson had considerable experience in negotiating oil and gas contracts with foreign governments, he had no government experience. Tillerson, however, "radiated the kind of authority admired by Trump," and Trump believed Tillerson and he could be "negotiators, the best negotiators, for America" (Zengerle, 2017)[2] owing to their business background. Nevertheless, even during his Senate confirmation hearings, Tillerson articulated policy positions at odds with Trump. Thus, Tillerson called for Washington to fulfill its NATO obligations and opposed Japanese and South Korean acquisition of nuclear weapons. Unlike Trump, he accepted the challenge of climate change, and he indicated he would have supported U.S. military assistance to Ukraine after Russia's annexation of Crimea. Finally, he emphatically supported the Trans-Pacific Partnership, from which Trump had previously announced America's withdrawal.

Owing to differences in views and style, Trump and Tillerson were frequently at odds with one another's policy positions, and these differences eventually led to Tillerson's dismissal in February 2018. Tillerson was repeatedly the target of critical tweets by Trump that undercut his diplomatic efforts. Two instances illustrate the difficulty that Tillerson faced. As we shall discuss later, when several Arab countries broke diplomatic relations with

Qatar, a U.S. ally, over alleged funding of terrorism and ties to Iran, Tillerson sought a negotiated settlement. However, Trump declared:

> I decided, along with Secretary of State Rex Tillerson, our great generals and military people, the time had come to call on Qatar to end its funding. They have to end that funding and its extremist ideology. The nation of Qatar has historically been a funder of terrorism at a very high level.
>
> (Cited in Woody, 2017)[3]

Not only was Tillerson "blindsided" by the presidential action, but he was furious that the White House and State Department were advocating different policies.

Another instance involved Tillerson's effort to negotiate with North Korea over nuclear testing. While in Beijing in September 2017, Tillerson indicated that Washington had direct channels to North Korea and was seeking a peaceful outcome. Within hours after his Secretary of State called for the "need is to calm things down" with North Korea, Trump tweeted "I told Rex Tillerson, our wonderful Secretary of State, that he is wasting his time trying to negotiate with Little Rocket Man . . . Save your energy Rex, we'll do what has to be done!" (cited in Watkins, 2017).[4] Regarding North Korean missile tests, Trump was especially confusing: "It is a situation that we will handle" (Landler et al., 2017).[5] Tillerson's policy differences with Trump, his derogatory remarks about the president, and his incompetence in managing the State Department foreshadowed his later dismissal.

Tillerson's successor was Mike Pompeo, a former member of Congress and Director of the CIA when appointed Secretary of State. His foreign-policy views were more in accord with Trump's on several issues, including those on North Korea, Iran, and the Paris Climate Accord. Unlike Tillerson, whom Trump characterized as having "a different mindset, a different thinking" than his own, Pompeo and he, Trump said, "have a very similar thought process" (cited in Parker et al., 2018).[6]

The appointment of James Mattis as Secretary of Defense, until 2019 when Trump fired him, was a more conventional choice. Mattis took office with a stellar military background. He was a four-star Marine general with considerable combat experience and was widely respected for his understanding of global affairs and for his skill in managing difficult issues. However, like Tillerson, Mattis's policy views were at odds with some of Trump's positions. During his confirmation hearing, the new Defense Secretary declared that he was skeptical of Russia, vigorously supported Washington's commitment to NATO, endorsed the Iran nuclear agreement (although calling it "imperfect"), and expressed great confidence in the intelligence community, which Trump had criticized because it had concluded that Russia had interfered in America's 2016 presidential election. In addition, Mattis recognized the crucial importance of diplomacy in conducting global affairs even as the president slashed the State Department's budget and failed to fill several crucial high-level positions in that agency. Mattis had declared some years before: "The more that we put into the State Department's diplomacy, hopefully the less we have to put into a military budget as we deal with the outcome of an apparent American withdrawal from the international scene" (cited in Locke, 2017).[7]

Despite Mattis's apparent decision latitude on defense matters owing to his military background, he also was sometimes caught off-guard by the president's comments. In early April 2018, for instance, Trump suddenly announced that the U.S. would be withdrawing from Syria "very soon." This was at odds with Mattis's and the Defense Department's position. Although the White House a few days later said that the withdrawal would not occur until the Islamic State (IS) was defeated, the differing pronouncements raised the issue of how much leeway Mattis had in shaping military policy (Worth, 2018).[8]

A third key appointee was the president's National Security Adviser, initially Lt. General Michael Flynn, who had been Trump's foreign-policy adviser during the campaign and had previously served as Director of the Defense Intelligence Agency during the Obama administration. Flynn's views largely dovetailed with the president's on foreign policy, and as the principal foreign-policy adviser, such views seemed to foreshadow a narrower, nationalist approach to the world. His appointment, however, lasted only twenty-four days when Flynn acknowledged that he had not been truthful to Vice President Mike Pence about his communications with the Soviet ambassador in December 2016. Subsequently, Flynn's contacts with Turkey and Russia, and perhaps other countries, came under scrutiny by special counsel Robert Mueller and congressional several committees investigating Russian meddling in the election. Flynn's subsequent resignation and admission of guilt about having lied to the Federal Bureau of Investigation (FBI) cast a cloud over foreign-policy decision-making in the Trump administration.

Flynn's replacement, General H.R. McMaster, continued the Trump administration's appointment of military personnel to key policymaking positions. McMaster was an active-duty, three-star army general, with more significant foreign-policy experience and a better reputation than his predecessor. Not only did he come to the position with extensive combat experience, but he also had a doctorate in history and had written a widely acclaimed book, *Dereliction of Duty*, in which he had sharply criticized the military for its failure to be more honest and open during the Vietnam War. He also had a reputation for "speaking his mind" to those in authority. More generally, McMaster's foreign-policy thinking reflected greater continuity than Trump's. Thus, he supported America's active role in maintaining the liberal global order – a position that seemed to clash with the commander-in chief's views. Yet, his views and style clashed with Trump's, and McMaster announced in late March 2018 that he would be resigning.

Trump then announced that John Bolton, who had served in the Reagan and George W. Bush administrations, including as U.S. ambassador to the UN, would replace McMaster. Immediately, the appointment produced sharp criticism from several foreign-policy analysts. Bolton, known for his hawkish views on foreign-policy matters, had argued in an op-ed piece how a preventive military strike against North Korea could be justified. He had also expressed interventionist and militant views regarding several other issues. Some of Bolton's views may prove to be at odds with the president's, and, given Bolton's antagonistic management style, an important question is how he will operate the national security bureaucracy at the White House.

Another military member of the President's national security team was General John Kelly as Chief of Staff in the White House. Originally appointed as Secretary of Homeland Security, Kelly moved to this position after Reince Priebus resigned in summer 2017. Like several other appointees, Kelly took positions at his confirmation hearing at variance with Trump's. Concerning the president's effort to build a wall on the border with Mexico to halt illegal immigration, Kelly stated that a wall would be insufficient to end the problem without using modern technologies like drones and sensors. Regarding the president's desire to ban Muslims from entering the U.S., Kelly was also more cautious, noting that while serving in Iraq, his troops successfully sought the assistance of Muslim clerics and community leaders.

Certainly, President Trump's most unconventional and controversial initial appointment to his national security team was Stephen Bannon. Bannon, former head of the rightwing Breitbart News, had helped to guide Trump's 2016 presidential campaign. After the election, Trump named Bannon "chief strategist" in the White House, and, in an unprecedented decision, appointed him to the NSC's Principals Committee. Bannon's populist foreign-policy views, through compatible with the president's desire to limit U.S. involvement abroad, directly clashed with those of Tillerson, Mattis, McMaster, and Kelly.

Bannon reportedly quarreled with the Secretary of Defense over Mattis's unwillingness to confront South Korea more directly in linking its trade surplus with America to the stationing of U.S. military personnel in that country. Bannon and McMaster also differed over the latter's support for increasing America's presence in Afghanistan. At one juncture, Mattis had to intervene to calm down McMaster at a particularly contentious meeting (*The Economist*, 2017a).[9] In August 2017, Bannon stepped down after clashing with President Trump who believed that Bannon was "leaking information to reporters" and "taking too much credit for the president's successes" (Haberman et al., 2017).[10] Nevertheless, even after resigning, Bannon remained in frequent contact with the president and began a campaign to replace Republican senators who he believed were not fully supporting Trump's policies. He also began to use Breitbart News to challenge the administration's domestic and foreign policies. Bannon subsequently resigned that position and has largely remained out of the limelight recently.

THE NSC AND THE TRUMP ADMINISTRATION

President Trump's initial reliance on "my generals" (as he called them) for the core of his national security team skewed decision-making in the NSC toward greater reliance on military options in American foreign policy. Several developments reflected this trend. First, the administration initially called for a $54 billion increase in the budget for the Department of Defense and a reduction in the State Department budget by 31 percent. Second, several long-serving diplomats in the State Department were fired, resigned, or demoted, and nine special departmental envoys intended to address issues in various regions (e.g., Afghanistan and Pakistan) and particular issues (e.g., climate change and the Six-Party Talks involving North Korea) were eliminated (Calamur, 2017).[11] Third, Secretary Tillerson and the administration were slow to fill vacancies in the State Department, and key assistant secretary positions (e.g., for Asia, the Middle East, and South America) and the ambassador for a crucial country, South Korea, remained vacant until Admiral Harry Harris, head of the U.S. military's Pacific Command, was nominated in April 2018. Fourth, the CIA and the military were allowed to initiate drone strikes against suspected terrorists without consulting civilian leaders, unlike in the Obama administration, which required high-level civilian approval for such strikes. Fifth, the National Security Strategy, the National Defense Strategy, and the Nuclear Posture Review issued by the administration in early 2018 emphasized increasing the size and role of the military in America's foreign policy.

In contrast, the role of diplomacy in foreign policy was reduced. Many of the top positions in the Department of State remained vacant, and top ranks of career ambassadors and career ministers were reduced from 39 to 19 by late 2017. Tillerson announced that he would undertake a restructuring of the State Department, intending to slash the overall size of the department by personnel cuts totaling 2,000 by October 2018, and, when he left, about 40 percent of Senate-confirmed positions at the State Department lacked even nominees (*The Economist*, 2018).[12] The proposal greatly reduced department morale and created difficulties for foreign leaders to get clear answers about the direction of American policy. The result has been that the office of policy planning, "which has traditionally functioned as the secretary of state's in-house think tank, is now tasked with handling day-to-day operations at the expense of formulations long-term strategy" (Zengerle, 2017).[13] However, Pompeo said he will seek to increase State Department morale and resume hiring of personnel, but his plans remain unclear at present.

Another view of reliance on the generals seems positive; they were "the grown-ups" in the room when discussing foreign policy and served to restrain a president who is unpredictable and impulsive. The generals have seen wars first-hand and have a greater understanding of global affairs than the president, who never served in the military. Consequently, they are likely to be cautious in using force. However, Trump still makes the final decisions, and his orders are likely to be followed by military professionals who are trained to obey their civilian commander-in-chief. Nevertheless, the military members of the national security team have been willing to speak out in support of long-time American policies and sometimes at odds with the statements of the president. Thus, after Trump's campaign comment approving the use of torture against terrorism suspects, General Mattis persuaded him to oppose the practice, which had been eliminated during the Obama years. Regarding the use of nuclear weapons, General John Hyten, head of U.S. Strategic Command, declared he would challenge an order by the president if he thought it to be illegal. "I provide advice to the President," Hyten said. "He'll tell me what to do, and if it's illegal, guess what's going to happen? I'm gonna say, 'Mr. President, that's illegal'" (Diaz, 2017).[14]

Are the NSC and the NSC system still important in the Trump administration? Indeed, the administration has organized the NSC system along the general lines of previous administrations, but the operation of this system has been faced with various challenges and afflicted by apparent dysfunction.

In its initial National Security Presidential Memorandum-2 (NSPM2) on the structure of the NSC system, the Trump administration made several key changes in who participated and in the distribution of various duties. Unlike past practice, the National Security Adviser and the Homeland Security Adviser, for instance, were *jointly* given responsibility to set the NSC's agenda, and the Director of National Intelligence (DNI) and the Chair of the JCS were *excluded* from regularly attending NSC meetings. The CIA Director, too, was excluded as a regular attendee. Instead, the president's chief political strategist (at the time), Stephen Bannon, was included in NSC meetings. Owing to the exclusion of these traditional members and the inclusion of Bannon, observers argued that the administration would lose professional advice and the process would be politicized.

Thus, several months later, the administration issued National Security Presidential Memorandum-4 (NSPM4) that made important adjustments to membership of the NSC and its Principals Committee. The DNI, the Chair of the JCS and the CIA Director were again made formal members of the NSC, and Bannon was no longer among the invitees.

The NSC agenda again became the sole responsibility of the National Security Adviser. Similar changes occurred with the Principals Committee where the Chair of the JCS and the DNI were again regular attendees while Bannon was excluded. Thereafter, the shape of the NSC system conformed to past practices.

Not surprisingly, the NSC bureaucracy experienced personnel and operational difficulties in the early months of the administration. An early political division emerged between those who took a highly nationalist approach to U.S. policy (e.g., the Bannon and Flynn faction) and those who had an internationalist view of America's role abroad (e.g., the McMaster and Kelly faction). This division reached a climax during the summer of 2017 when the National Security Adviser fired or reassigned several members of the NSC staff. A leading Middle East adviser was reassigned elsewhere, and the individual charged with strategic planning was cashiered over a rambling and conspiratorial-sounding memo alleging that bureaucrats were "attempting to destroy Trump's agenda." McMaster also fired a third high-ranking official, the senior intelligence director, owing to his inexperience and his close relationship with former National Security Adviser Michael Flynn.

Under John Bolton as NSC adviser, the personnel and operation of the NSC bureaucracy has already begun to change significantly as Bolton places his supporters on the NSC staff and works to remove McMaster's allies. Writes one observer, Bolton is also likely to use "his powerful perch at the National Security Council . . . to shape and influence policy and personnel at Foggy Bottom [the Department of State]" (Hudson, 2018).[15]

Staff competition and changes are part of the bureaucratic process, and other administrations have experienced similar cleavages. What appears different in the case of the Trump administration are both the number of staff turnovers and the resulting disarray. Indeed, despite Trump's opposition to promoting human rights and democracy, U.S. diplomats continue to do so, for example, in Cambodia and Hungary (*The Economist*, 2017b).[16] National Security Adviser McMaster and Chief of Staff Kelly sought to create a more orderly process in the NSC and the White House, but it has been difficult to maintain order with Bannon's supporters inside and outside undermining their authority – and with a president who pursues his own agenda and suddenly changes policy. Bolton now has a similar challenge. He is "tightening the NSC circle," and "reducing the frequency of formal principals' meetings" to gain greater control (Ignatius, 2018).[17]

CONCLUSIONS

Both the nature of the Trump's decision-making process and the impact of key policymakers have further concentrated foreign policymaking in the executive branch. Trump initially rejected many long-time U.S. policies and in some cases has been persuaded to revise his policy positions.

Among the changes, have been those associated with trade and the environment. Although Washington has historically promoted a free, open trading system and worked toward a climate-change agreement, Trump, with his emphasis on America First, challenged multilateral trade, the Iran nuclear deal, and the climate accord. Such actions produced criticism and opposition from several quarters – members of Congress, some states and cities, the business community, and the public at large. Trump's call for the renegotiation or cancelation of NAFTA sparked bipartisan opposition in Congress and elsewhere, alarming

Republicans who supported free trade and worrying Democrats who feared abandoning a successful trade pact. Moreover, lobbyists from America's auto industry and agricultural interests worked feverishly on Capitol Hill to reverse Trump's tariffs. The Chamber of Commerce, the country's largest business lobby, announced it opposed the demands that the administration were placing on Canada and Mexico and would rally support for the current agreement (Wiseman, 2017).[18]

Withdrawal from the Paris Accords also elicited opposition from Congress and leaders of several states and cities. The most visible expression of this opposition appeared at the 2017 Bonn summit on climate policy. Governor Jerry Brown (D-Ca.) and former New York Mayor Michael Bloomberg attended to express their commitment to this multinational accord despite the Trump administration's planned withdrawal. Several U.S. senators also attended the summit, and Senator Ben Cardin (D-Md.) summed up their concern: "We are here because it's our responsibility to be part of the global community. We're here because it's in our national security interests to deal with climate change" (cited in Tharoor, 2017).[19]

Trump has also waffled between accommodating and resisting Russia on issues related to Ukraine, Central Europe, and Syria and only reluctantly accepted continued sanctions for Russia after legislation passed Congress. In early 2018, Trump announced additional sanctions toward Russia over that country's involvement in a poisoning incident in the UK and threatened to impose tariffs on China over its trading practices. The week following the Helsinki summit with Putin were chaotic. "For Trump and his White House, the days that followed the Helsinki summit amounted to an unofficial Walk Back Week – a daily scramble of corrections and clarifications from the West Wing. Each announcement, intended to blunt the global fallout from the president's Russophilic performance in Helsinki, was followed by another mishap that fueled more consternation" (Parker et al., 2018).[20]

Although President Trump's leadership style has strengthened executive dominance, it has weakened support domestically and internationally for America. Domestically, presidential approval has hovered in the 30–40 percent range, only reaching 45 percent in mid-2018, and Trump has struggled to record a major foreign-policy success. The defeat of IS in Iraq and Syria in late 2017 was an exception, but vexing problems of Afghanistan, Korea, Ukraine, Iran, and China remain (although the summit with Kim may provide an exception if it has a favorable outcome). Globally, even greater doubts exist about the president and the direction of American policy. In June 2017, a Pew poll of 37 countries concluded:

> Trump and many of his key policies are broadly unpopular around the globe, and ratings for the U.S. have declined steeply in many nations . . . [A] median of just 22% has confidence in Trump to do the right thing when it comes to international affairs. This stands in contrast to the final years of Barack Obama's presidency, when a median of 64% expressed confidence in Trump's predecessor to direct America's role in the world.
>
> (Wike et al., 2017)[21]

Majorities of the global community also expressed disagreement with the Trump administration's policies, ranging from the travel ban on those from Muslim-majority countries and withdrawal from the climate accord to opposition to multinational trade agreements or building a wall along the Mexican border.

Trump's unpredictability and impulsiveness have created confusion about Washington's global role and damaged the credibility and reliability of America in world affairs. His unpredictability is made worse by his personal decision style in which "he trusts his instincts" and "glories in not listening to advisers" (Ignatius, 2018).[17] Indeed, on issues like North Korea, Iran, NATO, and Russia, Trump and his advisers recently seemed to be in entirely different worlds, with Trump appearing conciliatory and officials like Pompeo and Bolton articulating hardline positions. "There is a clear dissonance between what the president says and what his administration says," said Vali Nasr, "and it has been noticed by allies and adversaries around the world." (cited in Landler, 2018).[22]

If the standing of America in the global community is to improve in the near term, the policymaking processes, policy choices, and the president's style will likely need considerable attention and change.

ESSAY QUESTIONS

1) What are some examples of recent presidents shaping the direction of American foreign policy? Is President Trump following that pattern?

2) What are some key elements of the national security bureaucracy, and how have they contributed to presidential dominance of American foreign policy?

3) How are the principal foreign-policy appointees different from the appointees by previous administration? Use at least two examples of the appointees by the Trump administration to make your case.

4) What are some components of President Trump's worldview, and what foreign-policy issues did he emphasize at the outset of his administration?

5) To what extent do the positions of the Trump administration on foreign-policy issues reflect a sharp break from previous administrations? Use two or three issues in your assessment.

SHORT ANSWER QUESTIONS

Define and describe the importance of the following:

National Security Council
"Little Rocket Man"
John Bolton
NAFTA and Paris Accords
Presidential "tweets"

NOTES

1   Transcript: Donald Trump's Foreign Policy Speech (2016). *New York Times* [online]. Available at: www.nytimes.com/2016/04/28/us/politics/transcript-trump-foreign-policy.html [Accessed 25 Nov. 2017].

2   Zengerle, J. (2017). Rex Tillerson and the Unraveling of the State Department. *New York Times* [online]. Available at: https://nyti.ms/2zgP07r [Accessed 6 May 2018].

3   Woody, C. (2017). Mattis and Tillerson Are Trying to Soothe a Crisis in the Persian Gulf, but Trump Keeps Picking on a US Ally. *Business Insider* [online]. Available at: www.businessinsider.com/mattis-and-tillerson-try-to-sooth-gulf-crisis-as-trump-fights-qatar-2017-6 [Accessed 4 Nov. 2017].

4   Watkins, E. (2017). Trump: Tillerson 'Wasting His Time' Negotiating with North Korea. *CNN*. Available at: www.cnn.com/2017/10/01/politics/donald-trump-rex-tillerson-north-korea/index.html [Accessed 6 Nov. 2017].

5   Landler, M., Sang-Hun, C., and Cooper, H. (2017). North Korea Fires a Ballistic Missile, in a Further Challenge to Trump. *New York Times* [online]. Available at: www.nytimes.com/2017/11/28/world/asia/north-korea-missile-test.html [Accessed 4 Dec. 2017].

6   Parker, A., Rucker, P., Hudson, J., and Leonning, C. (2018). Trump Ousts Tillerson, Will Replace Him as Secretary of State with CIA Chief Pompeo. *Washington Post* [online]. Available at: www.washingtonpost.com/politics/trump-ousts-tillerson-will-replace-him-as-secretary-of-state-with-cia-chief-pompeo/2018/03/13/30f34eea-26ba-11e8-b79d-f3d931db7f68_story.html [Accessed 29 March 2018].

7   Locke, A. (2017). Mattis Once Said if State Department Funding Gets Cut 'Then I Need to Buy More Ammunition.' *Business Insider* [online]. Available at: www.businessinsider.com/mattis-state-department-funding-need-to-buy-more-ammunition-2017-2 [Accessed 29 Oct. 2017].

8   Worth, R. (2018). Can Jim Mattis Hold the Line in Trump's War Cabinet? *New York Times* [online]. Available at www.nytimes.com/2018/03/26/magazine/can-jim-mattis-hold-the-line-in-trumps-war-cabinet.html [Accessed 27 March 2018].

9   *The Economist* (2017a). Counsel of Warriors: Donald Trump's generals cannot control him, p. 22.

10 Haberman, M., Shear, M., and Thrush, G. (2017). Stephen Bannon Out at the White House after Turbulent Run. *New York Times* [online]. Available at: www.nytimes.com/2017/08/18/us/politics/steve-bannon-trump-white-house.html [Accessed 16 Nov. 2017].

11 Calamur, K. (2017). Why Keep State Department Special Envoys. *The Atlantic* [online]. Available at: www.theatlantic.com/international/archive/2017/08/tillerson-special-envoys/538377 [Accessed 20 Nov. 2017].

12 *The Economist* (2018). The Ballad of Mike and Ronny, p. 26.

13 Zengerle, J. (2017). Rex Tillerson and the Unraveling of the State Department. *New York Times* [online]. Available at: www.nytimes.com/2017/10/17/magazine/rex-tillerson-and-the-unraveling-of-the-state-department.html; see also Burns, N and Crocker, R. (2017) Dismantling the Foreign Service. *New York Times* [online] Available at www.nytimes.com/2017/11/27/opinion/dismantling-foreign-service-budget.html [Accessed 28 Nov. 2017].

14 Diaz, D. (2017). Top General Says He'd Push Back Against 'Illegal' Nuclear Strike Order. *CNN* [online] Available at: www.cnn.com/2017/11/18/politics/air-force-general-john-hyten-nuclear-strike-donald-trump/index.html [Accessed 6 May 2018].

15 Hudson, J. (2018). State Department Braces for Bolton's Return. *Washington Post* [online]. Available at: www.washingtonpost.com/world/national-security/state-department-braces-for-boltons-return/2018/03/27/ad3592d6-3143-11e8-9759-56e51591e250_story.html [Accessed 28 Mar. 2018].

16 *The Economist* (2017b). Relative Moralism: Donald Trump's administration is promoting democracy and human rights, Dec. 9, 2017, pp. 32–33.

17 Ignatius, D. (2018). Trump Can't Win at Foreign Policy the Way He Wins at Golf. *Washington Post* [online]. July 24. Available at www.washingtonpost.com/opinions/trump-cant-win-at-foreign-policy-the-way-he-wins-at-golf/2018/07/24/6887299e-8f83-11e8-b769-e3fff17f0689_story.html [Accessed 1 Aug. 2018].

18   Wiseman, P. (2017). U.S. Chamber of Commerce Sounds Alarm About a NAFTA Pullout by Trump. *Chicago Tribune* [online]. Available at www.chicagotribune.com/business/ct-chamber-of-commerce-nafta-20171006-story.html [Accessed 27 Nov. 2017].

19   Tharoor, I. (2017). Today's WorldView: Trump may be turning his back on the world, but America isn't. *Washington Post* [online]. Available at: https://s2.washingtonpost.com/camp-rw/?e=bWFuc2JhY2hAaWFkGF0ZS5lZHU%3D&s=5a126f34fe1ff6361c7b1a69 [Accessed 27 Nov. 2017].

20   Parker, A., Rucker, P., Dawsey, J., and Leonnig, C. (2018). Trump's Putin Fallout: Inside the White House's Tumultuous Week of Walk Backs. *Washington Post* [online]. Available at: www.washingtonpost.com/politics/trumps-putin-fallout-inside-the-white-houses-tumultu-ous-week-of-walk-backs/2018/07/20/7cfdfc34-8c3d-11 [Accessed 22 July 2018].

21   Wike, R., Stokes, B., Poushter J., and Fetterolf, J. (2017) U.S. Image Suffers as Publics Around World Question Trump's Leadership. *Pew Research Center*. Available at: www.pewglobal.org/2017/06/26/u-s-image-suffers-as-publics-around-world-question-trumps-leadership [Accessed 3 Dec. 2017].

22   Landler, M. (2018). There's Trump's Foreign Policy and Then There's His Administration's. *New York Times* [online]. Available at: www.nytimes.com/2018/08/03/us/politics/trump-foreign-policy.html [Accessed 4 Aug. 2018].

SUGGESTED READINGS

Daalder, I.H. and Lindsay, J.M. (2018). *The Empty Throne: America's abdication of global leadership*. New York: Public Affairs Press.

Haass, R. (2017). *A World in Disarray*. New York: Penguin Books.

Kroenig, M. (2017). The Case for Trump's Foreign Policy. *Foreign Affairs* 96:3 (May/June), pp. 30–34

Posen, B.R. (2018). The Rise of Illiberal Hegemony. *Foreign Affairs* 97:2 (March/April), pp. 20–27.

Part II

Regional issues

3 A poor China might be more dangerous than a rich China

Jonathan Hassid

INTRODUCTION

China has a long and turbulent history, and the last century has been no exception. China has endured revolution, governance by warlords, civil war, and the upheavals of the Mao Zedong era (1949–1976) that resulted in the deaths of millions of Chinese. Under Mao's successor, Deng Xiaoping, however, the country began a new era of "reform and opening," which has resulted in unprecedented growth and perhaps the most remarkable economic success story in history. Hundreds of millions of Chinese have been lifted from dire poverty into the middle class, and in just a generation the country has gone from one of the world's poorest countries to its second-largest economy. More impressively, China has done this peacefully; it has engaged in few external conflicts and, unlike Russia, has done little to threaten overtly the security of its East Asian neighbors or the U.S. But what would happen if China's economy finally slows? What would happen if paramount leader Xi Jinping's "China dream" is seen as an increasingly remote goal for millions of Chinese citizens? In that case, China's foreign policy may become increasingly aggressive, and the threat of military conflict in the region – and with the United States – will increase.

According to what scholars call the "scapegoat hypothesis," also called diversionary theory, governments may provoke conflict abroad to divert the public's attention from domestic woes, thus blaming others for those woes. In doing so, they invent an "enemy" against which the public can unite while ignoring contentious issues at home. Thus, Russian President Vladimir Putin's adventurist policy in Ukraine is regarded by some observers as a diversion from grim living conditions in Russia and its economic stagnation. The diversionary theory is the basis for the humorous 1997 American film, *Wag the Dog*, in which a scandal-ridden U.S. president initiates a fake war with Albania shortly before an election to distract the electorate's attention.

Although China has rapidly increased its "hard power," Beijing has long championed the idea of "nonintervention" in international affairs, that is, China has largely resisted intervening in the politics of other countries and has expected others not to intervene in its domestic affairs. Thus, China played a major role in the nonaligned movement during the Cold War, abstains frequently in the UN Security Council, vigorously resists foreign criticism of its human-rights record, pays little attention to human-rights abuses in countries in which it invests, and strongly defends its sovereign rights. Indeed, under the leadership of both Mao Zedong and Deng Xiaoping (1978–1989), the Chinese government was vocal about preserving and extending norms of noninterference globally. One measure of the seriousness with which Beijing applied these norms was that it even implied (in the so-called "Three Communiqués") that its relations with Taiwan – long considered a renegade province and thus a domestic issue for China – would be resolved through peaceful means. The 1972 Shanghai Communiqué, the most important of these documents, further clarified that neither China nor America – nor any other world power – should "seek hegemony in the Asia-Pacific region," with all disputes handled peacefully and without foreign interference. These communiqués are deliberately ambiguous, and Beijing has since made clear that it would take military action against Taiwan if the island declares independence or crosses other "red lines." The mere fact that China has been willing to negotiate with an outside power (the U.S.), however, over the fate of what it considers to be a renegade province itself represents significant adherence to international norms – at least for now.

While China considers Taiwan's status an internal matter and subject to no outside actor, Washington has also made clear that it considers the status of Taiwan to be important to U.S. national security. America's 1979 Taiwan Relations Act, which remains in effect, allows U.S. arms sales "of a defensive character" to the Taiwanese government and notes that the use of force in the region would be of "grave concern to the United States." Although Washington has no embassy in Taiwan the "American Institute" serves that function unofficially. The unsettled status of Taiwan remains a potential flashpoint and a source of regional tension.

This commitment to sovereignty and noninterference served the goals of the China's leaders, who focused on domestic issues. Rather than provoke its neighbors and risk destabilizing and expensive conflicts, Beijing directed its energy and attention first toward consolidating power and building a Communist society (under Mao) and then recovering from Maoism and getting rich (Deng and his successors). From the perspective of Mao and his successors, foreign conflict risked undoing the achievements of the Communist revolution and invited foreign meddling in Chinese affairs. As paramount leader Deng memorably announced in the late 1980s that it was official Chinese policy to be humble, "hide one's talents and bide one's time" (*taoguang yanghui*) before making a stir on the world stage.

MILITARY CONFLICT AND CHINA'S DOMESTIC POLITICS

Under Mao, China's economy grew slowly, and periodically the country was wracked by natural – and manmade – disasters. After an initial burst of prosperity through the mid-1950s, the growth rate of the Marxist-inspired centrally controlled economy was poor, arguably encouraging Mao and other Chinese leaders to use foreign policy to bolster their legitimacy. The spectacular failure of the Great Leap Forward (1958–1962), for example, resulted in the deaths of between eighteen and fifty-five million people, mostly by starvation. The Great Leap Forward did more than harm Chinese society: it also wrecked China's economy. Even the (likely underestimated) official figures from China's National Bureau Statistics show an astonishing *contraction* of 21 percent in economic growth in 1961, with additional contraction in 1962. This domestic economic crisis – and ongoing political events in Chinese elite politics – probably inspired Chinese leadership to look overseas for success and distraction.

They found distraction on the 4000-kilometer border between China and India. After British diplomat Sir Henry MacMahon established the "MacMahon Line" border on what was the then-British colony of India in 1914, the boundary remained a controversial source of tension with China. Thus, the dispute was hardly new, but China's 1962 invasion of India took nearly everyone, including the Indians, by surprise. Initiated partly to achieve China's strategic goals in the high Himalayas (and push back against perceived Indian aggression), the brief war was also driven by domestic Chinese concerns. After the spectacular failure of the Great Leap Forward, Mao and his allies desperately needed a military success.

Making matters worse, China's relations with the Soviet Union, its only major ally at the time, rapidly deteriorated. Ideological differences and rivalry between Mao and Soviet leader Nikita Khrushchev led to the withdrawal of Soviet advisers and technical help by 1960, further damaging China's economy. Moreover, "domestic stability was shaky with a serious rebellion in Lhasa in 1959 by Tibetan separatists supported by India and the U.S." (Feng, 2007: 56).[1] The failure of the Great Leap Forward, coupled with natural disasters and increasingly unfriendly Sino-Soviet relations probably contributed to the decision to go to war. The war itself went well for China, pushing India back across a number of key strategic border regions. And, as in subsequent conflicts, once the People's Republic achieved modest goals, it unilaterally declared a ceasefire to end the conflict.

Perhaps, the most glaring example of foreign conflict driven (at least in part) by internal Chinese political and economic woes was China's poorly planned and executed 1979 invasion of Vietnam. Disingenuously known in China as the "Defensive Counterattack against Vietnam," the nearly month-long war led to the deaths of tens of thousands of soldiers on both sides with little to show for the effort. Although complicated international political concerns contributed to the rationale for the invasion, it was driven in part by developments in Chinese domestic politics.

The death of Mao in 1976 sparked a protracted battle in the Chinese Communist Party (CCP) over who should be his heir and successor. Mao himself had chosen Hua Guofeng, a drab bureaucrat from Mao's home province of Hunan, to lead the country after his death and continue his economic and political policies. Hua, however, had a challenger in the charismatic and well-connected Deng Xiaoping, a politician and military leader with strong political survival instincts. Deng, three times purged from the Party and three times brought back, urged that China move away from doctrinaire Marxism and instead open its economic system to experimentation and freer markets. Deng argued that China urgently needed the "four modernizations," including reforming its armed forces, and, as the then-chairman of the Central Military Commission, he was the chief proponent of China's invasion of Vietnam. Deng cleverly realized that if the invasion went well, its success would increase his popularity at the expense of Hua; if it went poorly, then Deng could justify his argument that China urgently needed to adopt major reforms and jettison the ruinous legacy of Maoism. By most objective accounts, the People's Liberation Army (PLA) met its goals but exposed gross military incompetence and caused massive Chinese casualties. This outcome helped Deng gather support for further economic reforms – and additional personal power. By 1980, Hua Guofeng had been pushed aside, and Deng Xiaoping was in the driver's seat. He likely would have won the power struggle with Hua in the end, but the war assured Deng's political future.

There are other examples of how Beijing exploited foreign conflicts to divert its citizens' attention from domestic problems. Thus, the USSR and China experienced several border clashes beginning in 1969, just as Mao's Cultural Revolution was tearing China's government and society apart and new military leaders were assuming power at home. Just five years later, China and the Philippines briefly clashed over the disputed Paracel (or Xisha) Islands when Mao's health was deteriorating and the country was experiencing slow growth. In 1995 and 1996, China fired missiles near the coast of Taiwan, at a moment when newly installed leader Jiang Zemin was trying to assert more control over the PLA and intimidate potential rivals. All of China's conflicts and clashes during the past seventy years were fought for complicated reasons, but there is a pattern suggesting that Chinese leaders sometimes take a *Wag the Dog* approach to domestic problems, especially economic ones.

HOW HAS CHINA GROWN SO FAST?

Ever since Deng Xiaoping launched China on the path to economic reform in the late 1970s, the country's growth rate has been spectacular. Never before has a large country – let alone one as enormous as China – grown so quickly for so long. Since 1979, China has surpassed Japan as the world's second-largest economy and will likely overtake the United States in the coming decades. Hundreds of millions of people have been lifted from poverty to prosperity, and China boasts dozens of home-grown billionaires. The country's infrastructure – high-speed railways, new airports and modern highways – is among the immensely impressive achievements. Since 2001, the city of Beijing alone has built an astonishing twenty new separate subway *lines* in less time than it took New York City to build three new subway *stations*. Indeed, growth has been so extensive for so long that many observers believe that China will inexorably become a highly developed and wealthy country. How has China achieved this success, and can it continue?

There are several explanations for China's economic success, which has evolved in two distinct stages. During the first stage, between 1979 and 1992, China concentrated on opening its unproductive agricultural sector to market forces and encouraging the development of small and medium-sized businesses, often run and owned by local villages and small towns. During this period, China began to export low-tech and low-skill products and sought foreign direct investment to help produce manufactured goods less expensively than could the developed world. However, the results were relatively modest. Much of China's growth in this stage involved freeing the economy from the shackles of central planning, and letting market forces do their work domestically. China's government, which had previously owned virtually all major firms, started to step back and privatize many of these publicly owned entities. This policy of divestment forced many companies into bankruptcy, but also fostered many successful enterprises. By the early-to-mid-1990s, the state followed an explicit policy of "grabbing the big, but letting go of the small" (*zhuada fangxiao*), that is, the state would retain ownership of only the largest and most important firms in the economy.

Labor, too, was opened to the market. Under China's previous "iron rice bowl" system, urban state-owned enterprises (SOEs) provided lifetime employment to workers. These "work units," known in Chinese as *danwei*, provided cradle-to-grave services for employees. In addition to providing housing, the *danwei* built and ran schools and hospitals for workers and their families, provided food rations, and were even required to approve divorces and marriages. Although the *danwei* system created stability and predictability for employees, these services were expensive and inefficient, and provided few incentives for employees to work hard. College graduates, for example, were assigned by the government to jobs through the mid-1980s. With lifetime employment and little need to work hard, the result was a rigidly inflexible labor pool. Recognizing these problems, during the 1980s the *danwei* system was slowly reduced, and tens of millions of workers were encouraged to leave their "iron rice bowl" behind and "enter the sea" of commerce.

This "sea of commerce" increasingly became focused on export-led growth. Unlike the initial stage of growth, which had concentrated on small and medium-sized enterprises, often based in and owned by local villages, this stage, which began in 1992 and still continues, relied increasingly on large state- or foreign-owned companies producing goods for export. Unlike many countries in Latin America that unsuccessfully tried to enrich themselves by industrializing and replacing foreign purchases with domestically produced goods – a strategy known as "import-substitution industrialization" – the Chinese state vigorously encouraged "export-oriented industrialization" in which goods are produced for foreign markets. Pushing against hardline opponents who sought to limit foreign investment, Deng used his famous 1992 "Southern Tour" to promote "special economic zones" (SEZs) in coastal China. Enterprises in the SEZs paid fewer taxes and were less regulated than those elsewhere, and were designed to attract foreign investment and promote exports. The SEZs were successful, and growth became spectacular.

Not all growth is equally desirable, however. Economists point out that economic growth can be achieved in one of two (not mutually exclusive) ways. Either "inputs" such as land, labor and capital can be increased, or such inputs can be used more efficiently, improving what is known as "total factor productivity." Most developed countries have already extensively mobilized society's inputs, and so they grow by improving productivity, that is, increasing the amount produced by each worker. In the United States, for example, some economic growth results from more "inputs" of workers owing to population growth from births and immigration, but mainly from improved productivity. In most less developed countries, however, growth generally is the consequence of increases in the size of the labor pool or the amount of investment capital. Such countries generally employ many people in relatively unproductive small farms, thereby making it possible to increase economic growth simply by enticing people to leave their rural homes and move into urban factories.

Thus, when the reform era began in the late 1970s, China had vast numbers of workers involved in subsistence agriculture, who constituted a huge potential labor pool available for workers seeking higher wages in new urban factories. In time, several hundred million of these so-called "blind flow" agricultural workers moved – often illegally – from China's agricultural interior to growing coastal cities like Shanghai, enormously increasing the country's supply of labor "inputs." By some estimates, more than three hundred million people – almost equivalent to America's entire population – moved from the poor interior to the booming coasts, providing a vast new labor supply for foreign-funded factories that soon began to dominate world trade. Crucially, such economic growth relied mostly on increasing labor supply, not on making it more productive (Krugman, 1994).[2]

China's growth, of course, was not entirely the result of merely attracting more and more workers into factories. As time passed, productivity also improved, especially as the country improved its infrastructure to help move people and goods around the country and overseas. When China started the reform era in 1979, its infrastructure was minimal. Outside of major cities, there were few roads. Its rail network was small and virtually paralyzed by aging equipment, and airports hardly existed. Travel was arduous and expensive. A rail journey from southern China to Beijing, for example, took days to complete, generally in overcrowded carriages that froze in the winter and scorched in the summer. Steampowered locomotives were being built as recently as 1988 and used on some routes after 2000. Railroads were underfunded and poorly administered, giving scope to increasing efficiencies made possible by growing investment.

As China increasingly invested in infrastructure beginning in the 1980s, these investments often brought about spectacular increases in productivity. National savings and investment rates (including in infrastructure) rose from about 28 percent of gross domestic product (GDP) in 1980 to 46 percent in 2010, mirroring similar transitions that had taken place in Japan, South Korea, and Taiwan during their earlier economic "miracles" (Kroeber, 2016: 212).[3] Partly because China's roads, rails, ports, electric systems and water plants had been so undeveloped in the Mao era, this massive investment produced spectacular returns, as indicated in Figures 3.1 and 3.2.

FIGURE 3.1 China's annual GDP, 1952–2016

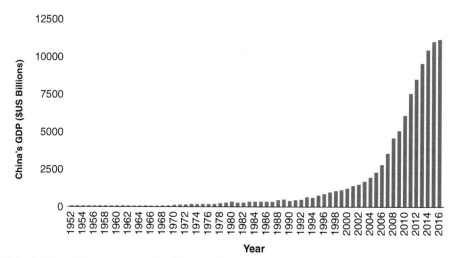

Source: Michael Ciabatti. Data source: National Bureau of Statistics of China

FIGURE 3.2 China's annual GDP growth rate, 1952–2016

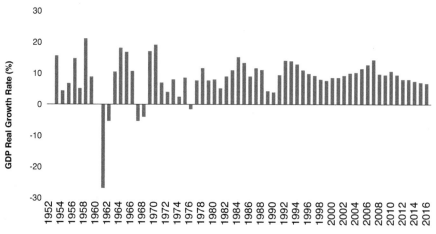

Source: Michael Ciabatti. Data source: National Bureau of Statistics of China

IS THE END IN SIGHT?

Thus, China reform-era growth has been extraordinary, but there are indications that it might be ending. As Arthur Kroeber (2016: 213)[3] notes: "At some stage, a country's capital stock approaches the rich-country level. There is then little benefit to be achieved by simply throwing more capital into the system . . . . Instead, growth must come from increasing the amount of output that a given unit of capital can produce – that is, by increasing the efficiency of resource use." Once a large city has an airport, building a second one will not produce the same economic benefit. Once road and rail systems connect all major cities and ports, each additional mile of road or track built has diminishing returns.

With appropriate economic and political policies, it is relatively easy for a very *poor* country to grow quickly. But after such a country "picks the low-hanging fruit" and receives an initial spurt of growth, it becomes increasingly difficult to sustain previous rates of growth. Economists refer to this as the "middle-income trap," and data increasingly suggest that China may be falling into that "trap" as it enters the ranks of middle-income countries – those with per capita GDP around $10,000. Among the major causes of this "trap" is that workers' wages rise, making exports increasingly uncompetitive globally. "As wages rise manufacturers often find themselves unable to compete in export markets with lower-cost producers elsewhere; yet they still find themselves behind the advanced economies in higher-value products" (*The Economist*, 2011).[4]

Wages have been rising rapidly in China's major coastal cities, the key drivers of China's export-led growth. Market research firm Euromonitor notes that in 2017, average hourly wages for factory workers hit $3.60, low by Western standards but up 64 percent since 2011 (Yan, 2017).[5] At such levels, a factory could employ nearly five Indian workers to replace a single Chinese worker, leading factories to relocate to lower wage countries. China's apparel and garment industries, in particular, have been moving overseas on a "massive investment spree outside of China," (Yan, 2017).[5] Vietnam, Bangladesh and similar less developed countries have benefitted from this trend, as labor-intensive, low-skilled manufacturing moves away from China's increasingly high-wage economy. Even some Chinese state-owned companies are moving factories overseas, something unheard of just a few years ago. The state-owned Shenzhou Group, for example, has recently opened huge garment factories in Vietnam. Rising wages assist China's workers, but they suggest that China's previous export-led growth model is reaching a tipping point beyond which China will become less productive in many highly competitive low-end industries.

Chinese leaders are keenly aware of this problem. President Xi Jinping has made "rebalancing" the economy away from exports and toward increased domestic consumption one of his priorities. The largest developed economies in the world, and the United States, in particular, rely heavily on consumer spending to drive economic growth. Thus, around seventy percent of America's economic activity is driven by consumer spending, compared to about half of that in China. By encouraging Chinese consumers to spend their money instead of saving it, Beijing hopes to move away from economic growth powered by increasingly uncompetitive exports to foreign consumers. This is an especially prudent move given Trump administration's imposition of high tariffs on Chinese goods. And in part this plan is working. Thus, China is now the world's largest market for automobiles, Western companies like Apple sell huge numbers of electronic products, and China's richer consumers purchase growing numbers of luxury goods. But, the transition to a consumer economy remains incomplete and has not met government goals. In theory, China's rising wages alone should promote consumer spending, but there are several reasons why China's hundreds of millions of middle-class consumers remain reluctant to spend their hard-earned money.

First, China's social safety net – including retirement plans, health insurance and unemployment payments – is in tatters. As noted earlier, most Chinese urban residents and many farmers were enrolled by their "work units" (the *danwei*), which enjoyed cradle-to-grave social and welfare services. Because workers were generally enrolled in their *danwei* for their whole careers, the services provided *were* the social safety net. As Deng's economic reforms spread during the 1980s, however, the *danwei* were slowly dismantled. Urban residents could increasingly change jobs and buy homes, food, cars, and vacations from the market economy, but the safety net the *danwei* had provided was not replaced. In the countryside, farmers took control over their land rather than working for huge farming communes, and here the safety net collapsed. Even now, hundreds of millions of farmers have virtually no access to medical care once provided for free by their rural *danwei*. The government has rolled out a national health insurance program that in theory covers virtually all citizens, but in reality provides so few benefits to poorer citizens as to be almost useless. The result is that many households must save most of their income to set aside a "rainy-day fund" in case of illness. The fact that retirees also receive virtually no government help further encourages savings, and thus even many richer citizens remain reluctant to spend their earnings on consumer goods. In part because of these reasons, progress from an export-driven to a consumer spending-driven economy has been slow.

A second obstacle to rebalancing China's economy and ensuring that growth continues has been a massive debt binge by China's local governments. Including debt from China's local governments, debt levels have risen from nearly zero at the start of the reform era to over 230 percent of GDP by the end of 2015, a level on par with richer countries like the United States. In the past, debt was used to finance local development projects, infrastructure and factories, which – because they improved the local economy – made sufficient money to cover the repayment of debt. Debt levels, although rising, were not a major concern. Recently, however, there has been mounting evidence that the local governments have been bingeing on debt to fund increasingly risky projects. Much of the debt has been assumed by China's SOEs to fund daily operations and pay workers' salaries, rather than toward making productive new investments. According to Steil and Della Rocca (2018),[6] these SOEs have increasingly sucked up public funding and amassed risky loans even while their profits – and ability to repay – have been declining. Steil and Della Rocca (2018)[6] argue: "Given the evidence that Xi has abandoned any pretense of concern with [bad debt], and our evidence that China is shoveling new loans to companies with the least ability to pay them back, we think China is heading towards a debt crisis."

Third, China's economy faces demographic challenges, especially as the number of young workers entering the workforce declines. From the early 1980s until 2017, China vigorously enforced a "one-child policy," restricting family size for most Chinese to a single child to limit population growth. The cultural belief that sons – and not daughters – should care for their aging parents, coupled with the collapse of the *danwei* social safety net, encouraged Chinese families to ensure that their single child was male. The result has been one of the world's most lopsided birth ratios. On average, about 118 boys are born for every 100 girls, creating a shortage of women that is being felt across China's society and economy. The one-child policy dramatically reduced the growth of the country's workforce, which is rapidly aging. Thus, demographers estimate that China will "get old before it gets rich," placing a burden on working-age adults to support not only their own children but their parents as well. The end result will be a society with many retirees in need of social services, especially medical care, but few workers to support them. This is a recipe for declining economic growth.

Finally, and perhaps most importantly, China's *economic* problems are intimately related to its *political* problems. Outsiders often imagine that China's central government in Beijing is all-powerful. After all, China is a huge, unified country ruled by the nearly eighty-three million members of the Chinese Communist Party (CCP). Its military forces are the world's largest as measured by numbers of personnel and is the second largest as measured by military spending. On paper, China has a unified political structure with no local political units like America's states to challenge central policy. Provinces, counties, and other sub-national political units exist, but they are merely units of administrative convenience. At 7:00 pm every broadcast TV station in the country transmits *Xinwen Lianbo (News Simulcast)*, the most-watched TV show on Earth. The country has a single currency, a widely spoken national language (Mandarin), and even a single time zone that improbably stretches across an area larger than the United States.

But this picture is misleading. China, in fact, is by some measures among the most decentralized countries in the world (Hassid and Watson, 2014),[7] and the central government in Beijing often finds it difficult to implement its policies. Without free media, local governments tend to be secretive and corrupt, and leaders in Beijing often have a difficult time controlling the behavior of subordinate political units. For example, China's environmental regulations are strict but are frequently ignored by local governments, resulting in air and groundwater that are widely toxic. An old Chinese saying notes that "the mountains are high and the emperor is far away" (*shangao huangdi yuan*), suggesting that local officials have been avoiding central government interference for a long time.

Part of the problem is simply related to size. China's government is like a dinosaur, with a huge body but a tiny brain. Despite the nearly eighty-three million members of the CCP, only 53,000 officials staff the central ministries (Fock and Wong, 2007).[8] Enormous block grants to the thirty-four province-level governments, accounting for hundreds of billions of dollars and about 40 percent of all local government spending, are overseen by only *four* (!) officials in the Ministry of Finance (Kroeber, 2016: 121).[3] Oversight is nearly impossible, and the end result is that serious economic reforms frequently are blocked or ignored at lower levels of government. When central officials urge the closure of polluting industries, for example, local officials often go out of their way to save those factories lest they lose a major source of local funding and employment. Major policy changes, in short, are often impossible to achieve when local officials remain hostile to them.

To reform China's economy, therefore, requires political reform, but President Xi has made clear that political reform is unlikely. Indeed, he has doubled down on the current system, by consolidating power in his office and aiming, in the words of some scholars, to become the "Chairman of Everything." The 19th Party Congress of 2017, which elevated Xi to his second five-year term as paramount leader, also made clear that Xi and other national leaders are resolutely opposed to major political reform. In particular, while the 19th Party Congress enshrined Xi Jinping's "important contributions" to socialist thought in the CCP constitution, no more than symbolic gestures were made to improve China's governance. The current political system will remain basically unchanged, meaning that major economic reforms are unlikely to be realized. Economic stagnation down the road may be the consequence.

CONCLUSIONS

China has several political differences and potential conflicts with the United States, some of which are summarized in Chapter 4. From China's vast maritime territorial claims, the anomalous status of Taiwan to America's alliances with Japan and South Korea, China's treatment of Tibetans and Islamic minorities like the Uighurs, and its reluctance to implement UN-sponsored sanctions to force North Korea to abandon nuclear weapons, there are many potential flash points in the Sino-U.S. relationship. Many analysts noted that at the 19th Party Congress Xi Jinping promoted a more aggressive and muscular foreign policy, promising that China would become a world superpower by 2050. This fact alone could presage eventual conflict with the current reigning superpower, the United States. Indeed, many in China and across Asia feel that President Trump's withdrawal from the U.S.-led Trans-Pacific Partnership has already signaled America's retreat from East Asia, opening the way for a more assertive Chinese foreign policy. Some analysts go further, arguing that China is even now trying to build its own world order and muscle out U.S. trade influence by signing new bilateral trade agreements with historical U.S. allies like Canada. These signs may point to potential conflict in the future. However, there are also reasons to be optimistic. Relations between the two giants were normalized in the 1970s, and thus far China and the United States have avoided serious conflict. In part, this has been a result of U.S. policies in the region and also because China has been able to increase its global status peacefully. But, perhaps the *most important* reason conflict has been avoided is because Beijing has looked inwardly, concentrating on generating economic growth within its borders rather than making trouble beyond them.

President Donald Trump has repeatedly argued that America must be more assertive in foreign affairs and in realizing its national interests regardless of the impact on others. His rhetoric has been highly combative, from vowing to declare China a "currency manipulator" on his first day in office – a claim he later abandoned – to arguing that China has been cheating America in trade deals, denouncing the U.S. trade deficit with China, its theft of U.S. technology and requirement that U.S. firms give Beijing access to their technology, and imposing tariffs on Chinese exports in 2018. Along with other economic problems, the threat caused China's stock market and the value of its currency to decline precipitously. A U.S.-China trade war could indeed cause significant economic problems for China, its Communist Party, and its leader, Xi Jinping (Bradsher and Myers, 2018).[9]

Trump appears to prefer confronting Beijing rather than engaging and cooperating with China. However, this appearance of confrontation may belie a different reality. Many have noted that Trump and his family have personal business ties with China, including large investments and numerous pending trademark applications. Actions like Trump's 2018 public support for state-owned Chinese telecom company ZTE – coming just two days after the Chinese government announced a $500 million investment in a Trump-branded property in Indonesia[10] – suggest to some observers that Beijing might be directly manipulating the U.S. president to benefit Chinese foreign policy. Thus, there was strong congressional opposition to Trump's removing penalties on ZTE that had been imposed for violating U.S. sanctions on North Korea. Combined with the perception, common in Chinese official circles, that America under Trump is actually retreating from its commitments in Asia, the result might be additional areas of potential conflict with China and misperception and misunderstanding between the two.

What might happen if there were an unintended Sino-American military confrontation in the South China Sea or the Sea of Japan, just as China's economy slumps and triggers labor unrest and disturbances at home? What might happen if Xi Jinping's goal of having "no poverty in China by 2020" proves impossible, and China's middle class becomes alienated from the regime and political dissent spreads owing to acute economic and/or environmental distress like widespread water shortages? Under such circumstances, China's history suggests that Xi and other leaders might decide a "minor" foreign conflict would be a way to divert the attention of Chinese citizens from their domestic woes.

In China's past, as we have seen, such "domestically influenced" conflicts have been contained, but the very success of these previous limited conflicts might make Chinese leaders overconfident about their ability to avoid military escalation. Mistakes are easy to make, especially if a potential foe has a leader who tweets militant threats. If Beijing sought to distract an unhappy population by stirring up Chinese nationalism toward the U.S., Taiwan, or Japan regarding maritime territorial claims, for example, and believes the Trump administration will not intervene, the two might career toward a war that neither wants. An incident caused by a trigger-happy U.S. pilot or Chinese naval officer might escalate into a war that neither Washington nor Beijing sought. In the end, then, it may arguably be better for the Trump administration that China continues to flourish economically. A prosperous China means that the United States has a valuable trading partner and – in certain issues – even a strategic partner. An impoverished China, however, might be bad news for everyone.

ESSAY QUESTIONS

1) China's wars with its neighbors have been sharp but short and limited. Why do you think China has not engaged in wars of conquest in the modern era?

2) If you were in Xi Jinping's shoes as leader of China, what would your foreign policy be in reaction to a sustained economic downturn?

3) What, if anything, should China do to reform its political system? What are some pros and cons of the current political model?

4) Why did China mostly pursue a policy of nonintervention in foreign conflicts? It is now time for China to take a larger role on the world stage?

5) How and why did China's economy grow so quickly? Do you think this growth rate will continue? Why or why not?

SHORT ANSWER QUESTIONS

Define and describe the importance of the following:

Noninterventionism
Shanghai Communiqué
Middle-income trap
Scapegoat hypothesis
Danwei (or "iron rice bowl") system

NOTES

1 Feng, H. (2007). *Chinese Strategic Culture and Foreign Policy Decision-Making: Confucianism, leadership and war*. London and New York: Routledge.
2 Krugman, P. (1994). The Myth of Asia's Miracle. *Foreign Affairs* 73:6, pp. 62–79.
3 Kroeber, A.R. (2016). *China's Economy: What everyone needs to know*. New York: Oxford University Press.
4 *The Economist* (2011). Running Out of steam. Available at www.economist.com/blogs/dailychart/2011/12/asias-middle-income-trap [Accessed 7 Jan 2018].
5 Yan, S. (2017). 'Made in China' Isn't So Cheap Anymore, and that Could Spell Headache for Beijing. *CNBC*. Available at: www.cfr.org/blog/china-heaping-debt-its-least productive-companies [Accessed 31 Jan 2018].
6 Steil, B. and Della Rocca, B. (2018). China is Heaping Debt on its Least Productive Companies. Council on Foreign Relations *Geo-Graphics* blog. Available at www.cfr.org/blog/china-heaping-debt-its-least-productive-companies [Accessed 19 Jan 2018].
7 Hassid, J. and Watson, B. (2014). State of Mind: Power, time zones and symbolic state centralization. *Time and Society* 23:2, pp. 167–194.
8 Fock, A. and Wong, C. (2007). China Public Services for Building The New Socialist Countryside. *The World Bank* report 40221-CN. Available at http://documents.worldbank.org/curated/en/527001468218981236/China-Public-services-for-building-the-new-socialist-countryside [Accessed 31 Jan 2018].
9 Bradsher, K. and Myers, S. (2018). Trump's Trade War is Rattling China's Leaders. *New York Times* [online]. Available at www.nytimes.com/2018/08/14/world/asia/china-trade-war-trump-xi-jinping-.html [Accessed 15 Aug 2018].
10 Unlike past presidents, Trump continues to be a direct beneficiary from his companies. He has not placed management of these companies in a so-called "blind trust," and many argue that as a result he is vulnerable to foreign financial pressure. On the Trump/China/Indonesia investment, see www.cbsnews.com/news/trump-project-in-indonesia-gets-chinese-government-partner [Accessed 6 Nov 2018].

SUGGESTED READINGS

Sheng, M.M. (2008). Mao and China's Relations with the Superpowers in the 1950s: A new look at the Taiwan Strait crises and the Sino-Soviet split. *Modern China* 34:4 (October), pp. 477–507.
Yan Xuetong (2011). *Ancient Chinese Thought, Modern Chinese Power*. Translated by E. Ryden. Princeton: Princeton University Press.

4 Expanding Chinese influence and China-United States relations

Yale H. Ferguson and Richard W. Mansbach

INTRODUCTION

As we have seen, China has grown increasingly powerful economically and militarily in recent decades and is widely perceived as a global rival to America. An assertive China has moved beyond Deng Xiaoping's foreign policy of "self-restraint." China seems determined to extend its influence using its military and economic capabilities, and by buying, guiding, and/or coercing overseas Chinese and local agents to achieve its objectives. It also uses "soft" power, notably by advertising its foreign-language media, economic model, technological achievements, and its overseas trade and investment to attract admirers globally.

We start by reviewing Sino-U.S. relations during the Cold War until hostility declined during the Nixon years. We then describe China's contemporary geopolitical objectives and American policy during the Obama years to "pivot" to Asia to counter these objectives. China's territorial claims and its repression of the cultural aspirations of minorities like the Muslim Uighurs and Tibetans and of political dissent in Hong Kong and China itself (sometimes violently as in the 1989 massacre of pro-democracy protesters in Beijing) have been widely criticized in America. These issues, as well as Washington's imposition of tariffs on Chinese imports and U.S. efforts to persuade Beijing to rein in North Korea, have attracted most U.S. attention.

Oddly, however, American policymakers in the Obama and Trump administrations paid relatively little attention to China's development aid to and trade with economically developing countries and its ambitious "Belt and Road Initiative" (BRI, also known as One Belt One Road – OBOR) that aims simultaneously to extend Chinese influence across Eurasia while reducing China's domestic economic woes.

SINO-AMERICAN RELATIONS DURING THE COLD WAR

After World War II U.S. foreign policy in Asia sought to counter Soviet expansion and the spread of communism in the region after Mao Zedong's victory in China's civil war and the establishment of the People's Republic of China (PRC) in 1949. U.S.-Chinese hostility encompassed two bloody wars, the first in Korea (1950–1953) and the second in Vietnam (1965–1975).

During the early decades of Mao's rule, Washington also provided security for the island of Taiwan where the defeated forces of Chiang Kai-shek had retreated and which Beijing claimed was a province of the PRC. Washington refused to recognize Mao's regime and influential U.S. politicians and anti-communist groups formed the so-called "China lobby," which fostered U.S. hostility toward Beijing while supporting Chiang's government in Taiwan.

For two decades, the U.S. sought to contain Chinese ambitions until the mid-1960s witnessed a growing schism between China and its Soviet ally. Mao had become increasingly alienated from Moscow after Soviet leader Nikita Khrushchev in 1956 denounced Joseph Stalin's purges, and declared that "peaceful coexistence" was possible with the capitalist West. Mao believed that Khrushchev was betraying communism, that the USSR had become a greater threat to China than America, and that therefore he was the true successor to Stalin as leader of the communist world.

Washington saw the Sino-Soviet schism as an opportunity, and in 1971 Secretary of State Henry Kissinger secretly journeyed to China and arranged for President Richard Nixon to visit Beijing. Nixon's visit produced a thaw in Sino-American relations that was accompanied by U.S. recognition of Mao's regime and of Beijing's claim that Taiwan was a PRC province. Beijing's "One China" claim was contained in the so-called Shanghai Communiqué. The 1979 Taiwan Relations Act, however, commits the U.S. to oppose the use of force to integrate Taiwan with the mainland, but growing Chinese military power would create a dangerous obstacle to U.S. efforts to defend the island. This situation, punctuated by disagreements over U.S. military sales to Taiwan and references to Taiwanese independence by some of its leaders, remained the status quo until President Trump questioned the "One China" policy. China's sharp reaction and the advice of Trump's advisers persuaded him to change his mind shortly afterwards. China also exerted additional pressure on Taiwan including "island encirclement" flights by bombers. Indeed, America's Taiwan Travel Act of March 2018, which encourages visits between U.S. and Taiwanese officials and the opening of new building to house America's de facto embassy called the "American Institute" further exacerbated Sino-American relations.

China's transition to capitalism began after its domestic economic reforms in 1979. Chinese trade in the 1950s had been almost entirely within the Soviet bloc, and the U.S. and its allies imposed an economic embargo on Beijing. The Sino-Soviet split increased China's isolation, and Beijing followed an economic policy of "self-reliance and independence."

In 1979, Beijing and Washington established formal diplomatic relations and concluded a bilateral trade agreement. During the following years each granted the other "most favored nation" status. Initial Sino-U.S. trade was subject to several conditions, notably, freedom of immigration and annual renewal, but the "most favored nation" norm became permanent after China joined the World Trade Organization (WTO) in 2001. China was regarded as a developing country under WTO rules that allowed it time to phase out discriminatory practices. China, however, claims it is *still* a developing country and has average tariffs three times higher than America. Beijing has been active in the WTO ever since as both a defendant and complainant in that organization's Dispute Resolution System. Over the years, China made remarkable progress as a trading nation, rising in world rankings from 32nd in 1978 to 1st in 2013.

TERRITORIAL ISSUES

China has a 22,000-kilometer land border that touches fourteen neighboring countries, and Beijing has minor border disputes lingering with a number of them, not least a continuing wrangle with India over Aksai Chin and Arunachal Pradesh. Other longstanding controversies have been the status of Taiwan and the evolving meaning of "one country, two systems" with respect to Hong Kong.

Most attention has centered on China's assertive pursuit of sweeping claims to sovereignty over the South and East China Seas – notably the Paracel and Spratly Islands, Pratas Islands, Macclesfield Bank, and Scarborough Shoal – that are also (variously) claimed by the Philippines, Malaysia, Vietnam, Taiwan, and Brunei. Control of the islands affords China strategic advantages, notably a naval ability to penetrate the Pacific beyond the U.S. controlled "first island chain" that stretches from Japan through Taiwan to the Philippines and which, in Chinese eyes, constitutes a strategic encirclement of China. Sovereignty over these islands and atolls would also give China exclusive legal control over the rich maritime resources like oil and fish in the "exclusive economic zones" around them. China's ambitions are also reflected in its first overseas naval base at Djibouti (near a U.S. naval facility) and its lease of a port in Darwin, Australia (also near a U.S. installation). As we shall see, China's maritime ambitions are also evident in its Belt and Road plan.

China's territorial claims are contentious. Beijing's claims are largely based on a so-called 9-dash (sometimes 10- or 11-dash) map originally issued by the then-Republic of China in 1947 that purportedly outlined China's "historical" sway over the entire area, but which violate the UN Law of the Sea Convention. Much of Asia's oil and trade pass through the East and South China Sea. There have been numerous clashes between China and rival claimants in the South China Sea including Vietnam, Indonesia and the Philippines, and tensions heightened after China began drilling operations near the Paracel Islands and conducted major landfill ("island building") operations on submerged reefs, several of which it militarized despite U.S. objections. Beijing's 2008 Olympics, China's influence in neighboring states, its tests of anti-satellite weapons, and warming relations with Russia are examples of China's growing status worldwide.

The Philippines successfully challenged China's claims in a high profile 2016 ruling by the Permanent Court of Arbitration in The Hague. During the Obama years the U.S. began regularly sending warships and reconnaissance aircraft into the disputed waters to underline its claim that the South and East China Seas were under no single country's sovereignty.

Concerned about China's growing military and economic capabilities, Beijing's territorial claims, and the deepening fears of America's Asian friends and allies, President Obama and Secretary of State Hillary Clinton in 2011 announced a strategic "pivot" to Asia. Washington also was concerned with Chinese hacking into U.S. national security networks and industrial cyberespionage. Thus, China's "rise" appeared to be decidedly less and less "peaceful" over time.

The pivot to Asia was diverted by turmoil in the Middle East and concern that China and Russia might form an anti-U.S. coalition. In the end, the pivot proved modest. During the Obama years, a contingent of Marines were stationed at Darwin, and several modern littoral combat vessels were sent to Singapore. Annual U.S. naval exercises were begun with Vietnam, and these were continued under Trump when a U.S. aircraft carrier visited the country. Washington also prepositioned equipment and rotated troops through the Philippines, and Washington and Manila signed an agreement for joint military exercises and U.S. access to Philippine bases. However, after Rodrigo Duterte was elected Philippine president in 2016, he declared a military and economic "separation" from the U.S., producing doubts about the continuation of U.S.-Philippine military cooperation. Duterte then ordered his country's military to take control of some the Spratly Islands that it claims, but shortly afterwards bowed to China's demand that he withdraw his troops. Thus, U.S.-Philippine military ties continue.

American naval forces in Asia remain stretched. Two collisions of U.S. naval vessels with commercial ships in Asia in 2017 that caused U.S. fatalities may have been partly the result of inadequate time for training rather than actively patrolling, and led to the ousting of the head of the U.S. Seventh Fleet.

The U.S. pivot to Asia was undermined by the anti-trade turn in U.S. politics with the election of President Trump. Trump decided to withdraw from the Trans-Pacific Partnership (TPP) trade liberalization treaty, which is more important for U.S. strategic engagement in Asia than for U.S. trade. The other TPP countries agreed to proceed without the U.S., and China, initially excluded, may join the negotiations. China, which already trades more with Asian countries than does America, also seeks to dominate the fledgling Regional Comprehensive Economic Partnership that also includes the Association of Southeast Asian Nations (ASEAN) countries (Brunei, Cambodia, Indonesia, Laos, Malaysia, Myanmar, Philippines, Singapore, Thailand, and Vietnam) plus six countries including China with which ASEAN has existing trade agreements. Finally, the Trump administration's willingness to cede its hegemonic leadership to China in Asia is revealed by comparing "America First" with the ambitious global vision of China's BRI plan.

In a shift from Obama's policy, President Trump agreed in May 2017 to send a National Security Council official, to a BRI conference. This concession, which recognized "the importance" of the plan, reflects the administration's unwillingness to resist the spread of China's economic and political influence and the desire of U.S. firms to participate in China's ambitious program.

ANTECEDENTS TO BELT AND ROAD

An antecedent of the "Belt and Road Initiative" (BRI) was China's growing role in the global economy as a source of foreign direct investment (FDI)[1] by state-owned enterprises and private companies. Beijing is a relatively recent overseas investor, going from little a decade ago to more than $100 billion in 2015, ranking China among the highest *current* exporters of FDI. Reflecting its late start, China's present stock of FDI is just 7 percent of its gross domestic product, compared with America's 38 percent, Japan's 20 percent, and Germany's 47 percent. However, China's foreign assets are growing rapidly. Beijing also spoke of a "digital Silk Road" to build "a community of common destiny in cyberspace" infrastructure according to a vice-minister of informational technology (cited in *The Economist*, 2018: 42).[2]

China's initial FDI focused on energy and natural resources in developing countries, although there has also been keen interest in America, the United Kingdom, and the European Union (EU). China's investments in Greece have provided it with an opening to the EU where it has organized a socioeconomic forum called "16+1" with eleven EU countries mainly in Eastern Europe and five Balkan states. European leaders regard this is an effort to divide them. China was long prevented from investing in America's potentially security-related high-tech and energy sectors. Thus, in 2005 Washington barred the China National Offshore Oil Corporation from purchasing UNOCOL, a U.S. oil company. In 2018 Trump refused to let Qualcomm, a leading U.S. digital chipmaker, be purchased by Singapore-based Broadcom, citing national security concerns. Several European countries are also concerned about Chinese acquisitions that might threaten their national security.

Other great powers seek resources abroad. China, however, has advantages over competitors because it can offer low-cost financing and Chinese labor, but Chinese companies have to contend with the perception that they are agents of Beijing, and sometimes suffer a "nationalist backlash." And, some companies that are not state-owned or even individuals – independent gold-seeking miners in Ghana, for example – embarrass Beijing when they ignore local laws and customs.

China has become Africa's largest trading partner, but its investments in Africa account for less than 5 percent of the region's FDI, well behind the EU, America, and even South Africa. Beijing provides low-interest loans to countries with poor credit ratings in exchange for concessions to develop oil, mineral rights, and in Sri Lanka even a port. Further, there have been complaints about poor safety and environmental standards, unfair business practices and violation of local laws. Thus, Chad castigated China National Petroleum for illegal dumping of crude oil, and Gabon withdrew an oil field permit from a Sinopec subsidiary because of environmental issues. China's policy of noninterference in authoritarian governments that abuse human rights allowed for a profitable flow of arms sales to Sudan and Zimbabwe. However, current Chinese FDI and trade are likely to be dwarfed by its new plan.

BELT AND ROAD

China's BRI plan that was unveiled in 2013 is a bold venture. Washington, however, has said little about this immense project although the Obama administration sought to prevent some of the new institutions established by China to fund it. The plan aims to address domestic problems, explore new investment opportunities abroad, and advance China's position as a global power in a rapidly shifting geopolitical environment. The BRI comes at a time when China's economy is slowing – or at least transitioning to a "new normal" of less-heated export-driven growth. Foreign investment in China has also somewhat slowed, and China has begun to use its huge reserves to become a net exporter of investment capital. The plan is still evolving and is highly ambitious and risky in economic terms.

Belt and Road can be interpreted as challenging both U.S. preeminence in the global strategic and liberal economic order and Russia's efforts to reconstruct its former imperial control over Eastern Europe and Central Asia. Although there is a "power politics" dimension to the plan, Chinese official pronouncements and the initial roll-out of the program were largely orthodox and "liberal" in economic terms. Thus, a more benign interpretation is that China is seeking to play the role to which it is entitled as a major economy in the existing order and looking for places to invest its money and improve its global national image.

Xi Jinping assumed office as China's president in March 2013, and announced his country's BRI plan a few months later. The plan involves two linked initiatives, a "Silk Road

FIGURE 4.1 Map of China's Belt and Road plan (showing China in blue)

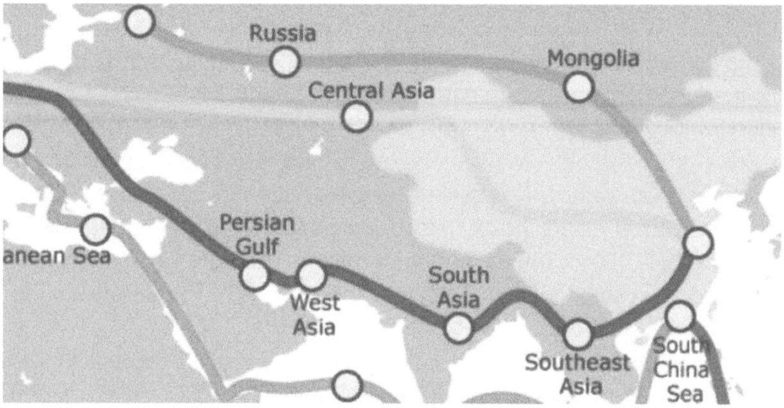

Source: Based on http://peoplesreview.com.np/2017/11/09/cpec-and-its-br-related-significance-for-various-regions-and-continents

Economic Belt" and a "21st Century Maritime Silk Road." The first "belt" is intended to run overland from Xian in central China, across Central Asia and Russia to Europe (eventually as far as Moscow, Rotterdam, and Venice). The importance of Central Asia is reflected in reports that China is building a military base on the Tajik-Afghan border and is providing arms to other regional states. The maritime part of the "road" will begin from China to ports in the South China Sea, the Indian Ocean, and Africa, and continue through the Red Sea and (via the Suez Canal) into the Mediterranean. Chinese official estimates proclaim that the BRI will ultimately affect more than 65 countries and that trade with those countries could reach $2.5 trillion within a decade (Stokes, 2015).[3] China is already the main trading partner of many of these countries.

The list of countries involved is still not entirely clear. Latin America and Africa – where China has already made substantial investments – are not (yet) directly included. However, Africa's participation seems probable because of two developments in 2015. China and the African Union signed a Memorandum of Understanding pledging the parties to link all of Africa through modern highways, high-speed railways, and upgraded airports; and former World Bank chief economist Justin Yifu Lin proposed adding Africa to the project. Latin America has been the recipient of massive Chinese loans, even as Washington retreats from involvement in the region, and China conducted unprecedented naval missions off Brazil in 2013 and Chile in 2014. Its investments in the region are linked to imports of commodities like oil from Ecuador.

The initial focus of the BRI is on infrastructure projects, including a network of roads and railroads, oil and gas pipelines, and improved ports along the entire circuit. Additional goals are financial integration involving the use of China's currency, trade and investment liberalization, and greater IT connectivity. Whether Chinese rhetoric emphasizing sovereignty and nonintervention, as well as adherence to international norms and the decisive role of the market, will be honored remains to be seen.

As of June 2017, China had committed $1.4 trillion or twelve times the size of the Marshall Plan's $120 billion (in today's dollars). It is intended to affect 4.4 billion people and entail investments of over $500 billion in the next five years (Meltzer, 2017).[4] Financing is to come from several sources. China's new $40 billion Silk Road Fund that began operations early this year is directly dedicated to the BRI. That Fund is supported by the China Investment Corporation (China's sovereign wealth fund), the China Development Bank (CDB), the Export-Import Bank of China, the State Administration of Foreign Exchange, and the Agricultural Development Bank.

In 2015 Beijing revealed a recapitalization plan that would inject $32 billion in foreign exchange reserves into the CDB, $30 billion into the Exim Bank, and an unspecified amount into the Agricultural Development Bank. These state-owned non-commercial lenders are known as "policy banks" because their principal mission is to finance China's high priority infrastructure projects at home and abroad. Probably starting with Central and Southeast Asia, the Silk Road Fund's initial concentration is expected to be on transportation infrastructure.

Another source will be the Asian Infrastructure Investment Bank (AIIB) that began operating in 2016. China's proposal for and offer of a substantial financial contribution to the AIIB accompanied the BRI initiative. The AIIB proposal met resistance from the Obama administration that was suspicious of China's geopolitical designs and argued that the new bank would undermine existing international financial institutions like the World Bank. The Obama administration was then embarrassed when some twenty regional states and 27 non-regional states quickly expressed an interest in joining the AIIB, and 50 states signed its charter in September 2015. Other states are in the process of joining. Although Japan chose to stay outside with the U.S., members include many U.S. friends and close U.S. allies like the United Kingdom, most EU states, Australia, and even Israel. The World Bank and the International Monetary Fund (IMF) also endorsed the AIIB, and President Obama changed his public stance to reluctant support when President Xi paid his first state visit to Washington.

The AIIB began with $50 billion capitalization and rapidly reached its target of $100 billion. China's share of the total is nearly one third, and China holds about a quarter of the voting rights. Beijing's argument for the AIIB was persuasive. China and other emerging countries had long been waiting for an increase in the resources and reform of the governance structures of existing international financial institutions to allow them greater voting rights. A treaty to that effect for the IMF and World Bank had been reached but seemed hopelessly stalled by Tea Party conservatives in Congress. However, in mid-December 2015, responding to the inauguration of the AIIB, Congress finally passed the reform measure. There were also complaints from potential applicants about the World Bank's stringent requirements for loans, its glacial review process for applications, and its shifting emphasis from infrastructure to poverty reduction projects. China also pointed out that estimates suggest that the future need for infrastructure investment in Asia alone will be about $8 trillion, or $750 billion a year, far beyond the lending capacity of traditional international institutions.

In October 2015 the Chinese president-elect of the AIIB declared that the new bank would insist on tough environmental and social standards while moving more rapidly with fewer bureaucratic barriers than existing international institutions. The AIIB will *not* have a resident board micromanaging policies and projects – rather a broadly representative non-resident board that will set general policies. The first set of four loans totaling $509 million were announced late June 2016 and included three projects co-financed with the World Bank and other existing international financial institutions. Beijing pledged to recruit an international staff, drawing even from non-member countries like the U.S., and to pay the staff tax-free salaries like the World Bank. Significant moves towards internationalization have been granting the United Kingdom one of the twelve seats on the AIIB's Board of Directors and the recruitment of the former chief secretary to the British Treasury as a senior executive.

An additional future source of funding for some projects might be the prospective Shanghai Cooperation Organization (SCO) Development Bank. The SCO was established in 1996 as the Shanghai Five and in 2001 adopted its new name with the addition of Uzbekistan to founding members China, Russia, Kazakhstan, Kyrgyzstan, and Tajikistan. SCO has two new members, India and Pakistan, four observer countries, and six so-called dialogue partners. As might be expected with such a diverse membership, SCO has thus far been underfunded, mainly a public relations forum, and at best a place for members to explore possible cooperation in energy. (Kazakhstan, Russia, and Turkmenistan have large oil and gas reserves.) In 2010 China proposed the establishment of a SCO Development Bank, which Russia was then unwilling to support. A less direct form of financing will come from China's bank card organization Union Pay, which is rapidly expanding its presence in BRI countries.

China's BRI ambitions have been closely connected to its drive for renminbi internationalization and formal acceptance as a global reserve currency in the IMF's Special Drawing Rights basket, which campaign finally succeeded late in 2015. BRI countries would help extend a "renminbi zone" that is bound to follow upon the Chinese currency's steady advance in recent years. The IMF's decision in 2015 to accept the renminbi as a reserve currency was, *at that stage*, primarily political – based on China's major power status, the sheer size of its economy, and Beijing's sensitivity to status "slights" – rather than economic. With easier currency convertibility, an important question remains about the degree to which China's government will be willing to permit a freer cross-border inflow of capital and foreign investment.

Belt and Road was announced only a few years ago, so it is still early in establishing the program's leadership, institutions, funding, and specific projects. It would be premature to describe China's implementation strategy in detail. Nevertheless, a widely cited survey by London-based merchant bank Grisons Peak found that Beijing has been fulfilling its commitment to countries along its BRI route. Excluding Latin America and West/Central Africa, 76 percent of overseas China state lending (2014 to March 31, 2015) went to such countries. There were 67 loans totaling $49.4 billion, of which 52 percent of loans went to infrastructure such as road, rail, and power projects. Some 70 percent of loans had some link with a China-based corporation. The survey also found that average interest rates charged have risen gradually from 2 or 2.5 percent to 4 or 4.5 percent (Kynge, 2015).[5]

China has also been rapidly building air connections with BRI countries. These are less expensive and easier to complete than roads and rail. Beijing has built fifteen new airports and expanded 28 existing ones, and in 2015 had 51 such projects in progress. In addition, Beijing has promised to allow carriers from Central and South Asia to establish more direct-link services to China.

All of China's provinces will participate in the BRI. For instance, western Qinghai is improving its air, road, and rail networks and is building a logistic center and bonded warehouse. The province's Xining Special Steel will provide products specially designed for infrastructure projects abroad. Wealthy coastal Guangdong is building a power plant in Vietnam, establishing banana plantations in Southeast Asia, and constructing an oil refinery in Myanmar (The Economist Intelligence Unit, 2015: 6).[6] One of the key regions involved in the BRI is the Xinjiang Uighur Autonomous Region, which has China's largest natural gas reserves, 40 percent of its coal, and 22 percent of its oil. It is also the gateway to even larger energy resources in Central Asia. State financial transfers to Xinjiang have grown significantly in recent years in part to increase the number of Han Chinese there. Xinjiang is also home to thousands of Muslim Uighurs who have sometimes violently expressed resentment of the growing numbers of Han Chinese.

Geopolitically, Pakistan is crucial to China and central to the BRI. Pakistan is in South Asia on the Arabian Sea. It has access to the Indian Ocean, the Persian Gulf, and the Middle East. Their relationship has been termed an "all-weather friendship" encompassing diplomatic cooperation, economic interests, and military matters. China is an alternative for Pakistan to America in providing military assistance, including aid in developing nuclear weapons, while Trump cut off aid to Pakistan for providing refuge for Afghan Taliban terrorists. His tweeted denunciation of Pakistan in late 2017 pushed that country closer to China, which has pledged much more aid to Pakistan than the U.S. aid in recent years.

Pakistan and China are rivals of India, which in recent years has begun working closely with America owing to the latter's concern about Beijing. India was the only country to turn down participation in BRI. U.S.-Indian relations improved after the 2008 Civilian Nuclear Agreement that initiated cooperation between them on developing peaceful uses of nuclear energy, although India's development of nuclear weapons had violated the Nuclear Non-Proliferation Treaty. This facilitated U.S.-Indian military coordination in an annual U.S.-India Strategic Dialogue in 2010, and military exercises among the U.S., India, and Japan in 2017 called "Malabar" and these are expected to continue. In addition, Prime Minister Shinzo Abe is seeking to revise Article 9 of Japan's constitution to free the country from limits on its military forces.

China is Pakistan's leading source of imports and its second-largest export destination. The two countries have cooperated on joint infrastructure projects, notably the Chinese construction of the Arabian Sea Gwadar port along the strategic Strait of Hormuz – allowing energy to reach China through connecting pipelines – and a highway between Pakistan and China over the Karakoram Mountains. China is currently investing a further $46 billion in Pakistan to improve the China-Pakistan Economic Corridor. Beijing will pay Pakistan's cost-share of the long-delayed Iran-Pakistani pipeline, but the "flagship project" will be a rail corridor across the two countries. The Karakoram highway will be upgraded, and the key goal is a link between the port of Gwadar and the city of Kashgar in Xinjiang. Indeed, some Indians fear that China's construction of port facilities in India's neighbors such as Pakistan, Myanmar, and Bangladesh constitute a "string of pearls" intended to encircle India.

President Xi has also promised new investments of $40 billion for infrastructure projects in Central Asia, which are especially welcome because of Russia's recession and falling commodity prices globally. China had passed Russia earlier as the region's major economic partner and is becoming Russia's political and economic rival in a region that Moscow regards as its sphere of interest. Chinese companies own a significant portion of Kazakhstan's oil production and China is constructing a rail link in a new town ("The Khorgos Gateway") that it is building, and is a key customer for Turkmenistan's natural gas. China National Petroleum Corporation has also ended Gazprom's Russian gas monopoly in the region, partly because of the China-Central Asia pipeline that is owned by China and Kazakhstan, Uzbekistan and Turkmenistan. China has also become the largest source of the region's development funding. Repaying resulting debts will consume much of those countries' gross national product in coming years.

Belt and Road is already contributing to China's influence. Nonetheless, serious challenges lie ahead. The most important is the outlook for China itself, especially its economy and concerns in Central Asia about China's growing presence. China's Communist Party has accomplished a difficult transition to a new generation of leaders, and Xi has proved to be a popular and effective president. However, over the long term, it is uncertain whether China's government is capable of managing a project as immense and complex as the BRI.

China's "rise" has been sustained over the years by record growth rates, which were the result of a boom in exports, and supported by a vast expansion of credit and government pump-priming. The years of "overheated" growth in China are drawing to an end, and China's leaders acknowledge that the export-oriented growth model must be supplemented by increasing domestic consumption, looser state controls, and greater openness to global market forces. Chinese leaders recognize that lower growth may lead to dangerous social strains. These concerns may be part of the reason for increasing domestic authoritarianism and fanning nationalist passions by pursuing territorial claims.

Moreover, China's bureaucrats and state enterprises have a poor record in executing sound and profitable projects abroad. In the future, some debtor countries will have difficulty repaying their loans, and some projects may create local political problems as they have in Africa and Asia. Sri Lanka is a case in point. Its former prime minister awarded large contracts to Chinese state enterprises with the result that nearly 70 percent of the country's infrastructure projects have been funded and built by China, and its national debt tripled. However, Sri Lanka's 2015 election brought a new prime minister to power, who alleged there had been widespread corruption and who halted two-dozen projects, including an enormous port project in the capital Colombo. Myanmar in 2011 tilted toward America and suspended a dam project to be built by China. A later government that was elected welcomes responsible investment from all sources, but under stringent rules.

However, regimes in Central Asia and the Middle East are capricious and in some cases unstable. Possible violence and terrorism are significant threats in several key states involved in the BRI. The Taliban in Afghanistan and Pakistan, the Islamic State in Iraq, Syria and elsewhere, al-Qaeda affiliates in Africa and the Middle East, and the Houthis in Yemen are some of threats China may meet. As these examples suggest, there are security concerns to the BRI that may entail military protection. There are also potential economic problems. Beijing has become concerned about whether its huge loans will be repaid by the countries to which it is lending. Thus, in 2018 China reduced the number of projects it is financing, and the new governor of China's central bank declared, "Ensuring debt sustainability – that is very important" (cited in Bradsher, 2018).[7] Moreover, Malaysia, a crucial geopolitical actor owing to its access to the strategic Malacca Straits that link the Indian Ocean with the South China Sea, like several other countries including Sri Lanka and Pakistan under its new prime minister, Imran Khan, is trying to back away from BRI commitments owing to fear of growing indebtedness to Beijing.

One observer notes that the BRI commits China to building an astounding 81,000 kilometers of high-speed railways, more than the current world total. He asks: "Who is going to protect so many projects covering so many countries?" and reminds us, as an example, that the Kashgar Gwadar economic corridor – designed to link western China and Pakistan with roads and pipelines, and send electricity to Pakistan – "passes through some of the world's most vulnerable and conflict-ridden territory" (Zhu, 2015).[8] Pakistan has promised 10,000 troops to guard Chinese projects, and U.S. forces have so far protected a Chinese copper mine in Afghanistan. Many other countries will surely pledge and attempt to provide adequate internal security as well. China will have to raise a rapid-response army, naval, and air units and may have to provide on-the-scene protection themselves. How receptive will countries be to having Chinese "boots on the ground"?

CONCLUSION

The historical Russo-British "Great Game" has a new set of players and geographical scope that includes but is broader than the Eurasian Heartland and even extends into Arctic regions. Gone are both the era of assured U.S. hegemony and its accompanying liberal political order. China has enjoyed a meteoric peaceful economic and military rise that seems to be transitioning to an uncertain "new normal," even as Beijing is embarking on its bold new strategy and threatening neighbors with pursuit of its sweeping maritime territorial claims. And it has assumed leadership on issues ranging from UN peacekeeping and funding to climate change and multilateral trade from which the Trump administration has retreated.

China's economic progress, its BRI, and the elevation of its currency confirm China's long-desired status as a leading global economic power. Trump's withdrawal from the TPP, along with its acceptance of the BRI, entail acceptance of Chinese economic and political leadership in Asia and beyond. This status propels China into the Great Game and "places" it on the playing board where major rivals – especially Russia and the U.S – have a strong presence. A struggle over competing national interests is likely, and perhaps even military confrontation.

Russia, for example, has long been concerned about Chinese migration and settlement into eastern Siberia and considers that its sphere of influence extends over resource-rich Central Asia. That history offers reasons both for and against it having closer ties with Moscow. Russia has made agreements with several Central Asian governments to build pipelines, as has China. As noted above, Russia to date has blocked the Shanghai Cooperation Association from undertaking major economic initiatives including establishment of the China-proposed SCO Development Bank. However, the geopolitical situation seems to be shifting as post-Ukraine Russia finds itself estranged from the West and suffering economic costs owing to sanctions. In consequence, Putin has drawn closer to Beijing and may find it necessary to cede influence in Central Asia for the benefits of Chinese investment in that region and in Russia itself.

In sum, Chinese-American relations are mixed. Since Trump's correction of his early gaffe regarding "One China," there have been issues on which the two countries cooperate, and others over which they have disagreed. We have discussed U.S.-China relations in recent years, emphasizing the extension of its global influence, but omitting friction over China's unwillingness to force North Korea to surrender its nuclear weapons (see Chapter 10). However, China has given self-interested support for UN peacekeeping, did not veto several UN Security Council resolutions regarding North Korea, and participated in both the diplomatic efforts to limit Iran's nuclear program and the anti-piracy campaign off the coast of northeast Africa. During the Obama years, there was also some encouraging bilateral progress on environmental goals and cyberwarfare.

At the top of America's foreign policy agenda with regard to China are trade and investment issues and threats to security in the South and East China Seas – *not* primarily China's extension of influence through "Belt and Road." However, China's strategy in Central Asia touches on some U.S. interests there, most of which touch on U.S. efforts to stabilize Afghanistan. Washington has been eager to see the emergence of a regional energy market, linked private-sector investments in Afghanistan and Pakistan, and the building of a Turkmenistan-Afghanistan-Pakistan-India pipeline. In all of these matters there is potential for rivalry between the U.S. and China, but also for mutual benefits.

The same is true about expanding mutual trade and investment. Were a future administration to reconsider joining the TPP along with China, the resulting growth in trade would benefit both countries. Thus, as some Chinese commentators have begun to recognize, the TPP might also offer benefits to China, as did its accession to the WTO. Much the same might be said of the innovative approaches even now taking shape in the Asian Infrastructure Investment Bank, as a spur to improve performance at the World Bank and other international financial institutions.

Already the AIIB's advent convinced Congress to approve long-overdue voting reforms in those international agencies. It may well be that just this sort of win-win thinking offers a possibility for constructive cooperation between the United States and China despite increasing Chinese global influence. Unfortunately, Trump's announcement in March 2018 of large tariffs on Chinese imports threatens a lose-lose trade war.

The real risk is hegemonic war as China threatens to replace the U.S. as a global hegemon (see Chapter 1). Graham Allison (2017)[9] called this the "Thucydides trap" because Thucydides argued that what caused the Peloponnesian War between Athens and Sparta in the 5th century BCE "was the growth of Athenian power and the fear which this caused in Sparta." Theorists who fear hegemonic war point to conflicts like the Seven Year War between England and France in the 18th century. Aware of the historical analogies, President Xi emphasized the need for "a new type of great power relations" during his 2015 visit to the U.S., and shortly before Trump's 2017 visit to China, Xi spoke of "Chinese wisdom and a Chinese approach to solving problems." Xi's "China dream" is equality with the U.S. in which China is a second global hegemon in a once-more bipolar world.

ESSAY QUESTIONS

1) China claims Washington is trying to "contain" its ambitions. Explain why China perceives this and defend the Chinese position.

2) Discuss the nature and significance of China's "Belt and Road" initiative.

3) Should countries participate in China's Belt and Road scheme? Discuss why. countries may wish to join or why they might resist joining?

4) What are the major issues about which China and America disagree? Describe the position of each on these issues, and how they might be resolved.

5) Trace the evolution of Sino-American relations from the Cold War to the present.

SHORT ANSWER QUESTIONS

Define and describe the importance of the following:

The "16+1" forum
Infrastructure projects
Malacca Straits
The Kashgar Gwadar economic corridor
The U.S.-India Strategic Dialogue

NOTES

1   Foreign direct investments are investments made by a company or government in one country in businesses in other countries, either by establishing business operations or acquiring business assets such as ownership of a foreign company. In contrast, portfolio investments involve purchases of stocks and bonds in foreign companies.
2   *The Economist* (2018). A Web of Silk: China talks of building a "digital Silk Road", p. 42. Available at: www.economist.com/china/2018/05/31/china-talks-of-building-a-digital-silk-road [Accessed 6 Nov 2018].
3   Stokes, J. (2015). China's Road Rules: Beijing looks West toward Eurasian integration. *Foreign Affairs*. Available at: www.foreignaffairs.com/articles/asia/2015-04-19/chinas-road-rules [Accessed 7 Dec 2017].
4   Meltzer, J. (2017). China's One Belt One Road Initiative: A view from the United States. Brookings [online]. Available at: www.brookings.edu/research/chinas-one-belt-one-road-initiative-a-view-from-the-united-states [Accessed 2 Oct 2017].
5   Kynge, J. (2015). Chinese Overseas Lending Dominated by One Belt, One Road Strategy. *Financial Times* [online]. Available at: www.ft.com/intl/cms/s/3/e9dcd674-15d8-11e5-be54-00144feabdc0.html [Accessed 8 Dec 2017].
6   *The Economist* Intelligence Unit (2015). Prospects and Challenges on China's 'One Belt, One Road': A risk assessment report [pdf]. Available at: https://static1.squarespace.com/static/529fcf02e4b0aa09f5b7ff67/t/554c49cee4b06fc215162cb4/1431062990726/One+Belt%2C+One+Road.pdf [Accessed 9 Dec 2017].
7   Bradsher, K. (2018). China Taps the Brakes On Its Global Push for Influence. *New York Times* [online]. Available at: www.nytimes.com/2018/06/29/business/china-belt-and-road-slows.html [Accessed 2 Jul 2018].
8   Zhu, Z. (2015). China's AIIB and OBOR: Ambitions and challenges. *The Diplomat* [online]. Available at: http://thediplomat.com/2015/10/chinas-aiib-and-obor-ambitions-and-challenges [Accessed 29 Jan 2018].
9   Allison, G. (2017). *Destined for War: Can America and China escape Thucydides's trap?* New York: Houghton Mifflin Harcourt.

SUGGESTED READINGS

Allison, G. (2017). *Destined for War: Can America and China escape Thucydides's trap?* New York: Houghton Mifflin Harcourt.
Rudolph, J. and Szonyi, M., eds. (2018). *The China Questions: Critical insights into a rising power.* Cambridge: Harvard University Press.

5 Realpolitik: United States-Russian relations and the emerging political order

Scott Feinstein and Ellen B. Pirro

INTRODUCTION

Russia has emerged as a competitor of America even as perceptions of U.S. decline have become widespread. Russian foreign policy is the sole prerogative of President Vladimir Putin, who has declared that he seeks to enhance global stability. To achieve this, he believes a multipolar world is necessary, and America's dominant role must be reduced. Putin wants to restore Russia's great-power status, giving Moscow a seat at every negotiating table. And, Russia wants to guarantee its security by asserting its sphere of influence over former Soviet republics, satellite states and near neighbors.

Moscow views relations with Washington as zero-sum in which one actor's gains equal the other's losses. U.S.-Russian geopolitical rivalry is illustrated by the eastern expansion of the North Atlantic Treaty Organization (NATO) and the European Union (EU), and Russia's aggression in Ukraine, its annexation of Crimea, and its involvement in the Middle East. Foreign-policy activism is crucial to Putin's domestic popularity, and he has swiftly advanced in transforming Russia into the major power the USSR once was – a force to be reckoned with. His success in this is fostering perceptions of a tri-polar world led by America, Russia and China.

President Donald Trump's admiration for Putin, Russian cyber-enabled interference in the 2016 U.S. elections, suspected collusion between Russia and Trump's campaign, Trump's reluctance to implement the sanctions against Russia demanded by Congress, and his unpredictable and continuously changing foreign policies have reduced U.S. world leadership and the potential for multilateral cooperation. Instead, Congress and an under-staffed State Department myopically guide foreign policy toward Russia.

Trump repeatedly expresses admiration for Putin, who epitomizes the "strong" leader Trump seeks to emulate. This admiration is repeatedly apparent. Thus, when the CIA uncovered a terrorist plot to bomb St. Petersburg, Trump immediately informed the Kremlin. This led to a "thank you" phone call from Putin and praise for America's president. Additional phone calls between Trump and Putin, including one just before Trump's summit with Kim Jong-un in June 2018, have fostered suspicion of Trump and a deep division with European allies that have sought to isolate Russia since its intervention in Ukraine. Standing next to Putin shortly after twelve Russians were indicted for hacking the Democratic National Committee, Trump horrified U.S. politicians by publicly questioning the conclusions of U.S. intelligence agencies about Russian interference in the 2016 U.S. elections. He declared that he saw no reason why Putin would try to influence the election. Shortly thereafter, the Justice Department indicted and arrested a woman whom it labeled a Russian agent. By August 2018, twenty-six Russians had been indicted. A former CIA Director called Trump's comments "treasonous." Even leading Republicans expressed horror. Senator John McCain declared, "No prior president has ever abased himself more abjectly before a tyrant"; Newt Gingrich, the former House speaker, declared it the "the most serious mistake of his presidency;" Mitt Romney, the 2012 Republican presidential candidate, called it "disgraceful and detrimental to our democratic principles" (cited in Stolberg et al., 2018).[1] Under a hail of criticism, he later said he had misspoken. Shortly afterwards, Trump declared that Russia was no longer targeting the U.S., thereby contradicting his own Director of National Intelligence. Thereafter, he reversed himself again, perhaps twice by admitting Russian hacking continued and then declaring the issue "a big hoax."

Trump's Russophilia places him at odds with other American views, especially those of Congress and U.S. national security and intelligence agencies, which view Russia as a dangerous foe. Trump's own National Security Strategy views Russia as a major threat to U.S. interests, and contradicts his public approach to relations with Russia at the expense of allied relations.

Russo-American rivalry predates the Trump administration. After two decades following the Cold War, which were called the "Cold Peace" and "reset," the two countries' relationship declined in 2011. Rivalry emerged concerning the fate of Syria's President Bashar al-Assad, with America and Russia taking opposing positions. The two countries also took antithetical positions toward U.S. government contractor Edward Snowden, who had leaked highly classified information from the National Security Agency in 2013. Snowden fled Hong Kong to Russia, and Moscow granted him asylum. In response, Washington imposed sanctions on Russia. Moreover, Moscow and Washington cannot reconcile Russia's annexation of Crimea and its aggression in eastern Ukraine, which triggered additional U.S. sanctions. Towards the end of the Obama administration's first term, these events reflected deteriorating U.S.-Russian relations.

This chapter examines how the relationship deteriorated and evolved. We review the policies pursued by President Obama and describe the situation Trump faced entering office. We then examine describe the policies and actions of the Trump administration toward Moscow and conclude by assessing where the relationship is heading with respect to key issues such as Ukraine/Crimea, Syria, NATO, and election interference.

PEREZAGRUZKA – RESET

Under Obama, U.S. foreign policy toward Russia took two opposite directions. Following Obama's election, U.S. relations with Russia improved modestly. America's election coincided with Dmitry Medvedev's election as third president of the Russian Federation (after Boris Yeltsin and Putin, who had to step aside after two terms in office). Putin became Russia's prime minister until he again became president four years later. Under Medvedev and Obama, the two countries began a 'reset' of U.S.-Russian relations and signed a new Strategic Arms Reduction Treaty (New START). Increasing cooperation encompassed a range of activities, including collaboration on missile defense in which Russia might even participate, multilateral military exercises, coordinated policies toward Iranian and North Korean efforts to acquire nuclear weapons, missions in space, and Russian membership in the World Trade Organization (WTO). However, following disruptive parliamentary Russian elections in 2011, which America condemned as flawed, and Putin's resumption as president of Russia in 2012, bilateral cooperation ebbed, as witnessed by inability to compromise regarding espionage, Ukraine, NATO and, at times, Syria.

Under President Obama, minimal but increasing cooperation began with the 'reset' and the New START treaty. The drafting of these two programs began in early 2009. The 'reset' was a largely symbolic gesture by Washington to improve relations with Russia after the 2008 Russo-Georgian War in which Moscow triumphed and occupied two breakaway Georgian provinces – Abkhazia and South Ossetia. Despite the misuse of a Russian word for 'implode' (*peregruzka*) instead of the correct word for reset/reload (*perezagruzka*), during Secretary of State Hillary Clinton's and Russian Foreign Minister Sergei Lavrov's announcement of plans to improve U.S.-Russian relations, the 'reset' initiated several bilateral cooperative efforts. In April 2010 the two agreed to a New START treaty that replaced both the original START I, signed in 1991 which had expired in December 2009, and the 2002 Strategic Offensive Reductions Treaty (SORT). New START continued reducing U.S. and Russian nuclear arsenals, limiting the number of nuclear warheads for each to 1,550, down from 6,000 in each country in the early 1990s.

Additional agreements followed the 'reset' with cooperation on missile defense and Iran. The Obama administration inherited and initially continued a program to establish a missile-defense system in Poland, claiming it was directed at Iran. President Medvedev stated that the missile-defense system threatened Russian security, declaring "the creation of a missile defense system, the encirclement of Russia with military bases, the relentless expansion of NATO – we have gotten the clear impression that they are testing our strength" (cited in Gutterman and Isachenkov, 2008).[2] Following new U.S. intelligence regarding Iran, however, Washington halted constructing its missile-defense system in Poland, lifted sanctions on Russian arms exporters, and U.S. and Russian leaders agreed to a UN resolution that imposed sanctions on Iran. In 2015 Washington and Moscow cooperated in achieving the Iran nuclear deal to slow Iranian uranium enrichment and Tehran's acquisition of nuclear weapons. Throughout this period, America continued cooperating with Russia regarding North Korea and space missions. Washington facilitated Russia's membership in the WTO in 2011.

Russo-American cooperation was not without difficulties. The extension of NATO into Albania and Croatia met vocal Russian opposition, but significant conflict did not occur until 2011 and 2012. Following domestic unrest in Russia's 2011 and 2012 elections and U.S. criticism of the latter, the two sides adopted opposing positions on Syria's civil war and controversy linked to the Snowden leaks. The Syrian civil war began in 2011. Russia vigorously backed Assad's regime, while Washington pressed Assad to resign, and supported the Sunni rebel opposition. After Russian intervention in Syria in 2015, the two accused each other of preventing progress in ending violence in Syria. Washington claimed that Russian aircraft attacked American-trained rebels, and Moscow contended that America bombed Syrian government targets. Moscow's intervention was largely driven by Putin's desire to prove that Russia was again becoming a global power and to distract Russian public attention from domestic economic and political problems.

Despite such differences, compromise still prevailed. By 2012 President Obama had established military training and covert operations to resist the terrorist Islamic State

(IS) in Iraq and Syria. Washington also agreed to coordinate military operations with Russia and permitted Russian military support of Assad. In short, Washington agreed to engage IS and refrain from anti-Assad activities, actions that fostered Russian influence in Syria.

However, the two countries continued to disagree over other issues. In 2012, the Obama administration implemented the Magnitsky Act to punish Moscow for the death of Sergei Magnitsky, an auditor at a Moscow law firm and a legal adviser for London-based Hermitage Capital Management, who had been imprisoned in 2009 after publicly claiming Russian officials were guilty of fraud. Bill Browder, who headed the hedge company, had hired Magnitsky to conduct his investigation. The Magnitsky Act sanctioned several Russian officials and businessmen linked to Magnitsky's death, preventing them from entering the U.S., freezing their assets in U.S. banks and preventing their use of U.S. banks. In retaliation Moscow barred American adoptions of Russian children. In 2016 Washington enacted the Global Magnitsky Act, which permitted the government to impose similar sanctions on individuals around world who committed human-rights abuses. Others, including non-Russians, were sanctioned in 2017 for violating the act.

In May 2013 events surrounding Snowden caused another U.S.-Russian confrontation after Putin granted Snowden asylum in Russia, refusing the Obama administration's demands for Snowden's return to America. In addition, Russia's intervention in Ukraine and annexation of Crimea and ensuing American sanctions increased U.S.-Russian tension. Following successful pressure by Moscow to end an economic agreement between Ukraine and the EU, protests erupted in Kiev in November 2013. Violent confrontation between Ukrainian President Viktor Yanukovych's government and protestors preceded an increase in the number of those in central Kiev demanding reform, and culminated in the ousting of Yanukovych, who fled to Russia.

Yanukovych's overthrow was seen by Moscow as an extension of creeping U.S. influence as part of a campaign to undermine Russia's government, a perception created by George W. Bush earlier support of NATO expansion. Thus, a low-level "frozen conflict" involving hybrid warfare began in Ukraine. Russian troops (known colloquially as 'little green men' because their uniforms had no identifying markings) entered Southern and Eastern Ukraine, arming local pro-Russian rebels with artillery and other arms. Russia sought to prevent Ukraine from joining NATO and to bring part of that country into Moscow's orbit.

The Obama administration responded decisively. Coordinating with the EU, Washington imposed economic sanctions on Russia. These included restricting access to Western financial markets and embargoing exports that would aid Russia's oil exploration and military modernization. The administration also placed visa restrictions on twenty Ukrainian officials and an undisclosed number of Russians believed to be destabilizing the Ukrainian government in collaboration with Moscow. Finally, to deter additional Russian aggression, President Obama introduced the European Reassurance Initiative and what became the largest increase of U.S. and NATO troops in Europe since the Cold War. The Trump administration continued this initiative, supporting the Department of Defense's request for over $6.5 billion for FY 2019 to increase NATO's military presence in Eastern Europe. The buildup also included greater allied military funding, positioned U.S.-led NATO troops in eastern Poland and additional military units in the Baltic region.

The events in Ukraine brought the final demise of the 'reset' and left the incoming Trump administration with issues that still impede U.S.-Russian cooperation.

THE TRUMP ADMINISTRATION AND RUSSIA

In a sense, the Trump administration's Russian policy has been schizophrenic. On the one hand, Trump and his surrogates have expressed admiration and friendship toward Putin and Russia. On the other, several agencies of the U.S. government including Congress and the State Department have followed the less friendly path taken by President Obama.

One of Trump's favorite tweets during the campaign and thereafter was: "Having a good relationship with Russia is a good thing, not a bad thing. Only 'stupid' people, or fools, would think that it is bad. We have enough problems around the world without yet another one. When I am President, Russia will respect us far more than they do now and both countries will, perhaps, work together to solve some of the many great and pressing problems and issues of the WORLD!" (cited in Scott, 2017).[3] There is some evidence that Trump's associates assured Putin that, if Trump were elected, U.S. sanctions would be quietly ended. For his part, Putin refrained from negative public comments about America during the U.S. electoral campaign. Trump seized opportunities to praise Putin, expressing the hope that when he was president relations would improve.

Trump still expresses admiration for Putin. Although no summit meeting occurred during Trump's first year in office, owing in part to Russia's interference in the 2016 U.S. election, in June 2018 the two agreed to meet shortly after in Helsinki, Finland. In addition, in defiance of his advisers, who wrote in his briefing materials in all-capital letters "DO NOT CONGRATULATE," Trump called Putin to do so after his March 2018 electoral victory.

Even as efforts to reconcile Moscow and Washington were taking place, intelligence sources were compiling information on Russian interference in the American presidential election. Intelligence reports and the Senate Intelligence Committee confirmed that Russia had utilized the Internet, especially social media in order to elect Trump and defeat Hillary Clinton. They hacked the Democrats, planted stories, and spread rumors and false information, especially in advertisements on Facebook and other social media. There is even evidence that attempts were made to hack into voting results in several states. It is hard to weigh the impact of these efforts, but the publicity they received was significant.

Simultaneously, the question arose about whether Donald Trump or any of his associates colluded with Russians in their efforts to aid his election. Trump has denied any Russian involvement in the election, calling it "fake news." Putin has denied his involvement and Trump has said that he believes Russia's president. Nevertheless, several investigations were initiated. Congressional committees have investigated both issues, and a special counsel, Robert Mueller, was appointed by the Justice Department (after Attorney General Jeff Sessions recused himself) to investigate these matters. Trump repeatedly refers to Mueller's investigation as a "witch hunt." Although there have been several indictments of Trump associates for wrongdoing, we have no final answer yet about what took place.

One problem is that the collusion investigation overshadowed the problem of Russian hacking, which intelligence agencies claim was continuing in the U.S. and Europe and was likely to occur in America's 2018 congressional elections. As long as Trump continues to deny any Russian interference, it will be difficult to develop countermeasures to protect U.S. campaigns and elections. Another problem is that Trump cannot advocate U.S.-Russian cooperation while a cloud hangs over his head.

Meanwhile, Washington and Moscow have engaged in a tit-for-tat conflict. Each has accused the other of espionage and other unfriendly acts. Each has retaliated for alleged violations of diplomatic norms, provoking additional retaliation. Between 2016 until 2018,

TABLE 5.1 DIPLOMATIC INCIDENTS BETWEEN THE UNITED STATES AND RUSSIA, 2016–2018

June 6, 2016	Russian police official attacks U.S. diplomat.
June 17, 2016	U.S. expels two Russian diplomats.
July 9, 2016	Russia expels two U.S. diplomats.
July 13, 2016	Moscow bans an Obama appointee from ever entering Russia.
October 3, 2016	Russia suspends an agreement on weapons-grade plutonium.
October 3, 2016	U.S. suspends plutonium agreement.
October 3, 2016	Russia claims the FBI is harassing its diplomats in U.S.
November 8, 2016	Russia threatens to ban U.S. observers from Russian elections.
November 10, 2016	Legislation introduced in Congress to restrict movement of Russian diplomats in the U.S.
December 7, 2016	Russia threatens to restrict U.S. diplomats' movements in Russia.
December 29, 2016	U.S. expels 35 Russian diplomats
July 1, 2017	Congress legislates new sanctions on Russia.
July 30, 2017	Putin orders U.S. diplomatic mission in Russia reduced by 755
July 30, 2017	U.S. closes and seizes Russian diplomatic buildings in San Francisco, Washington, D.C. and New York.
September 13, 2017	Russia removes parking at U.S. consulate in Moscow.
October 2, 2017	U.S. searches Russia's San Francisco consulate.
October 12, 2017	Russian Foreign Secretary Lavrov informs Secretary of State Tillerson that Russia will sue the U.S. over the properties it had seized.
February 16, 2018	Robert Mueller investigation indicts thirteen Russian citizens and three businesses, including Concord Catering and the Internet Research Agency, for interfering in the 2016 U.S. general election.
March 26, 2018	U.S. expels 60 Russian diplomats.
March 30, 2018	Russia expels 60 U.S. diplomats.
April 6, 2018	Treasury Department releases an outline of sanctions for Russian oligarchs
June 8, 2018	Robert Mueller investigation indicts Konstantin Kilimnik for conspiracy to obstruct justice and obstruction of justice.
July 12, 2018	Twelve Russian intelligence officers were indicted for hacking the Democratic National Committee shortly before President Trump's summit with President Putin.
July 16, 2018	Trump-Putin summit meeting.

diplomats have been expelled, consulates closed, and properties seized. Table 5.1 lists these. Trump has not commented on many of these incidents, and they are likely to continue.

ISSUES BETWEEN THE UNITED STATES AND RUSSIA CONFRONTING TRUMP

Ukraine and Crimea

Throughout his electoral campaign and early in his presidency, Trump seemed to support Russian actions in Ukraine. He told allied leaders that Crimea is Russian because its people speak Russian and that restoring Crimea to Ukraine would cause "World War III," apparently acquiescing in Crimea's annexation in 2014 (Sharkov, 2016).[4] Later he blamed President Obama rather than Russia for Crimea's annexation (*New York Times*, 2017).[5] Throughout the early months of his presidency, Trump proposed reducing U.S. foreign aid to Ukraine, and in April 2017 Secretary of State Rex Tillerson questioned his European counterparts about why Americans should care about the Ukrainian conflict (Blamer, 2018).[6] Nevertheless, amid accusation of Russian hacking, Trump continued Obama's policies, even increasing pressure on Russia through additional sanctions. Coming to terms with the issue in December 2017, Tillerson said: "We can have differences in other areas, but when one country invades another, that is a difference that is hard to look past or to reconcile," and Ukraine "stands as the single most difficult obstacle to us re-normalizing a relationship with Russia, which we badly would like to do" (cited in Morello, 2017).[7] Reluctantly, President Trump signed Congress's Countering Russian Influence in Europe and Eurasia Act of 2017. The act condemned Russia's annexation of Eurasian territories, including Abkhazia, South Ossetia, Transnistria, eastern Ukraine, and Crimea. It also established a State Department working group with authority to carry out political missions in countries where Putin has sought influence and territory. Russia's presence in Ukraine and seizure of Crimea, coupled with threats to U.S. and European interests, posed an intractable obstacle to improved U.S.-Russian relations.

Under Trump, then, Ukraine, Crimea, and economic sanctions remain central to U.S.-Russian relations. Washington continued to apply economic sanctions, demanding that Russia abide by the 2015 Minsk II agreements, which requires a ceasefire in Ukraine and the removal of Russian heavy weaponry and "foreign armed formations from Ukraine." According to Tillerson, "Absent a peaceful resolution of the Ukraine situation, which must begin with Russia's adherence to the Minsk agreements, there cannot be business as usual with Russia" (Tillerson, 2017).[8]

The 2015 Minsk Accords, however, have produced a stalemate between Kiev and Moscow. The agreements require Moscow to remove weapons and troops, *and* they require Kiev to hold elections in Donbass in the pro-Russian east. If Kiev holds elections before Russia leaves, the Russian occupation will promote a vote for self-governance, potentially leading to Ukraine partition that will trigger domestic opposition to Ukraine's government. If Russia removes its weapons and troops, Ukraine might reoccupy the region, which Russia claims will expose pro-Russian rebels to revenge. If the stalemate continues and Ukraine does not hold elections, the absence of elections may legitimate Russia's indefinite presence. Moreover, the 2018 assassination of one of Ukraine's separatist leaders who had signed Minsk II may invalidate the agreement.

While sanctions have frustrated President Putin and intensified Russia's alienation from the West, Donald Trump's recent actions have sought to minimize both. Approaching his first State of the Union address, Trump chose to ignore Congress's mandate to issue new sanctions on individuals who conduct significant business with Russia's defense and intelligence sectors. He also provided Congress with a list of Russian individuals who might face future sanctions. The list included two-hundred wealthy Russians with little regard or awareness about their political relevance. Moscow mocked the list, and Putin called it "an unfriendly act that complicates relations between Russia and the U.S. and damages international relations in general" (cited in Ioffe, 2018).[9] Nevertheless, the administration enforced these various sanctions and those later imposed in April 2018.

Trump has also intensified the stalemate by licensing the first sale of lethal weapons to Ukraine since the outbreak of violence. Although the weapons (Javelin anti-tank missiles) are 'defensive' and only valued at $50 million, well below China's loan to Ukraine, they are regarded as a military response to Russian aggression that may increase tension.

Russia's aggression in Ukraine and annexation of Crimea ended several post-Cold War trends, including peaceful EU and NATO eastern expansion and the absence of forcible seizure of sovereign territories in Europe. Sanctions on Russia, arms sales to Ukraine, and a buildup of NATO forces in Eastern Europe are intended to restore the pre-Ukraine status quo. These actions have refocused American and European attention on conflict in Europe and Russia's imperial aspirations. They also stand in the way of potentially cooperative ventures between Russia and the West. Despite the continued "frozen" Ukrainian conflict, Europeans alienated by Trump's unilateralism and trade policies may turn toward Russia as an economic and political partner, replacing America.

Washington has great interest in resolving the Ukraine conflict because it is inextricably linked to European and global security and stability. A proposed method for deescalating the conflict involves deploying a UN peacekeeping mission to Donbass in eastern Ukraine. President Putin has been open to this but has argued that peacekeepers should be deployed to separate Ukrainian government forces and the Russia-backed separatists. However, Kiev and its Western supporters object, claiming that the mission should be deployed on the border between Ukraine and Russia. In either case, the effectiveness of such a mission supposes that Russia's president has no interest in continuing another frozen conflict and that America's president is prepared to aid Ukraine economically and force its government to reform and eliminate rampant corruption if a deal is completed.

Syria and the Middle East

Although Obama initially sought Assad's ouster, he had largely abandoned that objective, and Trump did much the same. The Trump administration seems to want less U.S. involvement in the Middle East more generally. Focusing narrowly on the Islamic State, Trump no longer calls for the resignation of Assad. There is little interest in Washington in Syria's future since the terrorist threat has been eliminated. Trump is also very pro-Israel, and Russia and Israel have become friends as well, though Israel's conflict with Iran poses a dilemma for Moscow.

Russia has been eager to fill the vacuum. Moscow has a dominant role in Syrian peace talks in Sochi in which Washington is not a participant. Along with Turkey and Iran, Moscow has played a major role in defeating Assad's foes and aiding the Assad regime to recapture most Syrian territory. A UN-sponsored Geneva peace process is largely moribund, but Putin seeks to legitimize his efforts to end the civil war on terms acceptable to Moscow, Turkey and Iran. Russian influence in Turkey has also increased partly owing to U.S. support for Kurdish militias in Syria. Turkey's attack on Syrian Kurds and its purchase of a Russian S-400 anti-aircraft defense system and resulting U.S. sanctions, including suspension of a sale of F-35s to Ankara, signal erosion of the NATO alliance and deterioration of Turkish-U.S. relations. This has left Assad and his allies, Russia, Iran, and Hezbollah, in control of most of Syria. Russia, which has acquired bases in Syria, will likely play a major postwar role in that country and its reconstruction.

Indeed, Russia is expanding its interests throughout the Middle East, supporting Iranian interests, holding joint military exercises in Egypt, condemning America's recognition of Jerusalem as Israel's capital and moving its embassy to that city, expanding relations with Turkey, and possibly seeking to mediate the Israel-Palestinian conflict. As the United States under Trump retreats, Russia is moving in.

NATO

Notwithstanding President Trump's call for improved U.S.-Russian relations and his contention during the 2016 presidential campaign that NATO was "obsolete," Trump's rhetoric has not guided U.S. foreign policy regarding NATO-Russian relations. Instead, as noted above, the president's first year in office included a significant increase in U.S.-led NATO forces in Eastern Europe. This action fuels and responds to Russian military actions in Europe and the growing NATO-Russian security dilemma of recent years.

The buildup of NATO forces in Europe is part of both a long-term trend and, after a de-escalation of conflict during Obama's first term, a resurgence in NATO activity. Ignoring understandings in the early 1990s to avoid Western expansion into Russia's "near abroad," the EU and NATO expanded eastward, adding about two countries each year until 2010. The Russian government repeatedly made known its concern regarding the West's eastward expansion, with President Yeltsin describing it as a "conflagration war" and Putin labeling it as "new threats to national security" (cited in Farchy, 2016).[10] Putin's adviser, Sergei Glazyev strongly called it a war "to destroy the Russian World, to draw Europe into it, and to surround Russia with hostile countries" (cited in Zuesse, 2014).[11] Following Russia's intervention in Ukraine, NATO increased its concern with Eastern Europe, Turkey, and the Black Sea.

Notably, President Trump continues a schizophrenic relationship with NATO-Russian relations. After months of wavering support for NATO, in June 2017 the president reassured America's worried allies by reaffirming support for NATO's mutual defense treaty. Similarly schizophrenic, his administration has simultaneously called Russia a competitor (Mardiste, 2017),[12] a future partner (Xinhua, 2017),[13] and a threat to U.S. security (Talev, 2017).[14] Trump's advocacy of a friendly relationship with Russia seemed at odds with his request for nearly $700 billion in military spending (a $56 billion increase) as well as his support for Montenegro's NATO membership that was opposed by Russia. In addition, President Trump's demand for greater military spending by NATO members preceded increased funding from Romania, Poland, Lithuania, and Latvia. These actions have been perceived as hostile and threatening to Russian security.

Following these provocations, Russia initiated a major provocation of its own, deploying over 100,000 troops to Belarus for its threatening September 2017 Zapad war game. The war game displayed Russia's improved military technologies and growing military arsenals. European NATO posturing also triggered an increase in interaction – both "safe and professional" and "unsafe and unprofessional" – between NATO and Russian military aircraft. These "fly-bys" continue on a nearly bimonthly basis, increasing the need for and use of emergency communication channels to prevent conflict. Following Montenegro's entry into NATO in contrast to the opposition of Serbian Prime Minister Aleksandar Vucic to his country's entry, Russia announced plans for a large weapons sale to Serbia. In addition, a resurgence in Russian submarine activity has remilitarized the Atlantic. Russian submarines are stationed at strategic points, positioned to sever deep-sea cables and Internet communications. Other submarines have increased their nuclear-weapons capacity and new technologies have helped them to evade U.S. vessels in the Mediterranean (Barnes, 2017).[15] Finally, Russian construction in Belarus is viewed by some observers as auguring the stationing of nuclear missiles on the Polish border.

Wrapped in controversy and political scandal, President Trump's hands remain largely tied regarding the future of U.S.-led NATO-Russian relations. While a better relationship with Russia and a NATO arrangement that will not antagonize Russia are desirable, Trump has lacked the conviction and necessary leadership to repair U.S.-Russian relations.

North Korea

After Trump assumed office, North Korean dictator, Kim Jong-un provoked angry responses from Washington by continuing to test nuclear weapons and missiles that might be able to strike the U.S. homeland. Trump responded with a series of tweets using threatening and provocative language until a meeting was arranged between Trump and Kim in June 2018.

Russia had been instrumental in establishing the North Korean regime after World War II, and the USSR was a close ally of North Korea, with which Russia shares a border. After the demise of the USSR, Russia was no longer able to aid the North Korean regime and took a back seat to China's role in East Asia.

When Kim Jong-un became Supreme Leader of North Korea in 2011, Russia began once again to participate in activities involving Pyongyang. Putin saw the potential achievement of several goals with a change in the North Korean situation. With a shared border, North Korea's militancy and pursuit of nuclear weapon were a potential threat to Russia. It was not in Russia's interest to have a Pacific war involving Japan, the Korean peninsula, and, most importantly, America and/or China. Economically, it was to Russia's advantage to open North Korea to the world and to acquire greater access to the markets of both Koreas. In addition, the removal of U.S. forces from Korea would give Russia new opportunities in Asia and diminish America's global role.

Putin agreed with the basic premise that the Korean peninsula should be nuclear free and that a nuclear North Korea was a major danger. But, Putin also argued that UN and U.S. sanctions and threats were the wrong approach to the issue: "Russia believes that the policy of putting pressure on Pyongyang to stop its nuclear missile program is misguided and futile," he declared. "Provocations, pressure and militarist and insulting rhetoric are a dead-end road" (cited in Tarabay, 2017).[16] Instead, Washington and Seoul should immediately cease all joint military exercises, a step Trump announced after meeting Kim.

Russia flew bombers over the Korean peninsula during military exercises in late 2017 in support of Pyongyang, signaling its rivalry with America. Putin argued that Washington's potential military action constituted the greatest potential regional problem. Putin advocated immediate U.S.-North Korean talks. To cement Russia's intervention in this dangerous situation, Russia forgave $10 billion of North Korea's Soviet-era debt, and became the single largest food donor to Pyongyang. In January 2018, after North and South Korean officials held their first direct talks in over two year, Putin declared that the "North Korean leader, Kim Jong-un has 'won this match' in the contest to acquire nuclear weapons" (cited in Kravchenko, 2018: 1).[17] Simultaneously, Moscow and Beijing increasingly cooperated in East Asia; China even participated in Russia's immense military exercise in the region in September 2018 and sought Chinese economic aid in the face of Western economic sanctions.

Washington was critical of Russia's role in the Korean issue. Secretary Tillerson condemned Russian actions, and in January 2018 Trump accused Russia of evading UN sanctions by providing Pyongyang with oil and employing North Korean laborers, both vital to its economy. Observers viewed Moscow's actions as an additional effort by Putin to make Russia an indispensable world power, essential for solving major crises.

With the Singapore summit of June 12, 2018, Russia gained most of its objectives regarding North Korea. America yielded to Pyongyang and ceased, at least temporarily, joint military exercises, essentially agreeing with Russia's position. There is a commitment to denuclearization, removing the threat to Russia's border region. And, most important to Russia, North Korea is open to the world again with a trip to Moscow on the horizon for Kim Jong-un.

Afghanistan and the Taliban

In a reversal of policy since withdrawing its troops from Afghanistan in 1989, Russia began a process of rapprochement with the extreme Islamists in Afghanistan's Taliban. A diplomatic offensive led to meetings with Taliban leaders both in Afghanistan and elsewhere. In December 2017, a meeting was convened in Moscow among Russian, Chinese, and Pakistani diplomats about the situation in Afghanistan. Russia also began to provide the Taliban with weaponry, largely small arms and gear such as night vision goggles. Moscow's public reason for doing this was the Islamic State's challenge to the Taliban owing to the movement of large numbers of IS fighters to Afghanistan as the Islamic State disintegrated.

There are several reasons behind Russia's policies in Afghanistan. Many IS terrorists are Muslim Chechens who oppose their homeland's inclusion in the Russian Federation. Others threaten former Soviet Muslim republics like Uzbekistan that are Russian client states. Moscow seeks to protect itself from a terrorist threat from Islamic jihadists on its border with Afghanistan.

Russia also seeks to minimize American influence in Central Asia. Washington remains involved in Afghanistan, but its influence is waning. By arming the Taliban, Moscow seems to believe it can eliminate a terrorist threat and America's influence in the area. Although Russia supported America's invasion of Afghanistan after 9/11 and Russia and America still collaborate against global terrorism, the irony is that Moscow and the Taliban, enemies in the wars of the 1970s and 1980s, are now on the same side. Although Russia had even allowed NATO aircraft to use Russian airfields to supply its forces in Afghanistan, Russian weapons are now aimed at the U.S. troops who remain there.

CONCLUDING THOUGHTS

Since the collapse of the Soviet Union, U.S.-Russian relations have deteriorated after an initial honeymoon and the 'reset' of the Obama years, and the two are increasingly rivals globally. Since the 2011 and 2012 Russian legislative and presidential elections and Putin's return to the presidency, the two countries have reengaged in power politics. By the end of Obama's presidency, relations had substantially deteriorated. There were high hopes that Trump, who had hinted at removal of sanctions and talked positively about Putin and Russia, would turn things around.

It has not happened that way. One reason is the schizophrenic nature of America's Russian policies. While Trump as president may compliment Putin and Russia, Congress is angered by Moscow's interference in U.S. elections. As President Trump's personal relationship with Putin and campaign links to Russia have clouded trust in America's president to act robustly against Russia, that burden has fallen largely on Congress and its members who have frequently benefitted from labeling Russia as an enemy. Oddly, therefore, Trump has defended U.S. foes like Russia, while disparaging America's NATO allies.

For his part, Putin sees the world in terms of geopolitics and views America as the major impediment to the restoration of his country as a great power. Thus, he takes every opportunity to increase Russia's influence at America's expense, and has made significant strides toward realizing his goal. Few actively challenge his annexation of Crimea or are resisting his interference in Ukraine. Russia has new military bases in the Middle East where Moscow's influence is expanding with Assad regaining control of Syria, and it is reasserting itself in East Asia. Putin has also modernized his country's military forces, and this threatens a new arms race with the United States.

There are, of course, efforts to thwart Putin's steady march forward at U.S. expense. NATO remains the first line of defense in Europe, and Putin continues to complain about the threat NATO poses to Russian security. Moreover, the EU is discussing formation of its own military alliance. Russia continues to probe NATO at every opportunity, and Western sanctions harm its economy. Thus, Putin cheered Trump's initial refusal to implement congressionally mandated sanctions in January 2018. However, this was by no means evidence that existing sanctions will be lifted. Indeed, the EU renewed sanctions against Russia in June 2018.

Russo-American tit-for-tat relations are likely to continue as long as Trump and Putin remain in power, with Putin's thrust and Trump having to decide whether or not to parry. Trump may wish to compromise, but Congress and America's intelligence and diplomatic agencies may resist doing so. The consensus is that the Russian-American relationship has deteriorated still further under the Trump administration and is not likely to improve any time soon unless the investigations of Russia's role in America's 2016 election are concluded one way or the other.

ESSAY QUESTIONS

1) Since 2008, in what ways have the U.S. and Russia cooperated and how have they conflicted?

2) How has the U.S. campaign against the Islamic State in Syria affected Russia's goals in Syria?

3) Describe the Ukrainian conflict in Donbass. In doing so, discuss the potential impediments and pathways to reconciliation.

4) Presidential candidate Donald J. Trump proposed closer ties with Russia. Since President Trump took office what challenges face U.S.-Russian cooperation? Is cooperation possible? If yes, how? If no, why not? Is cooperation preferred? Explain why/why not.

5) Why has the U.S. financially sanctioned Russia and how have these sanctions affected Russian foreign policy and U.S.-Russian relations?

SHORT ANSWER QUESTIONS

Define and describe the importance of the following:

Zero-sum game
NATO and EU Expansion
New START Treaty
Tit-for-tat diplomatic expulsion
Minsk Agreement

NOTES

1 Stolberg, S., Fandos, N., and Kaplan, T. (2018). Republicans Rebuke Trump for Siding with Putin as Democrats Demand Action. *New York Times* [online]. Available at: www.nytimes.com/2018/07/16/us/politics/republicans-trump-putin.html [Accessed 18 Jul 2018].

2 Gutterman, S. and Isachenkov, V. (2008). Russia to Deploy Missiles near Poland. *San Francisco Chronicle* [online]. Available at: www.sfgate.com/news/article/Russia-to-deploy-missiles-near-Poland-3187024.php [Accessed 12 Feb 2018].

3 Scott, E. (2017). Trump: Only 'Stupid' People Think Warm Ties with Russia are a Bad Thing. *CNN* [online]. Available at: www.cnn.com/2017/01/07/politics/donald-trump-russia-relationship/index.html [Accessed 12 Feb 2018].

4 Sharkov, D. (2016). Trump Warns Taking Crimea from Russia Would Trigger World War III. *Newsweek* [online]. Available at: www.newsweek.com/trump-warns-taking-crimea-russia-would-trigger-world-war-iii-486226 [Accessed 4 Oct 2017].

5 *New York Times* (2017). Excerpts from the Times's Interview with Trump [online]. Available at: www.nytimes.com/2017/07/19/us/politics/trump-interview-transcript.html [Accessed 19 Jul 2017].

6 Blamer, C. (2018). U.S. Asks G7 Ministers Why it Should Care About Ukraine Conflict. *Reuters* [online]. Available at: www.reuters.com/article/g7-foreign-ukraine/u-s-asks-g7-ministers-why-it-should-care-about-ukraine-conflict-idUSKBN17D1P6 [Accessed 11 Apr 2017].

7 Morello, C. (2017). Tillerson Vows No Warming with Russia until it Leaves Ukraine. *Washington Post* [online]. Available at: www.washingtonpost.com/world/europe/tillerson-vows-no-warming-with-russia-until-it-leaves-ukraine/2017/12/07/2d1b8e0c-d7b6–11e7–9ad9-ca0619edfa05_story.html [Accessed 27 Dec 2017].

8 Tillerson, R. (2017). Rex Tillerson: I Am Proud of Our Diplomacy. *New York Times* [online]. Available at: www.nytimes.com/2017/12/27/opinion/rex-tillerson-state-department-diplomacy.html [Accessed 28 Dec 2017].

9 Ioffe, J. (2018). How Not to Design Russia Sanctions. *The Atlantic* [online]. Available at: www.theatlantic.com/international/archive/2018/01/kremlin-report-sanctions-policy/551921 [Accessed 31 Jan 2018].

10 Farchy, J. (2016). Putin Names NATO Among Threats in New Russian Security Strategy. *Financial Times* [online]. Available at: www.ft.com/content/6e8e787e-b15f-11e5-b147-e5e5bba42e51 [Accessed 2 Sep 2017].

11 Zuesse, E. (2014). The View that Putin's Advisor has on Obama's Ukrainian War. [Blog]. *Washingtonsblog.* Available at: www.washingtonsblog.com/2014/11/view-putins-advisor-obamas-ukrainian-war.html [Accessed 4 Dec 2017].

12 Mardiste, D. (2017). Britain Says Trump's Position Shifting on Russia. *Reuters* [online]. Available at: www.reuters.com/article/us-nato-russia-estonia/britain-says-trumps-position-shifting-on-russia-idUSKBN17M25L [Accessed 20 Apr 2017].

13 Xinhua (2017). Trump Expresses Desire for Better Relations with Russia. *China Daily* [online]. Available at: http://usa.chinadaily.com.cn/world/2017-08/29/content_31264158.htm [Accessed 20 Sep 2017].

14 Talev, M. (2017). Trump Adviser Calls Russia and China 'Threats' to U.S. Liberty. *Bloomberg News* [online]. Available at: www.bloomberg.com/news/articles/2017-12-12/trump-adviser-calls-russia-and-china-threats-to-u-s-liberty [Accessed 12 Dec 2017].

15 Barnes, J. (2017). A Russian Ghost Submarine, Its U.S. Pursuers and a Deadly New Cold War. *Wall Street Journal* [online]. Available at: www.wsj.com/articles/a-russian-ghost-submarine-its-u-s-pursuers-and-a-deadly-new-cold-war-1508509841 [Accessed 20 Oct 2017].

16 Tarabay, J. (2017). Russia's Power Play in North Korea Aimed at Both China and US. *CNN* [online]. Available at: www.cnn.com/2017/09/01/asia/russia-north-korea-analysis/index.html [Accessed 6 Dec 2017].

17 Kravchenko, S. (2018). Putin says North Korea's Kim 'Won this Match' on Nuclear Weapons. *Bloomberg News* [online] Available at: www.bloomberg.com/news/articles/2018-01-11/putin-says-north-korea-s-kim-won-this-match-on-nuclear-weapons [Accessed 11 Jan 2018].

SUGGESTED READINGS

Charap, S. and Colton, T.J. (2017). *Everyone Loses: The Ukraine Crisis and the Ruinous Contest for Post-Soviet Eurasia*. New York, NY: Routledge.

McFaul, M., Sestanovich, T., and Mearsheimer, J.J. (2014). Faulty Powers. *Foreign Affairs* 93(6), 167–178. Available at: www.foreignaffairs.com/articles/eastern-europe-caucasus/2014-10-17/faulty-powers [Accessed 1 Jun 2018].

Rumer, E.B. (2017). *Russian Foreign Policy Beyond Putin*. New York, NY: Routledge.

6 The Arctic: An emerging area of conflict

Lana Obradovic and Bethany Vailliant

INTRODUCTION

Although its harsh climate and near-impenetrable territory have discouraged countries from staking claims in the Arctic, climate change and melting ice are rapidly creating new environmental challenges, as well as creating potential economic and geostrategic opportunities for Arctic nations. As new sea routes, rich energy deposits and resources become accessible, the Arctic is likely to become one of the most disputed regions in the world and one of the most significant geostrategic theaters for the United States. In August 2018 the Danish-owned *Venta Maersk* was the first container ship to sail the Northern Sea Route (Booth and Ferris-Rotman, 2018).[1]

Despite international legal frameworks and institutions governing the Arctic, aggressive regional stakeholders, especially Russia, are seeking to alter the geopolitical landscape in coming decades to realize growing security and economic interests. By contrast, Washington has largely ignored the region until recently, and there remain significant gaps in U.S. Arctic policy to meet Russia's growing economic and military ambitions in the region. Russia's ambitions will pose serious security, energy, trade, environmental, and even human-rights challenges. If Russia remains unchecked, America's strategic interests and prosperity and those of its allies may be undermined. Unless the Trump administration acts quickly and makes Washington's Arctic strategy a priority, Russia, and perhaps even China, will continue to project power in this key strategic location at the expense of America and its allies.

This chapter describes the growing importance of the Arctic and U.S. policies in the region and the implications of those policies since the administration President William Howard Taft (1909–1913). While emphasizing the need to develop strategic responses to protect U.S. interests, it points to areas of concern for the Trump administration in the context of Russian expansionism, capabilities, infrastructure investment, and international law. Emerging risks and challenges need to be managed and understood, and Washington should pursue all avenues of international cooperation backed by military capabilities to deter threats posed by rivals in the Arctic.

FIGURE 6.1 Map of the Arctic region

ARCTIC REGION

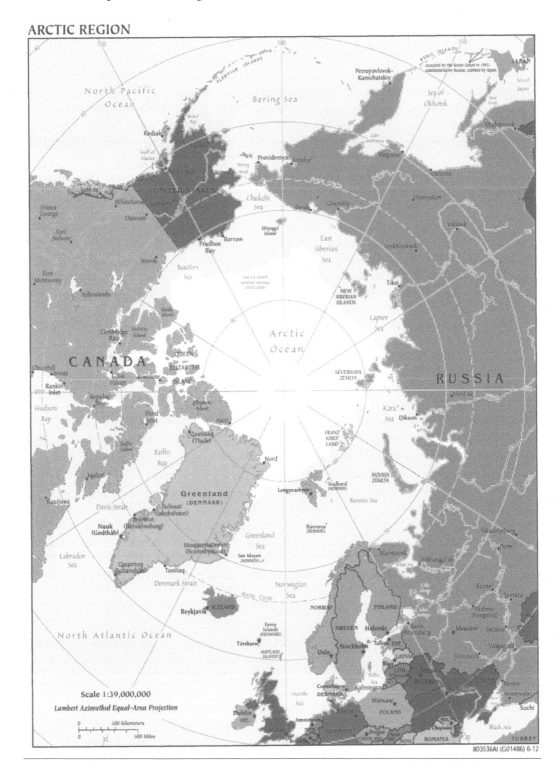

Scale 1:39,000,000
Lambert Azimuthal Equal-Area Projection

803536AI (G01486) 6-12

THE GROWING IMPORTANCE OF THE ARCTIC AND INTERNATIONAL GOVERNANCE

The National Oceanic and Atmospheric Administration's report for 2017 indicates that the Arctic environmental system has reached a "new normal," characterized by long-term losses in the extent and thickness of sea ice cover. Indeed, the average surface air temperature in 2017 was the second highest since 1900. Older ice now only comprises 21 percent of the cover, whereas in 1985, it was 45 percent (Arctic Report Card, 2017).[2]

The opening of the Arctic creates immense potential for economic resources as states compete for oil, gas, and other seabed resources, and as shipping grows in the region. According to the U.S. Geological Survey (USGS), the Arctic contains roughly 400 known oil and gas fields with 240 billion known barrels of oil and natural gas. This does not include the additional 90 billion barrels of oil, 1,669 trillion cubic feet of natural gas, and 44 billion barrels of natural gas liquids that are predicted to lie in unexplored areas of the Arctic (Bird et al., 2008).[3] To put this in perspective, the latter encompasses a quarter of the world's undiscovered recoverable petroleum. Moreover, according to one analyst (Burakova, 2005),[4] the Arctic seabed is the site of some $1.5 trillion to $2 trillion in other resources such as nickel, copper, tin, uranium and diamonds. As the ice continues to melt owing to climate change and the race to conquer this last great frontier intensifies among the Arctic's littoral states as well as non-Arctic contenders for resources, negotiations among competitors to realize their interests will have profound global environmental, financial, and security implications.

To limit disputes and share information, the littoral states began to coordinate their activities in the Arctic officially in the Arctic Environmental Protection Strategy adopted in 1991 and the Arctic Council established in 1996. Currently, the Arctic Council consists of eight member states – Canada, Denmark (including Greenland and the Faroe Islands), Finland, Iceland, Norway, Russia, Sweden, and the United States – that consult with six Arctic indigenous peoples' organizations that serve as Permanent Participants. The members of the Council collectively oversee and promote cooperation and coordination among regional stakeholders, especially on issues of sustainable development and environmental protection. Thirteen non-Arctic states, including China, Singapore and South Korea, in addition to thirteen intergovernmental/inter-parliamentary organizations and thirteen non-governmental organizations serve as observers. These countries and organizations are permitted to observe and engage in the Arctic Council primarily in one of six Working Groups, which deal with issues that range from protection of the Arctic marine environment and conservation of flora and fauna to emergency preparedness and pollution.

The Arctic Council is intended to serve as a consensus-based international forum and has neither an operating budget nor an international legal personality to implement and enforce its recommendations. Its mandate, described in the 1996 Ottawa Declaration, also prevents it from discussing any issues involving military security. Although the Council has been praised for its inclusiveness, its high level of cooperation, and its sharing of knowledge that informs much of our understanding of global warming, critics argue that its mandate should be revisited and revised to include security issues and unresolved boundary issues that might trigger disputes and to assure that the authority of littoral member states is not diluted by the growing number of those that have observer status.

Mediterranean countries, including Greece and Turkey, as well as landlocked Mongolia and Switzerland, are among new applicants for observer status. Observer states such as China have also announced their intention to seek a share of Arctic resources. China wishes to develop the so-called Polar Silk Road shipping lanes that overlap Russia's Northern Sea Route, thereby directly challenging the rights of the Council's member states, including Russia (State Council Information Office, 2018).[5]

The Arctic Council is not the only multilateral framework in which negotiations take place regarding sovereign rights and access to the Arctic's rich oil and gas deposits. Adopted in 1982 and in force since November 1994, the UN Convention on the Law of the Sea (UNCLOS) has been ratified by 168 UN members. In the Arctic and elsewhere, this treaty delineates the maritime zones and continental shelf boundaries of the littoral states and, therefore, defines both rights and responsibilities of states with respect to their use of ocean and seas, as well as the seabed.

UNCLOS also allows states to claim exclusive jurisdiction over areas on the continental shelf sections that are beyond their Exclusive Economic Zone (EEZ), that is, beyond 200 nautical miles to a maximum 350 nautical miles from their territorial sea baseline. Should a littoral Arctic state seek to claim an extended shelf beyond its EEZ, it must provide bathymetric data and maps demonstrating that the outer edge of its continental shelf exceeds those 200 nautical miles. Russia, Denmark/Greenland, and Norway have already sought to extend their legal boundaries in the Arctic by submitting their claims to the Commission on the Limits of the Continental Shelf (CLCS), a body of twenty-one experts in the fields of geology, geophysics, and hydrography, established under UNCLOS. The Commission has already issued a recommendation on Norway's 2009 submission, approving its claim over the Yermak Plateau, while Denmark/Greenland's 2014 submission and Russia's 2015 partially revised resubmission remain under consideration.

The Russian government's 2015 resubmission was actually its second attempt, after its 2001 claim had been rejected on the basis of insufficient scientific and technical evidence. In 2018, Canada also presented a claim to its Arctic continental shelf, including areas in the North Pole that would overlap with both the Danish/Greenland and Russian claims (Sevunts, 2016).[6] Although the U.S. is also as interested in staking claims, it has not ratified UNCLOS owing to partisan differences in Congress, and therefore, cannot make a submission to the Commission. President Trump's aversion to multilateral agreements makes it unlikely that the U.S. will ratify the convention in the near future.

UNITED STATES POLICIES IN THE ARCTIC: FROM TAFT TO TRUMP

In 1909 Admiral Robert Peary's telegram to President Taft regarding his expedition's success in the Arctic read: "I have the honor to place the North Pole at your disposal." President Taft thanked him for his offer but replied, "I do not really know what to do with it." In fact, despite the sensational news and media frenzy about whether Peary or his former colleague, Dr. Frederick Cook, reached the North Pole first, Taft was not attracted by the region. There is no consensus on whether Taft might have stayed out of the Arctic because he respected the international legal norms regarding claiming distant frozen oceans or simply because he saw no U.S. interests, economic or geopolitical (Steinberg et al., 2015: 40).[7] The Arctic reappeared briefly on Washington's agenda in the 1945 Truman

Proclamation – Policy of the United States With Respect to the Natural Resources of the Subsoil and Sea Bed of the Continental Shelf – that unilaterally extended Washington's claim to submerged lands and offshore resources of the continental shelf well beyond the seas' three-mile norm that existed at that time.

Although this was a watershed in the history of maritime law, to this day Washington has not made a serious effort to secure and advance its national security and economic interests in the region. The degree of investment in infrastructure, commercial development or resources still seems to reflect Taft's telegram. However, there have been efforts by several administrations to acknowledge that there are important U.S. interests in the region – national security, resource development, scientific inquiry, and environmental protection.

The Nixon administration's 1971 National Security Decision Memorandum 144, entitled United States Arctic Policy and Arctic Policy Group, called for increased international cooperation and establishment of an Interagency Arctic Policy Group (IAPG) that would supervise the implementation of U.S. Arctic policy, with the exception of issues that were deemed domestic, and therefore within Alaska's jurisdiction. The IAPG was to report to the National Security Council, chaired by the Department of State but including the Departments of Defense, Interior, Commerce, and Transportation, as well as representatives from the National Science Foundation, the Council on Environmental Quality and other relevant agencies.

In April 1983, the Reagan Administration's National Security Decision Directive 90 reaffirmed those commitments and requested that the IAPG submit a review of the policy on how to coordinate action with other Arctic states and federal agencies necessary to serve U.S. interests over the next decade. The following year, the Congressional Arctic Research and Policy Act of 1984 created a seven-member Arctic Research Commission (ARC) as an independent agency with the sole purpose of providing the president and Congress with integrated Arctic research policy reports and recommendations. The 1984 Act also made the National Science Foundation responsible for implementing Arctic research policy, and established an Interagency Arctic Research Policy Committee under its auspices, which was tasked with preparation of a comprehensive five-year plan and coordination of sixteen agencies, departments, and offices across the Federal government. In January 1985, both the Commission and Committee were formally created by President Reagan's Executive Order 12501.

Although President George H.W. Bush vigorously resisted Canada's proposal to establish the Arctic Council, the Clinton administration declared its support of new efforts at multilateral diplomacy in the region to address environmental as well as economic and social agendas (Nord, 2015: 20).[8] The 1994 Presidential Decision Directive 26 recognized that the new post-Cold war context allowed for greater cooperation among the eight Arctic littoral states on issues of environmental protection, sustainable development, scientific research, and indigenous peoples. This directive also recognized a continued need to focus on national security interests and protection of the country from attacks across the Arctic. In 1996, the U.S. joined the Arctic Council, but not without reservations. President Bill Clinton insisted that the Council have no permanent secretariat, that the Arctic Environmental Protection Strategy should merge with the new Council, and that the Council not discuss national security and defense (Berry et al., 2016).[9]

Late in his presidency in 2009, President George W. Bush released National Security Presidential Directive 66 and Homeland Security Presidential Directive 25 as part of an interagency review. Both directives were among the first U.S. policies concerning the

Arctic since 1994, and they were soon followed by the Obama Administration's 2013 National Strategy for the Arctic Region which defined America's three leading priorities in the region as advancing security interests, pursuing responsible Arctic stewardship, and strengthening international cooperation. It also recommended appointing a U.S. Arctic ambassador and developing a "robust" public diplomacy campaign involving federal, state, local, indigenous tribal authorities and the private sector. The Obama administration recognized the region's importance: "When historians look back at this critical opportunity to develop U.S. Arctic policy, we do not want the question to be posed 'Who lost the Arctic?' but rather, 'How did the United States win the Arctic?'" but "[c]rafting U.S. policy for the Arctic," it declared, "is a complex and challenging undertaking" (cited in Conley et al., 2013: viii).[10]

The Obama administration also published 2014, 2015 and 2016 implementation plans for Arctic strategy, setting additional milestones to be reached and detailing progress toward them. However, the U.S. Government Accountability Office report found evidence of policy overlap, lack of coordination, funding and follow-up mechanisms among the departments and agencies involved, which included the Departments of Defense, State, Homeland Security, Commerce, Interior, Energy, Transportation, NASA, the National Science Foundation, and the White House. Thus, President Obama issued Executive Order 13689 Enhancing Coordination of National Efforts in the Arctic, which established an Arctic Executive Steering Committee, chaired by his science adviser Dr. John Holdren, to coordinate the work in the Arctic region of twenty-five federal departments, agencies and offices.

Although the United States had made significant strides in its Arctic policy on paper, both the George W. Bush and Obama administrations were criticized for providing only planning documents, particularly in regards to homeland security and defense policy, and failing to allocate the funds necessary for effective implementation. Thus, the U.S. fell behind Arctic competitors in terms of capability and funding, and, according to Coast Guard Admiral Paul F. Zukunft, "is really not even in this game" (cited in Reiss, 2015).[11] It may become too late for Washington to join the race unless the Trump administration seizes the opportunities and addresses the challenges in a timely manner.

In November 2016, the Obama administration quietly began preparing a new Arctic policy on the understanding that it would be left incomplete until a new administration assumed office. The three primary policy goals outlined were protection of the Arctic environment, economic development by taking advantage of the region's potential for hydrocarbon extraction, and homeland protection by establishing a military presence in the region (Anderson, 2016).[12] Since April 2017, however, when President Trump issued Executive Order 13795 opening all previously closed and protected areas to offshore drilling development, it became clear that his administration was largely concerned with economic development. Besides putting America's energy needs first, this order was part of a decades-long congressional effort to open the areas of the Outer Continental Shelf, including the Arctic Wildlife Refuge, along with the Chukchi and Beaufort seas to oil and natural gas drilling – a provision that was added to the Republican tax bill in December 2017. In addition, President Trump's Executive Order prohibited the Secretary of Commerce from designating new National Marine Sanctuaries without first assessing that area's resource potential.

Although drilling may bring investment and infrastructure to the region, according to two RAND Corporation observers: "In the frigid North, the concept of 'America First' will take Americans only so far" (Tingstand and Pezard, 2017).[13] A number of questions remain regarding U.S. policy, particularly as it pertains to the Arctic Council's work on sustainable development, protection of unique Arctic ecosystems, and socio-economic development and cultural wellbeing of indigenous communities.

In his statement to the 10th Arctic Council Ministerial Meeting in Fairbanks, Alaska, in May 2017, then-Secretary of State Rex Tillerson recognized the Council's role as an important forum and pledged that Washington would continue to participate actively. However, he also emphasized that the Trump administration was reviewing its approach to the issue of climate change among other issues involving the Arctic (Department of State, 2017).[14] After reaffirming the administration's commitment to the Arctic Council, in his effort to overhaul the State Department, Tillerson announced that the positions of Special Envoy for Climate Change and Special Representative for the Arctic Region would be eliminated, and their functions and staff assumed by the Bureau of Oceans and International and Scientific Affairs. The Special Representative had been Admiral Robert J. Papp, Jr., 24th Commandant of the U.S. Coast Guard, who resigned in January 2017. As of 2018, among previously established federal institutional frameworks, the Arctic Research Commission and Interagency Arctic Research Policy Committee continued to carry out their work, while the position of chair of the Council on Environmental Quality remained vacant. Moreover, there are few signs of activity by the Obama-established Arctic Executive Steering Committee. Although he is yet to release a statement regarding the Arctic, Tillerson's successor, Mike Pompeo, during his Senate confirmation hearing to become CIA Director in 2017, declared that the idea of climate change as a national security issue is "ignorant, dangerous, and unbelievable" (cited in Friedman and Davenport, 2018).[15] Such a view will most likely inform his stance on the Arctic, particularly regarding environmental sustainability, and possibly affect the degree of urgency given to the region.

FUTURE CHALLENGES IN THE ARCTIC: THE TRUMP ADMINISTRATION AND BEYOND

As the Trump administration develops a strategy in the Arctic, let us examine more closely emerging challenges to America in the region and some possibilities about how to foster a policy that secures America's security and economic interests, and provide regional stability. Particularly important in this context are Russian intentions in the Arctic, the much-needed investment in constructing icebreakers and infrastructure for the sake of both emergency preparedness and homeland security, and the ratification of UNCLOS.

Russia's Arctic ambitions

In recent decades, Russian efforts to control over half of the traversable Arctic – an area that "may constitute the geographically largest unexplored prospective area for petroleum remaining on earth" (Bird et al., 2008: 1)[3] – have become increasingly more assertive.

Russian desire for supremacy in the Arctic dates back to the early explorer Uleb's eleventh-century voyage through the Yugorsky Strait. The establishment of the Solovetski Islands' monastery on Russia's remote northernmost White Sea coast (1436) and the Pechegenski monastery (1533) on the Murmansk side of the Barents Sea are symbols of the Russian Orthodox faith. This historic relationship reached mythic proportions from 1932 to 1938, during the golden age of Soviet Arctic exploration and conquest. The region was further embedded in Russia's national consciousness owing to Stalin's socialist realist narrative of polar heroes, notably, Otto Schmidt and his epic journey from the Barents Sea through the Northeast Passage to the Pacific Ocean in 1932. The Arctic was represented as an adversary that could only be tamed by a military campaign with the Soviet people as its only legitimate and worthy masters.

After the collapse of the USSR, Russia's northern territories were seen by Moscow as a burden and were largely abandoned. The ambitious revival of the mythic Arctic narrative started again to inform, at least symbolically, Russia's claim to the region in 2007 when two mini-submarines traveled to the Lomonosov Ridge, two and half miles under the North Pole, and there planted a titanium Russian flag (Chivers, 2007).[16] Although this was widely viewed as a publicity stunt, President Vladimir Putin awarded the title of "Hero of the Russian Federation" to Artur Chilingarov, a Duma member and leader of this expedition. This event reminded observers of how Stalin had named Otto Schmidt "Hero of the Soviet Union" in 1937.

Global warming has opened up opportunities for Russia and allowed it to initiate several projects. Among Moscow's principal interests and objectives in the region as identified in the 2009 Basic State Policy of the Russian Federation in the Arctic are developing and managing the Northern Sea Route, securing hydrocarbon resources and other raw materials, maintaining a military presence in the Arctic, and developing infrastructure to improve the quality of life for inhabitants. In an address to Russia's Federal Assembly in March 2018, Putin declared: "Our goal is to make it a truly global and competitive transport route" (cited in Johnson and Standish, 2018).[17]

Russia has sought to establish control over its Northern Sea Route, an expedited shipping route that connects the Atlantic and Pacific Oceans and falls entirely within Russia's Exclusive Economic Zone. To this end, Moscow has initiated a series of long-term construction projects including search-and-rescue stations and a system of shipping and cargo-handling hubs along its Arctic coast. This trans-Arctic shipping route cuts transit times in half, and dramatically reduces fuel consumption. In August 2017, a Russian-owned tanker completed the journey in record time from Europe to Asia, doing so without the aid of specialized icebreaking vessels. In addition, at Putin's urging, the State Duma passed a provision in December 2017 giving vessels traveling under the Russian flag an exclusive right to transport and store oil and gas products in the Northern Sea Route waters.

Russia is also increasing its economic investment in developing the region's oil and gas resources. The $27 billion Yamal liquefied natural gas facility in the Arctic Circle shipped its first cargo from a newly built port of Sabetta in December 2017 despite Western sanctions on Russia's energy sector. Partly owned by France's Total, the China National Petroleum Company, Russian Novatek, and China's Silk Road Fund, the Yamal project will allow Russia to remain competitive in energy markets (Foy, 2017).[18] Moreover, Russian energy giants Rosneft and Gazprom Neft, the only companies permitted to drill in the Arctic to date, continue to move forward with their projects with the aid of the Russian government. Between 2021 and 2025, Moscow plans to provide $414.5 million for equipment, machinery, and technological development for the region. According to Rosneft, 20 to 30 percent of Russia's total oil production in 2050 will come from the Arctic shelf (Rosneft, 2017).[19]

Besides securing natural resources, Russia is establishing a military presence in the region. In 2014, the Northern Fleet Joint Strategic Command was established as a dedicated military force and fifth Russian military district with "four new Arctic brigade combat teams, 14 new operational airfields, 16 deep water ports, and 40 icebreakers with an additional

11 in development" (Gramer, 2017).[20] There are also over a hundred capital construction projects on Russian military bases on Franz Josef Land, Novaya Zemlya, Sredniy Island (Northern Earth Archipelago), Cape Schmidt, the Wrangel Islands, and Kotelny Island (Ministry of Defence of the Russian Federation, 2017),[21] and in 2018 Moscow began construction of an anti-aircraft base at Tiksi.

President Putin has repeatedly emphasized the importance of developing defense infrastructure in the Arctic in order to station the four brigades there as soon as possible and equip them with weapons and vehicles suitable for extreme weather conditions. In March 2017, Russian Minister of Defense Sergei Shoigu announced that all infrastructure projects on Russian military installations would be completed by 2020. One is the northernmost permanent Arktichesky Trilistnik (Arctic Trefoil) complex that opened in 2017. Painted in the colors of the Russian flag, this 15,000-square-foot high-tech base is capable of sustaining 150 inhabitants for over a year without outside assistance. The first such self-sustaining installation, Severny Klever (Northern Clover), was opened in 2015 on Kotelny Island, in the New Siberian Islands archipelago.

Icebreaker capability

While Moscow has been building search-and-rescue stations and a flotilla of icebreakers to patrol the Northern Sea Route and announced in August 2018 that it would send a cargo vessel through the Russian Arctic for the first time, Washington has done little to establish its presence in the region. Potential increases in offshore drilling, oil spills, cruise ship tourism, and fishing suggest a need to increase America's ability to transit the Northwest Passage and map the continental shelf to back U.S. claims in the Arctic. Its shallow waters dotted with dangerous icebergs are currently navigable only during a seven-week period, but scientists expect it to be ice-free by 2050. This passage, although claimed by Canada as a domestic waterway, has been treated by America and other countries as an international strait in which they are entitled to the right of transit passage. Indeed, China's Maritime Safety Administration suggested that Beijing was preparing to open shipping lanes connecting the Atlantic and Pacific Oceans through North American Arctic waters. China's President Xi Jinping met with President Putin to discuss cooperation on planning and building infrastructure of a possible new trade route "frozen Silk Road." Thus "China, while not an Arctic nation by virtue of geography, is building icebreakers and preparing to be deeply engaged – hence the nascent partnership with the Russian Federation" (cited in Stavridis, 2018).[22]

Icebreakers are categorized by their brake horsepower (BHP), a measurement that determines a vessel's power, and only heavy icebreakers that operate at 45,000 BHP or above are capable of securing year-round access to the Arctic and operating independently with the presence of seasonal or multi-year ice. The Coast Guard operates heavy icebreakers, and these are an essential component of American strategy in the Arctic because they defend U.S. sovereignty and allow for a more robust presence. They also support scientific research, promote economic interests, monitor sea traffic, and other Coast Guard missions including search and rescue and law enforcement. While other types of naval vessels may occasionally carry out these missions, according to the Department of Defense Arctic Strategy, only heavy icebreakers provide assured sovereign presence (Department of Defense, 2013: 10).[23]

The U.S. and Russia are the only countries that currently have heavy icebreakers. Until recently, America had two such vessels – the *Polar Star* and the *Polar Sea* – commissioned in 1976 and 1977 respectively. After the *Polar Sea* experienced a major engine failure in 2010, only the *Polar Star* remained operational. In 2017, the Coast Guard decided that it was too costly to extend the life of the *Polar Sea*, and it is currently serving as a parts donor to extend the life of the *Polar Star*, which is also nearing the end of its service. Additionally, the United States has one medium icebreaker, the *Healy*, commissioned in 1999 and operating with significantly less power. The *Healy* can serve primarily as a scientific research vessel rather than a year-round icebreaker (O'Rourke, 2018: 5).[24]

By contrast, Russia has forty-six icebreakers, including eleven under construction and four planned. Six of those operate at 45,000 BPH or higher, of which two are non-operational. In the coming years, three additional heavy icebreakers will join Russia's fleet – *Arktika* (2019), *Sibir* (2020), and *Ural* (2021). The remaining Russian icebreakers operate at under 44,999 BPH, serving as scientific research vessels rather than projections of power. Moscow has also embarked on constructing an advanced nuclear-powered icebreaker named the *Lider (Leader)*.

In an address to the Coast Guard in May 2017, President Trump called icebreakers "truly vital to the United States Armed Forces and truly vital to our great country" (cited in Lamothe, 2017).[25] Acquiring funding for heavy icebreakers must be a strategic priority for this and future administrations if the United States is to remain a significant power in the Arctic. Icebreakers take time to build, and current projections, based on the expected life of the *Polar Star*, estimate that there will be a three-to-six-year gap in heavy icebreaking capability if construction of a new vessel – at an estimated cost of a billion dollars – does not begin now. Contracting the construction of naval vessels in a foreign shipyard is forbidden under U.S. law, and the possibility of leasing has raised concerns about a foreign vessel's ability to meet operational needs, as well as proving cost ineffective (Grover, 2016: 10).[26]

The process of updating and expanding the icebreaker fleet started during President Obama's second term, with the Coast Guard's 2013 budget request for $15.6 million through 2016, with an additional $25 million to the Coast Guard and $150 million to the Navy, to provide recommendations on general icebreaker design in FY2017. In October 2017, the draft request for the detailed design of one heavy icebreaker was released. In FY2018, the Coast Guard proposed a $19 million budget for acquisition of a new polar icebreaker and has requested $750 million for FY2019, with an additional request for $15 million to sustain the life of the *Polar Star* (United States Coast Guard, 2018: 13),[27] which already needs frequent repairs. In a statement in July 2017 to the House Subcommittee on Coast Guard and Maritime Transportation and the Committee on Transportation and Infrastructure, Ret. Rear Admiral Richard West recommended acquiring three new icebreakers for Arctic use, through a block buy contract, to be owned and operated by the Coast Guard (Subcommittee on Coast Guard and Maritime Transportation, 2017).[28] The schedule released in the Request for Information indicates that building would begin in FY2019, with delivery dates of FY2023, FY2025 and FY2026 respectively (O'Rourke, 2018: 17).[29]

The $750 million originally earmarked for the acquisition of the polar icebreaker is in jeopardy because the Trump administration reallocated these funds to immigration enforcement. According to a statement from the White House, while the administration will "continue to advocate for the full 2019 Budget request levels for a Coast Guard Polar Icebreaker," difficult decisions must be made in order to provide funding for its top priority: securing the nation's borders (The White House, 2018).[30] This development has triggered a backlash by some Democrats as well as the Senate Republicans whose budget version still includes acquiring the new icebreaker. As of late 2018, it remained unclear if the new icebreaker would make the cut, but there is still a possibility to save the funding as each version is passed in its respective chamber and differences are reconciled in conference. While the commercialization and militarization of the Arctic may seem a distant problem to many, the security of the southern border cannot be done at the expense of the Arctic. If America is to protect its national interest, it should appropriate the requested funds in the coming years and even consider further investments. Only by expanding the presence of icebreakers will Washington be able to increase the scope of the Coast Guard and Navy operations to prepare for the challenges in the Arctic.

International governance: UNCLOS ratification

Current international agreements are insufficient to manage the Arctic owing to America's nonparticipation in UNCLOS. There is a need to address this issue in order to establish the rules of crisis management and prevent efforts by Arctic rivals to impose maritime dispute settlements unilaterally. Washington participated for almost a decade in writing UNCLOS, and in 1994 even renegotiated the contentious Part IX regarding deep-seabed mining activities. While President Clinton thought that the renegotiated version could secure Senate ratification, Republicans continued to view UNCLOS as violating U.S. sovereignty.

Despite the decades-long refusal to ratify UNCLOS, Washington recognizes large parts of it as customary law, but this has not served American interests because Washington remains unable to assert its claims or contest the claims of other countries. Although America has potentially overlapping claims with Canada and Russia, it is not only prevented from filing an extended continental shelf claim with the CLCS, it also cannot participate in the CLCS process to evaluate and make recommendations about other countries' claims in the Arctic or elsewhere. Given the speed at which climate change is opening the Arctic Ocean to resource exploration and other activities, joining the other 168 nations, including all other littoral Arctic states in UNCLOS, is necessary to help Washington stabilize the region and reduce the likelihood of conflict.

Ratifying UNCLOS is a logical step for the Trump administration because it would also facilitate America's ability to explore and exploit energy resources. Critics have long disagreed with the view that ratification of UNCLOS is necessary to raise investment and acquire control over energy resources in the Arctic because the Truman Proclamation and bilateral agreements are sufficient to divide the Arctic Ocean and set the continental shelf boundary. Nevertheless, by ratifying UNCLOS, Washington would acquire legally recognized commercial development rights over as much as 350,000 square miles of ocean. This could further incentivize the private sector to explore and invest in infrastructure. To date, companies have been reluctant to explore and invest in oil drilling and deep-seabed mining owing to the contested nature of the Far North's territory.

Last but not least is the sensitive issue of balancing increased human activity and traffic with the threats they pose to indigenous Arctic communities and ecosystems unique to the region. UNCLOS contains provisions that require environmental protection and conservation, and Washington would be able to enforce those within its jurisdiction. Given the interest of many Arctic and non-Arctic countries in utilizing the Northwest Passage and Northern Sea Route and increasing economic activities, there is a growing threat of pollution, oil spills and damage to the marine environment and people living in the area. Only if America ratifies UNCLOS can Washington hold violating states legally accountable for their negligence and failure to observe their legal obligations.

CONCLUSIONS

We have traced the history of American policy in the Arctic and identified potential areas of conflict and cooperation for the future. As issues concerning the environment, geopolitics, and economics of the Arctic become more important, the degree of attention that it receives, not only from the littoral states but from the world at large, has dramatically grown. Coping with major Arctic issues including global warming, environmental protection, and sustainable development are inherently multilateral in nature, but Donald Trump, as noted frequently, dislikes and criticizes multilateral agreements and institutions.

Nevertheless, military and economic dominance in the region will be imposed during coming decades by those states that are not only willing to stake claims over their respective extended continental shelves within existing international legal frameworks, but also alter power dynamics in their favor by enhancing their military capabilities and infrastructure. U.S. policy must recognize that such strategic considerations in the Arctic involve rival great powers, including Russia and China. These states are achieving a competitive edge in the scramble for Arctic resources at the expense of American interests. Thus, Secretary of Defense Jim Mattis, while in Alaska in July 2018, declared "Certainly America's got to up its game in the Arctic. There's no doubt about that, "so the reality is that we're going to have to deal with the developing Arctic" (cited in Reuters, 2018).[31] That having been said, two analysts conclude that "other than the International Space Station, the Far North is perhaps the only setting in which the United States and the Russian Federation cooperate today on a variety of issues" (Sfraga and Brigham, 2018).[32]

ESSAY QUESTIONS

1) Discuss the significance of increased participation by non-Arctic states as Observers to the Council, and how, if at all, their efforts to promote economic development might undermine the Arctic Council's emphasis on sustainable development, Indigenous communities, and environmental protection.

2) Compare and contrast Arctic policies of different American administrations.

3) To date, Russia has abided by international laws governing the Arctic, such as UNCLOS, and has placed emphasis on cooperation through the Arctic Council. However, given Russia's recent tendency to push boundaries and disguise its operations in its near abroad, are the international frameworks governing the Arctic enough to prevent or mitigate escalation of conflict in the region?

4) Should the United States be concerned with the increase in investment in military capabilities and defense infrastructure in the Arctic by Russia?

5) What would be the most effective policy response to Russia in the Arctic? Discuss the costs and benefits of the Trump administration's decision to redistribute funds from the federal budget previously set aside for the commissioning of a new polar icebreaker for the Mexican border wall.

SHORT ANSWER QUESTIONS

Define and describe the importance of the following:

Arctic Council
United Nations Convention on the Law of the Sea (UNCLOS)
Icebreakers
Northern Sea Route
United States Arctic policy

NOTES

1   Booth, W. and Ferris-Rotman, A. (2018). Russia's Suez Canal? Ships start plying a less-icy Arctic, thanks to climate change. *Washington Post* [online]. Available at: www.washingtonpost.com/world/europe/russias-suez-canal-ships-start-plying-an-ice-free-arctic-thanks-to-climate-change/2018/09/08/59d50986-ac5a-11e8-9a7d-cd30504ff902_story.html [Accessed 10 Sep 2018].
2   Arctic Report Card (2017). Update for 2017. National Oceanic and Atmospheric Administration. Available at: www. arctic.noaa.gov/Report-Card/Report-Card-2017 [Accessed 4 Feb 2018].
3   Bird, K. et al. (2008). Circum-Arctic Resource Appraisal: Estimates of undiscovered oil and gas North of the Arctic Circle. Fact Sheet. United States Geological Survey. Available at: https://pubs.usgs.gov/fs/2008/3049 [Accessed 4 Feb 2018].
4   Burakova, I. (2005). Development of Arctic Areas to Bring Trillions Dollars of Profit to Russia.*Pravda* [online]. Available at: www.pravdareport.com/russia/economics/21-04-2005/8102-arctic-0 [Accessed 4 Feb 2018].
5   The State Council Information Office of the People's Republic of China (2018). Full Text: China's Arctic Policy. Available at: http://english.gov.cn/archive/white_paper/2018/01/26/content_281476026660336.htm [Accessed 4 Feb 2018].
6   Sevunts, L. (2016). Canada to Submit its Arctic Continental Shelf Claim in 2018. *Radio Canada International* [online]. Available at: www.rcinet.ca/en/2016/05/03/canada-to-submit-its-arctic-continental-shelf-claim-in-2018 [Accessed 18 Jan 2018].
7   Steinberg, P., Tasch, J., and Gerhardt, H. (2015). *Contesting the Arctic: Rethinking politics in the circumpolar North.* London: I.B. Tauris.
8   Nord, D. (2015). *The Arctic Council: Governance within the Far North.* New York: Routledge.
9   Berry, D., Bowles, N., and Jones, H. (2016). *Governing the North American Arctic: Sovereignty, security, and institutions.* London: Palgrave Macmillan. Available from: https://link.springer.com/book/10.1057%2F9781137493910 [Accessed 4 Feb 2018].
10 Conley, H., Toland, T., Mihaela, D., and Natalja, J. (2013). *The New Foreign Policy Frontier: U.S. interests and actors in the Arctic.* Center for Strategic & International Studies. Available at: https://csis-prod.s3.amazonaws.com/s3fs-public/legacy_files/files/publication/130307_Conley_NewForeignPolFrontier_Web_0.pdf [Accessed 4 Feb 2018].
11 Reiss, B. (2015). In the Race to Control the Arctic, the U.S. lags behind. *Newsweek* [online]. Available at: www.newsweek.com/2015/07/17/united-states-not-winning-race-control-arctic-349973.html [Accessed 23 Jan 2018].
12 Anderson, J. (2016). The US Quietly Re-writes Arctic Policy. *Global Risk Insights.* Available at: https://globalriskinsights.com/2016/11/23956 [Accessed 15 Jan 2018].
13 Tingstad, A. and Pezard, S. (2017). What Does 'America First' Look Like in the Arctic? *The RAND Blog.* Available at: ttps://www.rand.org/blog/2017/05/what-does-america-first-look-like-in-the-arctic.html [Accessed 4 Feb 2018].

14   Department of State (2017). Remarks at the Arctic Council Ministerial Meeting. Available at: www.state.gov/secretary/remarks/2017/05/270813.htm [Accessed 4 Feb 2018].

15   Friedman L. and Davenport C. (2018). Pompeo, Trump's Pick for Secretary of State, Is a 'Great Climate Skeptic'. *New York Times* [online]. Available at: www.nytimes.com/2018/03/13/climate/pompeo-state-department-climate-change.html [Accessed 16 Jun 2018].

16   Chivers, C. (2007). Russians Plant Flag on the Arctic Seabed. *New York Times* [online]. Available at: www.nytimes.com/2007/08/03/world/europe/03arctic.html [Accessed 4 Feb 2018].

17   Johnson, K. and Standish, R. (2018). Putin and Xi Are Dreaming of a Polar Silk Road. *Foreign Policy* [online]. Available at: http://foreignpolicy.com/2018/03/08/putin-and-xi-are-dreaming-of-a-polar-silk-road-arctic-northern-sea-route-yamal [Accessed 16 Jun 2018].

18   Foy, H. (2017). Russia Ships First Gas from $27bn Arctic Project. *Financial Times* [online]. Available at: www.ft.com/content/515d451c-dc11-11e7-a039-c64b1c09b482 [Accessed 24 Dec 2017].

19   Rosneft (2017). Offshore Projects. Available at: www.rosneft.com/business/Upstream/Offshoreprojects [Accessed 20 Dec 2018].

20   Gramer, R. (2017). Here's What Russia's Military Build-up In the Arctic Looks Like. *Foreign Policy*. Available at: http://foreignpolicy.com/2017/01/25/heres-what-russias-military-build-up-in-the-arctic-looks-like-trump-oil-military-high-north-infographic-map [Accessed 10 Jan 2018].

21   Ministry of Defence of the Russian Federation (2017). In 2017, More than 100 Military Infrastructure Facilities will be Completed in the Russian Arctic. *Military Encyclopedic Dictionary*. Available at: https://function.mil.ru/news_page/country/more.htm?id=12109324@egNews [Accessed 25 Jan 2018].

22   Stavridis, J. (2018). Avoiding a Cold War in the High North. Bloomberg [online]. Available at: www.bloomberg.com/view/articles/2018-05-04/russia-is-gearing-up-for-a-cold-war-in-the-arctic [Accessed 26 May 2018].

23   Department of Defense (2013). Arctic Strategy. Available at: http://archive.defense.gov/pubs/2013_Arctic_Strategy.pdf [Accessed 26 Nov 2018].

24   O'Rourke, R. (2018). *Coast Guard Polar Security Cutter (Polar Icebreaker) Program: Background and issues for Congress.* Congressional Research Service [PDF]. Available at: https://fas.org/sgp/crs/weapons/RL34391.pdf [Accessed 26 Nov 2018].

25   Lamothe, D. (2017). Trump Pledges to Build Coast Guard Icebreakers, but it's Unclear How Different His Plan is from Obama's. *Washington Post* [online]. Available at: www.washingtonpost.com/news/checkpoint/wp/2017/05/17/trump-pledges-to-build-coast-guard-icebreakers-but-its-unclear-how-different-his-plan-is-than-obamas [Accessed 10 Jan 2018].

26   Grover, J. (2016). Coast Guard: Agency could better assess its impact on Arctic capability gaps and is exploring icebreaker acquisition options. Washington, D.C.: United States Government Accountability Office. Available at: www.gao.gov/assets/680/678346.pdf [Accessed 5 Feb 2018].

27   United States Coast Guard (2018). 2019 Budget Overview: 2017 performance highlights. Available at: www.uscg.mil/Portals/0/documents/budget/2019%20BIB_FINALw.pdf [Accessed 20 Feb 2018].

28   Subcommittee on Coast Guard and Maritime Transportation Committee on Transportation and Infrastructure U.S. House of Representatives Hearing: West, R. Statement (2017) Building a 21st century infrastructure for America: Coast guard sea, land, and air capabilities, Part II. Available at: https://transportation.house.gov/uploadedfiles/2017-07-25_-_west_testimony.pdf [Accessed 20 Jan 2018].

29   O'Rourke, R. (2018). *Coast Guard Polar Security Cutter (Polar Icebreaker) Program: Background and issues for Congress.* Congressional Research Service [PDF]. Available at: https://fas.org/sgp/crs/weapons/RL34391.pdf [Accessed 26 Nov 2018].

30   The White House (2018). Statement from the Press Secretary on Border Wall Funding in the House of Representatives Homeland Security Appropriations Bill. Available at: www.whitehouse.gov/briefings-statements/statement-press-secretary-border-wall-funding-house-representatives-homeland-security-appropriations-bill [Accessed 6 Aug 2018].

31 Reuters (2018). 'America's Got to Up Its Game in the Arctic': Mattis. *New York Times* [online]. Available at: www.nytimes.com/reuters/2018/06/25/world/europe/25reuters-usa-military-arctic.html [Accessed 1 Aug. 2018].

32 Sfraga, M. and Brigham, L. (2018). U.S., Russia Can Look North to the Arctic to Find Common Ground. Wilson Center. Available at: www.wilsoncenter.org/article/us-russia-can-look-north-to-the-arctic-to-find-common-ground [Accessed 24 July 2018].

SUGGESTED READINGS

Sergunin, A. and Konyshev, V. (2015). *Russia in the Arctic: Hard or soft power?* Ed. A. Umland. St. Petersburg State University: Ibidem Press.

Zellen, B.S. (ed.) (2013). *The Fast-Changing Arctic: Rethinking Arctic security for a warmer world*. University of Calgary Press (Northern Lights Series).

7 The winds of change: Europe and the United States

Ellen B. Pirro

INTRODUCTION

Since World War II, the cornerstone of the liberal global order has been the intimate relationship between the United States and Europe. This partnership, forged during World War II, has persisted until now despite changing leaders and governments of different political complexions, and it has withstood political, economic and military crises. Indeed, the relationship has repeatedly been described as "stable" and "predictable."

In 2017, Donald Trump assumed America's presidency determined to upend the liberal global order. Nowhere is this more evident than in U.S. relations with its European friends. Trump's "America First" policies have challenged European perceptions of the United States and its willingness to follow the norms and practices of the liberal order. This chapter examines these changing perceptions concerning NATO, the European Union (EU), and it members and the impact of the Ukrainian conflict. It concludes by considering what the future holds for the U.S.-European relationship.

UNITED STATES-EUROPE IN THE POSTWAR LIBERAL WORLD

After World War II, U.S.-European cooperation fostered a complex network of ties in multiple arenas including security and defense, trade and finance, and collaboration in other regions.

Security and defense

Two multilateral institutions became the pillars of U.S.-European relations, the North Atlantic Treaty Organization (NATO) and the EU. The first was NATO. Established in 1949, NATO provided security against the Soviet Union during the Cold War. The alliance was central to America's containment strategy to prevent Soviet expansion. Its counterpart was the Soviet-led Warsaw Pact. Central to NATO was the commitment of Article 5 of the treaty that an attack on any member was an attack on all. Article 5 has been invoked only once, after al-Qaeda attacked the U.S. in 2001. The Afghan Taliban's refusal to turn over Osama bin Laden led NATO to invade Afghanistan to capture bin Laden. The NATO allies also participated in joint efforts during the conflicts against Serbia in the 1990s and the 2011 Libyan civil war.

Originally formed by twelve countries in Western Europe plus the United States and Canada, NATO grew in subsequent years, first adding Greece, Turkey, West Germany, and Spain. After the Cold War ended, NATO expanded eastward, adding former members of the Soviet bloc and several former Soviet republics in two waves, 1999 and 2004. It now has twenty-nine members (the most recent being Montenegro) and reaches Russia's border. The goals of the expansion were to maintain stability in these newly independent countries and help them establish liberal democratic systems. During this period U.S. forces in Europe were significantly reduced. During the Obama years there were additional reductions in NATO troop strength and military spending. In addition, President Barack Obama altered U.S. plans to place anti-missile installations in Poland and the Czech Republic to meet Russian objections. Nevertheless, Moscow viewed NATO's expansion eastward as violating the terms by which the Cold War had ended.

After Vladimir Putin succeeded Boris Yeltsin as Russia's president in 2000, a resurgent Russia began to challenge NATO. Moscow had enjoyed observer status in NATO councils, which ended at the onset of the Ukrainian conflict. NATO responded to Russian aggressiveness with economic sanctions, increases in NATO forces, and coordinated military exercises. The Barack Obama administration also sought to reassure Europe with the 2014 European Reassurance Initiative, which funds additional U.S. troops that rotate through NATO's eastern and Baltic member states, increased training and exercises, prepositioned military equipment, modernization of bases and airfields, and coordination among intelligence services against terrorism and cyber threats. Like his predecessors, Obama also urged that America's allies to increase their military contribution to NATO.

Trade and the European Union

While NATO was the security pillar, the EU was America's major transatlantic trade and financial partner. Although observers date the EU from the 1957 Treaty of Rome, its origins were America's 1948 Marshall Plan and the 1952 European Coal and Steel Community (ECSC). The former required European recipients to cooperate in distributing Marshall aid and to make progress towards integration and ECSC integrated the coal and steel industries of six Western European countries and established institutions for additional economic integration.

Additional integration took place, and in 1993, the Treaty of Maastricht established the European Union common market. The EU has built a dense network of agencies and policies that have further integrated them economically and politically. The EU expanded from the original "inner six" to include twenty-eight members, the most recent of which is Croatia (2013), and over half a billion people.[1] To join, members must have a democratic political system subject to the rule of law, and a free market subject to common regulations.

The EU has facilitated greatly increased trade with America, especially after nineteen members established a single currency, the euro (the Eurozone), elimination of borders, and common laws and regulations. U.S. trade with the EU in 2016 ranked second to China, totaling $1.1 billion in imports and exports. Of America's fifteen leading trading partners, six are EU members.

Transatlantic friendship

Notwithstanding occasional differences, every U.S. president and administration since World War II to Donald Trump have vigorously supported the transatlantic relationship. Each has also developed close ties with European leaders. As first declared by Winston Churchill (whose mother was American), America and the United Kingdom have a "special relationship," which has been reaffirmed by every president and prime minister. Franco-American friendship dates back to the American Revolution. The United Kingdom (UK), France, and America were allies in both world wars. After World War II, the U.S. and Germany developed complex economic, political, and military ties, and there are major U.S. military bases on German soil. Poland considered America its closest friend in throwing off the Soviet yoke, and many other former Soviet satellites and republics feel much the same.

In recent decades, ties have been particularly close. President Ronald Reagan had a warm personal friendship with British Prime Minister Margaret Thatcher whom he aided in the UK's 1982 Falklands War. A similar friendship existed between Bill Clinton and Tony Blair, and Blair followed George W. Bush in America's 2003 invasion of Iraq. This led British newspapers to label Blair as Bush's "poodle." Other European leaders had opposed the invasion. Public opinion polls confirm that President Obama is still highly regarded throughout Europe (Wike, 2016).[2]

Such ties fostered American-European cooperation in many respects including unified voting in the UN and other international organizations, and cooperation in out-of-area issues such as the 1991 Persian Gulf War, the 1992 Bosnia war, the 1999 Kosovo war, the 2011 Libyan civil war, and the Afghan campaign against the Taliban. There are numerous transatlantic links including shared criminal and terrorist intelligence. During the Obama administration, negotiations were begun on a TTIP (Transatlantic Trade and Investment Partnership) treaty designed to deepen transatlantic economic links.

THE TRUMP ADMINISTRATION AND EUROPE

President Trump has eroded traditional U.S.-European ties. Events in Europe itself have also contributed to changing transatlantic links. In America, the Trump administration has weakened America's support for democracy, free trade, multilateral alliances, and international institutions. Although some European populists who emulate Trump have lost recent elections in France, Germany, and the Netherlands, others have triumphed in Poland, Hungary, Austria, the Czech Republic, and, most recently, Italy. Trump has praised illiberal European populists like France's Marine Le Pen and has been praised by others, especially Hungary's Viktor Orbán.

Currently, the EU confronts major challenges to its survival and lacks the support of the Trump administration. After populist sentiments across the Atlantic culminated in Brexit, Trump tweeted, "[t]hey took their country back, just like we will take America back" and suggested that other members would be better off if they also left the EU.

The emergence of competing great powers, notably China and Russia, along with a perceived decline in U.S. dominance and the rhetoric and actions of Trump, have led Europeans to reassess their relationship with America. In the past year, the EU has negotiated a major trade deal with China, and Sino-European trade volume has surged past transatlantic trade. Despite American opposition, Germany and Russia have moved ahead with the Nord Stream pipeline project designed to avoid shipping gas from Russia to Europe through Ukraine and Georgia. Europeans have also embraced the Paris Accords on climate change, while Trump announced Washington would withdraw from them. In addition, Trump's withdrawal from the Iranian nuclear deal created consternation among America's European allies that along with Russia and China had been instrumental in negotiating that agreement. Finally, the EU also vigorously opposes Trump's decision to recognize Jerusalem as Israel's capital.

Trump's harsh rhetoric about "America First" raised several concerns across Europe about security, environmental, and economic issues. The president has questioned the utility of NATO and criticized Europe's contribution to the alliance, raising concerns about America's commitment to Europe's defense. Trump has also criticized the EU's multilateralism as well as other international organizations important to Europeans like the World Trade Organization (WTO) and, as we shall see, has embraced protectionism in trade. In sum, Trump has unilaterally sought to reshape transatlantic ties in ways to suit his ultra-nationalism.

TRUMP AND NATO

Trump questioned the utility of NATO early in his presidential campaign. He tweeted that NATO was obsolete and member states do not contribute their fair share to the alliance. His criticisms of NATO occurred even while Russia was acting like an expansionist power in Europe in its effort to regain its great-power status and foster U.S.-European differences. Russia's 2008 war with Georgia, its aggression against Ukraine, and its annexation of Crimea alienated America's European allies, leading them to re-examine America's reliability and to begin considering how to defend themselves without a U.S. presence. They are questioning, for example, whether Washington would aid small NATO Baltic members like Estonia if Russia were to invade.

There are four factors behind Trump's negativism about NATO. First, Trump admires authoritarian leaders like Putin. He has been reluctant to criticize Russia for its aggressive activities including annexing Crimea, intervening in Ukraine, and harassing European neighbors, especially Poland and the Baltic states. Second, Trump dislikes multilateral institutions, preferring bilateral negotiations dominated by Washington. Third, Trump stated in campaign speeches and interviews after the election that terrorism should be among NATO's main missions (Gove, 2017).[3] Finally, Trump believes that Europeans take advantage of America by failing to pay a fair share for their defense and, shortly before the NATO summit in July 2018, wrote threatening letters to NATO allies demanding increased spending. Indeed, after the 2008 financial crisis, European NATO members slashed defense expenditures still further. Washington, by contrast, continued spending about 3.6 percent of America's gross domestic product (GDP) on defense. NATO had agreed at its annual summit meeting in 2014 that all members should spend a minimum of 2 percent of GDP on defense and that all of them should meet that goal by 2024. By 2018, only a few – Belgium, Estonia, the UK, France, the Netherlands, and Poland – had reached the 2 percent goal. Indeed, during the past decade, several, notably Spain and Italy, had actually cut their military budgets to about 1 percent of GDP, and Germany spends only 1.2 percent of its GDP on defense. By contrast, several Eastern European members are increasing their defense budgets owing to their perception of a growing Russian threat.

Some European allies did begin to increase their defense budgets in order to meet to the 2 percent goal. The Czech Republic, for example, presented a budget, which would double its expenditures on defense and bring them into NATO compliance by 2020. It remains unclear, however, whether this was a response to Trump's pressure and/or perceptions of increased Russian threats.

East European NATO members like Poland, Estonia, and the Czech Republic, are understandably concerned about the threat from Russia. Since 2012, Russian provocations have significantly increased. Moscow repeatedly probes European defenses, routinely violating European air space with fighters, entering the maritime territory of countries liked Sweden and Norway with warships, and initiating cyberattacks, all with little response from the U.S. or NATO.

Europeans have become accustomed to using diplomacy first and, and previously believed they could rely on Washington in the event of a serious crisis when military protection might be needed. In the 2008 Georgia conflict, however, Putin challenged Washington by asking if America would trade its friendship/relationship with Russia for a small, impoverished Eastern European country (Cooper, 2008).[4] At that time, Europeans believed the answer was "yes."

Currently, however, there are growing doubts among Europeans whether Washington would honor its NATO commitments and come to the aid of small nations like Estonia, Latvia, or Lithuania. All three Baltic states and Ukraine have been subject to Russian harassment. Estonia was the victim of two Russian cyberattacks shutting down vital services, and Lithuania recently confronted a major Russian/Belarus military exercise along its border. Poland also has experienced Russian harassment. Indeed, the agreement between Trump and Putin in June 2018 to hold a summit in Helsinki, Finland greatly heightened European anxiety.

In May 2017 on his first post-election visit to Europe, Trump refused to acknowledge America's commitment to Article 5 of the NATO treaty, much to the distress of his advisers and America's allies. German Chancellor Angela Merkel concisely expressed European doubts about America's commitment when she declared in 2017: "The times in which we could fully rely on others are, to a certain extent, in the past. We Europeans must take our fate into our own hands more decisively than we have in the past" (cited in Barkin, 2017)[5] As recently as 2013, she had described America as Germany's "most important friend" outside Europe, but no longer used the "word" friend regarding the U.S. in 2017.

Trump responded to these fears by finally acknowledging America's commitment to Article 5 in June 2017 and by increasing the European Reassurance Initiative budget to nearly $4.8 billion in 2018 (an increase of $1.7 billion from 2017). According to General David Alvin, the Director, Strategy, and Policy, Headquarters U.S. European Command, this would provide "a more robust U.S. military rotational presence throughout the theater that is capable of deterring and, if required, responding to any regional threats" (cited in Pellerin, 2017).[6] Trump also sought to reinstate the missile-defense shield in Poland and the Czech Republic reversing Obama's 2009 decision. In July 2017, he moved to sell the Patriot missiles to Poland to be deployed within two years and promised missile defense to the Czech Republic if Prague wished it.

Owing to the fear that NATO under U.S. leadership would not come to Europe's aid, twenty-three EU countries signed a defense cooperation accord, Permanent Structured Cooperation (PESCO), in November 2017. This agreement committed EU members to additional defense expenditures and cooperation among those who choose to participate.

However, members could opt in or out of specific programs, exercises, and operations. Consequently, there are already suggestions that PESCO will accomplish little. Indeed, PESCO and NATO might compete for scarce resources (Valášek, 2017).[7]

America still remains the crucial player in NATO. Washington has begun to station additional forces in Europe with bases in twelve European countries. Washington is also involved in training forces in several countries and participates in joint exercises in military planning and preparation. Despite his criticism of NATO, Trump decided to attend NATO's annual summit in September 2018.

TRUMP, EUROPE, AND UKRAINE

As we discussed in Chapter 5, among the areas where America and its European allies confront Russia is Ukraine. Let us now examine the issue from the perspective of America's European allies. President Putin does not want NATO bordering Russia. Putin prefers a neutral buffer zone between Russia and NATO. Ukraine became independent after the collapse of the USSR, but Russia continued to influence its politics and elections. Inhabitants in western Ukraine, including in its capital Kiev, sought closer economic and political relations with Europe and membership in the EU and NATO. However, the Russian-speaking inhabitants in eastern Ukraine, notably the Donbass, wanted a closer relationship with Russia. The situation came to a head in 2014, when Ukraine's pro-Russian President Viktor Yanukovych refused to sign an agreement to allow the country to enjoy EU trade privileges and thereby receive encouragement to reform its corrupt political and economic systems. Ukrainians protested despite subzero temperatures in Kiev's Maiden Square, challenging the government and eventually forcing Yanukovych to flee to Russia with a trainload of loot. Ukraine wrote a new constitution; new elections were held; and Petro Poroshenko became Ukraine's president. In eastern Ukraine, however, pro-Russians took up arms and, with Russian "volunteers," resisted the government in Kiev, demanding autonomy or even secession from Ukraine.

The Obama administration applauded Ukraine's elections and supported the new pro-Western government with humanitarian and financial aid but not with arms. The administration also supported the efforts of the EU and the International Monetary Fund (IMF) to end corruption in Ukraine and help it become financially solvent. For its part, Russia seized Crimea from Ukraine and provided additional military support for pro-Russian militias.

The EU initially did little beyond providing humanitarian aid. It also condemned Russia's presence in eastern Ukraine, but it was only after the downing by pro-Russian separatists of a Malaysian plane in eastern Ukraine, which carried many Dutch passengers, that the EU began to increase its involvement. From the start, both the U.S. and the EU had condemned the annexation of Crimea, and Russia's military involvement in Ukraine's eastern region. In March and April 2014, Washington targeted economic sanctions against Russian officials and companies. These were expanded in late April to include additional Russian officials. Other sanctions targeted Russian energy firms, banks, and defense industries. In 2017, Congress voted further sanctions against Russia for supporting Ukrainian separatists and failing to carry out ceasefire and humanitarian agreements, but Trump refused to apply these sanctions until March 2018.

The EU swiftly followed Washington in imposing similar sanctions on Russian "entities" for interfering in Ukraine. However, not all EU members agreed to the sanctions. Italy,

Hungary, Greece, Cyprus, and Slovakia refused to comply with the EU decision. European firms also suffered economically, causing losses of an estimated 100 billion euros in trade per year. Germany estimated that over 30,000 of its firms were harmed by the sanctions. Nevertheless, the EU renewed sanctions against Russia in June 2018.

As noted in Chapter 5, Western economic and diplomatic pressure led to the Minsk Accords of 2015. This was essentially a ceasefire agreement that did not resolve the conflict. Negotiations took place among Russian, Ukrainian, French, and German leaders in which Washington did not participate. From its onset, both sides repeatedly violated the ceasefire. The EU continues to call for strict observance of these agreements, while sporadic fighting continued. As of late 2018 no resolution of the conflict is in sight although negotiations have occurred about a possible UN peacekeeping presence. Throughout the crisis, the EU has strongly supported the government in Kiev and Ukraine's economy with various forms of assistance, but it has failed to pressure Ukraine's government to eliminate corruption. The once-rejected EU partnership agreement with Ukraine was signed and came into force in April 2017. It put Ukraine on a path toward EU membership, although that remains in the distant future.

Donald Trump described the situation in Ukraine as "a mess," and contended that the conflict was the previous administration's fault because it had been "too soft" in reacting to Russia's occupation of Crimea. Nevertheless, throughout the election campaign, Trump seemed to imply that Russia had a legitimate right to Crimea. On several occasions he declared that Russia would not invade Ukraine, conveniently forgetting that Russian troops were already in the provinces of Luhansk and Donetsk. Trump largely ignored the Ukrainian situation, until he saw an opportunity for U.S. arms sales to Ukraine's government, and he decided in December 2017 to sell Ukraine a variety of small arms. In early 2018, a prisoner swap began, with Ukrainian soldiers freed in return for pro-Russian rebels (and Russian "volunteers"). Disrupting this process, Trump announced his approval of the sale of anti-tank missiles to Ukraine in January 2018.

THE EUROPEAN UNION AND THE TRUMP ADMINISTRATION

As the world's leading regional economic organization based on democracy and free trade, the EU is a pillar of the liberal global order. In all its forms it has survived seven decades – despite the vote for Brexit – and even earned a Nobel Peace Prize. Among its achievements, it has shepherded former Soviet allies and republics to democracy, capitalism, and prosperity. Every U.S. president has supported and encouraged the European Union since its inception until Trump.

Not only has Trump evinced his dislike of the EU, as noted earlier, he encouraged Brexit and lauded rightist populists like Nigel Farage and those who urged the UK's exit. He has criticized EU policies on terrorism, trade, migration, and climate. Thus, following her visit to Washington in 2017, Frederica Mogherini, the EU's Foreign Minister commented, "I think we are entering into a different phase of our relationship. A more transactional approach means Europeans will be more transactional, and we will base our approach on our interests" (cited in Gardiner, 2017).[8]

Trump has criticized the EU for several reasons. As noted above, he dislikes multilateral institutions, even successful ones like the EU, and believes that America gets a 'bad deal' by having to negotiate trade with Europe as a bloc instead of being able to deal with individual states bilaterally. Europe has been slow in recovering from the 2008 economic crisis, and it still suffers from issues such as Greece's indebtedness, the weakness of Italian banks, and widespread unemployment. Greater trade with non-members of the EU would accelerate Europe's recovery, but Trump ended TTIP negotiations early in 2017. Recently, Washington and Brussels have expressed an interest in renewing negotiations for this trade deal, but no concrete steps have been taken to do so.

Moreover, Trump does not publicly support the norms that the EU promotes, including the spread of democracy and human rights, and its reluctance to use military force. Trump views EU policies regarding terrorism as inadequate. As noted above, Trump withdrew America from the Paris Climate Accord, an agreement the EU strongly supports. Finally, Trump has not yet appointed a U.S. ambassador to the EU, although he has nominated Gordon Sondand, the founder and CEO of Provenance Hotels, for this post.

Starting in 2015, the European Union, and especially Germany, accepted over two million refugees fleeing violence in the Middle East, Africa and Central Asia. Trump condemned the EU and recipient countries for permitting such migration and their free movement among the twenty-six countries that are members of the Schengen area that dismantled internal border controls. He based his view on a fear of terrorists mingled among the refugees, contending that some will carry out the sort of 'jihadi' violence in Europe that has already occurred in cities such as London, Paris, Barcelona, Nice, Brussels, and Istanbul. At a tumultuous meeting in late June 2018, European leaders, however, reached a modest compromise to paper over their differences on the migrant issue. They agreed to strengthen their external borders and create voluntary centers for migrants in Europe, and possibly in North Africa as well, to house, screen, and determine swiftly whether they are genuine refugees and thereby reduce the burden on frontline countries like Italy and Greece. The agreement was expected to be helpful to Chancellor Merkel's political fortunes, but her support continued to decline owing to her liberal immigration policy, the losses by her party in German state elections, and the opposition to that policy of the Bavarian Christian Social Union (CSU), a long-time ally.

TRUMP AND EUROPEAN LEADERS

Despite a history of close ties between Germany and America, Donald Trump and Chancellor Angela Merkel did not get along. Since Trump took office, the warmth of German-American friendship has cooled. It was evident from the start that Merkel and Trump had different perceptions of the liberal global world. This was reflected in Trump's criticism of German policies. During America's presidential campaign, Trump accused Merkel of ruining Germany because of her admission of migrants. As we have seen, Merkel argued that Europe has to "go it alone." Nonetheless, German concerns about NATO were eased, largely because Merkel trusted U.S. Defense Secretary Jim Mattis.

There are several other issues where differences between Merkel and Trump were apparent. Merkel supports EU multilateralism as the keystone of her economic and political policies. Trump prefers bilateral arrangements. Merkel strongly supports the Paris Climate Accord and "lectured" Trump on the dangers of global warming before the G-20 summit in May 2017. Trump's administration accused Germany of currency manipulation to exploit the U.S. Merkel angrily defended the independence of the European and German Central Banks. Washington opposed the deal Merkel brokered to build a natural gas pipeline from Russia to Germany. Merkel expressed disapproval of Trump's ban on the entry of migrants from Muslim countries, suggesting it entailed religious bias, and Trump disapproved of Merkel's views on Islamic migration. A photo taken at the G-7 talks in June 2018 epitomized the Trump-Merkel relationship. Merkel is seen standing, finger pointed, lecturing an arms-crossed and defiant, seated Trump.

Chancellor Merkel was able to form a three-party coalition government in March 2018 only after months of negotiation and after paying a high price politically, immediately clouding her political future. In November 2018, Merkel announced that she would no longer seek to lead the Christian Democratic Union (CDU) after 2018 and that she will not serve as chancellor beyond her current mandate.

Trump has undoubtedly not helped Merkel's political fortunes. Unlike his predecessors' courteous behavior toward allied leaders, Trump failed to congratulate Merkel on forming a new government even though he had congratulated Vladimir Putin on his "reelection" in Russia. Her own party openly challenged her on the migration issue, and her political allies threatened to withdraw their support. At the G-7 talks, Merkel was forced to defend Germany against Trump's false claim that migration had led to an increase of 10 percent in crime in Germany. Merkel cited evidence that crime had actually dropped by 9.6 percent. Some thought that Trump's remarks would actually help Merkel retain power because Germans loathe Trump and his policies and resent attacks on their leader, but that has not been the case. Moreover, the Trump administration has not made any serious effort to improve relations with Germany. Notably, Washington only nominated an ambassador to Germany in April 2018. The new ambassador, Richard Grenell, quickly alienated Germans by demanding that German companies toe the U.S. line in sanctioning Iran again after Washington's decision to withdraw from the nuclear deal with Tehran.

In the case of France, Trump openly supported populist leader, Marine Le Pen of the Front National Party, in the 2017 French elections, largely because of her opposition to immigrants, desire for smaller government, and dislike of the EU. After Emmanuel Macron of the *En Marche!* Party won the election, defeating Le Pen by a 66 to 33 percent margin, Trump was forced to do a volte-face and embraced France's new president. While announcing cooperation with Washington. Macron is promoting very different views than Trump – globalism, strengthening the EU, and combating global warming. After several bone-crushing handshakes, which suggested that Macron was letting Trump know he was not going to be a pushover, Macron invited Trump to Paris where he reveled in the pageantry of Bastille Day celebrations. Macron also told Trump that moving the U.S. embassy in Israel to Jerusalem was a mistake. Although it appears that, despite protestations, the Franco-U.S. relationship is still on firm ground, Macron does not hesitate to criticize Trump's policies. Thus, at the G-7 meetings Macron criticized Trump's protectionist trade policies and for leaving before a discussion of policy toward climate change. After an acrimonious exchange of tweets, it seems the rapprochement between the two leaders was at an end.

In the UK, Prime Minister Theresa May sought to maintain the Anglo-American "special relationship." She was the first European leader to visit the White House after the U.S. elections and was insulted by being only the second visiting British politician. Trump had previously welcomed pro-Brexit ultranationalist Nigel Farage, who, Trump told May, would make an excellent ambassador to America. However, May seeks a bilateral trade deal with America after Brexit, to compensate for lost trade with Europe. Their initial meeting was cordial but cool. Thereafter, however, their personal relationship worsened after Trump criticized her government for being soft on terrorism after two terrorist attacks had occurred in the UK. In November 2017, Trump re-tweeted doctored anti-Muslim videos from a rightwing racist British fringe group called Britain First, and May rebuked the president. In turn, Trump again criticized May for her failure to curtail terrorism in the UK. In the ensuing tweet storm, Trump again took her to task, and she answered curtly by condemning his false claim that the British police knew the perpetrators of an explosion on a London tube train. Thereafter, the UK suspended sharing intelligence with Washington after information about a bombing in Manchester had been leaked to the U.S. press (Mason, 2017).[9] This led to debate over whether a proposed state visit to the UK by Trump would actually occur.

Every U.S. president typically receives an invitation for a state visit to London soon after assuming office. Trump only received such an invitation in January 2018 – much later than his predecessors. The British excuse was that the Brexit negotiations preoccupied the government. In fact, there was widespread discussion in the British media about such a visit, and in parliament, questions were raised about the wisdom of extending the invitation. Over a million Britons signed a petition opposing Trump's visit. London's Muslim mayor, Sadiq Khan, himself the subject of critical tweets by Trump, asked the prime minister to withdraw the invitation after Trump had shown the Britain First videos. "Many Brits who love America and Americans will see this as a betrayal of the special relationship between our two countries," declared Khan. "It beggars belief that the President of our closest ally doesn't see that his support of this extremist group actively undermines the values of tolerance and diversity that makes Britain so great" (cited in Vazquez, 2017).[10]

The high point of Trump's visit was to be the opening of a new U.S. embassy in London. Faced with mounting negative sentiment and the specter of thousands of British demonstrators, Trump refused the invitation, claiming that the new embassy reflected poor decisions by Obama. He argued that the embassy was in a bad location, its costs were too high, and there were flaws in the building's design, which he attributed to Obama. In early 2018, however, Trump and May conversed at the World Economic Forum in Davos, Switzerland and announced that their relationship was again "special" and cordial. Afterwards, the administration announced that Trump would be coming to the UK in September 2018, on a "working", not a "state visit." This descended to "dropping by" on his way to the NATO summit in July 2018.

Trump has applauded the rise of populist leaders in Eastern as well as Western Europe. Both he and Hungary's Prime Minister Orbán support "hard" borders and admire Putin. Although many in Europe condemn Orbán's illiberal views, he and Trump exchange telephone calls and share populist views. Orbán praised Trump's election as ending "liberal non-democracy" (cited in Pasha-Robinson, 2016).[11] Trump phoned Orbán to congratulate him on his reelection. In Poland, rising nationalism and Euroscepticism also led to populist leadership, and the EU condemned its leaders for reducing the independence of its judiciary. Trump and Polish leader Jarosław Kaczyński enjoy common ground in fostering their respective coal industries. Poland, where coal is a major industry, opposes EU efforts to use less polluting energy sources. In America, Trump made renewal of America's coal industry part of his campaign.

Instead of supporting liberal allies, Trump embraced Italy's new coalition government of the populist Northern League and Five Star Movement, inviting Prime Minister

Giuseppe Conte to the White House and declaring, "the people of Italy got it right" (cited in Griffiths, 2018).[12] Trump praised the program of the new government, which refuses to accept refugees and is skeptical about the Eurozone in which it has the third-largest economy.

THE INCIPIENT TRADE WAR

Since his election, Trump has repeatedly threatened to impose tariffs to protect America's economy. In April 2018, he imposed significant tariffs on imports of steel and aluminum, citing national security, which therefore prevents its being discussed at the WTO. Despite pleas and protests, Trump extended those tariffs to U.S. allies including Canada and Mexico, and in particular the European Union. "Please tell Prime Minister Trudeau and President Macron that they are charging the U.S. massive tariffs . . . The EU trade surplus with the U.S. is $151 billion" (cited in Qiu, 2018).[13] Some weeks later at a political rally, he denounced the EU: "It's going to stop, or we'll stop trading with them . . . like the piggy bank that everybody's robbing – and that ends" (cited in Shear and Porter, 2018).[14]

From the beginning, the EU had indicated it would retaliate if Washington imposed tariffs, and in late June 2018, the EU placed 25 percent tariffs on various U.S. products including motorcycles, steel, bourbon, peanut butter, cranberries, and jeans. These products were selected to target districts important to Republican congressional candidates. One industry that was hard hit is Harley-Davidson motorcycles, a major industry in Wisconsin, home of former House Speaker Paul Ryan. The firm, long praised by Trump and others as an American icon, announced it would be moving a portion of its manufacturing overseas to avoid the tariffs, thereby triggering angry threats by Trump to increase the company's taxes. Trump has also threatened to impose 20 percent tariffs on imported automobiles (especially important for Germany), arguing that the EU must remove all duties on U.S. cars exported to Europe. Trump believes he can "win" any trade war, but escalation of this incipient trade war would harm both Americans (especially, Trump's rural supporters) and Europeans. EU Trade Commissioner Cecilia Malmstrom said: "Today is a bad day for world trade. We did everything to avoid this outcome" (cited in Petroff, 2018).[15]

TRUMP, EUROPE, AND THE FUTURE

The gradual decline of U.S. interest and involvement in Europe after the Cold War has accelerated since Trump's election. Trump appears to have little or no knowledge of, as well as little or no interest in, the historical ties that have linked Europe and America. He seems to regard much of Europe as militarily weak and economically stagnant. The result is Washington's neglect of its European allies and their policies.

Meanwhile a new generation of leaders is emerging in Europe, both populist and globalist/anti-populist. For the globalists, Macron represents a new chapter for France, and Europe as a whole. He is seen as a new driving force in the EU, supplanting Chancellor Merkel, who is serving her final term in office. By British political norms, Theresa May should have resigned after the disastrous results of a snap election in 2017 for her Conservative Party, but she is determined to complete the Brexit negotiations with the EU. The United Kingdom's future remains to be seen, but it will almost certainly be under new leadership.

There has been speculation about the demise of the European Union. With the rise of Euroscepticism, especially in the UK and Eastern Europe; there are likely to be changes in the EU and how it operates after the conclusion of Brexit. There may emerge two groups – members that want a close union and those that seek to maximize national autonomy. It is difficult to see how the closely linked EU networks, which multiply each year, could evaporate. There are too many issues that require cooperation for the whole enterprise to disappear. Thus, the EU will probably continue in the future to "muddle through" until the next leap forward, perhaps stimulated by the ideas of Macron and other new leaders. From the American perspective and especially for American firms, it is easier to deal with a single unit like the EU and distribute products and services easily in many countries, notwithstanding Trump's preference for bilateralism.

Trump and his actions are widely disliked throughout much of Europe. His open support for populist movements and political leaders is seen as upending the order and stability of Europe. Despite NATO, there is a growing belief that America will no longer come to Europe's aid should the worst happen – especially if it involves one of the smaller European states. PESCO is seen by some as an initial effort to organize defense without the U.S. In the economic sphere, Trump's negative view of multilateral trade has led Europe to seek partners other than the U.S. Thus, the EU has implemented a major trade deal with Canada, and is negotiating with China for a trade agreement. Although the EU is under siege it is still the major player. The bottom line is that Trump neglects Europe, but Europe endures.

ESSAY QUESTIONS

1) Describe the historical ties that bind the United States and Europe.

2) Do you agree with President Trump's policies towards Europe, NATO, and the European Union? Explain your answer.

3) How has the dispute with Russia over Ukraine affected U.S.-European relations?

4) Why does President Trump dislike the European Union?

5) Discuss President Trump's relationship with major European leaders.

6) On what issues do the U.S. and Europe diverge?

SHORT ANSWER QUESTIONS

Define and describe the importance of the following:

Marine Le Pen
The Anglo-American "special relationship"
Brexit
Viktor Orbán
The Treaty of Maastricht

NOTES

1 Austria, Belgium, Bulgaria, Croatia, Cyprus, Czech Republic, Denmark, Estonia, Finland, France, Germany, Greece, Hungary, Ireland, Italy, Latvia, Lithuania, Luxembourg, Malta, the Netherlands, Poland, Portugal, Romania, Slovakia, Slovenia, Spain, Sweden, and United Kingdom. Albania, Macedonia, Montenegro, Serbia, and Turkey remain candidates for membership, and Georgia and Ukraine have expressed a desire to join.

2 Wike, R. (2016). As Obama Years Draw to Close, President and U.S. Seen Favorably in Europe and Asia. *Pew Research Center*. Available at: www.pewglobal.org/2016/06/29/as-obama-years-draw-to-close-president-and-u-s-seen-favorably-in-europe-and-asia [Accessed 1 March 2018].

3 Gove, M. (2017). Donald Trump Interview: Brexit will be a great thing. *The Times* [online]. Available at: www.www.www.thetimes.co.uk/article/donald-trump-interview-brexit-britain-trade-deal-europe-queen-5m0bc2tns [Accessed 25 March 2018].

4 Cooper, H. (2008). U.S. watched as a squabble turned into a showdown. *New York Times* [online]. Available at: www.www.www.nytimes.com/2008/08/18/washington/18diplo.html [Accessed 24 March 2018].

5 Barkin, N. (2017). U.S. No Longer a 'Friend' in German Election Program. *Reuters* [online]. Available at: www.www.www.reuters.com/article/us-germany-election-merkel-usa/u-s-no-longer-a-friend-in-merkel-election-program-idUSKBN19O1NS [Accessed 24 March 2018].

6 Pellerin, C. (2017). 2018 Budget Request for European Reassurance Initiative Grows to $4.7 Billion. U.S. Department of Defense. Available at: www.www.www.defense.gov/News/Article/Article/1199828/2018-budget-request-for-european-reassurance-initiative-grows-to-47-billion [Accessed 24 March 2018].

7 Valášek, T. (2017). The EU's New Defense Pact: Marginal gains. *Carnegie Europe*. Available at: http://carnegieeurope.eu/strategiceurope/74760 [Accessed 25 March 2018].

8 Gardiner, H. (2017). As Ties with US Cool, Europeans Look to Forge Other Alliances. *New York Times* [online]. Available at: www.www.www.nytimes.com/2017/02/10/world/europe/as-ties-with-us-cool-europeans-look-to-forge-other-alliances.html [Accessed 24 March 2018].

9 Mason, R. (2017). Theresa May Rebukes Donald Trump over Tube Bombing Tweets. *The Guardian* [online]. Available at: www.www.www.theguardian.com/us-news/2017/sep/15/donald-trump-blames-london-train-explosion-on-loser-terrorists [Accessed 18 March 2018].

10 Vazquez, M. (2017). London Mayor Hits Trump over Anti-Muslim Videos. *CNN*. Available at: www.cnn.com/2017/11/30/politics/sadiq-khan-trump-muslim-video-tweets/index.html [Accessed 24 March 2018].

11 Pasha-Robinson, L. (2016). Hungarian PM Viktor Orbán Celebrates Donald Trump Victory as End of 'Liberal Non-Democracy'. *The Independent* [online]. Available at: www.www.www.independent.co.uk/news/world/europe/donald-trump-us-election-win-hungarian-prime-minister-viktor-orban-end-liberal-non-democracy-a7413236.html [Accessed 3 March 2018].

12 Griffiths, B. (2018). Trump: Italy's Populist Prime Minister to Visit White House. *Politico* [online]. Available at www.politico.com/story/2018/06/09/Trump-Italy-prime-minister-White-House-Giuseppe-Conte-635009 [Accessed 23 June 2018].

13 Qiu, L. (2018). Trump Exaggerates Trade Deficit with European Union by $50 Billion. *New York Times* [online]. Available at: www.www.www.nytimes.com/2018/06/07/us/politics/fast-check-trump-trade-deficit-european-union.html [Accessed 25 June 2018].

14 Cited in Shear, M. and Porter, C. (2018). Trump Refuses to Sign G-7 Statement and Calls Trudeau 'Weak', *New York Times* [online]. Available at: www.www.www.nytimes.com/2018/06/09/world/americas/donald-trump-g7-nafta.html [Accessed 30 June 2018].

15 Petroff, A. (2018). Trump is Starting a Global Trade War. *CNN* [online]. Available at: http://money.cnn.com/2018/05/31/investing/us-steel-aluminum-tariffs-response/index.html [Accessed 26 June 2018].

SUGGESTED READINGS

Olsen, J. and McCormick, J. (2017). *The European Union: Politics and policies.* New York: Westview Press.
Kubicek, P. (2017). *European Politics*, 2nd ed. New York: Routledge.
Judis, J.B. (2016). *The Populist Explosion: How the Great Recession transformed American and European politics.* New York: Columbia Global Reports.

8 Crossing borders: United States foreign policy in Latin America

Ignacio Mamone and Amy Erica Smith

INTRODUCTION

Early twentieth-century Mexican dictator Porfirio Díaz once famously remarked to a journalist, "Poor Mexico. So far from God, and so close to the United States." Díaz captured the ambivalent familiarity of the relationship between the United States and its southern neighbors. Since most of Latin America became independent in the early nineteenth century, U.S. – Latin American relations have been marked by complex political maneuvering, with relationships ranging from overt mistrust to deep friendship. Throughout, steadily growing economic interdependence has increased U.S. political influence as a hemispheric powerhouse.

As both candidate and president, Donald Trump has expressed views that aim to restrict cross-border flows. Trump's general skepticism of the movement of people and goods between the U.S. and Latin America at times have led him to diverge from prior administrations and at others to continue earlier policies. Dating at least from the mid-twentieth century, prior administrations sought to increase legal trade and support diversity in legal immigration from Latin America, while vigorously opposing the illegal drug trade and illegal immigration. Trump, by contrast, has taken an isolationist and populist approach to U.S. – Latin American relations. The following sections deal with U.S. policy toward three types of cross-border flows: trade, immigration, and drugs.

TRADE

President Donald Trump has restored protectionism, retreating from international trade agreements and aggressively erecting tariffs against Washington's closest allies. The Trump White House's approach – with its zero-sum view of trade and disdain for multilateral rules – differs greatly from those of Presidents Clinton, Bush, and Obama. By forcing the renegotiation of major treaties under the threat of unilateral withdrawal, Trump has challenged the global order that Washington helped create in the postwar era. In this context, U.S. – Latin American commercial relations have become deeply strained. The renegotiation of the North American Free Trade Agreement (NAFTA), the establishment of barriers against Mexican steel and aluminum, and the withdrawal from the Trans-Pacific Partnership are breaking with the pro-integration strategy of previous administrations.

United States – Latin American trade before Trump

Free trade has historically been a cornerstone of U.S. policy toward Latin America. Past Republican and Democratic administrations argued that lower tariffs and fewer restrictions on cross-border movement of goods and services made everyone better off. After World War II, a hegemonic United States exercised leadership in establishing the General Agreement on Trade and Tariffs (GATT), which created a system of rewards for member country cooperation and penalties for cheating. In the mid-1990s, the GATT was replaced by the World Trade Organization, which reinforced a system for adjudicating trade disputes.

Within this multilateral system, U.S. presidents from George H.W. Bush to Barack Obama have pushed for bilateral and regional free trade agreements, many involving Latin America. Although the Constitution grants Congress responsibility for trade policy, the legislature has repeatedly delegated authority to the executive branch. The president received "fast track" authority to negotiate agreements that Congress could reject but not amend in the Trade Act of 1974; this power was renewed in 1988, 1994, 2002, and 2015. The U.S. Trade Representative (USTR), who reports directly to the president, is America's chief trade negotiator and oversees treaty implementation. The Department of Commerce also participates by investigating foreign subsidies and dumping, as well as patent, trademark, and copyright infringements, and by promoting exports through the U.S. Trade and Development Agency.

As noted in Table 8.1, of the fourteen free trade agreements (FTAs) that the U.S. has ratified, seven involve Latin America.[1] These instruments help account for the $1.8 trillion in trade in goods and services between the United States and the Western Hemisphere

TABLE 8.1 FREE TRADE AGREEMENTS WITH LATIN AMERICA[2]

AGREEMENT/ PARTNERS	DATE OF SIGNATURE	US PRESIDENT	DATE OF ENTRY INTO FORCE		US PRESIDENT
NAFTA	12/17/1992	Bush, G.H.W.	1/1/1994		Clinton
Chile	6/6/2003	Bush, G.W.	1/1/2004		Bush, G.W.
DR-CAFTA	8/5/2004	Bush, G.W.	El Salvador, US	3/1/2006	Bush, G.W.
			Honduras, Nicaragua	4/1/2006	Bush, G.W.
			Guatemala	7/1/2006	Bush, G.W.
			Dominican Republic	3/1/2007	Bush, G.W.
			Costa Rica	1/1/2009	Bush, G.W.
Peru	4/12/2006	Bush, G.W.	2/1/2009		Obama
Colombia	11/22/2006	Bush, G.W.	5/15/2012		Obama
Panama	6/28/2007	Bush, G.W.	10/31/2012		Obama
Trans Pacific Partnership	2/4/2016	Obama	Withdrew 1/2017		Trump

Source: World Bank DataBank (2017)

(Latin America, the Caribbean, and Canada). Many regional value chains are highly integrated, as when an automobile contains parts manufactured in different countries. Thus, the leading U.S. exports to Latin America are the also major Latin American exports to the U.S.: machinery, vehicles, and mineral fuel and oil. Agriculture, although a perennial source of conflict, is a small component of bilateral trade. For instance, Latin American countries "only" export $8.9 billion in fresh fruit to the U.S.

U.S. trade policy with Latin America took a decisively pro-globalization turn with NAFTA. The George H.W. Bush administration began trilateral negotiations with Mexico and Canada in 1991. NAFTA entered into force under President Bill Clinton in January 1994. Tariffs, duties, and quantitative restrictions (except for some agricultural products) were eliminated by 2008. NAFTA also regulates investment, trade in services, and protection of intellectual property. The agreement includes legal innovations such as dispute settlement procedures and "rules of origin" discrimination against non-NAFTA members.

The NAFTA experience influenced President Clinton to advocate an FTA covering the entire Western Hemisphere from Alaska to Tierra del Fuego. Owing to the opposition of leftist Latin American leaders such as Venezuela's Hugo Chávez, Bolivia's Evo Morales, and Argentina's Nestor Kirchner, negotiations failed, leading to the demise of the proposed "Free Trade Areas of the Americas" in 2005. By the early 2000s, Washington was instead advancing bilateral treaties. A U.S. – Chile Free Trade Agreement was written, signed, and ratified within six months in late 2003. This FTA eliminated Chilean duties on *all* U.S. consumer and industrial products, facilitated the establishment of U.S. banks and insurance companies in Chile, and granted "improved market access" to U.S. pork, beef, soybeans, grains, and potatoes. Then came the U.S. – Dominican Republic – Central America Free Trade Agreement (CAFTA-DR). Combined, the six countries represent America's sixteenth largest trading partner, with $53 billion in total goods traded in 2015 (U.S. Department of Commerce, 2016).[3] Although less aggressive in granting full liberalization than the Chilean FTA, the CAFTA-DR is important to the U.S. because it protects foreign direct investment (FDI). Central American countries benefit, too. For example, the agreement enabled unions to challenge Guatemalan labor law enforcement, leading to the first labor dispute ever filed under a FTA.

The Bush administration also fostered three innovative bilateral FTAs that were ratified during Barack Obama's presidency. The Peruvian FTA was the first agreement to incorporate environmental and labor protections, including regulations of forests. The agreement eliminated duties on more than two thirds of U.S. farm exports, as well as Peruvian requirements to hire local professionals and purchase local goods. Similarly, the Colombian and Panamanian FTAs eliminated tariffs for most U.S. consumer and industrial exports and guaranteed U.S. firms' access to large services markets.

Finally, in late 2009, the Obama White House unveiled a plan for a Trans-Pacific Partnership (TPP), which sought market access in eleven Pacific Rim countries (including Chile, Mexico, and Peru), balancing China's increasing economic and political role in the region. Together, the twelve prospective TPP partners accounted for 36 percent of world GDP and 43 percent of world trade (World Bank, 2016: 221).[4] The TPP would have slashed over 18,000 taxes on U.S. exports, protected intellectual property, opened bidding for foreign suppliers in government procurement, and stimulated the digital economy. It would also have regulated fisheries, illegal logging, and wildlife trafficking. However, President Trump abandoned the TPP almost immediately after taking office, thereby ceding U.S. leadership in Asia to China.

United States trade policy under Trump

President Trump's approach to trade policy has diverged sharply from the legacies of prior presidents. Trump has appointed critics of globalization to top government positions, bringing a zero-sum and protectionist vision of international trade. During the campaign, Trump declared his goal of reducing America's trade deficit, especially with China and Mexico. The U.S. annual trade deficit ran at $513 billion from January to November 2017, an 11.6 percent increase compared to 2016 (Gillespie, 2017).[5]

The rebirth of protectionism began with Trump's "America First" slogan and harsh rhetoric regarding U.S. trade partners and multilateral treaties. On the campaign trail, Trump labeled NAFTA a "disaster" and "the worst trade deal in history." Candidate Trump repeatedly threatened to establish a "border tax" for firms moving production overseas. Trump also bashed the TPP as a "job killer," forcing then-candidate Hillary Clinton to break with the Obama administration and criticize the deal. Differing dramatically from the Republican Party's traditional free trade position, Trump argued that the TPP was "another disaster done and pushed by special interests who want to rape our country. The TPP would be the death blow for American manufacturing" (cited in Cirilli and Knowles, 2016).[6]

The Trump White House quickly moved to appoint free trade skeptics. Industrialist Wilbur Ross, who thinks the WTO system is "broken," was appointed Secretary of Commerce. Robert Lighthizer, an experienced steel industry lawyer and former trade official in the Reagan administration, was appointed as U.S. Trade Representative and tasked with renegotiating trade deals. Peter Navarro, a heterodox professor of economics who had authored anti-China books and documentaries, was appointed to head a new White House Trade Council. Finally, former banker and conservative commentator Larry Kudlow was brought in as Director of the National Economic Council. The Trump White House developed the 2017 National Security Strategy (NSS), which denounced "[u]nfair trade practices" that "weakened our economy and exported our jobs overseas." It also claimed that America had helped "expand the liberal economic trading system to countries that did not share our values," and demanded that trade partners do more "to address trade imbalances" (The White House, 2017a: I, 17, 4).[7]

Protectionism soon became official policy. Three days after his inauguration, President Trump issued a memorandum withdrawing from the TPP. This unilateral action infuriated Mexico, Chile, and Peru. Nonetheless, the remaining eleven countries, including the three Latin American members, moved forward by signing a definitive deal in March 2018. Agricultural associations, representing business interests in rural states that Trump had won in the 2016 election, acknowledged Washington's withdrawal missed an opportunity for access to key growing economies.

After threatening to withdraw unilaterally from NAFTA in early 2017, Trump ordered America's trade representative to renegotiate the agreement. After multilateral talks to change NAFTA stalled, the president set out to reach trade agreements with Canada and Mexico separately. His demands included the lowering of U.S. trade deficits with Canada, higher U.S. content in North American-made automobiles, a dispute settlement system that largely exempts Mexico and Canada from U.S. anti-dumping tariffs, duty-free imports of textiles to the U.S. from Canada and Mexico that contain large amounts of Chinese yarn, and the mandatory five-year renewal of the treaty.

As multilateral negotiations to alter NAFTA ground to a halt, Trump entered into bilateral negotiations with Mexico. These negotiations reflected Trump's preference for bilateral rather than multilateral agreements. An agreement was reached in August 2018 that would only modestly change NAFTA. Mexican workers in the automobile industry would receive a minimum wage of at least $16 an hour for cars sold to the U.S., and at least 75 percent of such cars must be made in the U.S. or Mexico. The purpose of this was to reduce outsourcing of components from countries such as China, South Korea, Germany, and Japan. Canada was left out of U.S.-Mexican negotiations. If enacted, the result would be lower productivity, higher prices for consumers and a less competitive car-making industry in North America. It would also rearrange supply chains, probably at the expense of Mexico owing to the requirement that it grant workers higher wages, thereby reducing incentives for automobile companies to move south.

For Canadian Prime Minister Trudeau, joining the U.S. and Mexico was complicated by Canadian resentment at Trump's insults and his demand that Canada quickly accept the U.S.-Mexican deal with no changes. Both U.S. political parties, however, prefer a trilateral arrangement. Washington and Ottawa reached an agreement an hour before the U.S. deadline on September 30, 2018 that will rescue NAFTA (renamed "United States-Mexico-Canada Agreement" or USMCA, thereby listing the U.S. first). The U.S. agreed to retain NAFTA's tariff dispute settlement system ("Chapter 19") involving anti-dumping rules and countervailing duties that Trump had sought to eliminate, and Canada will afford greater access to its highly protected dairy industry. The agreement also upgraded environmental and safety rules such as higher safety regulations for Mexican trucks entering the U.S. The new agreement also increased protection of intellectual property. In addition, the deal must be reviewed after six years. Canada and Mexico would receive "accommodations" for their automobile industries in the event Trump decided to impose tariffs on imported cars and their components. The arrangements with Mexico such as those regarding automobiles were also retained. In addition, the new deal requires that by 2023 a tariff-free vehicle must contain at least 40 percent of its components made in a "high wage" factory, that is, a minimum wage of $16 an hour. This will reduce the number of automobiles made in Mexico, and North American auto manufacturers will it find it more difficult to compete with European and Japanese automakers.

The most serious challenge to U.S. – Mexican relations, however, came on June 1, 2018, when Trump imposed tariffs on steel and aluminum imported from Mexico and other major U.S. allies. The unprecedented action, grounded on executive powers to impose trade barriers in the interest of "national security," was mainly targeted at China over accusations that Beijing flooded the international market with cheap metals. The Mexican government quickly announced "appropriate and proportional" retaliatory measures, erecting tariffs on U.S. products such as steel and pork from key congressional districts (Reuters, 2018).[8] Other major Latin American producers of steel and aluminum (Argentina and Brazil) were excluded from Trump's aggressive move after voluntarily restricting the amount of their exports shipped to the United States.

IMMIGRATION

Immigration policy is arguably the area of foreign policy in which President Trump's rhetoric and policies have generated the most controversy. Although Presidents George W. Bush and Barack Obama were partisan rivals, their immigration policies appear fairly similar when contrasted with Trump's. Both of Trump's predecessors accepted the normative value of diversity in legal immigration from Latin America, while emphasizing the need to reduce illegal immigration. Trump's approach to immigration from Latin America is different than that of his predecessors in several ways, including rhetorical tone about immigrants, policy substance toward illegal immigration, and attitude toward legal immigration.

How United States immigration policy affects foreign affairs

Immigration encompasses both domestic and foreign policy. When U.S. immigration policy affects individuals living in the United States, it is considered domestic policy. However, immigration policy also affects foreign governments in several ways.

First, immigrants from Latin America typically maintain dual citizenship in, and family and cultural ties to, their home countries. Millions of Latin Americans living in the U.S. send home "remittances," or financial transfers, on a monthly or weekly basis. Remittances are critical sources of income in some countries. As Table 8.2 shows, in 2016 remittances

TABLE 8.2 UNITED STATES FOREIGN AID AND REMITTANCES TO LATIN AMERICA, 2016[9]

	US FOREIGN AID, 2016 (THOUSANDS US$)	GDP, 2016 (MILLIONS US$)	US FOREIGN AID AS PERCENTAGE OF GDP	REMITTANCES AS PERCENTAGE OF GDP, 2016
Argentina	550	545,476.10	0.0001%	0.1%
Bolivia	0	33,806.40	0.0000%	3.6%
Brazil	12,865	1,796,186.59	0.0007%	0.2%
Chile	700	247,027.91	0.0003%	0.0%
Colombia	300,095	282,463.00	0.1062%	1.7%
Cuba	20,000	N/A	N/A	N/A
Dominican Republic	22,209	71,583.55	0.0310%	7.7%
Ecuador	2,000	98,613.97	0.0020%	2.6%
El Salvador	67,900	26,797.47	0.2534%	17.1%
Guatemala	132,515	68,763.26	0.1927%	10.9%
Haiti	199,413	8,022.64	2.4856%	29.4%
Honduras	98,250	21,516.94	0.4566%	18.0%
Mexico	161,160	1,046,922.70	0.0154%	2.7%
Nicaragua	10,000	13,230.84	0.0756%	9.6%
Panama	3,350	55,187.70	0.0061%	0.9%
Paraguay	8,611	27,424.07	0.0314%	2.4%
Peru	72,700	192,207.34	0.0378%	1.5%
Uruguay	500	52,419.72	0.0010%	0.2%
Venezuela	6,500	N/A	N/A	N/A

Sources: US Foreign Aid: Meyer 2017, Table 2, p. 9;

Gross domestic product and remittances as percent of GDP: World Bank DataBank, 2017 constituted 29.4 percent of the gross domestic product (GDP) of Haiti, 18.0 percent of Honduras's GDP, 17.1 percent of El Salvador's, 10.9 percent of Guatemala's, and 9.6 percent of Nicaragua's. Remittances dwarf U.S. foreign aid in every country in Latin America. Even in 2016 during the Obama administration, U.S. foreign aid constituted far less than one percent of GDP in every country in the region except Haiti. Thus, immigration policy shapes the economies of many Latin American countries.

Second, U.S. immigration policy also affects Latin American economies by easing pressure on domestic labor markets, especially in countries with rapidly growing populations. Thus, scholars predict that the rapid return of Haitian and Salvadoran emigrants owing to Trump's policies (see below) may throw both economies into recession owing to the inability of their homelands to absorb returning workers.

Third, migrants from Latin America to the United States also affect their home countries through "cultural" or "social remittances." Migrants' changing attitudes can influence friends and families back home in ways that are compatible with U.S. foreign policy goals. Latin Americans living in the U.S. become emissaries of what are sometimes called "American values," including belief in capitalism, free trade, and democracy, as well as intolerance of corruption.

Fourth, Latin Americans living in the U.S. can also be the source of what one might call "negative remittances": the spread of gangs and guns to Latin America. U.S. gun laws are less restrictive than those in most countries in Latin America, and the market for firearms in the United States is very large. A recent report found 730 licensed firearm dealers in U.S. counties along the Mexican border (the number of unlicensed dealers may be larger) (Ingraham, 2016).[10] Almost three-quarters of the guns seized in Mexico by Mexican police had originated in the United States.

United States immigration policy before Trump

United States immigration policy under Presidents Bush and Obama was largely conducted under the rubric of legislation they inherited. The Immigration and Nationality Act of 1965 (henceforth INA 1965), signed by President Lyndon B. Johnson, dramatically rewrote U.S. immigration policy, which after 1920 had relied on quotas prioritizing immigrants from Northern Europe. The INA 1965 instituted a total cap as well as per-country limits for visas. It also created privileged categories of immigrant visas for high-skilled workers and relatives of U.S. citizens and permanent residents. These family preferences inadvertently remade the demographic profile of the U.S., tripling the foreign-born percentage of the population and dramatically increasing the number of Latin Americans in the U.S. When the legislation's sponsors instituted family preferences, they believed that the policy would maintain the predominance of Northern European immigrants (Gjelten, 2015).[11] Unexpectedly, however, it instead fostered immigration from developing countries by creating a mechanism for "chain migration," in which an adult who gets permanent residency in turn sponsors siblings and parents to join them.

The Immigration Act of 1990, signed by President George H.W. Bush, further liberalized certain aspects of U.S. immigration policy. Not only did the act substantially raise the cap on visas, but it created "Temporary Protected Status" (TPS) to provide "temporary safe haven" for nationals from countries experiencing national disasters or civil strife. Salvadorans were granted TPS in the act itself; TPS would later also be granted to Haitians, Hondurans, and Nicaraguans.

Meanwhile, other legislation dramatically restricted illegal immigration. The Immigration Reform and Control Act of 1986 and the Illegal Immigration Reform and Immigrant Responsibility Act of 1996 upped deportations, increasing the number of crimes for which legal residents could be deported, restricting detainees' access to attorneys, and allowing immediate deportation of immigrants apprehended within 100 miles of the U.S. border. All told, the 1996 statute led to a tripling of deportations by 2000 (Massey, 2011: 14).[12]

Despite partisan differences, Bush and Obama took similar approaches to immigration. On the one hand, they accepted the goal of diversity in legal immigration, and spoke forcefully of the U.S. as a country of immigrants. On the other hand, both worked to tighten border security and reduce illegal immigration. It was illegal immigration that consumed most legislative energy during the two administrations, both of which failed to pass "comprehensive immigration reform." In the parlance of contemporary immigration debates, the term "comprehensive" signals mixed objectives: to enable some illegal immigrants currently in the U.S. to remain legally, while also reducing the rate of future illegal immigration. Both presidents championed various proposals that would have created a path to citizenship for illegal immigrants.

Nonetheless, as Figure 8.1 shows, deportations increased rapidly under Bush and Obama, initially stimulated by a desire to increase security following the terrorist attacks of September 11, 2001. Deportations soared from 188,000 in 2000, Bush's first year in office to 360,000 in his last year, and then peaked at 406,000 in 2014 under Obama, before falling again to 340,000 in 2016. At the same time, what the Department of Homeland Security terms "returns" – that is, when unauthorized immigrants voluntarily leave or are removed from the U.S. without formal deportation proceedings – fell more than 90 percent across the two administrations, from 1,700,000 during Bush's first year to 106,000

FIGURE 8.1 Immigration statistics for removals and returns 1990–2016[13]

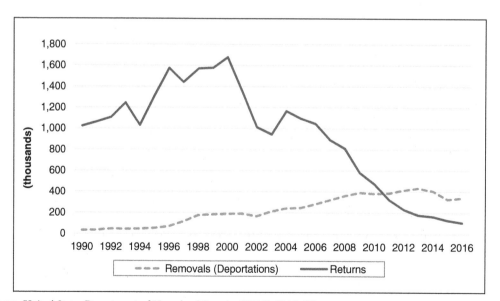

Source: United States Department of Homeland Security (2017), Table 39

in Obama's last year. Overall, total removals plus returns fell by about three quarters, from 1,900,000 in 2000 to 447,000 in 2016.

These intersecting trends reflect the two administrations' changing approaches. The high number of "returns" in the 1990s and early 2000s was a result of the revolving-door nature of much immigration enforcement during that era. Would-be undocumented immigrants caught in the U.S. were frequently simply dropped on the Mexican side of the border, only to attempt the crossing again – a practice critics called "catch and release." Both administrations sought to make illegal crossings into the United States harder and riskier. Not only was border security substantially improved, but immigrants were often driven hundreds of miles into Mexico, decreasing the ease of returning.

Finally, one important effort under Obama contravened the tendency toward rising enforcement. Frustrated by his inability to pass comprehensive immigration reform, in June 2012 Obama issued an executive order establishing Deferred Action for Childhood Arrivals (DACA), which as of 2017 protected about 800,000 individuals who had been brought illegally to the United States as children (called "Dreamers," after the name of failed legislative proposals). This executive order provided a pathway for Dreamers to live and work legally in the U.S. When additional legislative attempts to legalize Dreamers' status failed in the Republican-controlled. House of Representatives in November 2014, Obama announced his intention to expand DACA. He was immediately sued by several states, and the expansion was blocked by the courts.

Data depict the magnitude of these efforts and their impact. Budgets for U.S. Border Patrol more than tripled between 2000 and 2016. Meanwhile, budgets for Immigration and Customs Enforcement (ICE) nearly doubled between 2003, the year the agency was established, and 2016. Nonetheless, the overall impact was modest. Pew Research Center estimates that the number of Mexicans living illegally in the U.S. fell from 6,950,000 in 2007 to 5,850,000 in 2014. During the same time period, growing violence in Central America triggered increased illegal immigration from that region from an estimated 1,350,000 to 1,700,000. Overall, the number of illegal residents from Latin America and the Caribbean is estimated to have fallen from 9,700,000 in 2007 to 8,600,000 in 2014 (Passel and Cohn, 2016: 45).[14] One reason for the relatively modest decline may be rising crime and violence in Mexico and Central America. Recent research indicates that immigration driven by security concerns is less responsive to U.S. policy intended to deter illegal immigration than is economic migration (Hiskey et al., 2018).[15] Moreover, part of the drop that has been registered may be due to "push" factors in would-be immigrants' home countries beyond U.S. control. In addition, a declining gap in wages between the United States and Mexico diminished the attraction of illegal crossings.

United States immigration policy under Trump

Trump's approach to immigration from Latin America has veered sharply from the policies of Bush and Obama. The first major difference relates to Trump's rhetoric, which has been contemptuous toward Latin American immigrants. For example, Trump officially launched his presidential campaign in a speech in which he implied that most Mexicans in the United States were rapists. And in January 2018, he caused an international scandal by referring to Haiti, El Salvador, and other low-income countries sending immigrants to the United States as "shithole countries," indicating that he would rather have immigrants from countries like Norway.

Trump has also differed from his predecessors on policy. He stepped up enforcement of illegal immigration, while broadening the categories of illegal immigrants to be targeted. Trump's proposed 2018 budget for the Department of Homeland Security included a 22 percent increase for Customs and Border Protection, as well as a 29 percent increase for ICE. Moreover, in a February 2017 executive order, Trump gave immigration officials broader latitude to target non-criminal illegal immigrants. As a result, ICE arrests for civil immigration violations rose by 30 percent; arrests of non-criminal immigrants soared by 250 percent; and arrests in "community settings" (i.e., venues other than prisons) rose by nearly 50 percent. Overall, there was a 25 percent jump in "interior" deportations, meaning those based on arrests within the United States beyond the border zone (U.S. Immigrations and Customs Enforcement, 2017).[16] Nonetheless, despite an initial drop in illegal crossings during the administration's first year, illegal crossings rose sharply in 2018.

Finally, Trump has been skeptical of *legal* immigration from Latin America as well. Asylum recipients – a protected category of legal entry into the U.S. – have been targeted. In the spring of 2018, Trump's Justice Department began treating asylum recipients similarly to illegal immigrants, holding them in detention until their cases were resolved. This new policy aroused particular controversy because it did not allow exceptions for families with children. As children are not allowed into the same detention facilities with their parents, this policy change entailed separating children of all ages, including infants and toddlers, from their parents at the border. This practice was vigorously criticized even by Trump's supporters including evangelical Christians. Moreover, the Justice Department also announced that it would no longer grant asylum to victims of domestic or gang violence.

At the same time, Trump has rescinded several programs that had created protected categories of immigrants. In a September 2017 executive order he rescinded DACA, while allowing a six-month window for Congress to legalize the status of DACA recipients. After several congressional attempts to pass legislation that would provide legal protections for DACA recipients failed, federal courts blocked Trump's executive order. As of mid-2018, the controversy had not been resolved, although the Democratic majority in the midterm elections may facilitate a bilateral deal. Finally, the Trump White House has rescinded TPS protection for Haitians, Hondurans, and Salvadorans living in the country under the Immigration Act of 1990.

More globally, the White House, along with immigration hawks in Congress, has legislative ambitions to end the policy of "chain migration." In place of a family-centered model of immigration, Trump and his legislative allies are promoting a "points-based" system, similar to that practiced by Canada and Australia. They seek to restrict immigration overall, while favoring individuals based on merit-based criteria such as income, skills, and earning potential. Finally, Trump's demand for funding to build a wall along the Mexican border led to the longest government shutdown in U.S. history.

DRUGS

Illicit drugs have been a major issue in U.S. – Latin American relations for decades. Most of the prohibited drugs that American citizens consume come from Latin America. Massive demand for drugs such as heroin and cocaine is largely met by production in and trafficking from Mexico and Colombia, respectively. Other areas of production and trafficking include Bolivia, Peru, Honduras, El Salvador, and the Caribbean. The U.S. government has approached this problem by a policy of military cooperation with allied countries to eradicate the crops like coca from which narcotics are made, destroy the factories that are needed to make them, and interdict the movement of illegal drugs into the U.S. Contrary to other areas of foreign policy, President Trump's anti-drug policy in Latin America reflects continuity with regard to his predecessors. However, the consequences of failed policies, the changing landscape of the illicit drug trade, and a refusal to recognize that "demand" in America rather than "supply" from Latin America is the core of the problem still present challenges to the United States.

Military cooperation

Since the 1980s, the U.S. has launched regional and bilateral initiatives to deal with transnational criminal organizations. The Drug Enforcement Administration, Federal Bureau of Investigation, and Coast Guard participate in drug interdiction at the border and in international waters; crop eradication efforts; undercover infiltration; and intelligence gathering. They also lead special operations to target and capture drug lords from the Peruvian *sierras* to the streets of Bogotá (Colombia) and beach resorts in Cancún (Mexico). Most U.S. funding and personnel for these activities come from military training and arms supply programs. Washington allocates billions of dollars annually to train Latin America's armed forces and law enforcement agencies through the Department of State's Bureau of International Narcotics and Law Enforcement Affairs. In addition, the Department of Defense supplies the security forces of partner countries with arms and ammunition, vehicles, aircraft, and other military equipment. America's armed forces involved in training and counter-trafficking operations include elements of the Southern Command and the Navy's Fourth Fleet.

In early 2019, Trump appointed Jim Carroll as "Drug Czar" (as the Director of the Office of National Drug Control Policy is popularly known), and the White House is continuing programs inherited from the Obama administration. The 2017 National Security Strategy describes the administration's aim of "supporting local efforts to professionalize police and other security forces; . . . and improve information sharing to target criminals and corrupt leaders and disrupt illicit trafficking" (The White House, 2017a: 51).[7] Concluding his first official trip to Latin America, Vice President Mike Pence declared that "the United States is firmly committed to Latin America's security . . . [W]e'll continue to work with all the nations across our region to combat drug production and transnational criminal syndicates" (The White House, 2017b).[17] U.S. military and law enforcement agencies continue to focus on major drug transit and producing countries. In September 2017, Trump issued a memorandum noting that seventeen Latin American and Caribbean countries accounted for almost 80 percent of the world's major drug producing states that the administration's policies sought to curb.

Following his predecessors, President Trump renewed support for three major regional initiatives. First, the administration is continuing Peace Colombia, which was launched in 2000 as Plan Colombia, which aims to reduce that country's cocaine production and trafficking. Colombia has suffered from five decades of civil strife with irregular armed groups such as the left-wing *Fuerzas Armadas Revolucionarias de Colombia* (FARC) and right-wing paramilitary groups. The low intensity civil wars eroded state capacity and fueled the expansion of drug production that financed such groups. Infamous drug gangs such as the *Cartel de Cali*, *Cartel de Medellín*, and *Autodefensas Unidas* exercised control of much of the world's cocaine production. Under Plan Colombia, the U.S. sent thousands of "military consultants" and private contractors to train local security forces and capture drug lords. In September 2015, after years of counterinsurgency, Colombia announced a strategy that reduces the emphasis on coca eradication and focuses on local policing, judicial reform, and rural development. The new policy constitutes a key component of the 2016 Colombian peace accord with the FARC. The Trump administration, which has declared that Colombia remains America's "closest ally in the region," continued to provide aid requested by Colombian President Juan Manuel Santos.

The second major initiative that is being continued under the Trump administration is the Mérida Initiative. For years, Mexico has been a major source and transit country for heroin, marijuana, cocaine, and synthetic drugs destined for the United States. The Mérida Initiative was initially approved by Presidents George W. Bush and Felipe Calderon in 2008, but U.S. cooperation grew after brutal murders of American citizens by drug gangs in Ciudad Juárez in 2010. The Obama administration delivered about $1.8 billion in military equipment, training, and other support to build Mexican law enforcement capacity, reform the country's judicial system, and foster crime prevention. United States cooperation helped Mexico arrest leading drug lords, including the capture (twice) of Joaquín "El Chapo" Guzmán, who was sent to the U.S. for trial. Assistance also focused on modernizing border protection, even before this issue entered the 2016 U.S. presidential campaign.

Finally, the State Department is continuing the Central America Regional Security Initiative (CARSI) on the grounds that, in Secretary Rex Tillerson's words, "a secure and prosperous Central America contributes to a safer, more prosperous United States" (U.S. Department of State, 2017).[18] CARSI seeks to curb drug trafficking and neutralize gangs, which are fueling violence and a migration crisis in the region (Belize, Costa Rica, El Salvador, Guatemala, Honduras, Nicaragua, and Panama). A related program is the Caribbean Basin Security Initiative, which supports law enforcement, including maritime security, border control, and criminal justice. Partners include the Dominican Republic and the fifteen members of the Caribbean Community. In contrast to the Colombian and Mexican plans, the U.S. Agency for International Development is providing financial assistance to reeducate those in rural communities whose livelihood depends on coca and marijuana cultivation.

Balance and new challenges of the war on drugs

Despite spending $39 billion in Latin America between 2010 and 2015, America's antidrug policy has had little success in meeting its targets. The most immediate outcomes are usually shifts in where illicit drugs are produced and trafficked. Opioid abuse has emerged as the greatest drug threat to the United States. To meet demand yet avoid law enforcement efforts, drug cartels have used increasingly sophisticated techniques to smuggle drugs including submarines, aircraft, and tunnels, and periodically relocate within countries and across the region. Estimated flows of drugs from the region have risen, and Mexico has registered a spike in the supply and purity of heroin it sends northward.

Similarly, cocaine production in and trafficking from Colombia has increased significantly. This is due to production migrating to areas inaccessible to crop eradication, favorable terms of trade from currency depreciation, and reduction in illicit mining and greater security owing to the peace settlement with the FARC (Miroff, 2015).[19] Colombian authorities acknowledge this alarming trend, which risks destabilizing the peace agreement. The U.S. government is also deeply concerned, and President Trump has considered designating Colombia as a country that has not met its obligations to curb the manufacture and export of narcotics.

Among the effects of the militarization of anti-drug operations are increased violence, corruption, and human-rights abuses in Latin America. Policing by armed forces, mainly trained and armed by Washington, has claimed thousands of lives and weakened state capacity. Since the Mexican armed forces became involved, 200,000 people have been killed and 31,000 individuals are missing (Malkin, 2017).[20] This is not likely to change in the near future. In the run up to Mexico's 2018 elections, that country's legislature authorized its army to police anywhere in the country that the president designates. In Colombia, the militarization of anti-narcotics operations in the context of protracted civil war led to thousands of extrajudicial killings, disappearances, and displacements, as paramilitary groups targeted both suspected rebel sympathizers and drug operations (Paley, 2015).[21]

In sum, President Trump is continuing several past administrations' policies despite their material and human costs. Concern over the consequences of U.S. anti-narcotics policies in Latin America led Congress to create a Western Hemisphere Drug Policy Commission in late 2016. As yet, however, there has been no change in America's anti-drug strategy toward Latin America.

CONCLUSION

The Trump White House represents both change from and continuity with earlier policies toward Latin America. Trump has advanced efforts underway since the presidency of Ronald Reagan, and continued under subsequent Democratic and Republican presidents, to crack down on the illicit drug trade and illegal immigration. Mexico, Colombia, and many Central American and Caribbean nations continue to receive police training as well as American arms and equipment to prevent illicit drugs from entering the U.S. Border security and deportation remain central to U.S. efforts to curtail undocumented immigration from Latin America.

Nevertheless, Trump is often viewed in the region as an anomaly. Rescinding TPS and DACA potentially leaves millions of migrants vulnerable to deportation. On trade, Trump has abandoned the vision long embodied by his own political party. He has erected tariffs and is renegotiating NAFTA to protect American businesses he considers threatened by trade, and to reduce trade deficits that he believes reflect "unfair" practices.

In large measure, though, the sense that Trump is an anomaly is significantly related to his rhetoric and style. His administration views globalization with suspicion, and immigration with revulsion. The Trump White House portrays trading partners as "unfair," and as "raping" and "destroying" American firms and jobs. Recurrent tweets offer insults and threaten to break international agreements. Trump's apparent desire to distance the U.S. from Latin America is symbolized perhaps most strongly by his campaign promise to build a wall on its southern border and his modification of Obama's opening to Cuba. Bellicose language and shifting positions undermine bilateral relationships with countries like Mexico and El Salvador. Latin American leaders met Trump's 2017 threats of military intervention in Venezuela with a combination of disbelief and concern, fearing a return to an earlier era in which U.S. military intervention in the region was common. And Mexican leaders' plain refusal to discuss a border wall, led Trump to cease speaking of his insistence that Mexico would pay for such a wall.

What does the future hold? To some extent Latin American skepticism toward U.S. intentions is nothing new. However, shutting down trade and immigration could have major long-term negative implications for the U.S.'s regional "soft power," which has been based on those two major cross-border flows. The Trump administration's insistence on building walls and limiting imports and people not only fosters anti-U.S. sentiments in previously friendly neighbors, but also harms U.S. interests in the region, by restricting business and cultural opportunities.

ESSAY QUESTIONS

1) How has support for free trade with Latin America risen and fallen over the past three decades?

2) How have President Trump's policies with respect to free trade differed from those of his predecessors? In what ways have they exhibited continuities?

3) How is immigration from Latin America changing? What social and political forces are driving those changes?

4) In what ways do President Trump's policies with respect to immigration from Latin America continue policies of previous administrations? In what ways do they differ?

5) How have President Trump and his predecessors used military and civilian intervention to try to stop the flow of drugs from Latin America? Compare and contrast the Trump, Bush, and Obama administrations.

SHORT ANSWER QUESTIONS

Define and describe the importance of the following:

North American Free Trade Agreement (NAFTA)
Steel tariffs
Remittances
"Comprehensive immigration reform"
Peace Colombia/Plan Colombia
Mérida Initiative
The Central America Regional Security Initiative (CARSI)

NOTES

1   In addition to FTAs, the United States has signed 42 bilateral investment treaties (nine with Latin American and Caribbean countries), which protect American overseas foreign direct investment from expropriation and other forms of property violations. Data from the Organization of American States' Foreign Trade Information System. Available at www.sice.oas. org/agreements_e.asp [Accessed 17 Jan 2018].

2   World Bank (2017). World Bank Open Data. Available at: https://data.worldbank.org [Accessed 17 Jan 2018].

3   U.S. Department of Commerce, Census Bureau, Economic Indicators Division (2016). Top U.S. Trade Partners [online]. Available at: www.trade.gov/mas/ian/build/groups/public/ @tg_ian/documents/webcontent/tg_ian_003364.pdf [Accessed 31 Jan 2018].

4   World Bank (2016). Potential Macroeconomic Implications of the Trans-Pacific Partnership. *Global Economic Prospects*, January. Available at: http://pubdocs.worldbank.org/en/ 847071452034669879/Global-Economic-Prospects-January-2016-Implications-Trans-Pacific-Partnership-Agreement.pdf [Accessed 31 Jan 2018].

5   Gillespie, P. (2017) U.S. Trade Deficit with China and Mexico is Growing. *CNN Money* [online]. Available at: http://money.cnn.com/2017/12/05/news/economy/us-trade-deficit/index. html [Accessed 1 Feb 2018].

6   Cirilli, K. and Knowles, D. (2016) Trump Likens Trans-Pacific Partnership Trade Deal to Rape. *Bloomberg* [online]. Available at: www.bloomberg.com/news/articles/2016-06-28/ trump-channels-brexit-in-anti-trade-speech-at-pennsylvania-factory [Accessed 1 Feb 2018].

7   The White House (2017a). *National Security Strategy 2017.* Available at: www.whitehouse. gov/wp-content/uploads/2017/12/NSS-Final-12-18-2017-0905-2.pdf [Accessed 1 Feb 2018].

8   Reuters (2018). Mexico Aims Tariffs at Trump Country, sees NAFTA Complications. *Reuters:* Business News [online] Available at: www.reuters.com/article/us-usa-trade-mexico/mexico-aims-tariffs-at-trump-country-sees-nafta-complications-idUSKCN1IW1ZI [Accessed 1 Jun 2018].

9   Meyer, P. (2017). U.S. Foreign Assistance to Latin America and the Caribbean: Trends and FY2017 appropriations. Congressional Reference Service. Available at: https://fas.org/sgp/ crs/row/R44647.pdf [Accessed 2 Feb 2017].

10   Ingraham, C. (2016). Why Mexico's Drug Cartels Love America's Gun Laws. *Washington Post* [online] Available at: www.washingtonpost.com/news/wonk/wp/2016/01/14/why-mexicos-drug-cartels-love-americas-gun-laws/ [Accessed 1 Feb 2018].

11   Gjelten, T. (2015). The Immigration Act that Inadvertently Changed America. *The Atlantic* [online] Available at: www.theatlantic.com/politics/archive/2015/10/immigration-act-1965/408409 [Accessed 1 Feb 2018].

12   Massey, D. (2011). Chain Reaction: The causes and consequences of America's war on immigrants. Julian Simon Lecture Series VIII. Washington, D.C.: IZA Annual Migration Meeting [online]. Available at: http://conference.iza.org/conference_files/amm2011/ massey_d1244.pdf [Accessed 1 Feb 2018].

13   United States Department of Homeland Security (2017). Table 39. *2016 Yearbook of Immigration Statistics.* Washington, D.C.: U.S. Department of Homeland Security, Office of Immigration Statistics. Available at: www.dhs.gov/immigration-statistics/yearbook/2016 [Accessed 1 Feb 2018].

14   Passel, J. and Cohn, D. (2016). Overall Number of U.S. Unauthorized Immigrants Holds Steady Since 2009. *Pew Research Center's Hispanic Trends Project*, Appendix B. Available at: www.pewhispanic.org/2016/09/20/overall-number-of-u-s-unauthorized-immigrants-holds-steady-since-2009 [Accessed 2 Feb 2018].

15   Hiskey, J., Cordova, A., Malone, M., and Orces, D. (2018). Leaving the Devil You Know: Crime victimization, U.S. deterrence policy, and the emigration decision in Central America. *Latin American Research Review* 58:3.

16   U.S. Immigrations and Customs Enforcement (2017). Fiscal Year 2017 ICE Enforcement and Removal Operations Report. Available at: www.ice.gov/removal-statistics/2017 [Accessed 2 Feb 2018].

17   The White House (2017b). Remarks by the Vice President on Latin America, Our Lady of Guadalupe Catholic Church, Miami, Florida (2017). Available at: www.whitehouse.gov/briefings-statements/remarks-vice-president-latin-america (Accessed 2 Feb 2018).
18   U.S. Department of State (2017). Remarks at Conference on Prosperity and Security in Central America Opening Plenary Session. Available at www.state.gov/secretary/remarks/2017/06/271926.htm [Accessed 2 Feb 2018].
19   Miroff, M. (2017) For Veteran Drug Warrior and Diplomat, Retirement Comes with Tinge of Regret. *Washington Post* [online]. Available at: www.washingtonpost.com/world/national-security/for-veteran-drug-warrior-and-diplomat-retirement-comes-with-tinge-of-regret/2017/09/15/9ad1b6d2–9987–11e7-a527–3573bd073e02_story.html [Accessed 31 Jan 2018].
20   Malkin, E. (2017). Mexico Strengthens Military's Role in Drug War, Outraging Critics. *New York Times*, [online]. Available at: www.nytimes.com/2017/12/15/world/americas/mexico-strengthens-militarys-role-in-drug-war-outraging-critics.html [Accessed 3 Feb 2018].
21   Paley, D. (2015). Drug War as Neoliberal Trojan Horse. *Latin American Perspectives* 42:5, pp. 109–132 [online]. Available at: http://journals.sagepub.com/doi/pdf/10.1177/0094582X15585117 [Accessed 2 Feb 2018].

SUGGESTED READINGS

Hiskey, J., Córdova, A., Malone, M., and Orcés, D. (2018). Leaving the Devil You Know: Crime victimization, U.S. deterrence policy, and the emigration decision in Central America. *Latin American Research Review* 53:3.

Paley, D. (2015). Drug War as Neoliberal Trojan Horse. *Latin American Perspectives* 42:5, pp. 109–132.

Gries, P. (2016). Liberals, Conservatives, and Latin America: How ideology divides Americans over immigration and foreign aid. *Latin American Research Review* 51:3, pp. 23–46.

Gootenberg, P. (2012). Cocaine's Long March North, 1900–2010. *Latin American Politics and Society* 54:1, pp. 159–180.

9 America and the Middle East

Richard W. Mansbach

INTRODUCTION

The Middle East encompasses Israel, Iran, and the Arab states in western Asia and North Africa. It has been a focus of American involvement since before World War II owing to its oil resources and its geographic location as a link between Europe and Asia and Europe and Africa. These factors made the region a focus of European colonialism, and the United Kingdom (UK) and France established several Arab states and their boundaries as well as those of Palestine after World War I. America became the principal actor in the region after World War II owing to declining European influence and the growing desire for independence in the countries in the region.

During the Cold War, U.S. relationships in the region were relatively simple. The U.S. sought to enhance the security of Israel after that country was founded in 1948 and regarded it as an ally and an island of democracy surrounded by hostile Arab states governed by authoritarian rulers. To this day, Israel enjoys a robust lobby in America. Washington also sought to assure the security of the oil-rich conservative monarchies in the Persian Gulf, which were the largest source of U.S. oil imports. Iran, too, was a U.S. ally before that country's 1979 Islamic Revolution. The threats to the oil-rich Arab states were perceived to be the USSR and its regional proxies that for much the period included Egypt and Syria and their nationalist leaders, notably Egypt's President Gamal Abdul Nasser. Following the ending of the Cold War, issues in the Middle East became increasingly complex. The chapter emphasizes how regional actors exploit and institutionalize multiple intersecting issues and regional sectarian identities.

ISRAEL AND PALESTINE

Israel's victory in the 1967 Six-Day War and its occupation of territories on the West Bank, and in Gaza and East Jerusalem triggered intense efforts by Washington to find an equitable solution that would lead to an independent Palestinian state, assure Israeli security, and halt Israeli settlements in the occupied territories. These objectives remained largely unchanged in subsequent years. American efforts initially produced progress including a peace treaty between Egypt and Israel and a peace process begun by the Oslo Accords (1993 and 1995) that involved recognition of Israel and the Palestine Liberation Organization (PLO) as negotiating partners and established a Palestinian Authority (PA) with limited powers to govern the Gaza Strip and part of the occupied West Bank. The West Bank was divided into Area A, which the PA alone administers and includes most West Bank cities; Area B, which the PA and Israel jointly administer in order to ensure security; and Area C, encompassing the region near Jerusalem, which Israel alone administers.

The peace process, however, ground to a halt as Israeli voters rejected the liberal left-wing leaders of its early decades in favor of increasing rightwing and nationalist prime ministers like Ariel Sharon and Benjamin Netanyahu. While most Israelis favor a two-state solution, Netanyahu, although paying lip service to a two-state solution, pursued policies that made this outcome increasingly remote. Two "*intifadas*" (uprisings) – 1987–1991 and 2000–2005 – and a recent wave of violence some called a "knife *intifada*" (2015–2016), as well as wars with the Palestinian group Hamas, considered by the United States and many other countries as a terrorist group, and Hezbollah (a Lebanese Shia militia aided by Iran), produced profound insecurity among Israelis. Following an electoral victory, Hamas seized control of Gaza from the PA after Israel's withdrawal, dividing the Palestinian movement after 2006. There followed three bloody wars between Hamas and Israel (2008, 2012, 2014), and came close to a fourth in late 2018 in the midst of large Palestinian protests at the border with Israel, despite the latter's efforts to ease the impact of its blockade of Gaza. With Hamas to the south, Hezbollah to the north and growing Iranian influence in Syria, Iraq, and Lebanon, Israelis are reluctant to take steps toward resolving the dispute over the occupied territories. Moreover, they are encouraged by American evangelical Christians who overwhelming support President Trump and believe that Israel is special to God and whose expansion to Biblical boundaries will trigger the second coming of Jesus.

Although America and Israel remained allies, Israeli intransigence alienated President Barack Obama and Secretary of State John Kerry, whose arduous efforts to renew the peace process failed. Obama and Netanyahu came to dislike each other, especially over the 2015 agreement with Iran to curb Iran's nuclear weapons program. Shortly before leaving office, Kerry warned Israel that abandoning the two-state policy and expanding settlements would lead to "perpetual occupation" and warfare. And for the first time Washington did *not* veto a UN Security Council resolution condemning Israel settlement expansion, a resolution which candidate Trump called on Obama to veto. As Trump took office, the fragmented Middle East was in need of U.S. leadership owing to instability caused by civil wars and failed states, the fight against the Islamic State (IS), the growing influence of Russia and Iran, and the rivalry between Shia and Sunni Muslims.

On the Israel-Palestine issue, the Trump administration initially moved closer to Israel's rightwing positions than had the Obama administration. Trump's ambassador to Israel, David Friedman, is an outspoken hardliner who argues that settlement construction in the West Bank and East Jerusalem are legal. Despite vigorous efforts by many of the seventy countries attending a peace summit sponsored by France to persuade the new president of the need for a two-state solution, Trump's rhetoric – including a comment to Netanyahu that he was willing to consider either a one-state or a two-state solution – raised expectations that Washington would back Israel to the hilt. Thus, with Trump in office, Israel adopted outspoken pro-settler rhetoric, and its government announced additional housing units in East Jerusalem and in existing West Bank settlements as well as retroactively legalizing illegal settlements on Palestinian-owned land.

However, the president retreated as he has on so many issues, and the administration noted that additional Jewish settlements were untimely. Other U.S. officials, including America's UN ambassador, declared that Washington still supported a two-state solution. Trump appeared to move toward the center on this issue, asking Netanyahu to "hold back" on settlements for a while, even while recognizing Jerusalem as Israel's capital, a campaign promise. Nevertheless, in October 2017 Israel's prime minister, encouraged by Trump's support, approved plans to build thousands of additional units in West Bank settlements in areas like Hebron or east of Jerusalem that Palestinians view as crucial to a future state. Moreover, the administration cut off humanitarian funds to Palestinians, making violence increasingly likely.

Although a two-state solution would entail Israel's surrender of most of the territory it occupied in 1967, absorbing the Palestinians in Israel could entail granting them fewer rights than those of Jewish citizens, thereby violating the country's democratic norms. This became apparent after Israel adopted the Nation-State Law of the Jewish People in July 2018, which declared: "The right to exercise national self-determination in the State of Israel is unique to the Jewish people." The law was widely criticized because it excluded Palestinian residents of Israel. To have included them, however, would also dilute the Jewish nature of the Jewish state, especially because of the demographic fact that the Palestinian population is increasing more rapidly than Israel's Jewish population.

Nevertheless, after meeting PA President Mahmoud Abbas in 2017, Trump committed himself to resolving the Israeli-Palestinian dispute, declaring, "I've always heard that perhaps the toughest deal to make is the deal between the Israelis and the Palestinians. Let's see if we can prove them wrong." Aaron David Miller, who for years had sought to mediate the dispute, scoffed at Trump's comments: "When the president says we'll do this deal, he thinks in terms of a one-off real estate deal. And while that's partly true," the specific issues dividing Israelis and Palestinians "transcend the 'art of the deal' in ways I'm not sure he can now even begin to imagine" (cited in Baker, 2017).[1]

On visiting Saudi Arabia in May 2017, the president sought to engage key Sunni Arab states in promoting a solution to the Israeli-Palestinian stalemate, an idea called the "outside-in" approach also favored by Netanyahu. Owing to regional civil wars, the growing clout of Shia Iran, which Israel claims is building factories in Syria and Lebanon that build precision-guided missiles and establish military bases, Arab-Israeli interests overlap to a greater extent than at any time in recent decades. These states would provide aid to Palestinians in Gaza and persuade Hamas to cooperate with the PA. In late 2017, Hamas and the PA agreed to reunite and control Gaza jointly. However, the agreement proved moribund by early 2018 as Hamas refused to disarm, Egypt prevented entry into Gaza, and the PA ceased providing funds to public employees in Gaza. In addition, Washington cut funds to the United Nations Relief and Works Agency (UNRWA), the UN agency that aids Palestinian refugees and thereafter cut direct U.S. foreign aid to Palestinians in Gaza and the West Bank, pressuring them to negotiate with Israel.

Visiting Israel after leaving Saudi Arabia, Trump expressed optimism about Arab cooperation and declared that regional peace would require Israel to resolve its differences with the Palestinians. Trump's readiness to overlook Saudi human-rights abuses reflected a belief that such concerns impede security and economic ties. Thereafter, the president put his son-in-law, Jared Kushner, in charge of negotiating a solution to the "ultimate deal" and encouraging Arab leaders to restart the peace process. Kushner traveled to the Middle East in August 2017 and June 2018 where he met with Israeli, Arab, and Palestinian leaders. He confronts daunting difficulties and is unlikely to succeed where others like Kerry have failed. However, Saudi leader Mohammad bin Salman bin Abdulaziz Al Saud, a friend of Kushner, indicated his country would cooperate with Israel.

Kushner's diplomatic inexperience, his limited understanding of the region, the myriad tasks assigned him by his father-in-law, his investments in Israel and his contacts with Russians during the presidential campaign make him an improbable negotiator. In addition, he must constantly be concerned that the president might shift his views overnight. Moreover, like America's ambassador to Israel, Kushner is Jewish and close to pro-Israeli U.S. politicians, fueling Palestinian suspicions that he is not an impartial mediator.

Another problem is the political vulnerability of both Netanyahu and Abbas. Netanyahu is involved in a corruption scandal and his coalition has only a single vote majority, making him dependent on far-rightwing politicians like Naftali Bennett, leader of the Jewish Home party. The PA elected Abbas as its president in 2005 for a term ending in 2009, and new elections were postponed. Adding to the problem, U.S. congressional representatives denounced Palestinian payments to families of suicide bombers, claiming they encouraged violence. To date, Abbas has achieved little. He supports an Arab plan to establish a Palestinian state with 1967 borders in return for peace. He must, however, protect himself from accusations from Hamas and ambitious younger PLO politicians and avoid appearing to make concessions to Israel. An anti-Semitic tirade in April 2018 did not improve his position, nor did Palestinian militancy, which exploded in April 2018 in Palestinian demonstrations near Israel's border, causing numerous Palestinian casualties.

Thus, despite positive rhetoric from those he met, Kushner had achieved little. Trump himself, moreover, has raised concerns among Palestinians and Israelis respectively because of negative comments about Islam and reluctance to condemn neo-Nazi violence in Charlottesville.

Then, in December 2017, Trump announced that Washington would recognize Jerusalem as Israel's capital and move its embassy there. Trump's action complicated peace negotiations, augurs greater violence and alienated many Muslims. Although Trump omitted referring to the "entire" city, which Palestinians regard as their future capital, the action may preclude a two-state solution. Trump made his reckless decision despite the advice of senior advisers and allied leaders, and was condemned by overwhelming majorities in the UN Security Council and General Assembly. After Washington vetoed a Security Council resolution condemning Trump's decision, the president threatened to cut aid to countries that had voted for it. Enthused by Trump's decision, Israel's rightwing Likud party urged annexing Jewish settlements in the West Bank and extending Israeli law into occupied territory, further undermining prospects for a two-state solution. In Gaza, to publicize the Palestinians' plight, Hamas urged Palestinians to pull down the fence on Israel's border. In April and May 2018, Palestinians in large numbers tried to do so, and Israeli soldiers killed many. This humanitarian disaster was denounced around the world, although not by the Trump administration.

Israel's unwillingness to make concessions is partly a result of the violence and instability the Arab Spring produced in Syria, Iraq, Libya, and Yemen and the opportunities it gave Iran to extend its influence into Israel's neighborhood.

DEMOCRACY VERSUS AUTHORITARIANISM
AND ISLAMISM: THE "ARAB SPRING"

The Arab Spring with its demands for democracy and an end to corruption began in December 2010 after the death of a street vendor in Tunisia. It led to the overthrow of the country's dictator and, aided by social media, rapidly spread through much of the Middle East, producing violence, the overthrow of regimes in Libya, Egypt, and Yemen, the challenges to regimes in Syria and Iraq, and an upsurge in Islamic consciousness.

The Arab Spring posed difficult problems for the Obama administration because it involved widespread efforts to replace pro-American authoritarian leaders with democratic governments. In earlier decades Washington was prepared to support authoritarian leaders if they protected the region's oil, sided with Washington against Moscow, and aided U.S. efforts to combat terrorism. It also presented Washington with the prospect of Islamist regimes, which some observers believed would sponsor terrorism and/or would be incompatible with democracy because Islam would not accept that voters could support policies that would undermine the word of Allah. (Islamism means governing according to the precepts of the Koran.)

When the Arab Spring erupted, the Obama administration supported the spread of democracy even though several long-time pro-American despots including Egypt's President Hosni Mubarak were overthrown. Obama had previously given a speech in Cairo in which he encouraged regional leaders to foster democracy and assured his listeners that America was not anti-Muslim. Initially, Washington supported Mubarak's elected successor, President Mohamed Morsi, leader of the non-violent Muslim Brotherhood. Thus, Obama burnished his pro-democratic credentials to the dismay of some U.S. allies, notably Saudi Arabia's leaders who opposed democracy and Morsi. However, after the Egyptian army ousted Morsi and General Abdel el-Sisi became Egypt's president, the Obama administration supported Sisi. Consequently, Washington alienated both Islamists who had supported Morsi and moderates and secularists in Egypt and elsewhere in the region who were suspicious of Islamism. After Morsi's overthrow, Islamic terrorists became active in Egypt's Sinai Peninsula and attacked Shia Muslims and Coptic Christians elsewhere in the country.

Washington's criticism of Sisi's authoritarianism gave Russia an opportunity to extend its influence there. Thus, it acquired the right for its aircraft to use Egyptian airfields. Egypt has begun cooperating with Israel against terrorism in the Sinai, containing Iran, and restricting smuggled goods to Hamas in Gaza, and Moscow has acquired considerable influence in Lebanon.

The Arab Spring fostered violence and civil war throughout the region. Civil war in Libya triggered NATO's 2011 humanitarian intervention to protect civilians from the threat of massacre by the forces of Libyan dictator Muammar Qaddafi. Qaddafi was overthrown and killed in October 2011. Regime change, however, brought instability. Conflict arose among regional militias, some secular and others Islamist, and Libya became a failed state. The political vacuum enabled numerous migrants from sub-Saharan Africa to use local traffickers to transport them on the perilous voyage from North Africa to Europe. NATO's role in Libya also became the rationale for Russian criticism of Western intervention elsewhere, notably Syria, that might produce regime change.

The worst casualty of the Arab Spring was civil war in Syria and Iraq, which has caused hundreds of thousands of deaths and triggered a flood of millions of refugees to other regions in Syria (6.2 million) and to neighboring countries such as Turkey, Jordan, and Lebanon as well as into Europe (6.3 million). The Syrian civil war began in 2011 following a serious drought, which the government largely ignored, and protests, which the government violently repressed. The Arab Spring intensified a regional cleavage between a U.S.-supported Sunni Muslim bloc, led by oil-rich Saudi Arabia, and a Shia Muslim grouping led by Iran, which had become Washington's leading regional foe following its Islamic Revolution. IS drew its support in Iraq and Syria from Sunni Muslims, a majority in both countries.

The Obama administration limited U.S. military and political involvement in Syria, while helping stabilize Iraq and end President Bashar al-Assad's bloody rule. In consequence, it aided Assad's moderate Sunni foes, whom Assad declared were terrorists. Obama's political foes argued that the president's refusal to carry out his threat to use force against the Syrian government if it crossed a "red line" of using poison gas against its citizens in 2013 encouraged Assad and eroded the credibility of U.S. commitments throughout the region.

Iran, leader of the region's Shiites, aided Syrian President Assad. Iran and its proxy, Hezbollah, enabled Assad to remain in power despite the opposition of the country's Sunni majority. Simultaneously, Iran's ground forces tacitly coordinated with the American-led coalition in combating the Islamic State. For its part, Russia intervened militarily in Syria in September 2015 to aid Assad and to extend its influence in the region. Russia already had a naval base in Syria and signed a deal with Assad to keep an airbase in that country

President Trump, who is largely indifferent about democratic norms and human rights, supports authoritarian leaders like Egypt's President Sisi and the monarchs of the Persian Gulf states. Nevertheless, moved by photos of dead and dying children, he responded to Syrian President Bashar Assad's use of poison gas in Idlib province in April 2017 by describing it as an "affront to humanity" and blaming Obama for having failing to respond with military force to Assad's earlier use of toxic chemicals. Thereafter, he ordered a missile strike on the airfield from which Syria had launched its gas attack. Russia sharply criticized the American strike, deepening the divisions between Russia and Iran, on the one hand, and the regime's foes on the other. "It is in this vital national security interest of the United States to prevent and deter the spread and use of deadly chemical weapons," declared Trump. "Years of previous attempts at changing Assad's behavior have all failed."[2] However, in March 2018 Trump declared that U.S. troops would be leaving Syria "soon," but the Pentagon persuaded him to leave 2,000 troops for the time being. Shortly afterwards, Assad launched another chemical attack, provoking America, UK and France to launch over 100 missiles at three Syrian chemical weapons storage and research facilities.

Trump is suspicious of Islamist politicians whom he associates with terrorism, and the Supreme Court ultimately upheld his ban on visitors from several Muslim countries to the United States. The president repeatedly invoked fears of "radical Islam" during his campaign. American relationships with Arab states and other Muslim countries had become strained after the terrorist attacks of September 2001 against New York's World Trade Center and the Pentagon in Washington, D.C. that were carried out by al-Qaeda. Many of those involved were Saudi Arabians, and U.S. politicians, especially Republicans, accused Saudi Arabia of financing terrorists and sought to enable the relatives of victims of 9/11 to sue that country. This attack along with additional al-Qaeda terrorism in the Middle East and Europe triggered President George W. Bush's War on Terror and U.S. wars in Afghanistan (2001) and Iraq (2003).

After 2001, America succeeded in eroding al-Qaeda with drone strikes and Special Force commando units. As part of the War on Terror the Bush administration was criticized by opponents of violating human rights by using torture when interrogating suspects, often in CIA "black sites" in other countries and of holding prisoners outside America at Guantánamo Bay, Cuba in violation of the Geneva Conventions. Although President Obama did not succeed in closing Guantánamo as he had promised, he managed to have most of the prisoners released, and he did close down the "black sites" and end resort to torture. During his campaign, candidate Trump publicly supported using torture to interrogate suspected terrorists and even spoke of reopening the "black sites." However, he agreed not to pursue these policies owing to opposition from Secretary of Defense James Mattis. Thus, Trump is perceived as an enemy of Islam, a perception that has facilitated the efforts of Islamic terrorist groups to recruit Muslims in the region and around the world.

Under Trump, U.S. involvement in the region remains significant with drone strikes against al-Qaeda terrorists in Yemen, air strikes in Iraq and Syria, and advisers arming and training Kurdish and Arab foes of IS although the president has no intention to become involved in "nation building" as had the Obama administration in Iraq. IS originated as al-Qaeda in Iraq (and became a rival of the original al-Qaeda), migrated to Syria during that country's civil war, and then returned to Iraq. After seizing control of large swaths of territory in Syria and Iraq, including the city of Mosul, its leader, Abu al-Baghdadi, proclaimed a global caliphate, which espoused and practiced extreme violence against the West, its regional allies, the Syrian government, moderate Sunni foes, and Shia Muslims.

In response, the Obama administration provided aid to moderate anti-IS rebels in Syria and formed an international coalition, which began an aerial campaign against IS in 2014, first in Iraq and then Syria. Trump's position during the presidential campaign and thereafter has been that IS was a major threat to U.S. national security, and the president's initial National Security Adviser, General Michael Flynn, former director of America's Defense Intelligence Agency, argued that IS constituted an existential threat to America and that its elimination should be the country's principal foreign-policy objective. After Flynn resigned, Trump remained focused on IS, and his administration sought to coordinate its air strikes with Russia and Iran. Thus, Presidents Putin and Trump, although rivals regarding Assad, cooperated against IS. U.S. Special Forces and aircraft played a major role in Iraq's successful efforts to drive IS from Mosul and other Iraqi cities, and America's presence in Iraq increased significantly in 2017.

Assad's adversaries also included Turkey, a NATO member. Turkish President Recep Tayyip Erdoğan was among Assad's earliest foes along with other Sunni leaders in the region. However, Turkey's changing relationship with America and Russia reflect the complexity of Middle East politics. Erdoğan was deeply suspicious of Turkey's Kurdish minority and American-armed Kurdish allies – the Peshmerga – fighting IS. His reelection as president in June 2018 and his party's continued control of the legislature further enhanced his presidential powers, threatening the survival of Turkish democracy. .

In July 2016, however, Turkish army units launched an unsuccessful coup against Erdoğan, who blamed it on a religious scholar, Fethullah Gulen, who lives in Pennsylvania. Although Obama condemned the coup, Washington refused to deport Gulen to Turkey without compelling evidence, angering Erdoğan. In April 2017, Turkish voters approved a referendum granting Erdoğan greater power. Erdoğan also purged Turkish institutions of alleged "Gulenists." Angered by continued U.S. aid to the Kurdish Peshmerga, Erdoğan jailed several Turkish employees of the U.S. embassy and American visitors, seeking to trade them for Gulen. Both countries suspended visa services for each other in October 2017, and U.S.-Turkish relations plummeted. Trump imposed economic sanctions on Turkey after Erdoğan refused to release an American pastor from prison, and Turkey's president reacted by imposing tariffs on U.S. products. After the pastor's release, America withdrew its sanctions, and Trump also sought to find a reason to send Gulen back to Turkey. Thereafter, cooperation between the two increased owing to the murder of a U.S.-Saudi Arabian journalist, Jamal Khashoggi, in the Saudi consulate in Istanbul in October 2018.

The decision of Iraq's Kurds to hold a referendum about establishing an independent Kurdistan triggered fierce opposition from countries in which Kurds live, especially Turkey and Iraq. The referendum weakened America's anti-IS coalition, and Iraqi forces pushed the Kurds from the multinational city of Kirkuk and the surrounding oil fields. Many Kurds believe that the Trump administration had betrayed them after it ceased aiding Syria's Kurds in November 2017.

Turkey initially had opposed Russian intervention in Syria, and shot down a Russian plane in Turkish airspace, triggering a crisis between the two. However, Russo-Turkish cooperation increased owing to Turkey's fear of a Kurdish presence along its borders, which triggered its military intervention in Syria and growing coordination of Turkish policy with Moscow to defeat IS and bring peace in Syria even if it meant retaining Assad as Syria's president. Russia cooperated with Turkey in defeating IS and reducing the Kurdish role in seizing objectives like Raqqa, the IS capital city, in Syria. Thus, Turkey appeared to be tilting toward Russia and turning against the United States.

Russia and Turkey pressed Assad to be flexible, but Iran continued to support Assad's determination to reconquer the entire country. Notwithstanding the agreement with Iran to halt that country's nuclear enrichment program, Iranian hardliners continued to pursue efforts to extend their influence in Iraq, Syria and Lebanon at the expense of Sunni opponents like Saudi Arabia. Thus, Iran armed thousands of Shia volunteers in Iraq and Syria, and provided funding and arms to Shia groups in those countries. U.S. forces refused to aid Shia militias ("Popular Mobilization Forces") or Hezbollah because they are Iranian proxies. Nevertheless, U.S. planners have largely avoided confrontations between U.S.-supported rebels and Iranian- and Syrian-supported forces, a possibility that increased after the remnants of IS were squeezed between advancing U.S.-supported and Russian-supported forces. By 2018, IS had been defeated in Iraq and Syria although remaining capable of terrorist and guerrilla attacks there and elsewhere.

U.S. forces aided the anti-IS Syrian Democratic Forces but, unlike Obama initially, Trump cared little about ousting President Assad. Thus, the administration was marginalized in negotiating peace in Syria. Instead, Trump's interest was defeating IS and pushing back Iran. Turkey and Russia negotiated a partial ceasefire, along with Iran, and undertook peace talks with the Assad government and anti-Assad Sunni rebels. Additional talks began among Russia, Iran, and Turkey in Kazakhstan in March 2017 without a U.S. representative present, culminating in the establishment of several "de-escalation zones." Russia, Iran, and Turkey would each be responsible for one of these zones. The agreement legitimized Russia's military intervention in Syria. UN-sponsored peace talks in 2017–2018 went nowhere, and America remained absent from negotiations among Russia, Turkey, and Iran in April 2018.

Continued opposition to leaving Assad in power was impractical, and, with Russian and Iranian help, Assad reconquered much of the country, providing Russia and Iran with greater influence across the region. In November 2017, Putin (whom Assad thanked for "saving Syria") and Trump agreed to recognize Russia's leading role in Syrian peace negotiations while Russia acknowledged a U.S. presence in northeastern Syria, partly as a buffer against Iran. Assad and Russia may still have to deal with Washington and its Syrian allies, which control about a third of the country including its oil fields.

As IS withdrew, competing rebel groups and Russia, Iraq, Turkey, and the U.S. sought to consolidate control over areas in Syria. Another Turkish operation in early 2018 in the Kurdish enclave of Afrin sought to push U.S.-supported Syrian Kurds away from its border. The Turkish invasion risked a confrontation with Iranian-backed pro-Assad militias and risked a clash between Turkish and American troops. And in February 2018, Russian mercenaries aiding pro-Assad units were killed by U.S.-supported rebels aided by U.S. troops, and Israel bombed numerous Syrian sites after one of its aircraft, responding to an Iranian drone which had entered its airspace, had been downed by Syrian missiles. Then, the day after Trump pulled out of the nuclear deal with Tehran, Iranian missiles struck the Israeli-occupied Golan Heights, its first direct attack on Israel's army. Israel in turn unleashed a massive aerial attack on Iranian military facilities across Syria in May 2018. Russia, however, in concert with Israel has apparently acted to force Iranian troops and Shia militias away from Israel's borders (Bar'el, 2018).[3] Nevertheless, what had been a Syrian civil war threatens region-wide chaos.

THE SHIA-SUNNI DIVIDE

The Arab Spring deepened cleavages between a Shia bloc led by Iran and a Sunni coalition of Arab states led by Saudi Arabia. The origins of the Shia-Sunni split date back to the death of the Prophet in 632 AD. Most Muslims believed that the Islamic community should select Mohammed's successors ("caliphs") while a minority believed that only descendants of the prophet could succeed him. The former or Sunnis triumphed and regard the latter or Shia Muslims as heretics. Sunni terrorists in Pakistan, Iraq, Afghanistan, and elsewhere frequently murder Shias.

Although Iran had been an American ally until its 1979 Islamic Revolution, Iranians bitterly recall the Anglo-American role in overthrowing Prime Minister Mohammad Mossadegh in 1953. After foreign oil companies refused to accept the government's demand to split profits from the sale of Iranian oil, Mossadegh nationalized the British-owned Anglo-Iranian Oil Company, and the West imposed a boycott of Iranian oil. Thereafter, Iran's royal ruler Reza Shah Pahlavi, aided by America's CIA and the UK's MI6, overthrew Mossadegh. With U.S. backing, the Shah repressed opposition and governed until a revolution led by Ayatollah Ruhollah Khomeini, an anti-American religious leader who had returned from exile, overthrew him in 1979.

Khomeini assumed the title of Supreme Leader while the Shah, ill with cancer, was admitted to America for medical treatment. That triggered the occupation of America's embassy in Tehran by Iranian students in November 1979 who took Americans hostages. President Jimmy Carter sought to free them in a raid by U.S. Special Forces that proved disastrous. Finally, after 444 days, the students set their hostages free in January 1981 shortly after Ronald Reagan had become U.S. president. Iranian hostility to America, "the Great Satan," remains until the present day, and hopes that the U.S.-Iranian deal in 2015 to end Iran's nuclear weapons program would produce a reconciliation between the two countries were dashed, especially after President Trump withdrew from the Iran nuclear deal in May 2018.

As noted earlier, U.S.-Iranian tension was evident during Syria's civil war, and Iran enjoys considerable influence among Iraq's Shia majority. However, as the Syrian civil war ebbed, Iran opened a land corridor through Iraq and Syria to Damascus and to Syria's Mediterranean coast and Israel's border. This development increased Iranian influence throughout the region, and Iraq's refusal to agree to the Trump administration's demand that Iran's Shia militias return to Iran after IS's defeat reflected Iran's growing influence. The prospect of clashes between the Shia militias and U.S.-supported rebels was heightened as both sought to occupy territory from which IS retreated. Iraq's Sunni minority also remained alienated owing to the slow pace of reconstructing towns previously occupied by IS, and the continued role of anti-Sunni Shia militias provide fertile ground for the resurgence of Sunni terrorist groups like IS. Thus, by September 2018 IS had recovered and had grown to as many as 30,000 fighters though with no territorial control.

Iraq's Shia Prime Minister Haider al-Abadi has skillfully retained both U.S. and Iranian support and has tried to prevent his country from becoming a battleground between the two. He encouraged warm relations with Sunni states such as Turkey and Saudi Arabia. Syria is ruled by an Alawite minority – a branch of the Shia. Lebanon also has a Shia majority and hosts the Iranian-backed Shia militia, Hezbollah, which possesses a virtual veto over Lebanese policies and had been largely responsible for keeping Assad in power in Syria. However, the surprising electoral victory of followers of the radical nationalist Shia cleric Moktada al-Sadr in May 2018 threatened to destabilize Iraq again. The selection of a compromise Shia candidate, Adil Abd al-Mahdi, as the country's next prime minister calmed the political waters – at least temporarily.

Iran's land corridor through Iraq and Syria produced particular concern in Israel, which fears an Iranian presence on its borders as well as facilitating Iran's provision of arms to Hezbollah. "The development is potentially momentous, because, for the first time, it would bind together, by a single land route, a string of Iranian allies, including Hezbollah, in Lebanon; the Assad regime, in Syria; and the Iranian-dominated government in Iraq" (Filkins, 2017).[4] Those allies constitute a "Shiite Crescent", an Iranian sphere of influence in a region dominated by Sunni Muslims. Israel has bombed convoys in Syria that it believed were ferrying weapons to Hezbollah and bombed a Syrian factory in 2017 that it concluded was conducting military research for Hezbollah, thereby sending a message that it would act unilaterally if Iran or Hezbollah provoked it to do so. The "Shia Crescent" includes Iran, Iraq, Lebanon, and a majority population in Bahrain, which has a Sunni regime.

Indicating a desire for friendship with Saudi Arabia and other Sunni states, especially Egypt, Trump denounced the Muslim Brotherhood and considered labeling it a terrorist group, an act favored by Egypt's leaders and the Saudis, but which would alienate peaceful Islamist politicians elsewhere. In other ways, too, the Trump administration has indicated support for Sunni states in their quarrels with Iran, even though Islamic terrorism mainly involves Sunni extremists in IS, al-Qaeda and its affiliates.

American dependence on oil-rich Sunni states like Saudi Arabia has declined owing to growing U.S. energy independence resulting from "fracking" that has opened new sources of oil and natural gas in America, and the fluctuations in oil prices resulting from renewable energy and the abundance of oil and gas. Oil-producing countries such as Saudi Arabia and Russia cut production to raise prices, thereby countering the market effects of U.S. shale. They are also trying to diversify their economies.

FIGURE 9.1 The Shia Crescent

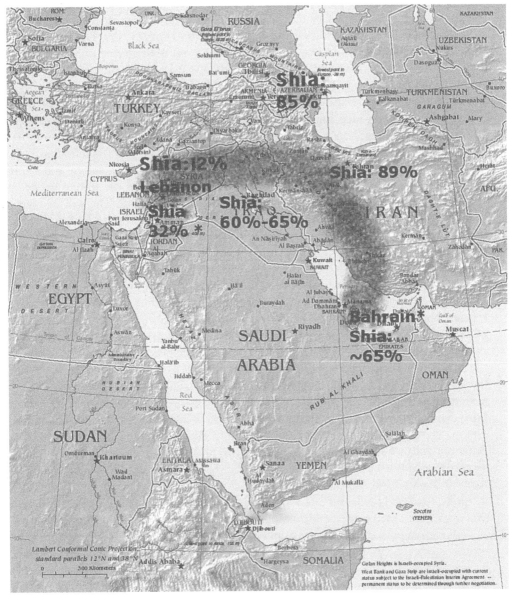

Source: Map and data sources: CIA World Factbook (2006). Available at www.cia.gov/ library/publications/download/ download-2006/index.html; *Mario von Baratta (2003). *Der Fischer Weltalmanach 2003.* Fischer Sachbücher

During President Trump's visit to the Middle East in 2017, he endorsed Saudi Arabia's claim that Qatar fostered terrorism and had become an ally of Iran even though Qatar hosts a major U.S. military base. The Saudis and their allies embargoed Qatar diplomatically and economically. Although Qatar is a sponsor of Hamas, has provided asylum to members of the Muslim Brotherhood and various Shia Muslims, and has normal diplomatic relations with Iran, the Saudi, Egyptian, and United Arab Emirates perception is exaggerated. Subsequent American efforts to mediate the quarrel merely exacerbated it. The president denounced Qatar about an hour after Secretary Tillerson had suggested the need for a "calm and thoughtful dialogue" to end the dispute. Unlike Tillerson's efforts to end the Saudi-led blockade, Kushner, the president's son-in-law, was apparently encouraging the Saudis to isolate Qatar. Tillerson's successor, Mike Pompeo sought to end Qatar's isolation during a visit to Saudi Arabia in April 2018.

Yemen, the region's poorest country, also collapsed into civil war, which drove from power Presidents Ali Abdullah Saleh in 2012 and Abd Rabbu Mansour Hadi in 2015. The Houthis, a Zaidi Shia religious-political movement aided by Iran, occupied much of the country. Iran has provided sophisticated weapons to the Houthis including anti-ship and ballistic missiles. Its presence triggered intervention by a Saudi Arabian-led Sunni coalition that launched repeated indiscriminate airstrikes, sent in Saudi and Emirati troops, and blockaded Yemeni ports, creating a humanitarian crisis involving famine and a cholera epidemic. Violence intensified when Houthi followers murdered the former president of the country, who had been their ally but sought to change sides. The violence led to a reduction in U.S. Special Forces in the country fighting al-Qaeda in the Arabian Peninsula, which along with the Islamic State, was able to seize several cities and enlarge the territory under their control. In May 2017, Trump praised the Saudis for their "strong action" in Yemen, but in December Secretary Tillerson criticized them.

Encouraged by the Trump administration, Saudi Arabia has focused its regional policies around its conflict with Iran. The war in Yemen continues, and any Saudi-Iranian detente remains remote. In addition, if President Trump insists (wrongly) that Iran is in violation of the nuclear deal (the Joint Comprehensive Plan of Action), despite contrary reports by the International Atomic Energy Agency (IAEA) and the belief of many of his advisers that the deal is in America's national interest. As of late 2018, Iran had continued to abide by the agreement, even as the Trump administration demanded major changes to the original agreement and reimposed heavy sanctions. Washington threatened to sanction countries and firms that continued to trade with Iran, especially those importing Iranian oil. The European Union, China, and Russia are trying to establish a means to trade with Iran without using American dollars – which are central to the global financial system – but they are unlikely to succeed. America has also given some countries including India and China temporary waivers to allow them to find substitutes for Iranian oil. If Tehran does resume developing nuclear weapons, Israel and perhaps the U.S. may attack that country. The Saudis might also develop similar weapons, thereby destabilizing the entire Middle East even more than it is at present.

Although imported oil from the Sunni-dominated states remains important, Trump vigorously advocates American energy independence and has opposed any limitations on the exploitation of U.S. shale natural gas deposits. He has approved several pipeline projects that the previous administration had halted, notably Keystone XL, which conservationists oppose because it will transport particularly dirty oil from Alberta, Canada to refineries in Texas. Indeed, Trump has suggested that belief in climate change and global warming are a "hoax."

CONCLUSIONS

Trump's policies in the Middle East have done little to stabilize relations among hostile states in a disorderly region. His policies have enabled Russia and Iran to gain a growing presence there. The election of the moderate Hassan Rouhani in 2013 had made possible the 2015 nuclear agreement. Rouhani was reelected president in May 2017, making it possible that Iran might adopt policies that are more moderate if the Trump made a serious effort to encourage Iran to do so. Nevertheless, Rouhani must confront the militants in his country, including the current Supreme Leader Ayatollah Khamenei, and Trump's withdrawal from the nuclear agreement has weakened him politically.

Trump continues to support Israel as well as Sunni Arab states, which he hopes can help negotiate a Palestinian-Israeli agreement. To date those efforts have failed, and the president's tweets have proved confusing and have raised concerns about what are his policies. Moreover, as the prospect of a two-state solution to the Israeli-Palestinian imbroglio fades and in light of Trump's recognition of Jerusalem as Israel's capital, the likelihood of a third intifada is growing.

Regarding the Arab Spring, Trump has been largely passive except for his efforts to eliminate IS. He allowed Russia to create de-escalation zones in Syria – areas in which they have inserted heavily armed military police. Moreover, Assad remaining in power has not perturbed Trump, and he terminated the CIA's covert effort to aid anti-Assad rebels. Thus, there is no foe in Syria capable of ousting Assad. In sum, Trump has done little to prevent the growing presence and influence of Russia and Iran in the region.

In the regional rivalry between the Shia bloc led by Iran and the Sunni allies of Saudi Arabia, Trump has vigorously supported the Sunni bloc, which depends on the U.S. for intelligence, training, logistics support, and security, and he enjoys a warm relationship to Saudi crown prince Mohammed bin Salman, the virtual ruler of his country. However, the murder of Jamal Khashoggi in the Saudi consulate in Istanbul was almost certainly ordered by crown prince Mohammed. This placed America's President Trump in a difficult position as he sought to maintain America's close relations with Saudi Arabia.

The monarchs of the Persian Gulf states were pleased that Trump opposed Islamists like those associated with Egypt's Muslim Brotherhood and that he is skeptical about climate change, advocating continued use of fossil fuels. Trump has increased U.S. economic sanctions in response to Iranian meddling in Iraq and Yemen and Tehran's efforts to weaken the power of the Saudis and its aid to Shia militias in Iraq, Lebanon, Bahrain, and Syria. Iraq has increasingly become part of Iran's Shia presence, and a confrontation between the U.S.-backed Syrian Democratic Forces and Iran remains possible. Moreover, U.S. policies in Yemen, Qatar, Lebanon, and over Jerusalem provide significant opportunities for Iran to exploit. Finally, Trump's withdrawal from the nuclear deal assures additional sanctions on Iran and greater Iranian belligerence.

ESSAY QUESTIONS

1) What are the key issues separating Israel and the Palestinians? Why are they so difficult to resolve?

2) In what ways have U.S.-Israeli relations evolved and what are President Trump's key policies toward that country?

3) Describe the "Arab Spring" including its accomplishment and failures, and America's policies regarding the events during the "Arab Spring."

4) Discuss the "Shia-Sunni" divide in the Arab world including key actors and divisive issues. What U.S. policies in the Middle East have involved America in this division?

5) What were the key actors in Syria's civil war and in what ways did they become involved in that conflict?

SHORT ANSWER QUESTIONS

Define and describe the importance of the following:

The Palestinian Authority
The Oslo Accords
Hamas
Hezbollah
"One-state" and "two-state" proposals in the Israel-Palestine relations
The Muslim Brotherhood
Fethullah Gulen

NOTES

1   Baker, P. (2017). Trump, Bullish on Mideast peace, Will Need More than Confidence. *New York Times* [online]. Available at: www.nytimes.com/2017/05/03/world/middleeast/mah-moud-abbas-trump-white-house.html [Accessed 5 May 2017].
2   Cited in Gordon, M., Cooper, H., and Shear, M. (2017). Dozens of U.S. Missiles Hit Air Base in Syria. *New York Times* [online]. Available at: www.nytimes.com/2017/04/06/world/middleeast/us-said-to-weigh-military-responses-to-syrian-chemical-attack.html [Accessed 7 April 2017].
3   Bar'el, Z. (2018). Syria Signals Willingness to Pull Hezbollah Back from Border with Israel, report says. *Haaretz* [online]. Available at: www.haaretz.com/middle-east-news/.premium-syria-signals-willingness-to-pull-back-hezbollah-from-israeli-border-1.6130666 [Accessed 1 June 2018].
4   Filkins, D. (2017). Iran Extends Its Reach in Syria. *The New Yorker* [online]. Available at: www.newyorker.com/news/news-desk/iran-extends-its-reach-in-syria [Accessed: 26 March 2018].

SUGGESTED READINGS

Dowty, A. (2017). *Israel/Palestine (Global Hot Spots)*, 4th ed. Cambridge, UK: Polity Press.
Mansbach, R. and Taylor, K. (2018). *Challenges for America in the Middle East*. Thousand Oaks, CA: Sage Publications.

Part III

Functional issues

10 Nuclear weapons: A new arms race?

Kirsten L. Taylor

On January 13, 2018, Hawaiians were alerted, "BALLISTIC MISSILE THREAT INBOUND TO HAWAII. SEEK IMMEDIATE SHELTER. THIS IS NOT A DRILL" (Fifield, 2018).[1] After widespread panic for over half an hour, the threat proved to be a false alarm. Four days later a similar alarm was broadcast (but quickly retracted) in Japan. Nuclear drills, a common practice in the 1950s and 1960s, have long been considered a Cold War relic. These events, however, highlight the dangers in relying on nuclear weapons for security.

NUCLEAR POLICY: PAST AND PRESENT

Until 1949 America was the world's sole nuclear power, and from the advent of the nuclear age, two important themes emerged in U.S. nuclear policy: crafting a policy for the use of nuclear weapons and limiting their proliferation. Although the world has changed dramatically in recent decades, the policies formulated during the Cold War remain influential.

After Moscow had acquired nuclear weapons in 1949 but not a delivery system capable of reaching America, U.S. policy emphasized developing a strong nuclear arsenal (including bombers and bases across Europe and Asia) to compensate for conventional military weakness relative to the USSR by threatening unacceptable nuclear retaliation should it attack America or an ally. Deterrence was the cornerstone of U.S. nuclear policy throughout the Cold War, although "massive retaliation" was abandoned once the USSR developed the technology for an intercontinental delivery system.

In the mid-1960s, once the U.S. and Soviet arsenals had become roughly equivalent, arms control became an important tool for managing the nuclear arms race by limiting or banning various weapons and removing incentives to use them quickly and preventing either side from gaining a military advantage that might lead it to launch a nuclear first strike. The 1972 Strategic Arms Limitation Treaty (SALT I) limited the number of new weapons, and the development of delivery and defensive systems. By then, both sides relied on a survivable, second-strike capability and the threat of mutual assured destruction (MAD) to prevent nuclear war. MAD remained a defining component of U.S. strategy until Ronald Reagan, who believed it might trigger the very nuclear apocalypse it was designed to avoid, abandoned it. SALT II (1979), which limited the number of missiles with multiple independent warheads (MIRV), heavy bombers, and the total number of strategic launchers, was never ratified owing to the Soviet invasion of Afghanistan.

Nuclear deterrence remains a key component of U.S. strategy, despite the evolution of military threats since the Cold War. Even President Barack Obama, who in 2009 spoke of "America's commitment to seek the peace and security of a world without nuclear weapons," argued that "as long as these weapons exist, the United States will maintain a safe, secure and effective arsenal to deter any adversary, and guarantee that defense to our allies" (White House, 2009).[2] The 2010 Nuclear Posture Review (NPR) that guided his administration's nuclear policy identified nuclear terrorism and proliferation as the most pressing challenges and described the "massive nuclear arsenal inherited from the Cold War era . . . [as] poorly suited to address" these challenges. The Obama administration adopted a view of deterrence that reduced the "role and numbers of U.S. nuclear weapons," sought to modernize "aging nuclear facilities," and integrated non-nuclear capabilities into U.S. deterrence policy, including missile defenses and conventional military capabilities as well as "assets in cyberspace and outer space" (U.S. Department of Defense, 2010: 33).[3]

Washington's interest in limiting proliferation goes back to the beginning of the nuclear era, but the 1963 Partial Test Ban Treaty constituted the first real progress. China's acquisition of the bomb in 1964 prodded Washington to agree to negotiations that produced the 1968 Nuclear Non-Proliferation Treaty (NPT) that was designed to prevent proliferation beyond those countries that had already tested a nuclear device by 1967 (U.S., USSR, UK, France, and China). The NPT and its watchdog agency, the International Atomic Energy Agency (IAEA), achieved modest success in stopping proliferation during the Cold War, but they have not prevented countries that view nuclear weapons as a viable regional security solution from proliferating – namely, Israel (which does not admit to having nuclear weapons), India, Pakistan, and North Korea.

After the Cold War, U.S. non-proliferation policy increasingly focused on the threat posed by "rogue" states, which flout international law and may be willing to share nuclear technology with others, including terrorists. Simultaneously, America began to modernize its own nuclear arsenal. This policy sends contradictory messages about the value of nuclear arms, risks fueling new arms races, and is incompatible with the interests of most non-nuclear powers, which in 2017 completed a Treaty on the Prohibition of Nuclear Weapons. The greatest nuclear challenges confronting U.S. administrations have been North Korea, Iran, and nuclear modernization.

North Korea

North Korea began acquiring nuclear technology in the 1950s with Soviet support, including training of scientists and technicians, development of a research reactor in Yongbyon in the early 1960s, and plutonium reprocessing technology several years later. Otherwise, Pyongyang pursued its nuclear program largely on its own, expanding it considerably in the 1980s.

American officials first became concerned about North Korea's program in 1983 and pressed Moscow to get Pyongyang to sign the NPT, which it did in 1985. North Korea, however, repeatedly delayed completion of IAEA safeguards agreements. Washington offered incentives to persuade Pyongyang to cooperate with the IAEA, including offers to negotiate trade and economic issues, unilateral withdrawal of its nuclear weapons from

South Korea, and suspension of nuclear exercises in the region. North Korea finally signed its safeguards agreement in 1992, but refused to work with the IAEA to verify its declarations of nuclear materials and facilities. Pyongyang threatened to withdraw from the NPT and continued missile research, including developing a missile capable of striking Japan in 1993.

Former President Jimmy Carter intervened to negotiate a deal, the Agreed Framework, by which North Korea would terminate its nuclear-weapons program, implement its safeguards agreements, and close its Yongbyon nuclear research complex. In exchange, Washington would lift sanctions, provide an annual supply of oil for energy, and contribute $4 billion for constructing two proliferation-resistant light-water reactors. In 1995 America, Japan, and South Korea established the Korean Peninsula Energy Development Organization to implement the agreement. However, owing partly to the election of a Republican Congress in 1994, the Agreed Framework was never fully instituted. Congress delayed promised oil shipments, refused to lift sanctions, and did not provide the light-water reactors. North Korea restarted its nuclear-weapons program in 1998, aided by the father of Pakistan's nuclear program, A.Q. Khan (Brown, 2015: 111).[4]

In his 2002 State of the Union address, President George W. Bush accused North Korea, along with Iran and Iraq, of constituting an "axis of evil" and promised to halt their efforts to acquire nuclear weapons. The following year, North Korea's Kim Jong-il announced his country had developed a nuclear weapon and would withdraw from the NPT. Pyongyang, however, was persuaded to return to the negotiating table, this time in multilateral talks in 2003 that included China, Russia, Japan, South Korea, and America. These Six-Party Talks produced an agreement by which North Korea would end its nuclear-weapons program (again) in exchange for food aid and its removal from America's list of state sponsors of terrorism. Sanctions, however, continued as did North Korea's weapons program, which in 2006 produced a successful test of a low-yield nuclear device (a fraction of the strength of the bomb dropped on Hiroshima in 1945).

Six-Party diplomacy finally collapsed in 2009, after Pyongyang's second nuclear test and ongoing missile tests. The prospects for denuclearization briefly improved following Kim Il-Sung's death in December 2011, and Washington pursued new bilateral negotiations with his successor and son, Kim Jong-un. The resulting 2012 agreement would have provided North Korea with food aid, but Kim refused to suspend North Korea's nuclear activities as promised and conducted a third nuclear test in February 2013. Thereafter, Obama's policy of "strategic patience" relied on diplomatic ostracism and escalating sanctions to pressure Pyongyang to denuclearize. However, North Korea detonated two more nuclear devices during Obama's presidency, in January and September 2016.

The Bush and Obama administrations sought China's help to denuclearize North Korea, but to little effect. Beijing's main interest is maintaining stability on the Korean peninsula, and it was reluctant to support economic sanctions imposed by the UN Security Council that might cause the regime in North Korea to collapse. Instead, China has evaded those sanctions. Without a strong diplomatic partner in Beijing, the Obama administration focused on countering North Korea's missile threat, deploying a Terminal High Altitude Area Defense (THAAD) system in South Korea. Designed to intercept and destroy incoming missiles in their terminal (downward) phase, THAAD complicated U.S. diplomacy in the region. It reassured South Korea but angered China, which views it as offering America a strategic advantage in tracking Chinese missiles.

Iran

Iran's nuclear program also began in the 1950s. Washington provided Iran's first research reactor as part of the Atoms for Peace program that sought to share peaceful nuclear energy with developing countries. Iran was among the earliest members of the NPT, but by the 1970s its plans for expanding its nuclear infrastructure raised concern among U.S. officials that Tehran sought nuclear weapons. Iran briefly halted its nuclear-weapons program after its 1979 Islamic Revolution, but by 1985 its uranium enrichment activities and construction of a heavy water reactor (which can produce plutonium) in Arak raised concerns. Iran's nuclear activities accelerated in the 1990s as it sought aid from Pakistan, China, and Russia to train personnel and acquire research reactors and uranium enrichment facilities.

A 2003 IAEA inquiry into Iran's nuclear program identified clandestine activities that violated Iran's safeguards agreement. During the following year, Tehran engaged in negotiations with France, Germany, and the United Kingdom (the EU-3) and agreed to sign (but not ratify) the IAEA's 1997 Additional Protocol that authorizes more intrusive nuclear inspections to monitor compliance with the NPT. Meanwhile, Iran was also improving its long-range missile capability.

Cooperation, however limited, began to end with the election of hardliner Mahmoud Ahmadinejad as Iran's president in 2005. During the ensuing years, the international community relied on a mix of diplomacy and economic sanctions to compel Iran to work with the IAEA to verify compliance with the NPT and its IAEA safeguards agreement. During this period, America, Russia, and China joined the EU-3 negotiations, creating the P5+1 (referring to the five permanent members of the UN Security Council and Germany). As diplomatic efforts stalled, the UN Security Council imposed painful sanctions between 2006 and 2010 that blocked the export of "sensitive nuclear equipment," froze financial assets of key participants in Iran's nuclear program, restricted Iranian banking, called for inspection of planes and ships believed to be carrying prohibited cargo to or from Iran, and prevented the purchase of heavy weapons (BBC, 2010).[5] Washington imposed even tougher sanctions including those banning the import of most Iranian goods and services in 2010.

An apparent breakthrough in the diplomatic impasse surrounded the election in Iran in 2013 of the more-moderate President Hassan Rouhani. Diplomacy began again following a telephone call between Rouhani and Obama in September. Within weeks, Iran and the P5+1 were negotiating an interim agreement to limit Iran's nuclear activities in exchange for lifting sanctions and unfreezing Iranian assets. A final deal, the Joint Comprehensive Plan of Action (JCPOA), was reached in July 2015 and was viewed as extending Iran's "breakout time" (time until it can build a bomb) to at least a year. Iran agreed to strict limits on its nuclear program, including reducing its stockpile of low-enriched uranium by 98 percent to 660 pounds for fifteen years and reducing the number of operating centrifuges used to enrich uranium from 20,000 to 5,060 older, less efficient centrifuges for ten years. Iran also agreed to redesign its Arak reactor to prevent production of weapons-grade plutonium and to send all of its spent fuel (the source of plutonium) and most of its heavy water (used in producing fissile uranium-235) out of the country. Iran also agreed to implement the IAEA Additional Protocol. In exchange, remaining sanctions on Iran's nuclear activities were lifted. A slap-back provision allowed sanctions to be re-imposed if Tehran violated the agreement.

Although supporters argued that this agreement was the only realistic way to ensure Iran did not acquire nuclear weapons, critics contended it left Tehran with a nuclear infrastructure and rewarded it by removing economic sanctions too quickly. Such concerns led Congress to pass the Iran Nuclear Agreement Review Act, requiring the president to certify Iran's compliance with the JCPOA every ninety days. If the President refused to issue the certification, Congress had sixty days to employ an expedited legislative process to re-impose sanctions (Davenport, 2017).[6] None of this necessarily abrogated the deal with Iran but, should Congress not act, the process would begin again in another ninety days.

Disarmament and Modernization

Disarmament and nuclear modernization pose a third challenge. All nuclear-weapons-possessing states pursue modernization because weapons systems have limited life-spans and must be updated and/or replaced to maintain an effective deterrent. Modernization advocates argue the nuclear landscape requires America update its own arsenal, citing modernization underway in Russia and China, North Korea's pursuit of nuclear weapons, and the threat of proliferation that might follow in South Korea and Japan. From this perspective, Washington needs to enhance its nuclear deterrent – possibly including the development of smaller tactical weapons to deter an adversary's use of similar weapons. Critics counter that modernization risks fueling arms races, arguing that smaller useable weapons will make the prospect of a limited nuclear war more attractive.

Despite Obama's early promises to decrease America's reliance on nuclear weapons, modernization was the price he had to pay to get Congress to support the 2010 New START Treaty that limited both America and Russia to 700 deployed intercontinental ballistic missiles (ICBMs), submarine-launched ballistic missiles (SLBMs), and heavy bombers with a combined total of 1,550 nuclear warheads. Many Republican senators viewed New START as insufficient to prevent Russian cheating and/or stop Russia from pursuing missiles prohibited by the 1987 Intermediate-Range Nuclear Forces (INF) Treaty (Paltrow, 2017),[7] which committed both states to eliminate all ground-launched ballistic and cruise missiles with a range of 500 to 5,500 kilometers.

New START, however, is a bilateral U.S.-Russia agreement focused on numerical limits, but saying nothing about modernizing systems or replacing them with something newer. Both Russia and China are making qualitative improvements to their arsenals, partly in response to U.S. efforts to deploy regional missile defenses in Europe and Asia. Russia is phasing out aging Soviet-era weapons and delivery systems and replacing them with new ICBMs, submarines, and heavy bombers. Its modernization will reduce Russia's overall number of delivery systems and nuclear warheads, but some would carry more warheads (Kristensen, 2017).[8] China, whose arsenal is smaller (about 260 warheads) and unlikely to grow substantially, is focusing on qualitative improvements to its retaliatory capability, including its first missile with MIRVed vehicles, more mobile and survivable missiles, and an improved SSBN (nuclear ballistic missile submarine) and SLBM (submarine-launched ballistic missile) capability.

U.S. modernization efforts have lagged behind those of Russia and China, in part owing to Washington's emphasis on counterterrorism since 2001. Washington began to pursue modernization late in the Obama administration to replace aging Minuteman III ICBMs and AGM-86B nuclear cruise missiles (Reuters, 2017),[9] transform the B61 gravity bomb (at $20.8 million per bomb) into a controllable smart bomb with a variable blast, and construct new heavy bombers and submarines to deliver these weapons. The Congressional Budget Office expects it will cost over $1.2 trillion over thirty years to replace all three legs of America's strategic triad (air, sea, and land) with weapons and delivery systems that will remain in service until 2080.

TRUMP'S NUCLEAR CHALLENGES

President Trump has no foreign-policy experience, and his administration has been slow in bringing in policy experts and filling key diplomatic assignments. By January 2018, for example, he had not appointed an Under Secretary for Arms Control and International Security or sent an ambassador to South Korea. Trump withdrew his first choice as ambassador, Korean expert Victor Cha owing to policy disagreements; his second nominee, Navy Admiral Harry Harris, was confirmed in June 2018. Moreover, Trump frequently tweets fiery rhetoric that contradicts officials, including the Secretaries of State and Defense, who are more likely to advocate diplomatic engagement. Trump's nuclear policy is reminiscent of Cold War-era thinking, with emphasis on a massive nuclear force and the threat of nuclear attack to deter aggression. In this era, this may very well produce the conflict it seeks to avoid.

North Korea

Initially, such a conflict seemed especially likely in the case of North Korea. Even before Trump was sworn into office, tensions were high, and the likelihood of diplomatic engagement receded when in early January 2017 Trump tweeted he would not permit North Korea to develop an ICBM capable of reaching the United States. North Korea then ratcheted up its nuclear and missile activities, which led to angry exchanges between the two leaders. North Korea launched its first ballistic missile during the Trump presidency in February and some weeks later launched another four missiles into the Sea of Japan. Additional missile tests followed, and in July 2017 North Korea launched its first "nuclear-capable ICBM" and a still more-advanced ICBM probably capable of striking America. The UN Security Council unanimously passed sanctions restricting North Korean banking and technology activities, banning North Korea's trade in coal, iron, and seafood, further restricting North Korea's technology trade, and increasing enforcement by banning vessels violating sanctions from entering foreign ports. Pyongyang insisted that "under no circumstances" would it negotiate to halt its nuclear-weapons and missile programs and, in the event of a U.S. attack, would "teach the US a severe lesson with its nuclear strategic force" (cited in Otto et al., 2017).[10]

Trump escalated the dispute further by declaring that any more threats would "be met with fire and fury like the world has never seen" (cited in Thrus and Baker, 2017).[11] Secretary of State Rex Tillerson explained the President "is sending a strong message to North Korea in language that Kim Jong-un would understand, because he doesn't seem to understand diplomatic language" (cited in Baker and Harris, 2017).[12]

Deterrence theory relies on clear signals of capability and intent to dissuade a rational adversary from attacking. Harsh language, however, can have the reverse effect and escalate an already tense situation. Thus, hours after a harsh exchange between Kim and Trump, Pyongyang announced a strike plan against the U.S. Pacific territory of Guam and threatened a preemptive strike if Washington continued its provocations. Within days, Tillerson and Defense Secretary Jim Mattis explained that the administration had replaced Obama's "failed policy of 'strategic patience' . . . with a new policy of strategic accountability" that relies on diplomacy "backed by military options" as a "preferred means of changing North Korea's course of action" (Mattis and Tillerson, 2017).[13] "Maximum pressure" became the descriptor of the administration policy.

North Korea continued to test the limits of this policy. In September 2017 it detonated a hydrogen bomb, and in November it tested an ICBM capable of reaching anywhere in the United States. Thus, Kim Jong-un dramatically accelerated North Korea's nuclear program, and analysts predict that Pyongyang would acquire an ICBM with a nuclear warhead and have sufficient nuclear material for as many as one hundred warheads by 2020 (Broad, 2017).[14]

Trump has pressed Beijing to compel Kim Jong-un to abandon his nuclear ambitions. Beijing had used its close economic and diplomat relations with Pyongyang to initiate the Six-Party Talks between 2003 and 2009. Since then, Sino-North Korean relations have deteriorated, particularly after Kim's accession to power in 2011. Despite North Korea's reliance on China for trade, in recent years China's leverage has waned.

One might conclude it would be in Pyongyang's interest to abandon its nuclear program and pursue security some other way. However, from Kim's perspective, there were good reasons to stay the course. First, sanctions are not a quick or efficient tool under the best of circumstances and had been ineffective in the case of North Korea. The Security Council had passed eight sanctions resolutions targeting North Korea's nuclear program after 2006, but China and Russia objected to the strongest sanctions, fearing the regime might collapse. China would then lose one of its last communist allies, a potential blow to the legitimacy of its Communist Party. Beijing also did not want an influx of North Korean refugees or, even worse, a reunited Korea allied with Washington. Moreover, at least forty-nine countries (including several in Europe) had systematically violated UN sanctions since March 2014, circumventing financial sanctions, ignoring bans on imported North Korean goods and minerals, employing North Korean laborers, and assisting in the transport of banned goods (Albright et al., 2017: 5).[15]

Second, Kim may have believed that nuclear weapons were his best bet to prevent Washington from pursuing regime change. If Kim accepted the doctrine of "asymmetric escalation," he might view nuclear weapons as necessary to prevent a U.S. attack. Accordingly, Pyongyang might deter America from attacking by launching a nuclear first strike against U.S. targets bases in Asia, followed by threats to attack an American city. Having thermonuclear-tipped missiles made such threats credible. The danger inherent in this is that, as the weaker country, Kim might also attack quickly to resolve a "use-it-or-lose-it" dilemma.

Finally, Pyongyang's nuclear capability affords potential political benefits by straining U.S. alliances with Japan and/or South Korea should Washington reject diplomacy, or should a crisis erupt that called into question America's military commitments. Currently, Washington provides military guarantees to South Korea and Japan, having installed the THAAD (Terminal High Altitude Area Defense) missile system in South Korea, conducting (separate) military exercises with both countries, and basing significant military forces in the region.

The U.S.-North Korean crisis, however, seemed to dissipate in early 2018, when North and South Korea began talks to ease tensions and the North agreed to participate in the

Winter Olympics in South Korea. Following the Olympics, North Korean officials indicated a willingness to negotiate with Washington. In preparation, Kim traveled to China twice to confer with Xi Jinping, and U.S. officials – including Trump's nominee to replace Tillerson, Mike Pompeo – traveled to Pyongyang to arrange details for a Trump-Kim summit. North Korea then released three American detainees and reportedly destroyed its nuclear testing site at Punggye-ri (although no foreign nuclear experts observed the event). Trump canceled the summit in late May, after North Korean officials called Vice President Mike Pence a "political dummy" and threatened a "nuclear-to-nuclear showdown" following Pence's televised warning that "this will only end like the Libyan model ended [where denuclearization had facilitated Muammar Qaddafi's overthrow in 2011] if Kim Jong Un doesn't make a deal" (cited in Noack, 2018).[16] Within days however, the summit was back on schedule.

The Singapore summit in June 2018 ended with a communiqué pledging to pursue a "lasting and stable peace" and "complete denuclearization of the Korean peninsula". Trump announced afterward that Washington would halt joint military exercises with South Korea (surprising U.S. and South Korean officials) but maintain sanctions until denuclearization was completed. Trump then tweeted that North Korea was "no longer a nuclear threat," but the summit communiqué neither defined "denuclearization" nor described a path to get there.

Critics accused Trump of making unilateral concessions while promoting Kim to a "superpower's peer" and sending a message to others that nuclear weapons might be worth pursuing (Fisher, 2018).[17] Although the threat of nuclear war had receded and Trump continued to exude optimism, National Security Adviser John Bolton declared that Pyongyang had made little progress toward denuclearization in the months after the summit and that Washington would maintain sanctions until it did so. U.S. intelligence revealed Pyongyang's efforts to conceal significant elements of its nuclear program and its continuing development of new missiles. In addition, Secretary Pompeo reiterated that sanctions would be lifted only after "complete denuclearization," while North Korea demanded that the president provide "security guarantees" (notably, a formal treaty to end the Korean War) and "lift sanctions" as negotiations continued (cited in De Young and Wagner, 2018).[18] Kim also demanded that Washington declare a formal end to the Korean War before Pyongyang would provide a written disclosure of its stockpiles of nuclear weapons, its nuclear production facilities and its missiles. South Korea's president diverged from U.S. policy to continue sanctions by offering Pyongyang economic incentives to begin denuclearization.

Washington and Pyongyang were speaking past each other. The Trump administration thought it had a reached a deal requiring for North Korea to begin denuclearizing by taking steps such as providing an accurate accounting of its weapons and beginning to dismantle them. By contrast, Kim viewed the first summit as simply an outline of what might become a deal. A second summit to clarify matters was likely to take place but, at best, the process would be lengthy and might collapse as had past negotiations.

Iran

When Trump was elected, it appeared the Iran deal would challenge the president-elect's nuclear agenda. Trump had been a strident critic of the JCPOA, calling it a "bad deal" which would not prevent Iran from acquiring nuclear weapons in the future. Speaking before the UN General Assembly, he declared: "We cannot abide by an agreement if it provides cover for the eventual construction of a nuclear-weapons program. The Iran deal was one of the worst and most one-sided transactions the United States has ever entered into" (cited in Kahl, 2017).[19]

American hardliners encouraged Trump to decertify Iran's compliance and renounce the deal. Trump floated the idea of resuming negotiations to make those provisions that expire in future years permanent and prohibit Iran from developing ballistic missiles. Israel, which regards Iran as an existential threat, supported this strategy, but Iran declined to revisit the deal's terms. America's European allies also lobbied against decertification and renegotiation. In a speech touted as articulating a new Iran strategy in October 2017, Trump announced his intention to decertify Iran, owing to its "destructive actions," including support for Hezbollah, testing ballistic missiles, and domestic repression.

Trump's decertification was controversial, particularly since IAEA inspectors repeatedly found Iran in compliance. Nonetheless, it initiated an expedited process for Congress to impose sanctions. Consumed with passing a tax bill, Congress did not act on Iran. In January 2018, the administration had two additional opportunities to scrap the deal in the 90-day deadline for certifying Iran's compliance and the requirement that the executive waiver on sanctions be reapplied every 120 days. Trump approved the waiver in mid-January and certified the deal again, but his conditions to do so again were that Iran allow "immediate inspections at all sites requested by international inspectors" and that the limits on the Iran's nuclear activities be made permanent.

With these conditions unmet, Trump withdrew from the JCPOA in May 2018 despite IAEA reports that Iran remained in full compliance. With Washington now widely viewed as violating the agreement, as noted in Chapter 9, the administration announced plans to reinstitute sanctions against Iran and foreign companies doing business in Iran beginning in August 2018 and to tighten sanctions to halt Iranian oil exports by November 2018. In July, Washington rejected calls from the EU to exempt European firms from the sanctions and announced it would only issue waivers for humanitarian or national security reasons. Iran repeatedly called the re-imposition of sanctions illegal (even taking its case to the International Court of Justice in July 2018), but continued to work with Europe, Russia, and China to implement the agreement. The JCPOA Joint Commission met in Vienna in July to discuss a path forward for the remaining parties, but without U.S. participation the JCPOA's future remains unlikely. In the months following America's withdrawal, Iran's economy suffered sharp declines as oil exports fell and the value of its currency plummeted. Popular protests erupted; investors fled; and, facing pressure from hardliners, Rouhani signaled that Iran might disrupt oils shipments through the Strait of Hormuz and/or end cooperation with the IAEA (Dehghan, 2018).[20]

Should Rouhani yield to domestic political pressure and pull Iran out of the JCPOA, its development of nuclear weapons would resume, and its "breakout time" would likely decrease from about one year to two-three months. Additionally, Iran's regional rivals, notably Saudi Arabia and Egypt, might seek their own nuclear weapons, triggering a Middle East arms race. Nevertheless, a few days after threatening war with Iran, Trump offered to meet Rouhani "any time" without "preconditions."

RUSSIA, CHINA AND NUCLEAR MODERNIZATION

Donald Trump has consistently sought to augment America's preeminence as a nuclear power, even if this meant reversing decades of arms control and disarmament. As president-elect, he tweeted in December 2016 that "the United States must greatly strengthen and expand its nuclear capability" (cited in Morello, 2016).[21] This tweet, sent after Vladimir Putin had described Russia's need to modernize its nuclear forces, signaled a possible new arms race.

Much of the administration's first year was devoted to compiling a Nuclear Posture Review (NPR). Every administration since Bill Clinton's has undertaken its own review, although there is no requirement to do so, and the strategies they articulate are not quickly (and sometimes never) put into practice. Nonetheless, the 2018 NPR was much-anticipated as offering a clarification of the administration's nuclear priorities.

Two issues dominated discussions about America's nuclear force during Trump's first year and were highlighted in the NPR: the prospect of continuing the arms reductions in the 2010 New START Treaty and Russia's development of intermediate-range missiles in violation of the INF Treaty. New START went into effect in February 2011 and will expire in 2021, with a possible five-year extension. Both Washington and Moscow met their treaty-mandated reductions by the February 2018 deadline and indicated they would abide by the treaty until it expires. Russian officials, including Putin, unsuccessfully proposed extension talks throughout 2017. In addition, American officials criticized Russia's violations of the INF Treaty. In late 2017, Washington identified Russia's land-based Novator 9M729 cruise missile as the violation. Trump, however, instructed Bolton (who once called New START "unilateral disarmament") to discuss extending the agreement in talks before the 2018 Trump-Putin summit, and Putin suggested extending New START for five years, and for a pitch to "reaffirm commitment" to INF. For its part, Congress approved funding to respond to Russia's violations, including the development of a new U.S. cruise missile in the same class as the 9M729.

The 2018 NPR reversed the post-Cold War emphasis on reducing America's reliance on nuclear weapons and elevated "great power competition" (Russia and China) and deterrence on Washington's national security agenda. "Given the range of potential adversaries, their capabilities and strategic objectives," the NPR "calls for . . . the diverse set of nuclear capabilities that provides an American President flexibility to tailor the approach to deterring one or more potential adversaries in different circumstances" (U.S. Department of Defense, 2018: 2).[22]

Trump's nuclear policy reaffirmed modernization of weapons systems approved by Obama but also called for new weapons like a cruise missile that could be fired from a submarine and then become airborne and low-yield warheads for those missiles. Republicans largely support the proposed upgrades, but critics insisted that low-yield weapons undermine deterrence because they obscure the line between nuclear and non-nuclear weapons, making nuclear war more, not less, likely.

CONCLUSION: NUCLEAR POLICY IN THE TRUMP ERA

Nuclear issues pose significant challenges for the Trump administration. Let us briefly examine Washington's options.

North Korea

Negotiate with North Korea: An objection to relying on negotiations is that they have been unsuccessful in the past. This may be a reason why Washington has been inconsistent in its diplomatic efforts. Before 2018, the State Department and president repeatedly issued conflicting messages about using diplomacy. In October 2017, Trump insisted talks were a waste of time, while Tillerson said diplomacy would continue "until the first bomb drops" (cited in Mohammed and Spetalnick, 2017).[23] In December, Tillerson reached out to Pyongyang, then backtracked shortly after, insisting "North Korea must earn its way back to the table" (cited in Sengupta, 2017).[24] Moreover, progress after the Singapore summit was slow. Trump and Secretary Pompeo, initially described "great progress" and "productive conversation," respectively, while North Korea has accused U.S. officials of "'gangster-like' tactics," and continued violating UN economic sanctions and updating its Yongbyon nuclear research center (Davis and Gladstone, 2018; 38 North, 2018).[25] Consequently, Trump deferred a second meeting with Kim even as South Korean President Moon Jae-in sought closer economic ties with North Korea.

Irreconcilable meanings of "denuclearization" produce mismatched perceptions. Most U.S. analysts believed that North Korea wanted to retain its nuclear weapons. U.S. officials continue to insist that Washington would not accept a nuclear North Korea. They view denuclearization as "a promise to unilaterally disarm," but Pyongyang sees it as "part of a larger package" to be considered after a stable peace and withdrawal of U.S. troops from the peninsula (Taylor, 2018).[26] Trump's unilateral abrogation of the Iranian nuclear deal revealed Washington might be an insincere negotiating partner. Yet, of available options, diplomacy is the one most likely to prevent nuclear war.

Intensify economic sanctions: This continues the status quo, although the sanctions regime has been difficult to implement, as described above, and increasing sanctions may be counterproductive as long as Pyongyang is willing to negotiate. For now, there is no reason to believe that additional sanctions will compel North Korea to denuclearize.

Press China harder to coerce Pyongyang: This would be difficult to accomplish even if Beijing agreed, because China no longer has the influence it once enjoyed with Pyongyang. Beijing may not want a nuclear North Korea, but, especially after the imposition of U.S. tariffs on China, they are unlikely to enforce sanctions rigorously. Moreover, Beijing and Washington have incompatible perspectives regarding this process. Washington insists on denuclearization as the starting point. Beijing, like North Korea, sees denuclearization as the outcome.

Use military force to compel Pyongyang to denuclearize: Although this option is less likely since the Singapore summit, it remains a dangerous option. Several events in early 2018 suggested that the Trump administration might be preparing to use force, including deployment of additional long-range bombers and naval vessels in the region.

Washington had earlier considered a "bloody nose" strategy that would entail responding to a North Korean nuclear or missile test with a limited attack on a North Korean facility. A military response, however limited, is risky. North Korea has massive conventional artillery within range of Seoul, South Korea's capital, which could cause innumerable casualties, including U.S. service personnel stationed near the demilitarized zone that separates the two Koreas. Pyongyang also has missiles capable of reaching America. Even the expectation of a U.S. attack might prompt North Korea to "lob a nuclear weapon at South Korea or Japan as a last, desperate act – or detonate it on North Korean territory to make occupation impossible" (cited in Sanger, 2017).[27]

How might China react should war occur? China's President Xi has promised that its mutual defense pact with North Korea would not apply if Pyongyang initiated a war, and U.S. and Chinese officials have discussed their mutual interests should such a war occur. However, what would happen if Washington were viewed as the aggressor? The possibility of Chinese intervention to aid North Korea and the larger war that would ensue cannot be discounted. Finally, even a costly war is unlikely to end permanently North Korea's nuclear threat. Past experience in Iraq, for example, suggests that preventive military strikes to eliminate a foe's nuclear program may only fuel its nuclear aspirations.

Accept a nuclear North Korea and practice deterrence: This option is antithetical to Trump's rhetoric, although it is not clear that any option can succeed in denuclearizing North Korea. There are two dangers in this option. First, if North Korea were more willing to use its nuclear weapons and if Kim were less rational than other leaders, the danger of nuclear war would increase dramatically. Second, North Korea's proliferation could easily spark proliferation in South Korea and/or Japan. Both countries have peaceful nuclear power programs that could be weaponized quickly, and there is some support in both for developing a nuclear deterrent, although at present there is not enough support to proceed. That might change if Washington accepted North Korea as a nuclear power.

Iran

Demand renegotiation of the nuclear deal: While Trump has talked about negotiating a better deal, most governments involved, including Iran, are not interested in renegotiating a deal they believe is successfully preventing Iran's proliferation. The administration has left little room for Iran to negotiate. Its demands include, in part, full disclosure of Iran's past nuclear activities, a permanent halt to all uranium enrichment and no plutonium reprocessing, "unqualified" IAEA "access to all sites throughout the country," ending all ballistic missile activities and support for terrorism and "militant partners" like Hezbollah (cited in Pompeo, 2018).[28] It may be difficult to get the remaining JCPOA partners back to the table with such rigid terms, and Washington's sanctions policy only reinforces this problem. In July 2018 Presidents Trump and Rouhani exchanged threats of war between their two countries.

Reinstitute painful economic sanctions: This scenario, pursued by Washington after withdrawing from the JCPOA, is risky. Sanctions take time and require widespread participation, and other JCPOA partners are reluctant to renew sanctions. Washington's threat to extend sanctions to governments and firms that trade with Iran alienates allies while squeezing Iran. Aggressive sanctions also risk undermining Iranian moderates. One reformist politician in Iran observed, if "Western countries . . . put too much pressure on Iran, it could unleash radical Shia forces and trigger a new wave of Islamic radicalism" (cited in Bozorgmehr, 2018).[29] Some U.S. sanctions were re-imposed by the Trump administration in August 2018 and others in November.

Nuclear Modernization

Abandon nuclear modernization: Washington is unlikely to select this option because all nuclear-weapons states are modernizing their forces and continue to emphasize nuclear deterrence. America has been slow to modernize its weapons, and, if Washington's capability is perceived to be declining, the credibility of U.S. deterrence would also decline. It could also cost more in the long run to maintain aging weapons and delivery systems than replace them with more efficient systems.

Pursue aggressive modernization: Congress has already approved several modernization projects, but the 2018 Nuclear Posture Review promises still more aggressive modernization. Aggressive modernization, however, can spark arms races and undermine other goals, including non-proliferation. Modernization signals to countries like North Korea that nuclear weapons are necessary for security.

Negotiate a five-year extension to the New START Treaty: New START offers many benefits that would be lost if it expires without a replacement. Washington would be allowed to increase its nuclear arsenal without limits if that occurred, but so would Russia. Indeed, there would be no mechanism in place to monitor the size or composition of Russia's nuclear forces. Resulting mutual mistrust would likely lead to an expensive and dangerous nuclear arms race.

Negotiate multilateral arms control and disarmament agreements: Most major arms control and disarmament agreements are bilateral U.S.-Russian agreements, but China, UK, France, India, and Pakistan are largely unconstrained if they wish to increase their arsenal or modernize their forces. Washington might be in a better position to persuade Russia to abandon its INF violations as part of a multilateral effort to prevent all countries from developing intermediate-range missiles. However, Trump dislikes multilateralism and prefers bilateral arrangements.

In sum, U.S. nuclear strategy poses difficult choices. Whichever option the Trump administration makes regarding the challenges we have discussed will have profound consequences for global peace and stability.

ESSAY QUESTIONS

1) Describe U.S. nuclear policy during the Cold War and discuss how it has evolved in the years after the Cold War.

2) What are the key issues in U.S. nuclear policy today? What challenges do they pose?

3) How have U.S. policies toward Iran's nuclear program evolved? How are President Trump's policies similar or different to those of his predecessors?

4) How have U.S. policies toward North Korea's nuclear program evolved? How are President Trump's policies similar or different to those of his predecessors?

5) Discuss the arguments for and against modernizing the US nuclear arsenal. Which option has the Trump administration pursued and why?

SHORT ANSWER QUESTIONS

Define and describe the importance of the following:

Six-Party Talks
P5+1
Joint Comprehensive Plan of Action (JCPOA)
New START
INF Treaty

NOTES

1 Fifield, A. (2018). First Hawaii, Now Japan Sends a False Alarm about Incoming North Korean Missile. *Washington Post* [online]. Available at: www.washingtonpost.com/world/asia_pacific/first-hawaii-now-japan-sends-a-false-alarm-about-incoming-north-korean-missile/2018/01/16/d8961ef4-fac1–11e7-b832–8c26844b74fb_story.html [Accessed 25 Jan 2018].
2 The White House, Office of the Press Secretary (2009). Remarks by President Barack Obama in Prague as Delivered. Available at: https://obamawhitehouse.archives.gov/the-press-office/remarks-president-barack-obama-prague-delivered [Accessed 25 Jan 2018].
3 U.S. Department of Defense (2010). Nuclear Posture Review Report. Available at: https://dod.defense.gov/Portals/1/features/defenseReviews/NPR/2010_Nuclear_Posture_Review_Report.pdf [Accessed 9 Nov 2018].
4 Brown, R. (2015). *Nuclear Authority: The IAEA and the absolute weapon* Washington, D.C.: Georgetown University Press.
5 BBC (2010). U.N. Sanctions against Iran. *BBC News* [online]. Available at: www.bbc.com/news/world-middle-east-10768146 [Accessed 27 Jan 2018].
6 Davenport, K. (2017). Understanding the US Compliance Certification and Why It Matters to the Iran Nuclear Deal. *Arms Control Now*. Available at: www.armscontrol.org/blog/2017-08-29/understanding-us-compliance-certification-why-matters-iran-nuclear-deal [Accessed 27 Jan 2018].
7 Paltrow, S. (2017). Special report: In modernizing nuclear arsenal, U.S. stokes new arms race. *Reuters* [online]. Available at: www.reuters.com/article/us-usa-nuclear-modernize-specialreport/special-report-in-modernizing-nuclear-arsenal-u-s-stokes-new-arms-race-idUSKBN1DL1AH [Accessed 31 Jan 2018].
8 Kristensen, H. (2017). Russian Nuclear Forces: Buildup or modernization? *Russia Matters*. Available at: www.russiamatters.org/analysis/russian-nuclear-forces-buildup-or-modernization [Accessed 31 Jan 2018].
9 Reuters (2017). U.S. Nuclear Arsenal to Cost $1.2 Trillion Over Next 30 Years: CBO. *Reuters* [online]. Available at: www.reuters.com/article/us-usa-nuclear-arsenal/u-s-nuclear-arsenal-to-cost-1-2-trillion-over-next-30-years-cbo-idUSKBN1D030E [Accessed 31 Jan 2018].
10 Otto, B., Watts, J., and Fassihi, F. (2017). North Korea Says it Would Use Nukes Only Against U.S. *Wall Street Journal* [online]. Available at: www.wsj.com/articles/no-north-korea-talks-while-missiles-are-flying-tillerson-says-1502084784 [Accessed 30 Jan 2018].
11 Thrus, G. and Baker, P. (2017). Trump's Threat to North Korea Was Improvised. *New York Times* [online]. Available at: www.nytimes.com/2017/08/09/us/politics/trump-north-korea.html [Accessed 31 Jan 2018].
12 Baker, P. and Harris, G. (2017). Deep Divisions in Trump Administration as North Korea Threatens War. *New York Times* [online]. Available at: www.nytimes.com/2017/08/09/us/politics/north-korea-nuclear-threat-rex-tillerson.html [Accessed 31 Jan 2018].
13 Mattis, J. and Tillerson, R. (2017). 'We're Holding Pyongyang to Account,' *Wall Street Journal* [online] Available at: www.wsj.com/articles/were-holding-pyongyang-to-account-150266025 [Accessed 31 Jan 2018].
14 Broad, W. (2017). North Korea Will Have the Skills to Make a Nuclear Warhead by 2020, experts say. *New York Times* [online]. Available at: www.nytimes.com/2016/09/10/science/north-korea-nuclear-weapons.html [Accessed 31 Jan 2018].
15 Albright, D., Burkhard, S., Lach, A., and Stricker, A. (2017). Countries Involved in Violating UNSC Resolutions on North Korea. Institute for Science and International Security. Available at: http://isis-online.org/uploads/isis-reports/documents/Countries_Involved_in_Violating_NK_UNSC_Resolutions_5Dec2017_Final.pdf [Accessed 19 Dec 2017].
16 Noack, R. (2018). How Kim-Trump Tensions Escalated: The more the U.S. said 'Libya,' the angrier North Korea got. *Washington Post* [online]. Available at: www.washingtonpost.com/news/world/wp/2018/05/24/the-more-pence-and-trump-say-libya-the-angrier-north-korea-gets. [Accessed 16 Jul 2018].
17 Fisher, M. (2018). What Happened in the Trump-Kim Meeting and Why it Matters. *New York Times* [online]. Available at: www.nytimes.com/2018/06/12/world/asia/trump-kim-meeting-interpreter.html [Accessed 18 Jul 2018].

18 De Young, K. and Wagner, J. (2018) Trump and Kim Declare Summit a Big Success, But They Diverge on the Details. *Washington Post* [online]: Available at: www.washingtonpost. com/politics/trump-says-korth-korea-no-longer-a-nuclear-threat-as-he-returns-to-washington/ 2018/06/13/b1d69566-6ef0-11e8-bf86-a2351b5ece99_story.html [Accessed 11 Aug 2018].

19 Kahl, C. (2017). The Myth of a 'Better' Iran Deal. *Foreign Policy* [online]. Available at: http://foreignpolicy.com/2017/09/26/the-myth-of-a-better-iran-deal [Accessed 3 Feb 2018].

20 Dehghan, S. (2018). Iran Threatens to Block Strait of Hormuz Over US Oil Sanctions. *The Guardian* [online]. Available at: www.theguardian.com/world/2018/jul/05/iran-retaliate-us-oil-threats-eu-visit-hassan-rouhani-trump [Accessed 20 Nov 2018].

21 Morello, C. (2016). Trump Says He Wants to 'Greatly Strengthen and Expand' U.S. Nuclear Capability. *Washington Post* [online]. Available at: www.washingtonpost.com/world/ national-security/donald-trump-says-he-wants-to-greatly-strengthen-and-expand-us-nuclear-capabilitiy-a-radical-break-from-us-foreign-policy/2016/12/22/52745c22-c86e-11e6-85b5-76616a33048d_story.html [Accessed 25 Jan 2018].

22 U.S. Department of Defense (2018). Nuclear Posture Review February 2018. Available at: https://thebulletin.org/sites/default/files/2018-NUCLEAR-POSTURE-REVIEW-FINAL-REPORT.PDF [Accessed 5 Feb 2018].

23 Mohammed, A. and Spetalnick, M. (2017). Exclusive: U.S. pursues direct diplomacy with North Korea despite Trump rejection. *Reuters* [online] Available at: www.reuters.com/ article/us-northkorea-missiles-usa-exclusive/exclusive-u-s-pursues-direct-diplomacy-with-north-korea-despite-trump-rejection-idUSKBN1D136I [Accessed 7 Feb 2018].

24 Sengupta, S. (2017). Tillerson in Apparent U-Turn, Says North Korea Must 'Earn' Its Way to Talks. *New York Times* [online]. Available at: www.nytimes.com/2017/12/15/world/asia/ tillerson-north-korea.html [Accessed 8 Feb 2017].

25 Davis, J. and Gladstone, R. (2018. Trump Cites 'Great Progress' in North Korean Nuclear Talks. *New York Times* [online]. Available at: www.nytimes.com/2018/07/12/world/asia/ north-korea-kim-jong-un-trump-letter-nuclear.html [Accessed 18 Jul 2018]; *38 North* (2018). North Korea's Yongbyon Nuclear Research Center: Testing of reactor cooling systems; construction of two new non-industrial buildings. Available at: www.38north.org/2018/07/ yongbyon070618 [Accessed 18 Jul 2018].

26 Taylor, A. (2018). North Korea May Have Offered its Clearest View Yet of Denuclearization. *Washington Post* [online]. Available at: www.washingtonpost.com/world/asia_pacific/north-korea-may-have-offered-its-clearest-view-yet-of-denuclearization/2018/07/08/4129e386-8246-11e8-9200-b4dee4fb4e28_story.html [Accessed 10 Jul 2018].

27 Sanger, D. (2017). A Tillerson Slip Offers a Peek Into Secret Planning on North Korea. *New York Times* [online]. Available at: www.nytimes.com/2017/12/17/us/politics/tillerson-north-korea-china.html [Accessed 19 Dec 2017].

28 Pompeo, M. (2018). After the Deal: A New Iran Strategy. U.S. Department of State [online]. Available at: www.state.gov/secretary/remarks/2018/05/282301.htm [Accessed 11 Jul 2018].

29 Bozorgmehr, N. (2018). Trump Sanctions Bolster Influence of Iran's Revolutionary Guards. *Financial Times* [online]. Available at: www.ft.com/content/81b4e9d4-89dd-11e8-b18d-0181731a0340 [Accessed 19 Jul 2018].

SUGGESTED READINGS

Bracken, P. (2013). *The Second Nuclear Age: Strategy, danger, and the new power politics.* New York, NY: St. Martin's Griffin.

Roberts, B. (2016). *The Case for US Nuclear Weapons in the 21st Century.* Stanford, CA: Stanford University Press.

11 America's energy transition and the global environment: Paradigm shift and policy challenges

Yu Wang

INTRODUCTION

America's energy usage and sources constitute a major factor in the global environment. Its energy sources have consistently evolved in response to technological and market changes. The growing reliance on natural gas, the concern with coal – among the highest polluting fossil fuels – and growing use of renewable energy constitute recent trends in U.S. energy usage policy. The shale gas boom and the reduction in renewable energy costs have played a major role in driving this trend. If these trends continue, they will lead to cleaner energy systems and a reduction in greenhouse gas emissions, commitments made by the Obama administration in the face of the existential common challenge of climate change.

However, President Donald Trump and his administration have tried to reverse these trends and foster climate-change denial. The revival of coal, however, is harming the oil and gas industries, which Trump also sought to aid. Trump had received generous campaign contributions from the fossil fuel industry during the 2016 campaign, and, as president, he has devoted substantial efforts to fulfill his promises of reviving America's coal industry and exporting U.S. fossil fuels abroad. Trump appointed Scott Pruitt (who was later forced to resigned owing to charges of corruption), a climate-change skeptic, to head the Environmental Protection Agency (EPA).

Early in his administration, Trump labeled climate change a "hoax," and announced America's withdrawal from the 2015 Paris Climate Accord. In January 2018, he imposed a 30 percent tariff on imported solar cells and modules during the first year, which would decline to 15 percent by the fourth year. This action will increase domestic energy prices, slow America's transition to solar energy, and harm America's own solar industry, which relies on imports, despite U.S. trade representative Robert Lighthizer's claim that such imports "are a substantial cause of serious injury to domestic manufacturers." Among those protesting the tariffs to the World Trade Organization are China, Taiwan, and U.S. allies in the European Union (EU).

Although environmental issues are seldom a decisive factor in presidential elections, the Trump administration's changes in energy policy reflect the prevalence of protectionism and national populism in American society. Trump's energy policies also reflect the Republican Party's opposition to government regulations and its desire for smaller government and "energy independence." Thus, Trump supporters tend to support greater fossil fuel production (onshore and offshore) and the use of alternative energy sources to secure reliable sources of energy. They believe that environmental regulation and emissions control impede economic growth and destroy jobs.

By contrast, Trump's Democratic opponents support environmental regulation and emission controls to slow climate change and promote economic growth. Thus, they oppose continued fossil fuel development and support "green" energy sources. Differences between the two parties on these issues have been growing, as reflected by voting in Congress on environmental issues (McCright and Dunlap, 2011).[1] In recent years, members of the House and Senate have become increasingly likely to vote along partisan lines on such issues, with a significant decline in Republican support for environmental policies. President Trump believes that expanding the use of "beautiful, clean coal" will bring back jobs in coal mining and that rescinding the Clean Power Plan will reduce costs for new (and old) power plants. Such claims appeal to those in states like West Virginia where economic growth and many jobs have long depended on coal mining and where environmental and energy regulations have become popular villains.

This chapter analyzes recent trends in and policies regarding the American energy market. The chapter examines the important energy issues and summarizes them. Five major factors are involved: (1) production of oil and gas and energy security, (2) coal production and environmental regulations, (3) declining costs of renewable energy, (4) energy efficiency, and (5) America's influence in multilateral climate negotiations. We will discuss major trends involved in each, and Trump's policies regarding them.

ENERGY SECURITY

In this environment, the Trump administration's energy policy stresses changing environmental regulations, expanding fossil fuel production, and bringing home manufacturing and mining jobs. To what extent will these priorities alter America's energy system and move that system in a new direction? Here, we review the policy shift and assess the potential impact of these changes on issues related to energy security, fossil fuel, renewable energy, and energy efficiency in the U.S. To place these changes in a larger context and assess their effect on the global energy market, we also draw some comparisons with other countries.

Since the late 1960s and early 1970s, the United States has been an oil importing country, dependent on crude oil produced overseas (Yergin, 2006),[2] but in recent decades, it has become self-sufficient and even an oil exporter. The source of this change is the emergence of hydro-fracking technologies to extract crude oil and natural gas from shale. According to data from the Energy Information Administration (EIA), America's total fossil fuel production increased 13 percent between 2006 and 2016 (Figure 11.1). Crude oil production, for instance, has increased by 72 percent during the past decade. Domestic consumption of oil, however, has remained flat. The production of dry natural gas has grown by 45 percent. Because of its rapid growth, natural gas has now become the principal energy source for America's economy. Since natural gas emits less carbon than other fossil fuels, it also has come to serve as a "bridge" fuel for the eventual transition to other energy sources.

The United States has recently made another important change involving fossil fuels. In recent decades, Washington banned the export of U.S. crude oil, but in 2016, Congress lifted the ban as the shale gas/oil boom grew. The U.S. thus became a net oil exporter and,

FIGURE 11.1 United States energy production by source

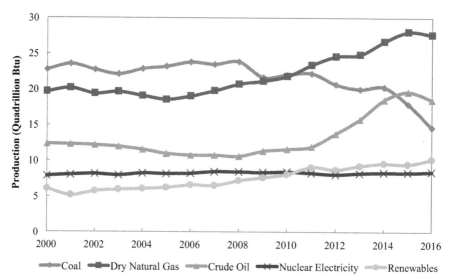

Source: Data from Energy Information Administration (2018) *Monthly Energy Review*, Table 1.2

FIGURE 11.2 United States natural gas retail price by sector

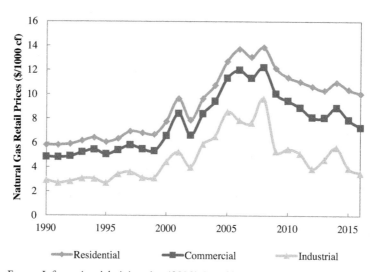

Source: Data from Energy Information Administration (2018) *Monthly Energy Review*, Table 9.10

in 2016, exported 10.0 quadrillion Btu of crude oil and petroleum, a dramatic 283 percent increase from 2006. The EIA now predicts that U.S. fossil fuel production will reach record levels in the coming years (U.S. EIA, 2018).[3]

Increased production of these fuels also produced fluctuating prices. Figure 11.2 describes the retail cost of natural gas from 1990–2016 for residential, commercial, and industrial customers. While natural gas prices increased for all of these customers during the first decade and a half of this period, the retail price for each declined significantly after 2010 owing to increased gas production. The price decline is even more striking if prices are adjusted for inflation. Retail prices for gasoline experienced a similar decline in recent years. The EIA predicts oil and gas prices will remain mostly "flat" for the near future.

Importantly, production increases and price reductions contribute to the security and stability of America's energy supply. We can assess energy security along four dimensions: availability, affordability, efficiency, and environmental stewardship (Knox-Hayes et al., 2013; Sovacol and Brown, 2010; Brown et al., 2014).[4] Based on the four dimensions, energy security in the U.S. has improved greatly since 2010. Table 11.1 demonstrates the changes in these energy security indicators since 2010. The fuel economy for on-road vehicles has increased by 2.3 percent, meaning vehicles travel more miles for every gallon of fuel used. The other indicators show improvement when their absolute value is lower in 2016 or the relative change is negative. For the past six years, energy security has improved significantly on all four dimensions. The availability dimension has improved the most; dependence on oil and gas imports has declined, and the transportation sector now depends less on petroleum. The International Energy Agency (2018)[5] judges that total U.S. energy self-sufficiency has increased from 78 percent in 2010 to 92 percent in 2015.

Fuel affordability has also improved for customers, as reflected by price indicators for electricity and gasoline. The average retail price for gasoline (all grades, including tax) decreased from $2.84 gallon in 2010 to $2.47 gallon in 2016 (although they began to rise in 2018). The average nominal retail price for electricity for all customers increased only slightly. Real electricity prices have actually declined when they are adjusted for inflation, and where prices are normalized to a 2005 dollar for comparison (Table 11.1). Although

TABLE 11.1 ENERGY SECURITY INDEX FOR THE U.S.*

DIMENSION	INDICATOR**	2010	2016***	RELATIVE CHANGE
Availability	Oil import dependence (%)	48.60%	24.40%	–49.8%
	Petroleum transport fuels (%)	93.10%	91.87%	–1.3%
	Natural gas import dependence (%)	10.80%	3.50%	–67.6%
Affordability	Retail electricity prices (¢/kWh)	8.65	8.27	–4.4%
	Retail gasoline prices ($/gallon)	2.50	1.99	–20.4%
Efficiency	On-road fuel economy (mile/gallon)	21.5	22.0	2.3%
	Energy intensity (thousand Btu/$)	6.0	5.2	–13.3%
	Electricity use (MWh/capita)	13.37	12.83	–4.0%
Environmental stewardship	Sulfur dioxide (SO_2) emissions (million tons)	6.8	4.7	–30.9%
	Carbon dioxide (CO_2) emissions (million tons)	5,637	5,269	–6.5%

*Data sources include the EIA's Monthly Energy Review, the Environmental Protection Agency (EPA)'s *National Emission Inventory*, and the Bureau of Transportation Statistics' *National Transportation Statistics*.

**All monetary values are normalized to 2005 dollars.

***Natural gas import, energy intensity, and CO_2 emissions are for 2015; SO_2 emissions are for 2014.

indicators are not included in this analysis, the prices for other fuels also experienced declines, suggesting once again that energy is more affordable to consumers today.

Energy usage is now more efficient and cleaner as reflected by a variety of measures as well. The on-road fuel economy for light-duty vehicles (gross vehicle weight of less than 8,500 pounds), for instance, has improved by 2.3 percent owing to improved cooperative average fuel economy (CAFE) standards. Per capita electricity usage across the U.S. has decreased by 4 percent. Increased efficiency in buildings, improved fuel economy for vehicles, and changes in industry structure are primarily responsible for the decrease in energy intensity. Overall, owing to these changes and improved supply-side technologies, emissions of carbon dioxide (CO_2) and sulfur dioxide (SO_2) were lower in 2016.

In sum, energy consumption in the United States has been flat since 2000, despite economic and population growth. Increases in fuel production during the past decade have largely been used to increase fuel exports. In addition, analysts project that domestic energy demand will grow slowly in the future, and Washington is encouraging exports of crude oil and natural gas in the future. In this sense, exports will likely be an important driver of greater fuel production. The economic benefits of these fossil fuel exports for the U.S. will be significant and will benefit other large energy-consuming countries. At the same time, however, the United States should be concerned by the impact of these exports on increasing emissions of global greenhouse gases (GHG).

COAL RETIREMENT AND ENVIRONMENTAL REGULATIONS

Coal had been America's leading source of energy until natural gas and crude oil surpassed it in 2011 and 2015 respectively. In fact, total coal production has decreased by over 38 percent since 2010. With such a reduction in coal production and increased use of natural gas, utility companies retired a significant number of coal-fired power plants between 2012 and 2017. In 2015 alone, more than 80 percent of retired generation capacity for electricity was attributable to coal. The EIA's Annual Energy Outlook projects that the reduction of coal-fired electricity generation will be 64 gigawatts in the next decade, that is, about a quarter of America's current coal power generating capacity.

The coal-fired units that have been retired are mostly older and smaller facilities. Natural gas is replacing some of the units that are being retired, while others are being closed because they do not comply with the EPA's Mercury and Air Toxics Standards (MATS). These impose emission limits on toxic air pollutants like mercury, arsenic, and metals from coal and oil-fired power plants. Older coal plants have high heat rates, and they do not have flue gas desulfurization systems to address these toxins. The older plants are closed largely because installation of the necessary technologies to control toxins is expensive and/or the older plants cannot utilize them. Even without the need for compliance with environmental regulations, older and less efficient coal generators cannot compete with those using natural gas. The trend seems irreversible. More coal plants and coalmines will cease production and some nuclear plants may be decommissioned as well. According to the EIA, most of the new generating capacity planned by utilities involves natural gas and renewables.

The closing of coal-fired power plants reflect the Clean Power Plan (CPP, see below), introduced by the Obama administration. Under the CPP, which the earlier Clean Air Act, section 111(d) made possible, coal and natural gas power plants must limit the emissions of carbon dioxide. The implementation of these standards are flexible. States were allowed to set their own targets and utilities allowed to choose from a variety of supply-side and demand-side options to meet them. Several states have already developed plans and strategies to decarbonize electricity generation in compliance with the CPP. For example, Iowa has developed an "Iowa Energy Plan" by involving stakeholder groups to encourage sector growth and sustainability. However, the Obama administration's CPP quickly became a focus of political and legal controversy. Energy companies and twenty-eight states filed lawsuits against it, arguing that the EPA did not have the authority to regulate a state's carbon emissions. The Supreme Court stayed the implementation of the regulation in February 2016 by a 5–4 decision, with the justices voting largely along ideological lines.

Once in office, the Trump administration moved quickly to seek a repeal of MATS and rescind the CPP, arguing that these standards harmed America's economy. In April 2016, the EPA had published a Supplemental Finding, concluding that MATS is a "necessary" regulation. A year later, under Trump, the EPA asked the Supreme Court to delay oral arguments involving the Supplemental Finding, but the Washington Circuit Court of Appeals rejected the request. However, the administration's other efforts to deregulate energy were more successful. Thus, President Trump revoked the Stream Protection Rule, which had prevented mountaintop mining operations near waterways. He also reversed the Obama executive order to protect oceans after the disastrous 2010 Deepwater Horizon oil spill. Trump also lifted the ban on coal mining on federally owned land, which is the source of some two fifths of coal mined in the U.S.

Trump's EPA also took steps to repeal Obama-era regulations limiting carbon emissions – the Clean Power Plan. That regulation sought to reduce the level of U.S. carbon emissions by 32 percent by 2030 compared to 2005 levels. The plan sought to achieve this largely by reducing emissions from coal-burning power plants. In August 2018, however, the Trump administration endorsed a plan designed by the EPA's top air pollution official, William Wehrum, to weaken the Clean Air Act. Wehrum is an attorney who had represented members of the coal-burning trade association, and the change will benefit his former clients (Lipton, 2018).[6] In addition, Trump proposed to let individual states decide how or even whether, to reduce carbon dioxide emissions from coal-fired plants or retire old coal-fired power plants, a development that threatens to release twelve times the amount of CO_2 into the atmosphere within a decade, compared with the Obama rule (Eilperin, 2018).[7]

The Trump administration's effort to reduce environmental regulations also influenced rules governing oil and gas production. In late 2017, the Bureau of Land Management (BLM) rescinded a rule requiring disclosure of the chemicals used in fracking on federal and Indian lands. The BLM also suspended the Methane Waste Prevention Rule that was designed to reduce methane[8] waste in oil and gas production by restricting flaring, venting, and leakage. In June 2017, the EPA also proposed suspending its Oil and Gas Methane 111(b) rule, which targets methane leakage and emissions from oil and gas fracking and transportation. However, the D.C. Circuit Court of Appeals rejected this. In March 2018, the EPA published a final amendment to the rule allowing leaks to go unrepaired during unscheduled or emergency shutdowns, arguing that repairing them could lead to service disruptions. Scientists announced a year later that methane emissions from oil and gas production were 60 percent higher than EPA estimates (Schwartz and Plumer, 2018).[9] Overall, observers estimate that the Trump administration has challenged some forty-four environmental regulations, including rules for pollution control, energy efficiency, renewable energy, and fossil fuel production (Environmental Law at Harvard, 2018).[10]

The EPA under the Trump administration has also taken initial steps toward eliminating the CPP, but environmental groups and state attorneys general have threatened legal action if the EPA ultimately rescinds it. Even if the administration succeeds in overturning the CPP, several major U.S. cities and states are seeking ways to cut their own carbon emissions despite Washington, and may enact their own plans.

RENEWABLE ENERGY

Renewables are another important emerging source of energy. The recent shale gas/oil boom places additional pressure on the development of renewable energy, but it has not halted its development. Low oil and natural gas prices would make renewables economically less attractive for large-scale investment. Nevertheless, renewables are becoming less expensive than before, and total renewable energy production increased 55 percent between 2010 and 2016 (Figure 11.1).

Figure 11.3 illustrates America's energy production from renewable sources between 2000 and 2016. Biomass, which releases energy by burning living or recently living organic material, produces biofuels. It is America's largest source of renewable energy. Although less significant at present than biomass, energy from wind has grown almost seven times, and solar energy provides roughly eight times more energy than it did a decade ago. Recent declines in the cost of renewables and the growing number of consumers seeking "green" electricity have sparked the growing production of renewables. Environmentally conscious consumer groups have expressed a strong preference for "green" electricity (Conte and

FIGURE 11.3 United States energy production from renewable sources

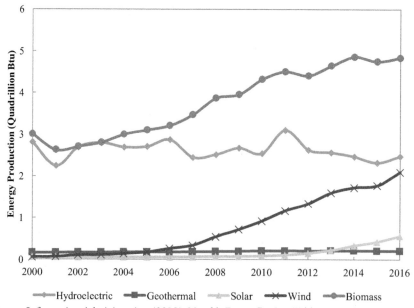

Data from Energy Information Administration (2018) *Monthly Energy Review*, Table 1.2

Jacobsen 2016, and Gerlach and Zheng, 2018)[11] and are willing to pay higher prices for power produced from renewable sources (Xie and Zhao, 2018).[12]

There is still resistance to renewable energy sources. There are, for example, objections to wind energy. NIMBY (not in my backyard) remains an objection to wind turbines, despite the disagreement over its impact among scholars (Petrova, 2016; Esaiasson, 2014).[13] Those individuals and groups that oppose wind projects do so because of sound and visual impact of turbines, and issues related to fairness, participation, and trust (Rand and Hoen, 2017).[14] Still, acceptance of wind technology is consistently higher in North America than elsewhere (Rand and Hoen, 2017).[14]

Financial incentives provided by the government contribute to the growth of renewable energy. The production tax credit (PTC) and investment tax credit (ITC) provided by Washington have had a significant positive impact on the development of wind and solar power. During the past decade, these incentives have expired from time to time, and they require continuous extension to be effective. One analysis has shown that newly installed wind capacity was near zero during years when the PTC had expired (Union of Concerned Scientists, 2015).[15] The high level of regulatory uncertainty is a significant market barrier to the development of renewables (Brown and Sovacool, 2011).[16] In December 2015, Congress passed a multiyear extension of the PTC for renewable electricity. The phase-down plan will cut the PTC by 60 percent in 2019. The multiyear PTC greatly reduces market risks for wind development, but, as the expiration approaches, the industry is uncertain about its future after 2019.

The Trump administration has provided a "dangerous" signal for the future by imposing a 30 percent tariff on imported solar panels. Solar industry analysts predict that this tariff will slow down the development of the industry by 11 percent through 2022 (Piper, 2018).[17] Thus, as the Trump administration's focus has shifted to fossil fuel production, the future trajectory of renewable electricity looks more uncertain.

Many of these problems affect the development of alternative transport fuels. The Renewable Fuel Standard (RFS) has been the most important driver for the growth of bioethanol and biodiesel production in the U.S. Since 2015, the regulation caps corn ethanol at 15 billion gallons, which constitute about 10 percent of gasoline consumption. Cellulosic biofuel from grasses and other plants can provide greater emission reduction than corn ethanol, and the RFS target for cellulosic biofuel increases to 16 billion gallons by 2022. Unfortunately, the EPA announces annual adjustments to this mandate, and it has repeatedly cut the mandatory volume for cellulosic biofuel. Without strong policy support, bio-refineries producing advanced biofuels frequently face financial problems that threaten their survival. For example, for these very reasons, one of the largest cellulosic ethanol plants, the DuPont ethanol plant in Nevada, Iowa, closed in November 2017. It is still unclear how the Trump administration is going to address the problem. What will happen to the biofuel industry after 2022 when the RFS ends?

Currently, the RFS has many critics owing to dissatisfaction on both sides of the issue. Opponents believe that the current ethanol-blending rate of 10 percent is already too high for the existing infrastructure to cope with. Biofuel advocates, however, believe that the regulation is inadequate because the mandatory requirement for advanced biofuels is too low. Experts appeal for a reform of the standard, but the Trump administration has done nothing to date because it has focused its attention on the battle over fossil fuel production. Thus, developing renewable energy and assisting society in transitioning to a renewable, low-emission energy system remain challenges for present or future administrations.

ENERGY EFFICIENCY

The efficiency of energy use by the U.S. economy has improved greatly as energy intensity decreased by 13.3 percent between 2010 and 2016 (Table 11.1). The market for energy efficiency has grown quickly as customer incentive programs increased from $3.2 billion in 2010 to $7.6 billion in 2016 (Berg et al., 2017).[18] A ratepayer-funded efficiency program can save significant amounts on electricity and natural gas for both residential and non-residential customers. Economic considerations and pro-environment behavior by individuals, cities, states, and countries are the principal drivers of improvements in energy efficiency. Adopting efficiency measures not only results in energy and cost savings, but also improves the comfort level of occupants (Zhao et al., 2016).[19] Energy customers come to value more efficient products, and buildings and homes that achieve efficient energy performance labels. And "green certificates" produce higher prices for homes and offices in today's real estate markets (Zhang et al., 2017).[20]

Although some analysts argue that expanding fossil fuel production will create additional jobs, the reality is that the clean energy industry creates more new jobs than does the fossil fuel industry (U.S. Department of Energy (DOE), 2017).[21] The U.S. Energy Employment Report finds that 467,648 jobs are in the mining and extraction industry (oil, gas, coal, and nuclear fuel stock), while the electricity power sector employs 1.9 million workers. About 800,000 of those jobs are associated with low-carbon-emission technologies (renewables, nuclear, and advanced natural gas). In total, the energy efficiency industry employed 2.2 million Americans in 2016, with renewables and energy efficiency industries as the biggest contributors to these new jobs (U.S. DOE, 2017).[21] The creation of jobs in industries that are innovative and environmentally beneficial is desirable and attractive in today's economy.

Nevertheless, the Trump administration has signaled its intent to roll back several energy efficiency policies, including the fuel economy standard for vehicles (both light- and heavy-duty vehicles), and appliance standards for air-conditioners and other products. An administration effort to cancel the planned penalty increases for violating the fuel economy standards was halted by the second Circuit Court of Appeals in April 2018. The Trump administration's putative purpose is to meet an "increasing demand for larger, low-efficiency vehicles." However, observers have repeatedly questioned the "benefits" of reducing current standards, because energy efficiency is actually an inexpensive option that saves consumers money because it saves energy and postpones expensive investments in new centralized power plants (Wang and Brown, 2014).[22]

What the Trump administration chooses to do also influences the policies of states, cities, local governments, and other countries. Some states have already begun to respond to the signals from Washington. Iowa for example, has proposed bills to cut the efficiency program to the "right size" by removing rebates provided to customers for adopting efficient appliances. Not all utilities support efforts to roll back customer efficiency programs. Large investor-owned utilities like MidAmerican Energy, a subsidiary of Berkshire Hathaway Energy, do not support Iowa's bill. After many years of practice, this utility has incorporated energy efficiency into its business model and rolling back the program does not guarantee the same rate of return. Furthermore, many utilities desire to incorporate environmental responsibility into their business model as well. Unlike Iowa, however, other states, along with environmental groups and non-profit organizations, have started legal proceedings against Washington's proposed rollback of efficiency policies.

GLOBAL CLIMATE NEGOTIATION

Climate change is a global problem, and addressing the issue requires the attention and cooperation of all countries. It is among the most dangerous problems in contemporary global life, and analysts regard it as a danger to America's national security. The burning of fossil fuels, the destruction of forests, and the resulting greenhouse gases are the principal sources of climate change. Among its effects are shrinking glaciers and Arctic ice, larger deserts, large-scale migrations in countries like Nigeria and India caused by unprecedented droughts, and increasingly violent storms. Rising coastal tides threaten major urban areas in Europe, China, and America's coasts, as well as the very existence of island countries such as the Marshall Islands, Kiribati, Tuvalu, Tonga, the Federated States of Micronesia, the Cook Islands, Antigua, Nevis, and the Maldives.

Greenhouse gases can remain in the atmosphere for hundreds of years, and they easily cross national borders. Combating such climate change requires collective action, and global climate negotiations are among the most important venues for producing meaningful actions.

In Kyoto in 1997, a protocol to an earlier UN treaty on climate change was negotiated under which thirty-five industrialized countries would have until 2012 to reduce emissions of greenhouse gases to five percent below 1990 levels. Although 140 countries ratified it, Washington refused to do so, demanding that the protocol should also apply to developing countries, especially China and India, both major sources of greenhouse gases that did not sign the protocol. Although Washington refused to sign the agreement, Russia's ratification in 2004 allowed the protocol to come into force. Additional meetings in Montreal (2005) and Bali, Indonesia (2007) made only limited progress in curbing carbon emissions, and as the deadline neared, it seemed unlikely to achieve the reductions agreed upon in Kyoto. A conference in Copenhagen in 2009 only achieved a nonbinding compromise among the U.S., China, India, South Africa, and Brazil to reduce emissions. The core of the problem was that, although developing countries like China and India had becoming the leading sources of contemporary emissions, they sought to industrialize like developed countries such as the U.S., which had previously been the leading sources of climate change.

The 2015 Paris Accord (signed on Earth Day in 2016) was an important step in this collective global effort to mitigate climate change, as 195 nations endorsed its aims. Under this comprehensive agreement, signatories pledged to take steps to limit warming to 3.6 degrees Fahrenheit above pre-industrial levels. However, the targets of individual countries were nonbinding, and each country was free to determine how to achieve them. The participants also agreed to take emission stocks and report their efforts every five years. In April 2016, the United States signed the Paris Accord and committed to reducing greenhouse gas emissions by 26–28 percent from its 2005 level.

Although President Obama pointed to the accord as a singular achievement in his commitment to combat climate change, President Trump shortly after taking office announced that the United States would withdraw from the accord. This decision is troubling because, although the U.S. is no longer the largest source of greenhouse gas emissions, it contributes the highest *per capita emissions* in the world. Moreover, although America's total carbon emissions have declined as noted earlier, the continuation in fossil fuel expansion and the proposed policy changes by the Trump administration may reverse that trend. In addition, America's withdrawal from the accord may influence other countries and makes it more difficult for developing countries to reduce their emissions. Thus, American participation remains crucial.

In June 2017, the Trump administration submitted formal notice to the United Nations that it intended to quit the Paris Climate Accord. According to the agreement, U.S. remains a party to the accord because no participant state can formally announce its intention to withdraw until November 4, 2019. Thereafter, it could withdraw one year after its announcement. However, Trump has recently suggested he might stay in the pact if the "deal is good".

Although no country can withdraw from the agreement until November 4, 2020, the Trump administration has started to remove climate change from domestic policies. In early 2017, President Trump disbanded the Interagency Working Group on the Social Cost of Carbon (SCC). The SCC monetizes the economic and environmental impact of carbon emissions to the society. The calculation of benefits from reducing pollution can have a significant political impact on regulating and controlling emissions. Trump has withdrawn the technical document on the SCC, and U.S. government agencies are not encouraged to consider the health and economic costs of carbon emissions.

In April 2018, EPA Administrator Pruitt determined that fuel-efficiency standards for light-duty vehicles were "not appropriate and unnecessary" even though the EPA projected the standards would reduce oil consumption and save American families more than $1.7 trillion in fuel cost. The EPA under Pruitt and his successor, acting Administrator Andrew Wheeler, was determined to roll back the Obama-era standards requiring automobiles sold in America to average more than 50 miles per gallon by 2025. In August 2018, the Trump administration announced it would freeze Obama's fuel-efficiency requirements. This will create a legal confrontation with states like California that wish to retain such requirements in their states. The change would emit an additional 321 million to 931 million metric tons or more of carbon dioxide by 2035 and could be Trump's "most consequential climate-policy rollback yet" (Plumer, 2018).[23]

In comparison with Washington's vacillation, other countries figure prominently in addressing the future of global energy and climate change. In early 2018, the European Commission announced that the European Union (EU) would not sign trade agreements with countries that did not ratify the Paris Accord. Many countries have announced plans in compliance with the Paris Agreement and in curbing carbon emissions. Since most countries do not have the range of energy resources that the U.S. has, renewable energy is a critical factor in increasing energy independence and reducing carbon emissions. Many countries have made significant efforts to incentivize innovation in renewable energy technologies.

The EU, for instance, has aggressively sought to reduce fossil fuel consumption and carbon emissions. The EU passed binding legislation to meet the 20–20–20 targets by 2020: to cut greenhouse gas emissions by 20 percent from the 1990 level, achieve 20 percent of energy consumption with renewables, and improve energy efficiency by 20 percent. The EU is also developing targets for 2030 to encourage additional emission reductions, utilize more renewables and ensure greater efficiency. In 2005 the EU instituted emissions trading, under which firms have a limit to emissions but can buy and sell emissions allowances, and the scheme is central to Europe's effort to reduce emission. The scheme encompasses about 45 percent of all EU emissions. Each country has binding annual targets for those sectors not covered by the trading system.

The EU also provides financial incentives to support renewable energy and carbon capture and storage, and funds energy research and innovation through its Horizon 2020 program. The European Commission's energy research and development budget prioritizes energy efficiency and renewable energy, which accounts for about a quarters of its total research and development (R&D) budget. In contrast, fossil fuel only accounts for 6 percent of the total energy R&D budget. Major countries in Europe, including Germany, Spain, Italy, and Sweden, utilize renewable energy sources that already exceed the EU's 2020 target.

Another major player is China, the world largest source of greenhouse gas emissions. China's role in is increasingly crucial owing to the U.S. retreat from the effort to slow climate change. China announced its commitment to peak emissions in 2030 and "increase the share of non-fossil fuels in primary energy consumption to around 20% by 2030" in the U.S.-China Joint Announcement of November 2014. The U.S. also announced its commitment to reducing emissions to 26–28 percent below the 2005 level by 2025. In announcing the targets, both countries hoped to encourage other countries to accelerate their efforts to combat climate change. In December 2017, China initiated a national emission-trading scheme to cut emissions from power generation. The new rule also contains a multiyear plan to expand the coverage of the emission-trading system to other industries. Currently, renewable electricity accounts for a quarter of China's total electricity production, much of which is hydroelectric power. As part of China's effort to reduce air pollution, Beijing has decided to reduce dependence on coal by using more natural gas and renewables. China also provides financial incentives to support the development of wind and solar electricity. In 2016, for instance, China invested $32 billion in clean energy technology and increased that total to $44 billion in 2017. After President Trump's announcement of his intention to withdraw from the Paris pact, China faced growing pressure from the international community to assume leadership in dealing with global climate change.

The European Union and China are not alone in moving toward more renewable energy. With the shift to a focus on fossil fuel production, the Trump administration appears to be out of step with this global trend. Several U.S. cities and states like California however, have committed to continue cutting emissions and developing clean energy technologies, and California will retain higher emissions regulations for autos than Washington, forcing automakers either to make different types of cars or to maintain higher mileage standards nationally despite Washington's deregulation. However, the Trump administration is trying to outlaw California's ability to determine auto emissions.

State regulations and incentives provide considerable motivation for low-emission technologies. Popular policy efforts include the Renewable Portfolio Standard, building energy codes, appliance standards, procurement and other financial incentives, and the Energy Efficiency Resource Standard under which twenty-six U.S. states are setting long-term, binding energy savings targets. States have taken several approaches to setting targets, including legislation to enact formal energy efficiency standards and setting long-term energy savings targets through utility commissions. In addition, twenty large U.S. cities joined a national initiative, the City Energy Project, to continue making efforts to improve energy efficiency of buildings. As the Trump administration moves in one direction, U.S. states and cities are moving in a different direction in addressing climate change.

CONCLUSIONS

The energy system in the United States has moved to a new natural-gas-dominant, self-sufficient paradigm. This new paradigm features low oil and gas prices, oil exports, coal retirement, and the rapid development of renewables. Energy security, too, has improved greatly in recent years, although challenges remain for reducing America's greenhouse gas emissions.

The energy policies of the Trump administration have imposed shocks to this transition to a low-emission energy system. These include efforts to repeal the Clean Power Plan, imposing a 30 percent tariff on imported solar panels, and efforts to remove several of the country's environmental and energy regulations. However, it is difficult to reverse the trend of retiring old, low-efficient coal-based power plants. The market for energy efficiency and renewable energy is likely to grow, as state and local policy incentives for such initiatives increase.

Overall, although American policymaking on energy issues is decentralized, the federal government often seeks to incorporate additional factors including job creation, deregulation, and political considerations in its national energy policy. Instead, decision-making on energy policy should be rational and science-based, and less politically driven – with an emphasis on immediate economic effect. Decision makers need also pay attention to the long-term impacts and the symbolic power of domestic policies in the global regime of combating climate change.

ESSAY QUESTIONS

1) Explain the concept of energy security and discuss the current status and recent trend of energy security for the United States.

2) Describe and discuss the advantages and disadvantaged of increased fossil fuel production in recent years in the United States.

3) Explain why coal retirement is an irreversible trend and discuss the impacts on jobs.

4) Summarize the Trump administration's policy on clean energy – renewable energy and energy efficiency – and discuss impacts of the policy changes.

5) Describe and discuss the role that the United States plays in the global negotiation of combating climate change.

SHORT ANSWER QUESTIONS

Define and describe the importance of the following:

Energy intensity
Cooperative average fuel economy (CAFE) standards
NIMBY
Energy efficiency
Climate change

NOTES

1   McCright, A. and Dunlap, R.E. (2011). Cool Dudes: The Denial of Climate Change among Conservative White Males in the United States. *Global Environmental Change* 21:4, pp. 1163–1172. Available at: www.sciencedirect.com/science/article/pii/S095937801100104X [Accessed 1 April 2018].

2   Yergin, D. (2006). Ensuring Energy Security. *Foreign Affairs* 85:2, pp. 69–82.

3   U.S. Energy Information Administration (2018). EIA Expects Total U.S. Fossil Fuel Production to Reach Record Levels in 2018 and 2019. *Today in Energy* [online]. Available at: www.eia.gov/todayinenergy/detail.php?id=34572 [Accessed 2 April 2018].

4   Knox-Hayes, J, Brown, M, Sovacool, B, and Wang, Y. (2013). Understanding Attitudes Toward Energy Efficiency: Result of a cross-national survey. *Global Environmental Change* 23, pp. 609–622; Sovacool, B. and Brown, M. (2010) Competing Dimensions of Energy Security: An international perspective. *Annual Review of Environment & Resources* 2010:35, pp. 77–108; Brown, M., Wang, Y., Sovacool, B., and D'Agostino, A. (2014). Forty Years of Energy Security Trends: A comparative assessment of 22 industrialized countries. *Energy Research & Social Science* 2014:4, pp. 64–77.

5   International Energy Agency. IEA Country Statistics [online]. 2018. Available at: http://data.iea.org [Accessed 21 August 2018].

6   Lipton, E. (2018). As Trump Dismantles Clean Air Rules, an Industry Lawyer Delivers for Ex-Clients. *New York Times* [online]. Available at: www.nytimes.com/2018/08/19/us/politics/epa-coal-emissions-standards-william-wehrum.html [Accessed 20 August 2018].

7   Eilperin, J. (2018). New Trump Power Plan Would Release Hundreds of Millions of Tons of CO_2 into the Air. *Washington Post* [online]. Available at: www.washingtonpost.com/national/health-science/new-trump-power-plant-plan-would-release-hundreds-of-millions-of-tons-of-co2-into-the-air/2018/08/18/be823078-a28e-11e8-83d2-70203b8d7b44_story.html [Accessed 19 August 2018].

8   Methane is a Powerful Greenhouse Gas, which has Estimated Global Warming Potential 28–36 Times Higher than CO_2.

9   Schwartz, J. and Plumer, B. (2018). The Natural Gas Industry has a Leak Problem. *New York Times* [online]. Available at: www.nytimes.com/2018/06/21/climate/methane-leaks.html [Accessed 22 June 2018].

10 Environmental Law at Harvard (2018). Available at: http://environment.law.harvard.edu/policy-initiative/regulatory-rollback-tracker [Accessed 4 April 2018].

11 Conte, M. and Jacobsen, G. (2016). Explaining Demand for Green Electricity Using Data from all U.S. Utilities. *Energy Economics* 60, pp. 122–130; Gerlach H. and Zheng X. (2018). Preferences for Green Electricity, Investment and Regulatory Incentives. *Energy Economics* 69, pp. 430–441.

12 Xie, B. and Zhao, W. (2018). Willingness to Pay for Green Electricity in Tianjin, China: Based on the contingent valuation method. *Energy Policy* 114, pp. 98–107.

13 Petrova, M. (2016). From NIMBY to Acceptance: Toward a novel framework – VESPA – For organizing and interpreting community concerns. *Renewable Energy* 86, pp. 1280–1294; Esaiasson, P. (2014) NIMBYism – A Re-Examination of the Phenomenon. *Social Science Research* 48, pp. 185–195.

14 Rand, J. and Hoen, B. (2017). Thirty Years of North American Wind Energy Acceptance Research: What have we learned? *Energy Research & Social Science* 29, pp. 135–148.

15 Union of Concerned Scientists (2015). Production Tax Credit for Renewable Energy [online]. Available at: www.ucsusa.org/clean_energy/smart-energy-solutions/increase-renewables/production-tax-credit-for.html [Accessed 2 April 2018].

16 Brown, M. and Sovacool, B. (2011). Barriers to the Diffusion of Climate-Friendly Technologies. *International Journal of Technology Transfer and Commercialization* 10:1, pp. 43–62.

17 Piper, J. (2018). New Tariffs to Curb US Solar Installations by 11% through 2022. *GreenTechMedia* [online]. Available at: www.greentechmedia.com/articles/read/tariffs-to-curb-solar-installations-by-11-through-2022 [Accessed 2 April 2018].

18   Berg, W., Nowak, M., Kelly, S., Vaidyanathan, M., Shoemaker, A., Chittum, A, DiMascio, M., and DeLucia, H. (2017). The 2017 State Energy Efficiency Scorecard. American Council for an Energy Efficient Economy. Available at: http://aceee.org [Accessed 4 April 2018].

19   Zhao, D, McCoy, A, and Du, J. (2016). An Empirical Study on the Energy Consumption in Residential Buildings after Adopting Green Building Standards. *Procedia Engineering* 145, pp. 766–773.

20   Zhang, L., Li, Y, Stephenson, R., and Ashuri, B. (2017). Valuation of Energy Efficient Certificates in Buildings. *Energy and Buildings* 158, pp. 1226–1240.

21   U.S. Department of Energy (2017). The 2017 U.S. Energy and Employment Report. Available at: www.energy.gov/downloads/2017-us-energy-and-employment-Report [Accessed 2 April 2018].

22   Wang, Y. and Brown, M. (2014). Policy Drivers for Improving Electricity End-Use Efficiency in the USA: An economic-engineering analysis. *Energy Efficiency* 7:3, pp. 517–546.

23   Plumer, B. (2018). How Big a Deal is Trump's Fuel Economy Rollback? For the climate, maybe the biggest yet. *New York Times* [online]. Available at: www.nytimes.com/2018/08/03/climate/trump-climate-emissions-rollback.html [Accessed 5 August 2018].

SUGGESTED READINGS

Hughes, L. and Lipscy, P.Y. (2013). The Politics of Energy. *Annual Review of Political Science* 16:1, pp. 449–469.

Yergin, D. (2006). Ensuring Energy Security. *Foreign Affairs* 85:2, pp. 69–82.

12 Trump and terrorism: A major focus of foreign policy

Ellen B. Pirro

INTRODUCTION

This chapter examines U.S. policies toward terrorism to determine what changes and developments have occurred over time. It sketches the links between terrorists and terrorism and U.S. policies toward Afghanistan, Iraq, the so-called Islamic State (IS) and elsewhere. It also addresses terrorism attacks within the United States by extremist groups and "lone wolves."

In each section, we examine the policies of George W. Bush, Barack Obama, and Donald Trump to see what changes and developments have occurred and whether Trump has made a significant contribution to the fight against terrorism or in reducing the terrorist threat to America. Terrorism is not new in the U.S. Indeed, the assassinations of President Abraham Lincoln, William McKinley, and John F. Kennedy as well as Robert Kennedy and Martin Luther King were terrorist acts.

Investigating U.S. policies toward terrorism is complex. First, terrorism, which constitutes threats and/or violence against innocent civilians for political ends, is both national and transnational. For the U.S., terrorism involves both domestic and foreign groups and individuals. Overseas terrorist acts are directed at U.S. interests, for example, attacks on the U.S embassies in Kenya and Tanzania in 1998, and the interests of close allies, for example, the 2004 Madrid train bombings. For intelligence services, and for necessary terrorist surveillance, this presents a considerable and ongoing challenge. In consequence, there are many loci of response and security within the U.S. government. Overseas security is the responsibility of the Defense Department and the Central Intelligence Agency (CIA), while domestic terrorism falls under Homeland Security and other agencies like the Federal Bureau of Investigation (FBI). Nevertheless, their responsibilities overlap considerably.

Second, several types of perpetrators are included under the "terrorist" label. 9/11 presents a purely foreign case involving foreign activists, trained overseas and covertly entering the United States to carry out terrorist acts. By contrast, "lone wolves" may be individuals trained abroad who have fought overseas and returned to the U.S., or they may be domestic converts affiliated or not affiliated with an ideology/religion and/or a group like IS. They may also be American or non-American citizens. In addition, they may simply be mentally deranged individuals without any attachment to a movement, ideology or cause.

A third complicating factor is the growing number of terrorist enemies. During the Clinton, George W. Bush, and Obama presidencies, al-Qaeda led by Osama bin Laden was seen as uniquely threatening. Established by Muslim volunteers fighting the Soviet occupation of Afghanistan in the late 1970s and headquartered in Sudan, then again Afghanistan, and finally Pakistan, al-Qaeda acquired disciples around the world, and carried out attacks against U.S. interests and America's European and Middle Eastern allies. Al-Qaeda's success prompted "copycat" movements some of which claimed affiliation, others which were loosely affiliated and still others which were totally outside the al-Qaeda framework. IS entered the global jihad as only one of a large number of entities dedicated to promoting worldwide terrorism to gain their objectives.

The civil war in Syria reflected a complex array of Sunni terrorist groups and militias, some allied and some rivals in their struggle against the Syrian regime. These groups repeatedly splinter and merge, and frequently change names. Washington has had difficulty determining which to support and which are antithetical to U.S. interests. In addition, Shia militias, notably Hezbollah, which Washington regards as a terrorist group, supports Syria's government and serves as an Iranian proxy, even while the U.S. has trained several Iraqi Shia militias to support Iraq's government the war against IS.

Under the slogan, "Make America Safe Again," Donald Trump made fighting terrorism a cornerstone of his presidential campaign. In fact, as we shall see, despite loud declamations and numerous tweets, to date he has offered few innovative approaches to combating terrorism, no new counterterrorism strategies, and little of note for preventing attacks. Indeed, Trump's policies resemble those of his predecessors. Although the number of terrorist attacks has decreased slightly, this is probably due to the defeat of IS in Iraq and Syria, rather than anti-terrorist measures undertaken by the U.S. or its allies.

Nevertheless, Trump continues, at least rhetorically, to emphasize defeating terrorism as one of his priorities, and eliminating IS was his major foreign-policy goal. He links terrorism with immigration, contending that terrorists are slipping into the U.S. among illegal immigrants, despite evidence to the contrary (Barrett, 2018).[1] He claims he seeks to reduce America's footprint around the globe unless U.S. interests are directly involved (although, as we shall see, not in the case of Afghanistan) Thus, he is content to leave much of the Middle East to Russia and much of Asia to China. The exception is a foreign policy that emphasizes combating terrorism against the U.S. and its overseas interests.

TERRORISM TARGETS THE UNITED STATES

While many observers discuss terrorism as though it began with the al-Qaeda attacks against New York's Twin Towers and the Pentagon in Washington, D.C. on September 11, 2001, there were several earlier attacks by al-Qaeda against U.S interests. Indeed, owing to the perceived threat of al-Qaeda, the CIA established a Counterterrorism Center in 1986, which later added a unit to kill or capture bin Laden.

In 1995, U.S. facilities in Riyadh, Saudi Arabia, established after the first Persian Gulf War, were car bombed, probably by al-Qaeda. In 1998, al-Qaeda operatives bombed the U.S. embassies in Kenya and Tanzania, resulting in a large loss of life, and prompting President Bill Clinton to order missile strikes against al-Qaeda targets in Afghanistan and a pharmaceutical factory in Sudan. In 2000, an al-Qaeda attack on the U.S.S. Cole in the Yemeni harbor of Aden left seventeen U.S. sailors dead and many injured. Terrorist attacks on hotels in Jordan frequented by Westerners in 2005 attacks also caused many deaths and injuries.

In retrospect, one domestic terrorist attack stands out as a predecessor to 9/11. On February 26, 1993, a truck bomb was detonated by Ramzi Yousef beneath the World Trade Center in Manhattan killing six and injuring over one-thousand. Ramzi Yousef's uncle was Khalid Sheikh Mohammed, regarded as a key architect in the 9/11 attack.

Overall, however, there have been few genuine attacks in the U.S. after 9/11. According to one source, there had been only eight major attacks between July 2002 and November 2017 (Jacobs, 2017).[2] By contrast, there were more than 11,000 terrorist attacks globally in 2006 alone, of which almost 3,000 took place in Iraq, and over 1,300 occurred in India (Statista, n.d.).[3] Overwhelmingly, most attacks were initiated in Muslim countries against Muslims.

9/11 AND AFGHANISTAN

It was the attacks on 9/11 in New York and Washington which awakened most Americans and their leaders to the terrorist threat and ushered in a new era of surveillance and homeland security concerns. Although these attacks took place on U.S. soil, the terrorist threat was largely shaped overseas. Although al-Qaeda condemned all infidels (non-Muslims), especially those in its "far enemy," the United States, the group's initial goals involved eliminating the Saudi monarchy and Israel. After 9/11, President George W. Bush announced a "War on Terror" both at home and abroad. With congressional and public approval, the U.S. invaded Afghanistan to capture bin Laden and his followers and overthrow his protectors, Afghanistan's Islamic Taliban government.

In Operation Enduring Freedom, the U.S, NATO, and other allies aided Afghanistan's Northern Alliance to oust the Taliban and install President Hamid Karzai. However, the Afghanistan campaign failed to capture Osama bin Laden. Both the Taliban and al-Qaeda retreated to mountain caves, and many crossed the border to Pakistan where the Taliban reconstituted itself as a guerrilla movement.

George W. Bush began the use of drones (UAVs or unmanned aerial vehicles) to track and kill Afghan and al-Qaeda militants in remote areas. Obama greatly intensified the use of drones both in Afghanistan and elsewhere such as Somalia and Yemen. From 2004 to 2015 there were almost 400 drone strikes. The strikes decimated al-Qaeda. Under Obama, too a U.S. military unit was able to find and kill bin Laden in Pakistan on May 2, 2011.

Obama viewed the conflict in Afghanistan as a "good" war adding troops in a "surge" even as the U.S. withdrew from a "bad" war in Iraq. During his presidency, Secretary of State John Kerry brokered a power-sharing deal in Afghanistan after Karzai, who had become a U.S. foe, was voted from office. The deal established a relatively stable government in which power was shared among major ethnic groups and warlords. While many U.S. allies have pulled troops out of Afghanistan, fighting continues to this day in what has become America's longest war in history. U.S. troops remain there to train Afghan forces and combat the resurgent Taliban.

The U.S. public remained relatively detached from Afghanistan and operations there, but there was a desire for a speedy withdrawal among those in Washington who are aware of its drain on personnel, resources, and funds. Obama's later policy was generally directed at removing U.S. troops from Afghanistan, and he published timetables for withdrawal, a strategy condemned by Trump during the presidential campaign as allowing the Taliban to avoid negotiations and wait for the withdrawal.

Although Trump announced he wanted the U.S. to withdraw all troops from Afghanistan, he changed his mind after advice from the military. In August 2017, he announced a five-point strategy for dealing with Afghanistan. First, U.S. troops were no longer restricted in their mission. They could target Taliban and other terrorist groups, especially IS (which had established a presence there), and not simply defend themselves and train Afghans. The Pentagon was authorized to expand the forces in Afghanistan, and no announcements would be made about the size of U.S. forces. Second, terrorists would be targeted and destroyed wherever and whenever they were found. Trump has continued using drones, but has not supervised targets as had Obama and has given the CIA discretion to target whom they want. Third, there would be no timetables for withdrawal. Like Obama, Trump sought a political solution, but was skeptical that one could be achieved, although Washington continued trying to start talks with the Taliban after a brief ceasefire ended in June 2018, and the group announced the next month it would cease attacking civilians. Fourth, he demanded that Pakistan cease harboring terrorists, and he cut off aid to that country until it did so. Finally, Trump was adamant that the United States would no longer be involved in nation-building. America's sole goal in Afghanistan would be a military victory to destroy terrorism (Herb, 2017).[4]

Although there are certain new elements in Trump's Afghan strategy, much of it dates back to Obama. His goal is to get the U.S. out of Afghanistan as quickly as possible, although, unlike Obama, he believes another troop surge and military operations could accomplish what his predecessors failed to achieve.

IRAQ AND THE ISLAMIC STATE

On March 20, 2003, George W. Bush initiated Operation Iraqi Freedom to remove Saddam Hussein from power. Falsely claiming that Iraq still possessed weapons of mass destruction despite inspections after the first Persian Gulf War waged by his father, and that Saddam had aided bin Laden, Bush launched a conventional war with the significant support of only one ally, the United Kingdom (UK). The conventional war was successful, Baghdad was soon captured, and thereafter Saddam was hunted down and executed. Chaos ensued, however, owing to a combination of infrastructure devastated by the war and the elimination of trained pro-Saddam Sunni government and military personnel that left a power vacuum. This vacuum was swiftly filled in Iraq by sectarian violence between the Shias, Sunnis and Kurds, and the terrorism of al-Qaeda.

Despite indications that the situation in Iraq was worsening, Obama withdrew U.S. troops from the "bad" war in 2011. This facilitated the growing influence of IS in Iraq, its terrorism against the country's new Shia government, and its expansion into Syria as the so-called "Islamic State" led by a former prisoner and thug, Abu Bakr al Baghdadi. Unlike the original al-Qaeda with which it feuded and which criticized its brutality, IS sought to emulate Islam's medieval caliphate and occupied and began to govern large areas in Iraq and Syria on which they imposed a harshly "pure" version of Islamic law.

Utilizing social media, IS recruited Sunni sympathizers globally from countries as diverse as Russia and China to Tunisia, the U.S., France, and the UK. Establishing its capital at Raqqa, Syria, IS declared its caliphate and with ruthless brutality subjugated all those it captured, forcing women into marriage, indoctrinating and then arming children, and publicly killing many of the Christians, Shia Muslims, Westerners, and Sunni foes it encountered. Much was recorded on video and publicized globally on social media, which at once horrified many observers while also attracting additional recruits.

In 2014 IS captured several major Iraqi cities including Mosul, and Iraq's government requested U.S. help. That year Iraq's pro-Iranian Shia prime minister since 2006 Nouri al-Maliki, who was widely unpopular among Sunnis and Kurds, was replaced by Haider al-Abadi, who set out to empower Sunni and Kurdish Iraqis against IS. U.S. involvement consisted of extending airstrikes into Syria, sending U.S. military advisers to Iraq, and providing support for moderate Islamic and Kurdish rebels seeking to overthrow the Syrian regime. Iraqi and Syrian Kurds in particular found considerable U.S. support in battling IS. Despite Turkey's concern that Iraqi and Syrian Kurds would seek independence for Turkey's large Kurdish population, Obama managed to assemble an anti-IS coalition among these groups, several NATO allies, and several conservative Arab governments.

In 2015, Obama sent 1,500 troops to Iraq to help train Iraqi forces and deployed naval vessels in the eastern Mediterranean for air and missile strikes. Congress authorized $5 billion to supply and support anti-IS military operations and train anti-IS groups. Faced with U.S., Russian, and Iranian troops, militias, and air power, IS gradually retreated. After bitter combat, Mosul was retaken by Iraqi troops, and IS-occupied areas in Iraq and Syria, including Raqqa, were liberated.

The Trump administration continued these operations in Syria and Iraq. There were no major campaigns, and the Trump administration worked hard to avoid a confrontation with Russia, whose presence in Syria propped up the Syrian regime. Although the Obama administrations had demanded that Syria's President Bashar al-Assad step down, the Trump administration retreated from that position.

By allowing Moscow to dominate Syrian politics (see Chapter 9), Trump sought to reduce U.S. presence in the Middle East. To some extent, both Obama and Trump share similar ideas about Syria's civil war. It is expensive for the U.S., destabilizes the region, and enhances Iranian influence in the Middle East. Both presidents agreed that the U.S. had an obligation to destroy IS, but, once accomplished, the U.S. should reduce its presence in the region (Cook, 2018).[5] How quickly to leave, however, remained unclear. In late March 2018, Trump surprised and contradicted his own advisers by declaring: "We'll be coming out of Syria, like 'very soon.' Let the other people take care of it now" (cited in Liptak and Cohen, 2018).[6] However, less than a month later, after meeting France's President Emmanuel Macron, Trump shifted, declaring that before withdrawing from Syria, "we want to leave a strong and lasting footprint" (cited in Burns, 2018).[7] Moreover, although IS was defeated in Syria and Iraq, it still has the capacity for hit-and-run attacks in Syria and Iraq and "lone wolf" attacks overseas, and home countries are unwilling to accept IS members imprisoned in Syria.

ISLAMIC TERRORISM ELSEWHERE IN AFRICA, ASIA, AND THE MIDDLE EAST

Several other terrorist groups in these areas that have emerged in recent decades that are loosely linked affiliates (or franchises) of the original al-Qaeda and/or IS and pose significant threats to the U.S. homeland and overseas interests as well as local governments. Terrorists in Africa find refuge in that continent's fragile or failed states from Mozambique to the Central African Republic, and several of them have links to the United States either through recruits, or successful operations.

Al-Qaeda in the Arabian Peninsula (AQAP)

Al-Qaeda in the Arabian Peninsula was established in 2003 in Saudi Arabia, and merged in 2009 with jihadists in Yemen. While primarily targeting foes in Yemen, AQAP became extremely dangerous to the U.S. homeland, owing to the world's most sought after terrorist bomb maker, Ibrahim Hassan Tali al-Asiri, for whom Washington has offered a $5 million reward. Asiri has made bombs for terrorists with plastic explosives that are virtually invisible to airline detectors. These included two "underwear" bombers, the first on Northwest Flight 253 to Detroit in 2009 and the other prevented in advance in the Middle East by the CIA in 2012, and in 2010 two bombs hidden in printer cartridges, the first discovered on a FedEx plane's stopover in the UK en route to the U.S. and the second a week later which AQAP claimed caused United Parcel Service Airlines Flight 6 to crash in Dubai, killing its American pilot and copilot.

Perhaps, the best known victim of a U.S. drone strike was an American-born Islamic cleric Anwar al Awlaki, one of AQAP's leaders. His death caused controversy in the U.S. because some believed that Awlaki had been denied his right to a trial as a U.S. citizen. Washington had begun drone strikes against AQAP in 2002 and over the years killed many of their leaders, including Awlaki. The U.S. sent Special Forces to train Yemeni soldiers, but after civil war in Yemen erupted in 2011 they had to be removed. AQAP still retains territory in southern Yemen and controls the oil resources there and continues to plan attacks against the United States.

Al-Shabab

Al-Shabab is largely involved in Somalia, and neighboring Kenya. Although the group was temporarily vanquished in 2007, the involvement of Ethiopian troops enraged many Somalis who contributed to Shabab's resurgence in about half the country by 2009. With the help of the African Union, the group was driven out of much of this area in 2011. It continues launching terrorist attacks, and pledged loyalty to al-Qaeda in 2012, shifting its allegiance to IS in 2015.

Al-Shabab threatens the U.S. in two ways. First, it has been successful in recruiting young men originating from overseas, including Minneapolis, home to many Somali refugees, a few who returned home to the U.S. to commit terrorist acts. Second, the group continues to mount terrorist attacks in the Horn of Africa against U.S.-supported governments in Kenya and Uganda. Its attack on Kenya's Westgate shopping mall in 2013 and the country's Garissa University in 2015 caused numerous fatalities, and it remains a threat to Mogadishu, Somalia's capital.

Al-Qaeda in the Islamic Maghreb (AQIM)

Emerging from civil war in Algeria in 2006, al-Qaeda in the Islamic Maghreb (AQIM) pledged its allegiance to al-Qaeda. The group sought to establish militant Islamic regimes across North Africa and targets European, Israeli, and American interests in the region. In addition, several of its members lived and plotted in Europe. The group took advantage of weak governments in Mali and Libya. In Mali, AQIM seized the northern part of the country including major cities, and moved toward Bamako, the capital. It was only the intervention of France, Mali's former colonial ruler, in 2013, which forced the group to retreat to remote areas in northern Mali, southern Algeria, and Niger. The Obama administration provided France with logistical aid and intelligence. Washington remains involved in the region, having established an African Command and sending Special Forces to Niger.

In Libya, a civil war in 2011 and the overthrow of the regime of Muammar Qaddafi with U.S. and NATO military assistance created a failed state and the spread of Libyan weapons and terrorists across northern Africa nations including Niger and Mali. Libya remains a failed state with regional and ethnic militias forming different governments that have had to deal with a significant IS presence. Overall, despite Western troops, of which there are relatively few, terrorist groups control much of Africa's Sahel region.

Washington has left much of the fight against AQIM to the French, but it established a small base in Niger, and helped finance with other Western powers, the G5 in West Africa, utilizing troops from Burkina Faso, Chad, Mali, Mauretania, and Niger. In Niger, a combination of errors by U.S. commanders led to the ambush and death of four U.S. soldiers in October 2017. Uncharacteristically the White House remained silent for almost two weeks. Congressional investigation uncovered the presence of some 900 U.S. troops in Niger and over 6,000 based in countries across Africa. Their principal mission has been to assist weak African governments to combat the jihadist threat from groups like AQIM. Some of the African terrorist groups have pledged loyalty to al-Qaeda, including al-Shabab, Boko Haram, and Nusrat al-Islam wal Muslimin in MaliJama'a. The Niger ambush was attributed to a splinter group operating near the village of Tongo Tongo, which has experienced many attacks in recent years (Tharoor, 2017).[8]

President Obama supported the U.S. presence in Africa, and the Trump administration has done little to change this. However, unlike the Obama administration's considerable attention to Africa, as of this writing, the Trump administration has still not appointed an Undersecretary of State for Africa and has appointed few ambassadors to African countries.

Boko Haram

The jihadist group Boko Haram controls much of northern Nigeria and is second only to IS as regards the number of fatalities it has caused in recent years. Nigeria is a U.S. friend and a major source of sweet crude oil. Boko Haram, whose name means "Western education is forbidden" has destroyed villages, killing indiscriminately, and bombed city centers. It is perhaps best known in Western media for kidnapping school girls who were then forced to marry their captors, sold into slavery, or used as suicide bombers.

Nigeria has repeatedly asked for U.S. aid to combat the terrorists, many of whom also terrorize other countries in West Africa, such as Cameroon, Chad, and Niger. However, the Obama administration was reluctant to give aid to Nigeria's corrupt government and poorly trained army. Instead, Washington has sent a few trainers and some funding but has mainly limited its assistance to local officials. Obama did send 300 soldiers to Cameroon in October 2015. While the level of mistrust between the U.S. and Nigeria declined some-what after Muhammadu Buhari became Nigerian president in 2015, Washington has been reluctant to provide weapons and funding owing to Nigeria's poor human-rights record and government corruption. Trump met Buhari in April 2018 and arranged a sale of $600 million for combat aircraft and counterterrorism. Nevertheless, he insulted African countries including Nigeria with a vulgar phrase over continued African immigration to the U.S , and does not seem to regard Boko Haram as a priority.

Terrorists no more

It is worth noting that in Europe several indigenous terrorist threats involving Marxists and/or secessionist groups have been eliminated, including Italy's Red Brigades and Germany's Red Army Faction (Baader Meinhof Gang). In Northern Ireland, the Good Friday Accords of 1998 produced a truce between the Irish Republican Army (IRA) and the British government resulting in power sharing and participation in governance, which has lasted for twenty years. A small fringe group calling themselves Continuity IRA (CIRA) has attempted to continue terrorist activities but they have been largely thwarted. More recently, the Basque terrorist group, ETA, has disbanded as a terrorist organization to contest elections and participate in Spanish politics.

TERRORISM IN THE UNITED STATES

"Lone wolves"

There is a significant difference between terrorism in the Middle East and Africa and those occurring on U.S. soil. Overseas terrorism is largely conducted by well-organized and armed groups made up of trained individuals.

Within the United States, however, most terrorist attacks are carried out by unaffiliated individuals described as "lone wolves." These individuals fall into two categories. First, there are ideologically and religiously driven individuals, usually young men, who commit terror attacks by themselves or occasionally with a partner. They are disproportionately second-generation young Muslims or Muslim converts, who lack a sense of self-identity and feel neither at home in America nor members of the societies from which their parents emigrated. Some have traveled to Syria, Iraq, or Pakistan, received training in terrorist techniques, and have participated in terrorist acts, and whose return home is feared by Washington as well as other countries like Belgium and Russia. Such battle-hardened former soldiers could prove dangerous operatives in Western societies. To date, however, most terrorists on U.S. soil with links to overseas terrorist groups have received guidance online where social media provide them with propaganda, bomb making directions, and plans for proposed operations. American intelligence agencies make great efforts to penetrate clandestine online communication and social media posts between these individuals and terrorist groups overseas.

A second type of "lone wolves," who may be even more dangerous because their behavior is so difficult to predict, consists of mentally deranged individuals without ideological or religious ties. Thus, Timothy McVeigh, the 1995 Oklahoma truck bomber, had no links to terrorist groups. The individual who shot nine African-American worshipers at a South Carolina church in 2015 had racist motivations, and the individual who used automatic weapons to kill fifty-nine people and injure over five-hundred at a Las Vegas concert in 2017 had no apparent ties to jihadism, radical Islam, or any other ideology or religious motivations.

In the wake of each mass shooting in the United States there have been calls for tighter gun regulations and background checks. George W. Bush never pursued such reforms, yielding to pressure from the National Rifle Association (NRA). President Obama made several attempts to impose additional gun regulations but failed to get Congress to act. President Trump initially made public promises to impose reforms, including a minimum age to purchase guns, but, shortly after doing so, endorsed the views of the NRA, arguing instead that something needed to be done to help mentally ill individuals.

Indeed, Trump tends to views terrorism in the U.S. through an immigration lens, and he argues that homeland terrorism will be eliminated in part by strong measures including travel bans on Muslims and a reduction in illegal and legal immigration. Trump's emphasis on reducing immigration involves the border patrol, which has received additional funding (U.S. Customs and Border Protection), the U.S. Immigration and Customs Enforcement, and a wall on the Mexican border. In February, April, and May 2018, in campaign-style speeches and tweets, he blamed Mara Salvatrucha or MS-13 (a Central American gang that originated in and had been driven out of Los Angeles) for much U.S. crime. He also claimed that America's immigration policies made it possible for gang members to enter the U.S. freely as unaccompanied minor children. He condemned random chain migration and the immigration lottery system for allowing terrorists and criminals to come to the United States, and asked both Congress and the Justice Department to examine ways to address these problems.

The War on terror at home

After 9/11, Congress created the Department of Homeland Security which moved agencies from different departments into a mega-agency which would be able to share information quickly and deal with threats in a number of different ways. Agencies as diverse as the Customs and Border Protection and the Federal Emergency Management Agency were joined with the Coast Guard and the Transportation Security Administration. Its effect was to place another layer of bureaucracy between major intelligence agencies and the president but also to integrate security agencies with one another. Congress also named a Director of National Intelligence (DNI) whose mandate was to ensure sharing of information and cooperation among sixteen intelligence agencies. The DNI briefs the president on perceived threats. While this integration of agencies has led to cooperation, the Director has little authority over member agencies, especially those in the military.

During the George W. Bush administration, these changes were implemented and began to work. Under Obama it appeared that the War on Terror was enjoying success domestically. Several plots were uncovered before execution. Under Trump the effectiveness of this re-organization has been reduced by his mistrust of bureaucracies. The Trump administration has been slow to make appointments, leaving key agencies without leaders. Trump took almost a year before naming Kirstjen Nielsen as Secretary of Homeland Security in October 2017 after General John F. Kelly became White House Chief of Staff.

The Trump administration was also preoccupied by questions regarding the firing of FBI Director James Comey and the allegation of collusion between Russia and the Trump campaign. After repeated criticisms by Trump of the CIA, FBI, and the Justice Department, these agencies suffer from low morale and effectiveness, and this climate affects the entire intelligence community. Finally, there is a tendency in the Trump White House and the president himself to ignore the information provided by the intelligence agencies. The president reads few intelligence reports and seems to regard Fox News as a better source.

In an effort to make the intelligence community "more agile" and reduce the influence of the National Security Agency (NSA), the CIA, and FBI, Trump appointed Dan Coats, a former Republican senator from Indiana, as DNI. Coats overhauled the organization of the sixteen intelligence agencies that report to him. The administration appointed four new deputy directors, and Coats's office focused on four major tasks. The first is to integrate the intelligence streams coming from the various agencies. Second, it is tasked with allocating resources among these agencies. Third, it will promote national security partnerships between the administration and both private civilian groups (including corporations) and foreign intelligence services. Fourth, it will develop strategies to address future threats (Kitfield, 2018).[9]

While Coat's operation produces multiple threat assessments, and devises methods to deflect them, the Trump White House seems to ignore many of his reports and those of the U.S. intelligence community. In sum, Trump's priority is not gathering, processing, and digesting intelligence, or even assessing future threats but, as noted above, using terrorism as an excuse to reduce immigration.

CONCLUSIONS

Under the Trump administration, terrorism continues to be a focal point of foreign policy. Trump' speeches and tweets make it clear that the main task of the U.S. intelligence community and armed services should be preventing terrorism on American soil. Moreover, 2017 was the third consecutive year that the number of terrorist attacks globally had decreased, mainly owing to the military defeat of IS (START, 2018: 1).[10]

When it comes to overseas terrorist groups, Trump's view, "let the generals do it," has allowed the armed services and CIA to act with little oversight from civilian authorities. He insists on "victory" without a clear idea of what that means. Thus, he declared victory over the Islamic State, even while the Pentagon resisted his announcement of a U.S. withdrawal from Syria.

The conflicts waged in Iraq, Syria, and Afghanistan continue the policies of George W. Bush and Barack Obama. "Trump has borrowed elements from Bush's approach, [but] he has also embraced the burden sharing aspect of Obama's 'indirect' strategy to combating terrorism" (Tankel, 2017).[11] A major difference is that Washington no longer reveals what it is doing concerning operations, troop deployments, and outcomes.

Domestically, there is little that is new in fighting terrorism other than opposition to immigration and building the border wall, which Trump had promised during the presidential campaign. The president has seen his efforts to ban travel from majority Muslim countries stopped by the courts although a limited ban may be approved by the Supreme

Court. Nothing has been done about the children of illegal immigrants brought to the United States when young, the so-called "dreamers." Residency rights are being revoked for many aliens who have fled natural disasters or wars in their home countries in Central America and elsewhere. And, Trump has had difficulty getting funding from Congress to build his wall. During his campaign, Trump had advocated using torture to make terrorist suspects talk, a policy Obama had revoked. Trump retreated from this as well after criticism from Secretary of Defense James Mattis and the late Senator John McCain, himself a victim of torture in North Vietnam.

In sum, the Trump administration's anti-terrorist policies are similar to those implemented by George W. Bush and Barack Obama, and they are likely to remain so throughout his presidency.

ESSAY QUESTIONS

1) What major domestic measures has President Donald Trump undertaken to thwart domestic attacks?

2) How has the terrorist threat changed from Obama to Trump?

3) What are Trump's goals/objectives regarding terrorism in the Middle East? How is he trying to achieve them?

4) What are Trump's goals/objectives in Afghanistan? How is he trying to achieve them?

5) How do terrorist attacks around the world affect the United States? Why should the United States get involved?

6) What group has the United States used to fight IS in Syria? Why is this causing problems for the United States?

7) How does Trump link terrorism and immigration? What is his policy to deal with this?

SHORT ANSWER QUESTIONS

Define and describe the importance of the following:

Lone wolf terrorists
Islamic State
Osama bin Laden
Taliban
Kurds
Anwar al Awlaki

NOTES

1   Barrett, D. (2018). Trump Administration Links Terrorism and Immigration, but an Expert Doubts the Math. *Washington Post* [online]. Available at: www.washington post.com/world/nationalsecurity/trump/administration/links/terroirsm/and/immigration/but/an/expert/doubts/the/math [Accessed 3 May 2018].

2   Jacobs, B. (2017). America Since 9/11: Timeline of attacks linked to the 'war on terror'. *The Guardian* [online]. Available at: www.thcguardian.com/us-news/2017/nov/01/america-since-911-terrorist-attacks-linked-to-the-war-on-terror [Accessed 14 May 2018].

3   *Statista* (n.d.) Number of Terrorist Attacks Worldwide between 2006 and 2016. Available at: www.statista.com/statistics/202864/number-of-terrorist-attacks-worldwide [Accessed 14 May 2018]; *Statista* (n.d.) Number of terrorist attacks in 2016, by country (n.d.). *Statista*. Available at: www.statista.com/statistics/236983/terrorist-attacks-by-country [Accessed 14 May 2018].

4   Herb, J. (2017). Five Key Pieces of Trump's Afghanistan Plan. *CNN*, [online]. Available at: https://edition.cnn.com/2017/08/21/politics/trump-afghan-plan-five-things/index/html [Accessed 18 April 2018].

5   Cook, S. (2018). Trump's Syria Policy Isn't Retrenchment. It's pandering. *Foreign Policy* [online]. Available at: www.foreignpolicy.com/2018/04/09/trumps-syrian-policy-isnt-retrenchement-its-pandering [Accessed 1 May 2018].

6   Liptak, K. and Cohen, Z. (2018). For Trump, Syria Policy is All About the Economy – And private jumbo jets. *CNN* [online]. Available at: www.cnn.com/2018/04/03/politics/donald-trump-syria-middle-east-policy/index.html [Accessed 20 April 2018].

7   Burns, R. (2018). Trump Backtracks on Syria after Talks with French Leader. *Chicago Tribune* [online]. Available at: www.chicagotribune.com/news/nationworld/sns-bc-us-trump-staying-in-syria-20180424-story.html [Accessed 13 May 2018].

8   Tharoor, I. (2017). Trump's Niger Uproar Shines Light on the U.S.'s Murky African Wars. *Washington Post* [online] Available at: www.washingtonpost.com/news/worldviews/wp/2017/10/24/trumps-niger-uproar-shines-light-on-the-u-s-s-murky-african-wars [Accessed 25 April 2018].

9   Kitfield, J. (2018). Coats Rolls Out Overhaul of Top Intelligence Office. *Politico*. Available at: www.politico.com/story/2018/03/15/dan-coats-dni-intelligence-overhaul-466619 [Accessed 4 May 2018).

10 START (2018). Global Terrorism in 2017. National Consortium for the Study of Terrorism and Response to Terrorism. Available at: www.start.umd.edu/pubs/START_GTD_Overview 2017_July2018.pdf [Accessed 15 August 2018].

11 Tankel, S. (2017). Trump's Plan to Defeat Terrorism is Self Defeating. *Foreign Policy* [online]. Available at: www.foreignpolicy.com/2017/06/06/trumps-plan-to-defeat-terrorism-is-self-defeating [Accessed 4 May 2018].

SUGGESTED READINGS

Hoffman, B. (2017). *Inside Terrorism*. New York: Columbia University Press.

White, J.R. (2017). *Terrorism and Homeland Security*, 9th ed. Boston: Cengage Learning.

13 Failed and fragile states: The unfinished agenda

David Carment, Mark Haichin, and Yiagadeesen Samy

INTRODUCTION

President Donald Trump has inherited a world where the institutions and orthodoxies that were once unquestioned are now overwhelmed. The world order we have known for decades may be undergoing a second post-Cold War shift. Trump's 2017 National Security Strategy (NSS) (White House, 2017)[1] reflects that great power geopolitics has returned and balances of power are shifting with far-reaching effects, especially as China and Russia challenge U.S. hegemony. This chapter examines the continuity and change in U.S. government policy towards failed and fragile states (FFS)[2] in the developing world of Africa and Asia after the 9/11 attacks in 2001. The analysis encompasses the George W. Bush era with the release of the 2002 NSS (White House, 2002),[3] followed by Obama's, and into the Trump era. 9/11 was a turning point because it led to increasing attention towards FFS as safe havens for terrorist organizations such as al-Qaeda. The purpose is to highlight key areas where Trump's policies are consistent and different from those of his predecessors. We argue that with its sustained focus on security there has been significant continuity in FFS policy from Bush to Trump. U.S. foreign policy has largely focused on those FFS that affect U.S. strategic interests. To demonstrate this point, we examine and compare U.S. policy toward Afghanistan, Ethiopia, and Pakistan.

The choice of these three cases is based on several factors. They are countries that we consider trapped in fragility and have been among the worst performers globally, based on their fragility scores. Afghanistan is the most fragile of the three and has been the subject of U.S. intervention as part of the Global War on Terror. Despite receiving billions of dollars in foreign aid from Washington during the last decade, its situation has not improved very much. As one of the fastest growing economies in the world, Ethiopia's economic and social indicators continue to improve. However, it remains a fragile country, lacking in capacity, and among the largest recipients of US foreign assistance. Finally, we consider the case of Pakistan, which has received significant economic and military assistance from America over time and whose relationship with Washington has been complex.

FAILED AND FRAGILE STATES AND UNITED STATES NATIONAL SECURITY STRATEGY OVER THE YEARS

By 2018, U.S. foreign assistance for reconstruction in Iraq and Afghanistan had exceeded the amount spent on the Marshall Plan to help Western Europe recover from World War II. While the Marshall Plan was a success, Afghanistan and Iraq are arguably not better off today than when the U.S. first intervened in those countries. Both remain unable to exercise full control of their territory, and lack the institutions and bureaucratic capacity necessary for effective reforms. If throwing money at a problem could fix it, we would not be discussing Fragile and Conflict-Affected States (FCAS) today. As early as 2012, Carment and Samy (2012)[4] argued that more states were becoming increasingly fragile over time. The fragility index developed by the Country Indicators for Foreign Policy (CIFP) project showed that progress had been uneven or in some cases non-existent[5] and identified several countries trapped in fragility, and several others that had moved in and out of fragility and were unable to build resilience over time. Since then, several reports relying on incidents of terrorism, battled-related deaths, and levels of internally displaced people and refugees, have made the case that the world had become more turbulent during the last decade.

This stands in sharp contrast to what had happened during the previous two decades. At the end of the Cold War, between 1989 and 1993 or so, conflict was on the rise, commensurate with an increase in the number of FFS around the world. Thereafter, from about 1994, large-scale violence declined largely owing to international efforts to mitigate the destabilizing effects of weak and unstable states and invest heavily in their reconstruction. In addition to declining large-scale violence, additional ethnic groups around the world acquired independence, and more democratic governments emerged. Indeed, at this time democracies outnumbered authoritarian states by a ratio of 2 to 1.

During the Clinton era, the State Failure Task Force (which would later evolve into the Political Instability Task Force) came to dominate policy discourse. State failure, the overarching concept, as defined by the Task Force, was the collapse of authority of a central government to impose order in situations of civil war, revolutionary war, genocide, politicide, and adverse or disruptive regime transition. The original Task Force definition weighted conflict, environment, genocide, and governance factors significantly in its analysis, and thus its principal concern was with instability and security as they related to underlying structural problems and only secondarily proximate factors.

The Turning Point

It was only after 9/11 that policymakers explicitly tied the presence of FCAS to American geopolitical interests. It was around this time that we also witnessed a renewed escalation of violence globally. There were several reasons for this change, chief among them the complex relationship between state failure, poverty, crime and terrorism, such that they were seen to be reinforcing one another. Weak governments motivated impoverished citizens to engage in illicit activities such as drug production and providing ungoverned spaces for terrorists to enjoy safe haven. Indeed, up until then, the tolerance for weak and even failed states meant that the West was an unwitting contributor to creating spaces for terrorist groups to recruit and begin to operate.

After 9/11, all that changed as U.S. policymakers began to equate America's national security with stability and order in the world's impoverished and poorly governed regions. The goal would no longer be development, but security. Thus, FFS were seen as threat to American national security and the global order more generally. America's 2002 National Security Strategy (NSS) discounted Cold War strategies of deterrence and containment in a world of amorphous and ill-defined terrorist networks, arguing that the threats in the world were so dangerous that the U.S. should "not hesitate to act alone, if necessary, to exercise our right of self-defense by acting pre-emptively" (White House 2002: 6). The 2002 NSS also stated that the U.S. aimed to create a new world order that favored democracy and defeats terror at the same time.

In the immediate aftermath of 9/11, media reports indicated that the primary countries harboring terrorists included Afghanistan, Sudan, and Algeria. Eventually that list would be expanded to include U.S. intelligence and law enforcement efforts in the over thirty countries in which terrorist networks were believed to have cells. As a result of this expansion, American efforts evolved to include a variety of policies other than military intervention. U.S. initiatives included training foreign armies and police forces to deal with terrorism, for example, in the Philippines, Pakistan, and Yemen; increased American participation in bilateral and multilateral aid programs in which aid was tied to "good governance" by recipient countries; and the pursuit of global integration through assistance to countries trying to join the international systems of trade and finance.

Thus, under President George W. Bush, and then President Obama, America's FFS policies became most concerned with national and international security, thereby encouraging ideas that promoted immediate stability, such as strengthening domestic security forces, limiting opportunities for international terrorists, and suppressing transnational crime. Policies most concerned with building resilience in less weak states where terrorist activity was less pressing focused on programs that enhanced opportunities for education and employment, reducing disease and malnutrition, increasing standards of living, and supporting concepts such as "good governance."

In brief, the emphasis of the United States Agency for International Development (USAID) on poverty reduction must be seen in the context of Bush and Obama's strategies with their focus on threats to American interests with development subordinate to security. Both administrations sought to build authority and capacity, but there were other issues involving America's focus on government legitimacy and democratization in fragile states. Considerable academic literature debated the link between peace and democracy or trade, or a combination of the two. Poor countries that are making the transition to democracy are actually more likely to engage in conflict, either civil or interstate, in the years immediately following the transition. Under Presidents Bush and Obama, USAID took the lead in implementing the U.S. strategy toward fragile states, including the development of a fragility-oriented analysis and monitoring, with considerable attention given to states' political legitimacy and effectiveness in extracting and distributing resources or public goods.

Under Trump, America's strategy reduced its preoccupation with terrorism and emphasized America's rivalry with China and Russia. Nevertheless, in examining those countries on which Trump sought to impose a visa ban, all but one (Iran) are fragile states, and all have been previous targets of U.S. covert or overt military operations. Where an emphasis on FFS overlaps with this Trump's agenda on geopolitics are those fragile states such as Yemen and Syria, in which powerful rivals have a keen interest. Trump's emphasis on supporting proxy wars in fragile states such as Libya, Syria, Ukraine, and Yemen reflects the linkage between geopolitics and fragile states.

The numbers

As Figure 13.1 shows, during the Bush administration, bilateral foreign aid to FFS increased from about $2.2 billion in 2000 to $20.0 billion in 2005 before declining to $12.6 billion in 2008, the final year of George W. Bush's presidency. The initial increase reflected large amounts of foreign aid to Iraq and Afghanistan. The year 2005 was exceptional as more than 75 percent of U.S. aid to FFS went to Afghanistan and Iraq alone. While this concentration of aid to the so-called "aid darlings" is not unusual among Western donors, U.S. policy is more extreme owing to its extensive involvement in these two countries. Under President Obama, the amounts spent stabilized during the first few years but then declined to roughly $10 billion in Obama's second term as funding for Iraq and Afghanistan gradually declined.[6] The difference in heights of the two sets of columns indicates the importance of these two countries for aid allocation. Thus, overall, we see an increase in foreign aid followed by a decline, but, if Afghanistan and Iraq are excluded, we see an increasing (linear) trend over time. Data from USAID indicates that the amounts of aid given by the US to fragile states declined further in 2017, the first year of the Trump presidency. This is perhaps a sign of further changes to come, given Trump's "America First"

FIGURE 13.1 United States foreign aid to fragile states, 2000–2016

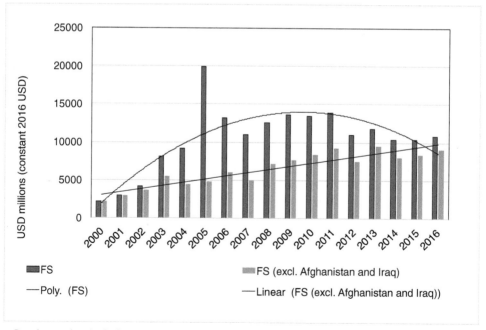

Source: Based on authors' calculations using data from CIFP and the OECD-DAC

FIGURE 13.2 Share of United States foreign aid to fragile states, 2000–2016

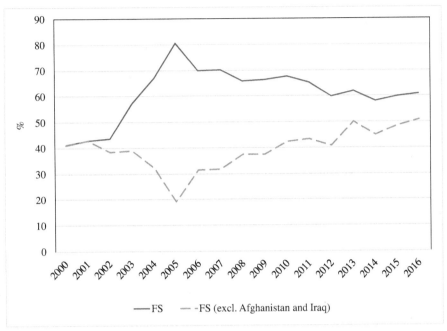

Source: Based on authors' calculations using data from CIFP and the OECD-DAC

rhetoric and its focus on investments that serve U.S. strategic interests. However, Trump's reluctance to intervene in countries like Syria is not very different from Obama's policies. Instead, other than the precision airstrikes against Syria following the latter's chemical attacks, the focus has remained on defeating IS, supporting Kurdish militias fighting the Assad regime, and using diplomacy – not a major change from the Obama administration.

Figure 13.2 examines shares of U.S. bilateral aid going to fragile states relative to total U.S. bilateral aid to all developing countries. Here again, the numbers are skewed by U.S. involvement in Afghanistan and Iraq, and we can see an important turning point in 2005. When we compare the Obama presidency with the Bush presidency, the share of U.S. aid going to fragile states declined slightly in the case of the former but increased in the case of the latter. During Obama's second term, when the share of aid to Afghanistan and Iraq stabilized and then declined, other fragile states consequently saw an increase in their shares.

It is important to remember that the numbers from the *OECD* Development Assistance Committee (*DAC*) are only related to development aid (long-term development and humanitarian assistance). However, Washington also provides significant amounts of military and security aid to assist its allies, and this includes such things as the purchase of military equipment and training of military personnel. While the data are less precise, in part because of the secretive nature of "security" assistance, all available evidence indicates that U.S. security aid has increased significantly since 9/11. The number of security assistance programs almost doubled between 2001 and 2017, and the funding has also increased. Among the largest recipients of U.S. security assistance are several fragile states such as Afghanistan, Egypt, Iraq, and (until recently) Pakistan. Overall, there was continuity between the Bush and Obama presidencies, in investing in long-term development to reduce threats of instability and terrorism. The main difference between the Bush and Obama presidencies, however, is a decline in foreign aid to Afghanistan and Iraq over time. Under Trump's "America First" policies, we may see more disengagement (or simply a reluctance to engage) in countries that have no strategic relevance for America.

 ## CASE STUDIES: AFGHANISTAN, ETHIOPIA, AND PAKISTAN

Afghanistan

United States policy in Afghanistan is the single longest military intervention in American history and has cost over a trillion dollars since 2001. Afghanistan is also a good test case for the support of previous U.S. administrations for innovative policies to stabilize fragile states. In 2001, U.S. intervention in Afghanistan was premised on a belief that it was possible to aid that country with priority being given to supporting mechanisms of defense, diplomacy, and development simultaneously and thereby secure it from terrorists like al-Qaeda and Islamic radicals like the Taliban. Under Obama, there was a reversal of that strategy around 2008 when greater emphasis was placed on security and a de-emphasis on institutionalization and development. In the context of nation-building, the initial approach to intervening in Afghanistan after 2001 was framed as "fighting a three-block war" (conducting full-scale military action, peacekeeping operations and humanitarian aid within three contiguous city blocks). More broadly, it was understood as a "whole of government" approach (integrating the resources and skills of multiple agencies).

The reversal of the strategy under Obama was partly the result of recognition that a "small footprint" was simply not sufficient to deal with growing instability in specific Afghan provinces like Kandahar, and a growing political and terrorist crisis in Pakistan and the spillover effects it was having on neighboring Afghanistan. Subsequent events in Afghanistan have demonstrated that while development and diplomacy are of great value and crucial to overall success, getting military security right at the outset is crucial as it is a pre-condition for other forms of engagement.

A 2018 report by Special Inspector General for Afghanistan Reconstruction (SIGAR) found that, despite heavy investments, stabilization efforts that have been central to military and foreign policy in Afghanistan since the U.S. invaded in 2001 have largely failed. Projects were poorly planned or mismanaged, fostering widespread mistrust among Afghan civilians. Many projects failed after American troops left an area. Afghanistan shows that, despite that country's strategic importance to U.S. security interests, interagency coordination is difficult to achieve. Interagency cooperation depends on agreement among the various arms of government in several different areas. First, they must have a mechanism for shared assessment and early warning to determine in which countries to intervene and when to do so. If America intervenes, its agencies must share a general conceptualization of the problem. This includes the primary sources of instability in the country, a strategy for how best to intervene that specifies both short-term priorities and long-term goals for the national effort, a common pool of resources to ensure that funding flows to the true priority areas in the country, and an integrated administration and decision-making structure to ensure that the efforts of each U.S. government agency do not impede, or actively undermine, the efforts of the others.

The Trump administration's Afghanistan policy has largely continued the trend of de-emphasizing nation-building in favor of security. Early in the 2016 presidential election, Trump described the invasion of Afghanistan as a "mistake" due to it having become a quagmire, although he quickly backtracked and denied his previous remarks in favor of considering the conflict necessary owing to Afghanistan's proximity to Pakistan and its nuclear arsenal. After winning the election, Trump's 2017 National Security Strategy stated that the administration would commit to supporting FFS whose weakness threatened American security, with Afghanistan being explicitly referenced (White House 2017: 40).[1] It became clear early on that the Trump administration would take a more militarily aggressive stance in Afghanistan than its predecessors, having used a high-yield Massive Ordnance Air Blast bomb against Islamic State forces in that country in April 2017.

President Trump's actual Afghanistan policy, however, was not announced until August. The administration declared that it would end nation-building efforts in favor of focusing specifically on combating terrorism, though few specifics were provided. Additionally, Trump's policy announcement stated that the American forces would remain indefinitely in Afghanistan, with the intention of following Pentagon recommendations for increasing the number of deployed troops. By September 2017, America had increased the number of troops deployed in Afghanistan to 14,000, with an additional 1,000 having been sent in early 2018. Additionally, Trump stated in January 2018 that Washington would not negotiate with the Taliban, indicating that the administration would seek a military victory. Despite the apparent focus on military efforts, agencies like USAID continued to fund non-military projects like energy services (USAID, 2018a).[7]

To date, the Trump administration's approach to Afghanistan has not been successful. At present, the Taliban is believed to either control or have an active presence in about 70 percent of Afghanistan's territory that contains approximately fifteen million Afghans. The situation has deteriorated with Afghan security forces suffering high desertion and casualty rates. Thus, they were reduced to just under 300,000 personnel by April 2018 – a drop of about 10 percent compared to twelve months earlier (SIGAR, 2018).[8] The Taliban insurgency seems sufficiently powerful that President Ashraf Ghani offered to negotiate with its leaders, notwithstanding the Trump administration's position. Ghani even proposed that the Taliban could become a legitimate political party if it ceased its attacks. The security situation in Afghanistan thus does not appear to have improved in spite of the Trump administration's militant approach, and indeed seems to have worsened owing to the relative lack of focus on good governance.

Ethiopia

American foreign policy towards Ethiopia since 2001 has largely revolved around two main objectives. The first is eliminating, or at least containing, the presence of terrorist organizations based in East Africa. Ethiopia is regarded as crucial owing to its relative military strength and proximity to Somalia where terrorists have a major presence. During George W. Bush's presidency, Ethiopia gained prominence as an important ally in fighting terrorism in East Africa. This is due in large part to its proximity to Somalia, which has been a haven for terrorist groups like the Islamic Courts Union and al-Shabab as well as al-Qaeda in the Horn of Africa. Ethiopia has become part of Washington's Partnership for Regional East Africa Counterterrorism (PREACT), since its establishment in 2003 (Bureau of Counterterrorism, 2018; Emerson, 2014).[9] Under this initiative, America aids the Ethiopian government in developing counterterrorism capabilities, including enhancing border security and attacking the operational capacity of terrorist networks, and in return is provided with relevant intelligence and can use the country as a base for fighting Islamic militants in Somalia with airstrikes and special forces (Fisher and Anderson, 2015; Gordon and Mazzetti, 2007).[10]

A second goal for the U.S. in Ethiopia has been to fund development in order to address domestic challenges such as the absence of democratization, famine relief, and the spread of HIV/AIDS. This has its origins in the 2002 NSS, which stated that aid to developing economies for crisis relief and economic and political reform are necessary for U.S. national security. Much of the funding provided by Washington to Ethiopia during this period was spent on humanitarian and development programs. The U.S. also kept Ethiopia on the list of countries given greater access to American markets through the African Growth and Opportunity Act (AGOA), which sought to encourage the implementation of market reforms and democratization (International Trade Administration, 2009).[11]

Ethiopia's importance in fighting terrorism in the 2000s meant that it faced little pressure from the United States to implement domestic reforms. Despite the importance of democratization among the Bush administration's broader foreign-policy objectives, the Ethiopian government faced only occasional criticism. This was apparent in the Bush administration's response to the rigged 2005 elections, when Washington merely voiced concern about "voting irregularities" (Bruton, 2009).[12] This stood in vivid contrast with the action of the European Union, which cut off $88 million in aid in response to electoral fraud and the government's use of deadly force against protestors (Abbink, 2006).[13] In order to maintain Ethiopian support for the War on Terror, the U.S. administration also took no action in response to war crimes committed by Ethiopian forces in Somalia (Plaut, 2013).[14] The Bush administration even took steps to defend the Ethiopian government's actions on some occasions, such as opposing a Democratic bill in 2007 that would have required ending aid to Ethiopia if that country failed to take steps to democratize and improve human rights. The bill ultimately died in the Senate. Moreover, the Ethiopian government failed to meet AGOA's requirements to protect human rights and combat corruption, but the Bush administration chose to keep it on the list of eligible states. Taken together, these suggest that the Bush administration was willing to compromise its democratization objectives in Ethiopia in favor of its security interests in the region.

Much like his predecessor, President Obama considered Ethiopia to be a key counterterrorism ally. Many Bush-era policies regarding U.S.-Ethiopian cooperation, including intelligence-sharing and the provision of military funding and training, continued during the Obama years (Mariam, 2017).[15] The administration also received permission from the Ethiopian government to use a base in Arba Minch in southern Ethiopia for launching drones between 2011 and 2016. Although the Obama administration claimed that these drones were only used for surveillance, it is suspected that they were also used to attack al-Shabab members in Somalia (BBC News, 2016).[16] Foreign aid continued as in the Bush years to focus on development-related programs, and, much as in the Bush administration, these programs were justified in the Obama National Security Strategies as beneficial to U.S. national security (White House, 2010; White House, 2015).[17] Aid for military training and equipment increased relative to Bush-era funding levels, although publicly released figures suggest they remained around $5 million per year, with a maximum of $12 million out of a total of $808 million in funding in 2015 (USAID, 2018b).[18]

Like the Bush administration, the Obama administration did little to address domestic reform in Ethiopia owing to its role in counterterrorism. Although the 2010 and 2015 Ethiopian elections were widely viewed as shams due to the *Ethiopian People's Revolutionary Democratic Front's* legislative dominance, America's response was minimal, with a simple expression of concern regarding subsequent political irregularities. During a visit to Addis Ababa in July 2015, Obama himself referred to the Ethiopian government as having been democratically elected (Arriola and Lyons, 2016).[19] Much as in the preceding administration, Ethiopia was not disqualified from AGOA despite failing to meet the outlined criteria owing to its election rigging, suppression of popular dissent, and human rights abuses (Allo, 2017).[20] Counterterrorism goals in the Horn of Africa thus continued to supersede development and democratization objectives in Ethiopia under the Obama administration.

To date, President Trump appears to lack a coherent Ethiopian policy, but it appears to continue prioritizing counterterrorism. The proposed 2018 budget emphasized military spending more than diplomacy or development assistance. Thus, America's Department of Defense received a 9 percent increase in funding, while the State Department (including USAID) had its budget slashed by 29 percent. This reduction included cuts to programs like the President's Emergency Plan For AIDS Relief (PEPFAR), which provides treatment for HIV/AIDS patients in countries like Ethiopia, as well as emergency response programs for alleviating food shortages (Campbell, 2017).[21] The administration has, however, continued to provide aid funding to Ethiopia, including $454 million in food and medical aid in 2017, but has demanded that the Ethiopian government make greater contributions as well (Morello, 2017).[22] The administration has been perceived as relatively uninterested in African issues and has left many important diplomatic positions unfilled, although former Secretary of State Rex Tillerson condemned the Ethiopian state of emergency during a visit in March 2018 (Ansley, 2018; Schemm, 2018).[23] At present, the most senior US official with Africa-focused duties is AFRICOM commander General Thomas Waldhauser, due to there being no Assistant Secretary of State for African Affairs. In short, the Trump administration's priorities regarding Ethiopia, insofar as they can be discerned, appear to be more military-oriented than development-focused.

Pakistan

While Afghanistan and Ethiopia are heavily dependent on American aid, Pakistan is less so and therefore is less amenable to overt manipulation. The aid the U.S. has given Pakistan is largely military and has been used to shore up a centralized and corrupt military-dominated authority structure whether perceived to be legitimate or not (Carment and Samy, 2017).[24] Externally, the risks that Pakistan poses have been shaped by its historical rivalry with India and influence in Afghanistan. In addition to supporting separatist movements in India, Pakistan has provided sanctuary and training as well as arms to participants in conflicts in Asia, including the Muslim resistance to Russian occupation of Afghanistan.

American policy towards Pakistan is exemplified in Bush's and Obama's long-term aid program in support for allies in the War on Terror. At the height of the war in Afghanistan, Washington was willing to turn a blind eye to Pakistan's domestic problems in exchange for that country's support in fighting al-Qaeda. General Pervez Musharraf's ascension to become Pakistan's president in 2001 was followed by a crackdown that reduced civil liberties, saw the arrest and torture of opposition politicians, restricted media outlets, and banned public rallies (Shah, 2008).[25] While political parties were allowed to operate during this period, their influence was curtailed by party factionalism, a lack of leadership and army influence. The combination of silencing political opponents and restricting political liberties would eventually challenge the legitimacy of the Musharraf regime, leading to his resignation in 2008.

Linked to his rise and fall was President Musharraf's decision to support the American anti-terrorist campaign in Afghanistan. That effort coincided with a crackdown on Islamic political action in Pakistan (Polity IV, 2010).[26] In addition, the alliance forged between Washington and the Musharraf regime against "global terror" reduced the government's authority over the contested Federally Administered Tribal Areas bordering Afghanistan and the Baluch region (Carment et al., 2007; Brown et al., 2012).[27] Despite being legally owned by Pakistan, these areas, particularly North and South Waziristan, are largely ungovernable, host both the Afghan and Pakistani Taliban, and remain linked to Afghanistan (Carment et al., 2007).[27] The region affords a sanctuary for terrorist networks, a training and recruiting ground for the Afghan Taliban, and a breeding ground for indigenous militants (Schofield 2011).[28] Between 2004 and 2007, the Pakistani government was engaged in sustained fighting in the region against al-Qaeda and Taliban militants. However, this proved ineffective because it created additional jihadists who turned against the Pakistani state (Polity IV, 2010,[26] Grare, 2012).[29]

In 2011, after a 10-year search, Osama bin Laden was killed by U.S. Special Forces. There was considerable debate about whether Pakistani authorities had knowingly providing bin Laden with safe haven. Indeed, he had resided in the country for over nine years. Debate also focused on the legality of the killing with Obama condoning the act not as a state-sponsored assassination or violation of Pakistani sovereignty but as an act of self-defense. Between 2004 and 2013, the Bush and Obama administrations conducted numerous targeted drone killings in Pakistan of al-Qaeda operatives. The use of drones resulted in considerable collateral damage with casualties in excess of 3,000. A UN special rapporteur described these attacks as war crimes, and Pakistan's legal authorities declared them illegal.

In 2013, Pakistan held the first democratic transition between governments in its history. Hailed as a "watershed" moment in Pakistan's political history, the government of Nawaz Sharif, a once-exiled Prime Minister and leader of the Pakistani Muslim League party, took power amid a backdrop of deep-seated anti-Americanism following the stalemate in Afghanistan, strained civil-military relations, and a declining security situation in Baluchistan (Grare, 2012).[29] Since then Pakistan has witnessed spreading extremist violence including attacks carried out by the Islamic State. Intermittent violence and terrorist acts included the Peshawar school attack in 2014 that led to the death of 150, many of whom were children.

When Donald Trump became president, he signaled U.S. dissatisfaction with Pakistan's border disagreements with Afghanistan and its perceived involvement in the security situation in Afghanistan and asylum for the Afghan Taliban, and he threatened to end U.S. aid. Politically, however, many Pakistanis considered U.S. drone attacks and continued U.S. interventions on their soil as violations of their country's sovereignty. Against this backdrop the decline in U.S. influence over Pakistan coincided with America's failures in Afghanistan. And, in January 2018, Trump carried out his threat and suspended military aid to Pakistan. "The United States has foolishly given Pakistan more than 33 billion dollars in aid over the last 15 years, and they have given us nothing but lies & deceit," Trump tweeted, "They give safe haven to the terrorists we hunt in Afghanistan, with little help. No more!" (cited in Aleem, 2018).[30]

When Trump announced that his government would focus on a renewed security strategy in Afghanistan, the U.S. also signaled it would be engaging other regional partners who could provide air base and logistical support, like Uzbekistan. This shift in strategy coincided with a rise in China's influence over Pakistan with the two countries opening trade routes, developing joint weapons programs, and signing agreements and initiatives to attract Chinese investment. Reflecting this transformation, a 2013 Pew study found that 81 percent of Pakistanis responded favorably to China. Only 11 percent of Pakistanis had a favorable view of America, with a large majority supporting the withdrawal of U.S. troops from Afghanistan (Pew Research Center, 2013).[31]

CONCLUSION

What lessons have we learned from US policies towards FFS since 9/11? On the one hand, we have seen more continuity than might have been expected, with three different presidents who have focused on security. While the precarious situations in the three cases we have examined cannot be tied to specific U.S. involvement, such involvement cannot be totally discounted. Afghanistan has deteriorated in all aspects of stateness – authority, legitimacy and capacity. Ethiopia, despite improvements in capacity, has seen an erosion in authority and legitimacy. In the case of Pakistan, improvements in the government's legitimacy have been offset by deterioration in authority and state capacity. Overall, each of these cases has experienced a deterioration in fragility since 2001. Afghanistan and Pakistan are clearly stuck in a fragility trap, and Ethiopia is not far behind even if it has a better chance of improving over time (Carment and Samy, 2017).[24]

On the other hand, there is one glaring discontinuity between Trump and his predecessors on climate change and its link to FFS. Going back to the Clinton era, one of the main concerns of post-Cold War presidents has been the impact that climate change has had on state stability. This was a core part of the original State Failure Task Force in the 1990s and has been central to national security ever since. This linkage is discussed in many studies, specifically the relationship between desertification, famine, and refugee flows as a source of instability in the Middle East and Africa (Carment et al., 2016).[32] Donald Trump's withdrawal from the Paris Accords and his interest in revitalizing American producers of fossil fuels through exploitation of known resources suggests that America's commitment to battling climate change and in turn addressing the problems it generates for fragile states is on hold and perhaps reversed.

A less obvious development has been the revival of geopolitics. Over time, it appears that geopolitics is playing a larger role in fragile states, as Chinese and Russian influence increase owing to economic and/or military assistance increase. Thus, the Trump administration will focus primarily on the direct effects these rivals have on core American interests. Fragile and Conflict-Affected States will be more or less relevant accordingly. Are these changes simply window dressing or is there a meaningful shift? In the absence of a grand strategy guiding Trump's engagement with FCAS, we surmise that many of these countries, including Afghanistan and Pakistan, will continue to remain the targets of major competitors. Strategic FCAS will become the objects of intervention by rivals, assuring that civil strife will become more prolonged and deadly. We have witnessed extreme outcomes in the case of the lengthy civil war in Syria (with direct Russian and U.S. intervention) and the humanitarian catastrophe in Yemen (with geopolitical proxies Iran and Saudi Arabia vying for control).

ESSAY QUESTIONS

1) What are the characteristics of failed or fragile states, and what has been the trend with these states over the past decades?

2) Discuss how the events of 9/11 were a turning point in U.S. policy toward failing and fragile states and how the Bush and Obama administrations viewed these states.

3) What have been the patterns in the distribution of U.S. foreign aid to fragile states over the past decades? To what extent do the authors indicate the likely trend with the Trump administration?

4) Select one of the states from the case studies analyzed in the chapter (Afghanistan, Ethiopia, and Pakistan) and compare the policy approaches of the Obama and Trump administrations in addressing that state.

5) To what extent do the authors argue that the Trump administration's policy toward failed and fragile states reflect continuity and discontinuity with the recent past?

SHORT ANSWER QUESTIONS

Define and describe the importance of the following:

NSS 2017
Political Instability Task Force
SIGAR Report on Afghanistan
Trump's Ethiopian policy
Suspension of military aid to Pakistan

NOTES

1   White House (2017). National Security Strategy. Available at: www.whitehouse.gov/wp-content/uploads/2017/12/NSS-Final-12–18–2017–0905.pdf [Accessed 9 June 2018].

2   Fragile and Conflict-Affected States (FCAS) is another term used to describe fragile states. In this chapter, we will use FCAS and FFS interchangeably. Initially US administrations referred to FFS, which evolved under Obama to become FCAS.

3   White House (2002). National Security Strategy. Available at: www.state.gov/documents/organization/63562.pdf [Accessed 7 June 2018].

4   Carment, D. and Samy, Y. (2012). An increasingly fragile world. In Sean Clark and Sabrina Hoque (eds.) *Debating a Post-American World: What lies ahead?* London: Routledge, pp. 176–182.

5   According to CIFP's conceptualization, a state must possess three attributes – *authority, legitimacy* and *capacity* – to function properly. *Authority* refers to the state as having a monopoly on violence and the ability to pass binding legislation over its population, control its territory, and provide core public goods and a stable and secure environment for its citizens. *Legitimacy* refers to how much a state commands loyalty to the governing regime and supports the government's legislation and policy. *Capacity* refers to the ability of a state to mobilize and use resources for productive ends. States that build capacity are more resilient to exogenous shocks.

6   We used CIFP's latest ranking of fragile states to calculate how much aid is provided. The 40 most fragile states in the world for 2015 are selected, and the amount of bilateral development aid (using data from the OECD Development Assistance Committee, or OECD DAC, in constant dollars) provided to these countries is then tracked over time.

7   USAID (2018a). U.S. Foreign Aid by Country: Afghanistan. Available at: https://explorer.usaid.gov/cd/AFG [Accessed 6 May 2018].

8   SIGAR (2018). SIGAR April 30 2018 Quarterly Report to the United States Congress. Arlington: Special Inspector General for Afghanistan reconstruction. Available at: www.sigar.mil/pdf/quarterlyreports/2018-04-30qr.pdf [Accessed 7 June 2018].

9   Bureau of Counterterrorism (2018). Programs and Initiatives. U.S. Department of State. Available at: www.state.gov/j/ct/programs/index.htm#PREACT [Accessed 14 May 2018]; Emerson, S. (2014). Back to the Future: The evolution of US counterterrorism policy in Africa. *Insight on Africa*, 6:1, pp. 43–56.

10   Fisher, J. and Anderson, D. (2015). Authoritarianism and the Securitization of Development in Africa. *International Affairs* 91:1, pp. 131–151; Gordon, M. and Mazzetti, M. (2007). U.S. Used Base in Ethiopia to Hunt Al Qaeda. *New York Times* [online]. Available at: www.nytimes.com/2007/02/23/world/africa/23somalia.html [Accessed 4 May 2018].

11   International Trade Administration (2009). Summary of AGOA I. U.S. Department of Commerce. Available at: www.trade.gov/agoa/legislation/index.asp [Accessed 1 May 2018].

12   Bruton, B.E. (2009). U.S. Policy Shift Needed in the Horn of Africa. *Council on Foreign Relations*. Available at: www.cfr.org/expert-brief/us-policy-shift-needed-horn-africa [Accessed 3 June 2018].

13   Abbink, J. (2006). Discomfiture of Democracy? The 2005 election crisis in Ethiopia and its aftermath. *African Affairs*, 105:419, pp. 173–199.

14   Plaut, M. (2013). "How Unstable is the Horn of Africa?" *Review of African Political Economy*, 40:136, pp. 321–330.

15   Mariam, A. (2017). US Doesn't Need Ethiopia in its War on Terror in the Horn of Africa. *The Hill*. Available at: http://thehill.com/blogs/pundits-blog/foreign-policy/332093-us-doesnt-need-ethiopia-in-its-war-on-terror-in-the-horn-of [Accessed 7 February 2018].

16   BBC News (2016). "US Shuts Drone Base in Ethiopia." *BBC News*. Available at: www.bbc.com/news/world-africa-35220279 [Accessed 5 June 2018].

17   White House (2010). National Security Strategy. Available at: http://nssarchive.us/NSSR/2010.pdf [Accessed 8 June 2018]; White House (2015). National Security Strategy. Available at: https://obamawhitehouse.archives.gov/sites/default/files/docs/2015_national_security_strategy_2.pdf [Accessed 9 June 2018].

18   USAID (2018b). U.S. Foreign Aid by Country: Ethiopia. Available at: https://explorer.usaid.gov/cd/ETH [Accessed 6 May 2018].

19 Arriola, L. and Lyons, T. (2016). The 100% Election. *Journal of Democracy* 27:1, pp. 76–88.
20 Allo, A. (2017). Protests, Terrorism, and Development: On Ethiopia's perpetual state of emergency. *Yale Human Rights & Development Law Journal* 19:1, pp. 133–177.
21 Campbell, J. (2017). Trump's Dangerous Retreat from Africa. *Foreign Policy*. Available at: http://foreignpolicy.com/2017/11/03/trumps-dangerous-retreat-from-africa [Accessed 14 May 2018].
22 Morello, C. (2017). United States to Give Ethiopia $91 Million in Drought Aid for Food and Medicine. *Washington Post* [online]. Available at: www.washingtonpost.com/world/africa/us-gives-ethiopia-91-million-in-drought-aid-for-food-and-medicine/2017/08/31/0f8d381e-c101-4a08-86e4-562fae028a2c_story.html [Accessed 1 May 2018].
23 Ansley, R. (2018). Trump's Tough Approach to Ethiopia. Atlantic Council. Available at: www.atlanticcouncil.org/blogs/new-atlanticist/tillerson-in-ethiopia [Accessed 6 June 2018]; Schemm, P. (2018). Trump's Comments on Africa Cast Pall Over Tillerson's Long-Awaited Trip. *The Washington Post*, 7 March. www.washingtonpost.com/world/africa/trumps-comments-on-africa-cast-pall-over-tillersons-long-awaited-trip/2018/03/07/d4e12ea8-2211-11e8-946c-9420060cb7bd_story.html [Accessed 14 April 2018].
24 Carment, D. and Samy, Y. (2017). Exiting the Fragility Trap. UNU Helsinki Working Paper Series. Available at: www.wider.unu.edu/publication/exiting-fragility-trap [Accessed 5 May 2018].
25 Shah, A. (2008). Pakistan after Musharraf: Praetorianism and Terrorism. *Journal of Democracy*, 19:4, pp. 16–25.
26 Polity IV 2010. Country Report 2010: Pakistan. Available at: www.systemicpeace.org/polity/Pakistan2010.pdf [Accessed 7 March 2018].
27 Carment, D., Prest, S., and Fritzen, A. (2007). Pakistan. Ottawa: Country indicators for foreign policy democracy & governance. Available at: https://carleton.ca/cifp/wp-content/uploads/1044-1.pdf [Accessed 3 May 2018]; Brown, M., Dawod, M., Irantalab, A., and Naqi, M. (2012). Balochistan case study. Available at: https://carleton.ca/cifp/wp-content/uploads/1398-1.pdf [Accessed 5 June 2018].
28 Schofield, J. (2011). Diversionary Wars: Pashtun unrest and the sources of the Pakistan-Afghan confrontation. *Canadian Foreign Policy Journal* 17:1, pp. 38–49.
29 Grare, F. (2013). Pakistan's Foreign and Security Policies after the 2013 General Election: The judge, the politician and the military. *International Affairs* 89:4, pp. 987–1001.
30 Aleem, Z. (2018). Trump's Sudden New Fight with Pakistan, Explained. *Vox*. Available at: www.vox.com/world/2018/1/8/16850116/trump-pakistan-suspend-aid [Accessed 8 June 2018].
31 Pew Research Center (2013). On Eve of Elections, a Dismal Public Mood in Pakistan. Available at: www.pewglobal.org/2013/05/07/on-eve-of-elections-a-dismal-public-mood-in-pakistan [Accessed 3 March 2018].
32 Carment, D., Langlois, B., and Samy, Y. (2016). Assessing State Fragility with a Focus on Climate Change and Refugees. Available at: https://carleton.ca/cifp/wp-content/uploads/CIFP-2016-Fragility-Report-March-16-2016.pdf [Accessed 7 June 2018].

SUGGESTED READINGS

Carment, D. and Samy, Y. (2012). An increasingly fragile world. In Sean Clark and Sabrina Hoque (eds.) *Debating a Post-American World: What lies ahead?* London: Routledge, pp. 176–182.
Brock, L. and Holm, H. (2012). *Fragile States*. Cambridge, UK: Polity Press.
Plaut, M. (2013). How Unstable is the Horn of Africa? *Review of African Political Economy*, 40 (136): 321–330.
Ghani, A. and Lockhart, C. (2008). *Fixing Failed States*. New York: Oxford University Press.

14 Is weak cyber security an existential threat?

Steffen W. Schmidt

INTRODUCTION

Cyber refers to the culture and systems of computers, information technology, networked society and systems, the Internet, social media, and virtual reality, and is the fifth dimension of warfare. It is a relatively new environment and therefore society and governments have yet to fully grasp its opportunities and threats because it surpasses traditional modes of communication.

The scale of the cyber environment is staggering. In 1994 there were fewer than 3,000 online websites. Today, there are over a trillion. There are over three billion e-mail accounts. Facebook had 2.07 billion monthly active users by 2018. The analytics firm Twopcharts reported there were over 974 million Twitter accounts, and Morgan Stanley predicted that 75 billion devices would be connected to the Internet by 2020. Most are insecure and can be hijacked for nefarious activities (LaFrance, 2015).[1]

CYBER-CHALLENGES

In cyberdefense, warfare, crime, espionage, or terrorism we are faced with an "uncertainty vector." Cyber-challenges are fundamentally different than past threats. Emily Parkerasks:

> How does a government respond to an invisible attacker, especially without clear rules of engagement? How can officials convince other governments and the public that they have fingered the right suspects? How can a state prevent cyberattacks when without attribution, the logic of deterrence – if you hit me, I'll hit you back – no longer applies?
> (Parker, 2017)[2]

A challenging problem for the Trump administration is "diagnostic," including, "Was this a cyberattack?" and, if so, "who is responsible and how can we respond?"

Because the cyber-domain is non-transparent and secretive, it produces uncertainty and asymmetrical knowledge, and the speed of "information," including rumor and false news, means that there is little time between an alert and a necessary response. The lack of transparency of cyberspace was evident in Russia's Facebook and Twitter networks that spread disinformation and propaganda. The Internet and the anonymity of its user-identity make possible clandestine operations using social media that are a menace to Western democracies. Imperialist U, True Pundit, and similar websites are shadowy Twitter megaphones that amplify Russian efforts to shape Western public opinion and elections. Their impact was virtually unseen until the 2016 U.S. elections, when hacks of Democratic Party accounts by Russians were exposed.

CYBERATTACKS

The opportunities and risks of the Internet in recent decades evolved slowly from the Advanced Research Projects Agency Network (ARPANET), a closed military/academic precursor of today's Internet. Incidents of cyberattacks during the past decade reflect the Internet's vulnerability:

- In 2005 U.S. and Israeli intelligence agencies placed the Stuxnet virus in Iran's nuclear centrifuges. This "worm" targeted industrial computer systems and caused substantial damage to Iran's nuclear weapons program. Stuxnet was part of an intelligence operation called "Operation Olympic Games," initiated under President George W. Bush and expanded by President Obama. The Obama administration also had a secret program, code-named "Nitro Zeus," involving a massive cyberattack on Iran if negotiations over Iran's nuclear program collapsed and America were to go to war (Sanger and Mazzetti, 2016).[3]
- In 2010, leaks of classified government information by Bradley (now Chelsea) Manning to WikiLeaks, an international non-profit entity that releases secret information provided by anonymous sources, proved highly damaging to U.S. intelligence agencies.
- In 2013, the data theft and its release by former CIA contractor Edward Snowden were devastating for America's National Security Agency (NSA).
- In 2015, suspected Chinese hackers broke into the U.S. Office of Personnel Management computers compromising the personal data of 25.7 million of current and former federal employees, including U.S. intelligence operatives, their friends and family members. FBI Director James Comey called this attack the most damaging cyberbreach in U.S. history.
- In 2015, after numerous hacks of U.S. companies, Washington and Beijing agreed not to steal each other's corporate data. The cybersecurity firm CrowdStrike reported additional attacks on U.S. technology companies a few days later.
- In March 2017, WikiLeaks leaked information about cybertools called "Vault 7", revealing CIA electronic surveillance and cyberwarfarecapabilities.
- In April 2017, the hacker group Shadow Brokers released information about sophisticated cyber-capabilities developed by the NSA's best hackers, the "Tailored Access Operations" group (Reeve, 2017).[4] Called WannaCry and NotPetya, the ransomware revealed the NSA's EternalBlue exploit and DoublePulsar "backdoor" tools. The Shadow Brokers provided EternalBlue and DoublePulsar to the criminal world, resulting in massive breaches of Microsoft systems. The ransomware attacks from NotPetya alone affected 12,500 computers in at least sixty-four countries. The disturbing reality was that U.S. intelligence agencies had lost control of their "cyber weapon arsenals,"

a vast array of hacking tools used to penetrate computer systems to gather intelligence and conduct cyberwarfare.

- In 2017, the cybersecurity firm Equifax was breached. According to the company, personal information including Social Security numbers, birth dates, addresses, and credit card numbers were stolen, affecting about 147 million people.
- In 2017, the NSA experienced an extensive hack on its classified cyber counterintelligence information and its own cyber-weapons. Some of these tools were used against U.S. agencies. Former Defense Secretary and CIA Director Leon Panetta argued that every time a hack like this occurs, agencies are forced to "start over" (Shane et al., 2017).[5] A year of investigations has still not revealed who was behind this attack.
- In late 2017, the Trump administration Homeland Security Adviser claimed that North Korean hackers were behind the global WannaCry ransomware attack, which had crippled computers in over 150 countries with demands for ransom. Such events reveal the cyber-problems with which American leaders have to cope.

CYBERPOLICIES BEFORE THE OBAMA ADMINISTRATION

Although there was some attention to cyber security by the Clinton administration (Boys, 2018),[6] cyber was not a priority for most U.S. policymakers. Clinton's Vice President, Al Gore, was among the first political leaders to recognize the emerging importance of the Internet. Even earlier, as a U.S. senator, Gore had promoted the importance of high-speed communications technology. The Internet was a nascent system and there were no smart phones, much less innumerable smart devices (actually mini-computers) in cars, refrigerators, TV sets, children's toys, home thermostats, collectively called "The Internet of Everything." "As recently as 2007, malicious cyber-activities" did not on appear on America's "list of major threats to national security. In 2015, they ranked first" (Nye, 2016/17).[7]

The George W. Bush administration addressed the threat with the Comprehensive National Cybersecurity Initiative (CNCI), established by National Security Presidential Directive 54 and Homeland Security Presidential Directive 23.

Elements of the CNCI were:

- Creating or enhancing shared situational awareness within the federal government, and with other government agencies and the private sector;
- Creating or enhancing the ability to respond quickly to prevent intrusions;
- Enhancing counterintelligence capabilities;
- Increasing the security of the supply chain for key information technologies;
- Expanding cyber-education;
- Coordinating and redirecting research and development efforts; and
- Developing deterrence strategies.

In 2009, Washington established the U.S. Cyber Command.

> USCYBERCOM plans, coordinates, integrates, synchronizes and conducts activities to direct the operations and defense of specified Department of Defense information networks and prepare to, and when directed, conduct full spectrum military cyberspace

operations in order to enable actions in all domains, ensure US/Allied freedom of action in cyberspace and deny the same to our adversaries

(US Department of Defense, 2010).[8]

In 2011, the NSA began building the first of several data centers to be developed from CNCI, the Community Comprehensive National Cybersecurity Initiative Data Center.

The Obama administration gave cybersecurity considerable visibility. In 2010, President Obama signed Executive Order 13549, which declared: "There is established a Classified National Security Information Program designed to safeguard and govern access to classified national security information shared by the federal government with state, local, tribal, and private sector (SLTPS) entities" (Ellis, 2014: 24).[9] The order offered an ambitious list of provisions and actions intended to defend and protect classified information at all levels of government and private companies doing classified work with the government. While admirable in hindsight, it is unlikely that there existed then or now sufficient resources, trained personnel, and/or hardware/software to achieve these goals. The numerous hacks, data breaches, and thefts of sensitive information that have occurred since 2010 confirm this.

The Cybersecurity Enhancement Act of 2014 was designed "to provide for an ongoing, voluntary public-private partnership to improve cybersecurity, and to strengthen cybersecurity research and development, workforce development and education, and public awareness and preparedness, and for other purposes." The act encompassed an ambitious set of objectives including funding for robust cloud computing, authentication, "interoperability among identity management technologies," and "improving privacy protection in identity management systems, including health information technology systems, through authentication and security protocols" (P.L. 113–274, 2014).[10] Few of the objectives listed in the law were realized.

The Cybersecurity Act of 2015 provided "important tools necessary to strengthen the nation's cybersecurity, particularly by making it easier for private companies to share cyber threat information with each other and the Government" (The White House, 2016).[11] Thereafter, the Obama administration launched the Cybersecurity National Action Plan. According to the White House, this plan, "takes near-term actions and puts in place a long-term strategy to enhance cybersecurity awareness and protections, protect privacy, maintain public safety as well as economic and national security, and empower Americans to take better control of their digital security" (The White House, 2016).[11]

Nevertheless, during the Obama administration's two terms, massive cyberattacks against private companies and government agencies proliferated. In retrospect, the Obama administration responded rather meekly to Russian efforts to interfere in America's 2016 elections, expelling diplomats, telling Russian President Putin to "cut it out," and closing a Russian facility. While we do not know whether other attacks were successfully prevented, it is clear that overall, America has been vulnerable, and its greater emphasis on cybersecurity may still remain ineffective. The task of the Trump administration is to realize the objectives of previous initiatives.

CYBERPOLICY IN THE TRUMP ADMINISTRATION

In dealing with cybersecurity as with other issues, the Trump administration is not following the traditional foreign policy-making model, involving the president and major foreign-policy agencies like the State and Defense Departments, and the NSC. President

Trump has repeatedly tweeted attacks on what he calls the "deep state," that is, government bureaucrats whom he believes have conspired against him. Thus, he has assailed U.S. intelligence agencies and the FBI, which are responsible for cybersecurity and cyberdefense. On July 13, 2018 the Special Counsel's office issued indictments against twelve Russian military intelligence officers accusing them of hacking the e-mails of Hillary Clinton's campaign and other Democratic Party sites and providing great detail of their activities. This came just a day before President Trump was to meet with Russian President Vladimir Putin. Following his meeting, to the dismay of U.S. politicians, Republican and Democratic, standing next to Putin, Trump refused to acknowledge Russian cyberattacks in the face of detailed evidence by seven federal agencies and congressional committees.

In addition to the president's apparent unwillingness to accept documented evidence of Russian cyberthreats, two key issues confront the Trump administration. First, is it safe to source crucial technology components and software from countries that are adversaries? Is it farfetched to imagine that Chinese or other foreign suppliers might deliberately embed malware in devices for American defense contractors, foreign-policy decision makers, or military services? This would be a classic asymmetrical military technique. Current adversaries could close the strategic gap by literally "moving" cyber components directly into America. Second, does relying on foreign suppliers of critical parts also make the U.S. vulnerable to a supply choke-off in which these components could be withheld at a crucial moment, paralyzing U.S. cybercommand.

Both Presidents Obama and Trump prevented Chinese investors from buying American chip manufacturers. Observers point out that U.S. manufacturers, including companies in the delicate information and communications technology (ICT) sector are outsourcing production overseas, notably to China. Trump must examine how to preserve a healthy U.S. manufacturing sector for computers, electronic communications devices, microchips, and other components of networked systems. In 2018 Washington prohibited the merger of a Chinese company with American tech giant Qualcomm, suggesting that a hard line on mergers has become the norm.

One consideration that will affect the foreign-policy and security ecosystems is the security of five enormous ICT companies, Alphabet (Google's owner), Apple, Microsoft, Facebook, and Amazon, which control the Internet. This is a sensitive issue for the Trump administration and Congress because they are committed to deregulation and are reluctant to interfere with the vast private-sector ITC companies.

We have noted the damage that Microsoft operating system vulnerabilities caused when hackers were able to attack computers around the world. It is largely private-sector products such as servers, computers, software, and smart phones that are used by U.S. military and intelligence agencies. Thus, these five and other smaller but crucial ITC companies are indispensable for the security of cyberspace. Indeed, the ability of these tech giants to mine personal information about U.S. citizens as well as others globally has major implications for government policy. Ultimately, these companies will have access to more information than the U.S. government. Moreover, these companies, as well as telecoms like Verizon and AT&T, are also potential sources of information for law enforcement and intelligence agencies.

There have already been confrontations, in one instance between the FBI and Apple, because the iPhone is encrypted and government agencies cannot easily access information on the smart phones of, for example, terrorist suspects. Similar standoffs will feature

Facebook, Twitter and other social media as government tries to access information about users to solve crimes, terrorist plots, and other objectives. Once again, then, the Trump administration must make difficult decisions regarding whether or not and/or how to compel private companies to collaborate with government agencies responsible for national security.

Another daunting issue facing the administration involves foreign investment in Silicon Valley companies. Huge investments by Saudi Arabian and Russian investors in Facebook and other social media have produced concern because these media were prominent in Russian hacking and use of aggressive Info-Bots. These robotic devices and software can execute commands, reply to messages, post and execute comments, do searches, and perform routine tasks such as spreading misinformation automatically without or with only minimal human intervention.

Russian engineering, mathematics, and computing talent has been prominent in developing American tech companies. After the collapse of the USSR, much of what is called "Russian talent" migrated to the U.S. There are tens of thousands of Russian and other innovative immigrants in Silicon Valley, and in other American cities such as New York and Miami. These include Google co-founders Sergey Brin and Yuri Milner, who invested large sums in Facebook. Russian immigration was viewed as positive for U.S. companies and led to many startups and innovations especially in technology (Manjoo, 2017).[12] Owing to concern about Russian interference in the U.S., gifted Russians and Ukrainians have come under suspicion.

Some of the cyber-activities of concern in the Trump administration involve Russian activities. The most prominent was Russian interference in the 2016 American elections, including the hacking of the Democratic National Committee and the use of social media like Facebook and Twitter to affect U.S. public opinion. These social media campaigns were carried out by non-governmental individuals and groups on behalf of Moscow. Thus, one issue that arose as a consequence of Russia's disinformation program was the role of the Russian company Kaspersky, which sells antivirus software. Resulting apprehension led to a ban of Kaspersky software in U.S. government agencies. There was also alarm about private companies using this software because many of them are also contractors on government projects involving national security.

Indeed, a significant policy concern involves foreign component and software sourcing more generally. Thus, another threat involves the vast number of Chinese-designed and manufactured semiconductor components. The U.S. government is dangerously vulnerable to Chinese espionage or cyberattack because of its dependence on electronics and software made in China, a risk that threatens to grow as Beijing seeks global technological dominance, according to a study for a congressionally chartered advisory commission (Lynch, 2018).[13] Thus, China has a hand in half the world's hardware designs, cellphones, and wireless devices. This is not an idle concern, as reflected in the shipment of flawed Chinese-manufactured microchips intended for U.S. Navy helicopters. If installed, the chips would have prevented the firing of missiles.

In another area of urgent concern, congressional hearings were held beginning in 2017 on the role of social media like Facebook in hacking American political websites. The hearings revealed evidence of the lack of desire or inability of major social media websites to "curate" (carefully manage, sort, and vet) fake and/or dangerous foreign government accounts. The hearings also revealed the use of bots to post comments to blogs and websites, and articles to divide American society.

Another alarming development involved the Russian hacks of NATO soldiers' cell phones. Initial information indicated that the attacks focused on the roughly 4,000 NATO troops deployed in Eastern Europe near the Russian border. The fear is that Russia might access sensitive military information and even interfere with how NATO would respond to Russian military actions, for example by sending false commands to NATO troops.

Members of Congress and intelligence experts argue that Washington needs a "Cyber Doctrine," a coherent and integrated program, to deal with cyberthreats. Congressional leaders contend that Facebook, Twitter, and other social media must help the U.S. government push back against the Russian interference. Facebook has released a tool that lets users see if they liked or were influenced by Russian propaganda during the 2016 election. This was an admission by the Internet giant that it had inadvertently given potentially dangerous clients access to its social media platform.

CONGRESS, BUREAUCRACIES, AND CYBERSECURITY

These events remind us that there are numerous actors involved in fighting a cyberwar. America's president is only the most visible. Congress also plays a significant role. Executive agencies such as the intelligence services like the CIA and NSA are also involved. Such agencies have continuity and are largely independent of the president or Congress. Finally, especially in America, private companies have a major role since they are often the engines that drive Internet traffic.

Congress has shown interest in the cybersecurity. In December 2017 Senators James Lankford (R-OK) and Amy Klobuchar (D-MN) as well as Senator Kamala Harris (D-CA) and Senator Lindsey Graham (R-SC), drafted bipartisan legislation that would require the Department of Homeland Security to establish information-sharing processes and improve election cybersecurity. This was in response to Russian interference in the U.S. elections including its hacking a U.S. voting systems software company and hacking the e-mails of at least one hundred election officials. Senator Klobuchar also led a group of twenty-six senators in calling for a full account of the Election Assistance Commission's efforts to address Russian cybersecurity threats. Senator Lankford, for his part, has indicated that the Trump Homeland Security Department is engaged with this effort even though the president himself has continued to insist that Russian hacking and influence over the 2016 election results is fake news (*Fox News*, 2017).[14]

Looking ahead, Congress and the Trump administration must decide whether to limit, oversee, or even ban investment from foreign individuals or entities that may be undesirable. This would be a game changer for a capitalist economy such as America's, which has a global market economy that attracts investment. China, for example, has purchased billions of dollars in U.S. government bonds that help bankroll U.S. government deficits. Chinese companies are also building manufacturing facilities in the United States, including some in sensitive areas such as computing and ICT. Should such investments be prohibited? What would be the consequences for U.S. companies and the American economy?

Another issue that arose early in the Trump administration was the use of private e-mail by staff and family members raising the alarm that government-related business might be compromised by these private servers. Thus, former White House Chief of Staff Gen. Kelly's phone was hacked in May 2018, and it was revealed that someone had spied on smartphones in the White House, using a Stingray -like international mobile subscriber identity-capturing device (Nichols, 2018).[15]

Initial response to the cyberthreat has been Bill S. 1815, the Data Broker Accountability and Transparency Act (2017), which would set new accountability and transparency requirements for data brokers selling consumers' sensitive information. This bill was introduced not by the administration but by Senator Edward Markey, a Democrat from Massachusetts. A second piece of potential legislation, Bill H.R. 3806, the Personal Data Notification and Protection Act of 2017 (PDNP Act) would provide for a single national data breach notification standard. This bill was introduced by Rhode Island Representative James Langevin.

An interesting development was President Trump's order for a "broad pressure campaign against North Korea." That led Washington to conduct a denial of service attack against the Reconnaissance General Bureau (RGB), North Korea's spying agency (Shaikh, 2017).[16] The action apparently flooded the RGB's servers with traffic that choked its Internet access. It also disabled the Bureau 121 group, the unit responsible for North Korea's substantial hacking campaigns. Oddly, this campaign was short-lived, lasting only half a year. On the other hand, it made it harder in the short run for North Korea to continue hacking projects. However the campaign did not cripple or eliminate those activities, and in September 2018 the Justice Department identified a North Korea hacker in the RGB as involved in a group implicated in the theft of $1 billion from the Bangladesh Bank, and in the WannaCry virus (Nakashima and Barrett, 2018).[17]

There has also been serious discussion about funding for cybersecurity, which remains inadequate given the challenges associated with the Internet. Years of neglect concerning U.S. cyberdefense and an emphasis on offensive hacking tools led veteran intelligence officers to believe that American cyberdefense is neglected, leaving U.S. agencies vulnerable.

MULTILATERALISM AND CYBERSECURITY

One challenge to effective cyberpolicy facing the Trump administration is that an effective cyberdefense and protection policy would entail multilateral implementation agreements. That is because cyberattacks rely on protected physical environments. They need safe houses, cyber cafés, or business premises, electricity, and a communications highway (telephone system at minimum) or fiber optics in order to deliver attacks. Cyber-criminals, hackers, cyber-terrorists, and national cyber threats will persist as long as local and national law enforcement authorities in countries where hackers operate with impunity tolerate or even encourage malicious activity.

There is a strong consensus in the ICT community that if cyberattacks are to be reduced, there is an urgent need for a strong international agreement and multilateral cooperation. Without it, the United States becomes "cyber-isolated" and global cyber-defenses are greatly endangered. Repeatedly, however, Trump has rejected multilateralism and has exacerbated the cyber problem by openly criticizing key intelligence agencies.

Some international agreements that help reduce cybercrime include the Council of Europe's Convention on Cybercrime (2001) and the United Nations Transnational Organized Crime Convention (2003). The former was the first international treaty focused on cybersecurity issues and has been ratified by thirty-seven countries. The convention seeks to harmonize national laws on cybercrime, improve national capabilities for investigating such crimes, and increase cooperation on investigations. In addition to COE member states, others including the United States participated in drafting the convention as "observers."

In October 2004, the London Action Plan was established to "promote international spam enforcement cooperation and address spam related problems, such as online fraud and deception, phishing, and dissemination of viruses" (Kleiner et al., 2013: 12).[18] The Action Plan also established a voluntary code of conduct for private companies to prompt greater spam enforcement cooperation.

There is broad agreement that the United States should be a more aggressive and active supporter and leader of these multilateral efforts. However, as we noted, President Trump is less interested in such multilateral efforts. That said, we must remember that national policy consists of more than the personality and style of a president. Trump's cabinet has generally been more supportive of cooperative relations with U.S. allies on many issues including cybersecurity. Former Secretary of State Tillerson, White House Chief of Staff Kelly, Defense Secretary Mattis, and UN Ambassador Haley frequently try to restrain President Trump's aggressive opposition to international agencies and agreements.

It is noteworthy that Trump nominated Kirstjen Nielsen, an aide to Chief of Staff Kelly and longtime national security official, to be Secretary of the Department of Homeland Security. She is a national security expert with cybersecurity expertise who served in the George W. Bush administration's Department of Homeland Security. Her cyber credentials are substantial. She was a senior fellow and member of the Resilience Task Force of the Center for Cyber & Homeland Security, a think tank at George Washington University. Nielsen also served on the Global Risks Report Advisory Board of the World Economic Forum. She was president of the Alexandria, Virginia company Sunesis Consulting, and president and general counsel for the homeland and national security arm of the consulting firm Civitas Public Affairs Group.

However, it is also starkly clear that some of the key players in the Trump administration are unfamiliar with the complexities of cyberthreats and cybersecurity. When Attorney General Jeff Sessions testified before the Senate Judiciary Committee in October 2017, his testimony showed little interest or concern with Russia's interference in the 2016 American elections. "In the final moments of the hearing, Sessions admitted that the Trump administration did not have 'an effective strategy' to counter cyber threats to the United States, having asserted that neither he nor Trump had demonstrated any interest in the Russian hacking attack" (Korn, 2017).[19]

Compounding the problem of cybersecurity was the sudden, shocking revelation in January 2018 of two security flaws in the microprocessors of almost all computers worldwide (*The Economist*, 2018).[20] The flaws, called Meltdown and Spectre, afford access to hackers who might then steal the full memory contents of hacked computers. Also vulnerable were mobile devices, personal computers and even the servers running cloud computing for the Amazon, Microsoft, and Google systems. This revelation came at a moment when the Trump administration was distracted by the publication of the book *Fire and Fury* written by Michael Wolff, which revealed highly critical information about the president and the chaotic conditions in the White House. To the extent that Meltdown and Spectre required quick and decisive government assistance to computer and cybersecurity firms and a rapid response to secure all government computer systems, the roiling atmosphere at 1600 Pennsylvania Avenue posed a daunting challenge (Metz and Perlroth, 2018).[21]

There was also the shocking discovery that Facebook had given access to 250,000 accounts, and with its permission an academic had been allowed to study the social media data from these accounts. It was also found that this individual had passed on the data and that of fifty million "friends" and links of the original group to Cambridge Analytica, a global corporation dealing in information management. This company had then provided detailed information about these individuals to Trump's 2016 campaign. This revelation triggered a critical and ongoing examination of Facebook and other social media and their violation of user privacy. In addition, Facebook shares data with four Chinese electronics companies including Huawei, which U.S. intelligence officials regard as a national security threat (LaForgia and Dance, 2018).[22]

The persistent insecurity of the Internet was highlighted by a report from the news site *Axios* that a senior member of the National Security Council had suggested creating a nationalized, government-built 5G wireless communications network to counteract China's "dominant position" in 5G. The proposal refers to China as "the dominant malicious actor in the Information Domain," and warned of its dominant position in the manufacturing and operation of advanced network infrastructure. This prompted the Trump administration to weigh the benefits and risks of the government competing with private companies such as AT&T, which normally are the innovators and investors in wireless and which already are developing 5G. However, Ajit Pai, chairman of the Federal Communications Commission opposed the idea of a government-controlled network (Villas-Boas, 2018).[23]

CONCLUSIONS

Future cyberespionage and cyberattacks and America's responses are among the most serious challenges facing the Trump administration. The cyberthreat to the United States is real and enormous in scope as we have demonstrated. Many actors including criminals, "dark web" hackers, and terrorist groups as well as state actors have been penetrating American systems. Procurement of sensitive computing and communications technology from foreign sources has been identified as risky. There is also a potential "quantum gap," with the United States lagging behind China, Russia, and others in this important technology. All of these pose dangers to the American economy, trade, individual credit cards and bank accounts, healthcare systems, and critical infrastructure (power plants, fiber optic cables, airports, train facilities, ports, and water treatment plants among others) as well as government and military institutions. Thus, the Department of Homeland Security (DHS) recently added 32 states and 31 local governments to a system that scans Internet-connected systems in the federal government every night for cyber vulnerabilities. DHS is then providing weekly reports on weaknesses and makes recommendations for fixes.

Cyber is so critical to U.S. national security that in early 2018 the Pentagon drafted a new U.S. nuclear strategy for President Trump. It would apparently permit the use of nuclear weapons to respond to a range of "devastating but non-nuclear" attacks on American infrastructure. While not explicitly stated, and obviously an extreme option, it might include the possibility of using nuclear weapons in case of "crippling cyberattacks" that can cause physical destruction of major infrastructure. That would include attacks against America's power grid, cellphone networks, dams, transportation systems, and the Internet. This would entail a dramatic ramping up of the concept "Cyber Deterrence." Such deterrence is critical because Russia has placed malware called "BlackEnergy" in American utility systems but to date has never activated the malware (Eilperin and Entous, 2016).[24] Moscow has also deployed cable-cutting submarines along the path of undersea fiber optic cables that connect the continents, but not yet disrupted any of these (Birnbaum, 2017).[25] In addition, Iran had prepared a plan to launch crippling denial-of-service-attacks on American and European electric grids, water plants, healthcare, and technology companies

(Reints, 2018).[26] Thus, in August 2018, Washington changed the rules on cyber-weapons making it easier to use cyberwarfare for deterrence.

Perhaps the most stunning news was the announcement in February 2018 by special counsel Robert Mueller that thirteen Russians and three Russian companies were being indicted for interfering in American politics during the 2016 elections. The indictment described a conspiracy that began in 2014. Termed "Translator Project," this multimillion-dollar Russian initiative sought to undermine Hillary Clinton, bolster Donald Trump, and turn Americans against one another. The Russians described the goal of their mission as "information warfare against the United States of America," and spreading mistrust in the "the American political system in general" before they focused on helping Trump win the 2016 election. "The indictment alleges that the Russian conspirators want to promote discord in the United States and undermine public confidence in democracy," Rod Rosenstein, the deputy attorney general overseeing the inquiry, said (cited in Apuzzo and LaFraniere, 2018).[27]

At a Senate Intelligence Committee hearing in February 2018, Director of National Intelligence Dan Coats also warned that cyberthreats were a daunting challenge to U.S. democracy and security. "Frankly," he declared, "the United States is under attack." He said threats to U.S. cybersecurity from abroad coming from state and non-state actors using technology to target "virtually every major action that takes place" are one of his "greatest concerns and top priorities." Coats noted that intelligence officials expect Moscow to continue using propaganda, social media, "false-flag personas," sympathetic spokespersons and other venues to "try to exacerbate social and political fissures" in the U.S. (cited in Nordlinger, 2018).[28] Further, "there should be no doubt that Russia perceives its past efforts as successful and views the 2018 U.S. midterm elections as a potential target for Russian influence operations," Coats (2018) said. In fact, there was much less Russian meddling in the midterm elections than in the earlier presidential election.

The president's son-in-law, Jared Kushner, initially assumed leadership in modernizing the government's technology and computing infrastructure even though it is not clear what his credentials are for such a task. However, after a year and a half in the Trump administration,

[t]he White House has failed to name chief information officers for nine major agencies, including Defense, Treasury and Homeland Security. Even the federal chief information officer is only an acting official, and the White House's Office of Science and Technology Policy is largely a ghost town.

(LaFraniere et al., 2017)[29]

Overall, little has been accomplished in the area of cybersecurity. The Trump administration has been averse to supporting and staffing government agencies to execute policy. On Cyber, the State Department was allocated $120 million to fight Russian meddling. By March 2018 none of that had been spent because former Secretary of State Tillerson and President Trump had little confidence in State Department personnel or its bureaucracy despite the fact that it was revealed in March 2018 that Russian hackers had gone from infiltrating business networks of energy, water, and nuclear plants to worming their way into control rooms that manage systems for critical infrastructure sites.

Declared former NSA chief, and head of U.S. Cyber Command until May 2018, Admiral Michael S. Rogers in testimony before the Senate Armed Services Committee: "We're taking steps, but we're probably not doing enough." He added that Russian President Vladimir Putin "has clearly come to the conclusion that 'there's little price to pay here and therefore I can continue this activity.'" Asked whether he'd been authorized by either Trump or Defense Secretary Jim Mattis to do more against Russian attacks, Rogers said: "No, I have not" (cited in Blake, 2018).[30]

Moreover, in June 2018 the Office of Management and Budget issued a report that 71 of 96 government agencies had cybersecurity programs that were either at risk or high risk (Lanier, 2018).[31]

The cyberprotection agenda is like an iceberg. Much of what is happening is below the surface. Thus, there is a risk that because cybersecurity, cyberdefense, and cyberwar preparation are not visible, President Trump and his team can ignore it. That poses a serious, dangerous risk to the United States. Is weak cybersecurity an existential threat? The answer is unequivocally yes (Sanger and Broad, 2018).[32] In all the chaos of the first year of the Trump government, cyber threats were identified by the business community and military as the most serious security danger facing the United States. *New York Times* reporter, David Sanger, noted, "We [the USA] have the most fearsome cyber-weaponry on the planet, yet we're afraid to use it for fear of what will come next" (Sanger, 2018a).[33] Sanger also reported that the United States Cyber Command has quietly decided to take risky "constant, disruptive 'short of war' activities" against cyber threats, including taking proactive action, without any leadership from the White House (Sanger, 2018b).[34]

ESSAY QUESTIONS

1) Describe and discuss the structural weaknesses of the Internet, which makes it so vulnerable to hacking. Provide specific examples.

2) What were three initiatives of the Obama administration cyberprotection policies?

3) The 2016 United States elections were controversial because of Russian hacking and social media interference. What were the major incidents of each of these?

4) The head of U.S. Cyber Command Admiral Michael S. Rogers said in testimony before the Senate Armed Services Committee, "We're taking steps, but we're probably not doing enough." Discuss and analyze what the cyber threat challenges are for the United States.

SHORT ANSWER QUESTIONS

Define and describe the importance of the following:

Malware
Ransomware
Phishing
Stuxnet
The Convention on Cybercrime
WannaCry and NotPetya

NOTES

1   LaFrance, A. (2015). How Many Websites Are There? *The Atlantic* [online]. Available at: www. theatlantic.com/technology/archive/2015/09/how-many-websites-are-there/408151 [Accessed 14 Jan 2018].

2   Parker, E. (2017). Hack Job: How America invented cyberwar. *Foreign Affairs* [online]. Available at: www.foreignaffairs.com/reviews/review-essay/2017-04-17/hack-job [Accessed 17 Jul 2017].

3   Sanger, D. and Mazzetti, M. (2016). U.S. Had Cyberattack Plan if Iran Nuclear Dispute Led to Conflict. *New York Times* [online]. Available at: www.nytimes.com/2016/02/17/world/middleeast/us-had-cyberattack-planned-if-iran-nuclear-negotiations-failed.html [Accessed 19 Jan 2018].

4   Reeve, T. (2017). WannaCry Not First to Exploit NSA Eternal Blue, DoublePulsar Malware. *SC Media*, May 16 [online]. Available at www.scmagazineuk.com/wannacry-not-first-exploit-nsa-eternalblue-doublepulsar-malware/article/1474651 [Accessed 7 Aug 2018].

5   Shane, S., Perlroth, N., and Sanger, D. (2017). Security Breach and Spilled Secrets Have Shaken the N.S.A. to Its Core. *New York Times* [online]. Available at: www.nytimes.com/2017/11/12/us/nsa-shadow-brokers.html [Accessed 14 Nov 2017].

6   Boys, J.D. (2018). *Clinton's War on Terror*. Boulder and London: Lynne Rienner Publishers.

7   Nye, J. (2016/17). Deterrence and Dissuasion in Cyberspace. *International Security* 41:3, p. 45.

8   US Department of Defense (2010). U.S. Cyber Command Fact Sheet: Mission statement, May 25 [pdf]. Available at https://nsarchive2.gwu.edu/NSAEBB/NSAEBB424/docs/Cyber-038.pdf (Accessed 17 Nov 2018).

9   Ellis, J. (2014). *Fundamentals of Homeland Security: An operations perspective*. Springfield, IL: Charles C. Thomas.

10 Public Law 113–274 (2014). Cybersecurity Enhancement Act of 2014. 113th Congress [pdf]. Available at: www.congress.gov/113/plaws/publ274/PLAW-113publ274.pdf [Accessed 19 Jan 2018].

11 The White House (2016). FACT SHEET: Cybersecurity national action plan. Available at: https://obamawhitehouse.archives.gov/the-press-office/2016/02/09/fact-sheet-cybersecurity-national-action-plan [Accessed 8 Jul 2018].

12 Manjoo, F. (2017). Why Silicon Valley Wouldn't Work Without Immigrants. *New York Times* [online]. Available at: www.nytimes.com/2017/02/08/technology/personaltech/why-silicon-valley-wouldnt-work-without-immigrants.html [Accessed 8 Aug 2018].

13 Lynch, D. (2018). What's Inside Made-in-China Electronics Should Worry Federal Customers, Study Says. *Washington Post* [online]. Available at: www.washingtonpost.com/business/economy/whats-inside-made-in-china-electronics-should-worry-federal-customers-study-says/2018/04/18/d06c5252-433c-11e8-ad8f-27a8c409298b_story.html [Accessed 8 Aug 2018].

14 *Fox News* (2017). Sen. Lankford Urges DHS to Prioritize Election Cybersecurity after Russian Cyberattacks. *Fox 23 News* [online]. Available at: www.fox23.com/news/sen-lankford-urges-dhs-to-prioritize-election-cybersecurity-after-russian-cyberattacks/666300832 [Accessed 10 Jan 2018].

15 Nichols, S. (2018). Stingray Phone Stalker Tech Used Near White House, SS7 abused to steal citizens' date – just Friday thins. *The Register*. Available at: www.theregister.co.uk/2018/06/01/wyden_ss7_stingray_fcc_homeland_security [Accessed 4 Jun 2018].

16 Shaikh, R. (2017). Cyberwarfare: US Launched DDoS Attacks Against North Korean Spy Agency. *WCCFTECH*. Available at: https://wccftech.com/cyberwarfare-us-ddos-north-korea [Accessed 8 Aug 2018].

17 Nakashima, E. and Barret, D. (2018). U.S. Charges North Korean Operative in Conspiracy to Hack Sony Pictures, Banks. *Washington Post* [online]. Available at: www.washingtonpost.com/world/national-security/justice-department-to-announce-hacking-charges-against-north-korean-operative-the-charge-stemming-from-the-2014-sony-pictures-case-is-the-first-against-a-pyongyang-spy/2018/09/06/f477bfb2-b1d0-11e8-9a6a-565d92a3585d_story.html [Accessed 7 Sep 2018].

18 Kleiner, A., Nicholas, P., and Sullivan, K. (2013). Linking Cybersecurity Policy and Perfor-mance [pdf]. Available at: www.ilsole24ore.com/pdf2010/SoleOnLine5/_Oggetti_Correlati/Documenti/Tecnologie/2013/02/SIR-Special-Edition-Security-Atlas-whitepaper.pdf [Accessed 18 Jan 2018].

19 Korn, D. (2017). The Most Shocking Revelation From the Sessions Hearing. *Mother Jones* [online]. Available at: www.motherjones.com/politics/2017/06/the-most-shocking-revelation-from-the-sessions-hearing [Accessed 22 Nov 2017].

20 *The Economist* (2018). Silicon Meltdown. *The Economist*, January 13, pp. 57–58.

21 Metz, C. and Perlroth, N. (2018). Researchers Discover Two Major Flaws in the World's Computers. *New York Times* [online]. Available at: www.nytimes.com/2018/01/03/business/computer-flaws.html [Accessed 5 Jan 2018].

22 LaForgia, M. and Dance, G. (2018). Facebook Gave Data Access to Chinese Firm Flagged by U.S. Intelligence. *New York Times* [online]. Available at: www.nytimes.com/2018/06/05/technology/facebook-device-partnerships-china.html [Accessed 6 Jun 2018].

23 Villas-Boas, A. (2018). The Trump Administration Explored a Government-Controlled 5G Network for Phones and Internet Because 'We are Losing' to China, *Businessinsider* [online]. Available at: www.businessinsider.com/trump-administration-exploring-national-ized-5g-wireless-network-report-2018-1 [Accessed 8 Aug 2018].

24 Eilperin, J. and Entous, A. (2016). Russian Operation Hacked a Vermont Utility, Show-ing Risk to U.S. Electrical Grid Security, Officials Say. *Washington Post* [online]. Available at: www.washingtonpost.com/world/national-security/russian-hackers-penetrated-us-electricity-grid-through-a-utility-in-vermont/2016/12/30/8fc90cc4-ceec-11e6-b8a2-8c2a61b0436f_story.html [Accessed 8 Aug 2018].

25 Birnbaum, M. (2017). Russian Submarines are Prowling around Vital Undersea Cables. It's making NATO nervous. *Washington Post* [online]. Available at: www.washingtonpost.com/world/europe/russian-submarines-are-prowling-around-vital-undersea-cables-its-making-nato-nervous/2017/12/22/d4c1f3da-e5d0-11e7-927a-e72eac1e73b6_story.html [Accessed 8 Aug 2018].

26 Reints, R. (2018). U.S. Officials Warn of Potential Cyber Attacks from Iran. *Fortune* [online]. Available at: http://fortune.com/2018/07/20/iran-cyber-attacks-aspen-forum [Accessed 8 Aug 2018].

27 Apuzzo, M. and LaFraniere, S. (2018). 13 Russians Indicted as Mueller Reveals Effort to Aid Trump Campaign. *New York Times* [online] Available at: www.nytimes.com/2018/02/16/us/politics/russians-indicted-mueller-election-interference.html [Accessed 4 Jun 2018].

28 Nordlinger, J. (2018). 'Frankly, the United States is under Attack'. *National Review*. Avail-able at: www.nationalreview.com/corner/frankly-the-united-states-is-under-attack [Accessed 4 Jun 2018].

29 LaFraniere, S., Haberman, M., and Bakernov, P. (2017). Jared Kushner's Vast Duties, and Visibility in White House, Shrink. *New York Times* [online]. Available at: www.nytimes.com/2017/11/25/us/politics/jared-kushner-white-house-trump.html [Accessed 15 Jan 2018].

30 Blake, A. (2018). NSA Director Mike Rogers's Remarkable Comments about Trump's Rus-sia Efforts – or Lack Thereof. *Washington Post* [online] Available at: www.washingtonpost.com/news/the-fix/wp/2018/02/27/nsa-director-mike-rogerss-careful-indictment-of-trumps-anti-russia-efforts [Accessed 4 Jun 2018].

31 Lanier, C. (2018). OMB Releases Damning Report on U.S. Govt's Inability to Counter Cyber Threats. *bleepingcomputer.com* [online]. Available at: www.bleepingcomputer.com/news/security/omb-releases-damning-report-on-us-govts-inability-to-counter-cyber-threats/ [Accessed 4 Jun 2018].

32 Sanger, D. and Broad, W. (2018). Pentagon Suggests Countering Devastating Cyberattacks with Nuclear Arms. *New York Times* [online]. Available at: www.nytimes.com/2018/01/16/us/politics/pentagon-nuclear-review-cyberattack-trump.html [Accessed 19 Jan 2018].

33 Sanger, D. (2018a). We Can't Stop the Hackers, *New York Times*, p. 4sr (Sunday Review).

34 Sanger, D. (2018b). Pentagon Puts Cyberwarriors on the Offensive, Increasing the Risk of Conflict. *New York Times* [online]. Available at: www.nytimes.com/2018/06/17/us/politics/cyber-command-trump.html [Accessed 3 Jul 2018].

SUGGESTED READINGS

Knake, R. (2018). The Next Cyber Battleground. *Foreign Affairs* [online, July 19]. www.foreignaffairs.com/articles/north-america/2018-07-19/next-cyber-battleground.

Rogers, A. (2018). The Tipping Point: We predicted the digital revolution with all the fervor of true believers. Then the revolution conquered all, *Wired* (October), pp. 60–61.

Microsoft (2018). Microsoft Security Intelligence Report. Volume 23. https://info.microsoft.com/ww-landing-Security-Intelligence-Report-Vol-23-Landing-Page-eBook.html.

Futter, A. (2018). *Hacking the Bomb: Cyber threats and nuclear weapons.* Washington, D.C.: Georgetown University Press, 2018.

Rudner, M. (2013). Cyber-Threats to Critical National Infrastructure: An intelligence challenge. *International Journal of Intelligence and Counter Intelligence* 26:3, pp. 453–481.

15 Trump's challenges in international political economy

Mark D. Nieman

"AMERICA FIRST" AND THE UNITED STATES ECONOMY

The world is beginning to emerge from the grip of the weakest recovery from an economic recession of the post-World War II era. The Great Recession, which began with the collapse of a housing bubble in the United States, quickly spread through the financial system to much of the rest of the world. Real income growth stagnated at most income levels and inequality within countries increased. In response, governments around the world engaged in a mix of stimulus and austerity programs, with the former intended to jump-start the economy and the latter to limit public debt. Many central banks utilized near-zero interest rates and engaged in quantitative easing programs – purchasing financial assets – limiting the extent of further monetary intervention. The failure of these various efforts to encourage economic growth to be more widely felt has led to a reevaluation of the pre-existing economic order, with the rise of isolationist and national populist sentiments among those who perceived a globalized world to be leaving them behind.

The United States was no exception and has experienced its own populist sentiments. The Trump administration has not only avoided pushing back against economic isolationist and protectionist impulses, but has actively fanned their flames. From mixing incentives and threat to the refrigeration company Carrier, placing tariffs on Canadian aircraft and Canadian and European Union (EU) aluminum and steel, and placing tariffs on Chinese products, to ending U.S. participation in the Trans-Pacific Partnership (TPP), criticizing the World Trade Organization (WTO), and threatening to pull out of the North American Free Trade Agreement (NAFTA), which he did not do. Bucking the long-time U.S. preference for free trade and financial liberalization, Trump has advanced his "America First" economic agenda, with a focus on increasing manufacturing jobs and reducing trade deficits, and demonstrating a preference for bilateral rather than multilateral trade accords. Trump's policies, and the reaction to them, are having wide-ranging effects as the world economy remains tightly interconnected. Efforts that reduce or undo trade, investment, and human capital interdependence may be a painful price to pay in exchange for greater US economic autonomy.

STATE OF THE UNITED STATES ECONOMY

The U.S. economy has experienced steady, if unspectacular, growth since the Great Recession ended in June 2009. Fed by low interest rates, low inflation, and increasing consumer demand, America's economy has encountered low unemployment, record corporate profits, and a record high stock market. At the same time, manufacturing jobs are being replaced by automation and, to a lesser degree, corporate offshoring, while inequality in income (Piketty and Saez, 2003)[1] and wealth (Saed and Zucman, 2016)[2] are reaching levels not seen since the late 1920s.

Economic trends, of course, do not change overnight; rather, the economy we see today is the outcome of number of decisions made by previous presidential administrations, central bank officials, regulators, legislators, and firms, as well as consumers and foreign governments and investors. In order to understand America's current economic condition, and the political feelings of the public and the officials they elect, we must briefly describe how it reached this point.

The housing bubble and the Great Recession

The Great Recession, which began in December 2007, had a number of complex, related causes, both short and long term. The origins of this crisis began in the 1980s/1990s, as a combination of government spending and tax cuts resulted in increases in the U.S. ratio of debt to gross domestic product (GDP) from 26 percent in 1983 to 49 percent in 1993 (Chinn and Frieden, 2011: 3–4).[3] While increases in debt are not, on their own, necessarily problematic, the fact that this occurred during a period of relatively good economic health, should have raised some concern. One reason that concern was not greater was that financial liberalization helped to offset the standard economic expectation that domestic borrowing hurts private lending. As foreign investors continued to seek a secure home for their assets, U.S. lenders remained flush with cash and continued to provide private loans. While the 1990s saw a return to budget surpluses, that money was not used to reduce the budget deficit. The 2000s saw a return to deficit spending, the result of tax cuts and multiple wars, while investors continued to park their money in safe U.S. investments such as U.S. government bonds – including a dramatic increase in petrodollars and Asian currency reserves (Chinn and Frieden, 2011: 9–12, 16–19).[3]

A combination of legislative policy choices and Federal Reserve Bank decisions produced low interest rates, feeding a housing market that home owners could easily borrow against (Chinn and Frieden, 2011: 31).[3] Government policies to promote home ownership and a capital surplus led to a doubling of housing prices in just five years (Chinn and Frieden, 2011: 34, 57–86).[3] Arguments that the high prices of the housing market constituted a housing "bubble" were offset by those who contended that increases in prices was evidence of the superiority of the U.S. financial system, with its complicated securities, and by those who lacked the political will to question an economy that was seemingly generating tremendous wealth for the average household (Chinn and Frieden, 2011: 41–47).[3]

The housing bubble did burst, of course, and upended the U.S. economy, and with it the global economy as well. Many financial instruments and models created by American banks and financial institutions included mortgage assets and assumed that housing prices would continue to rise. When they fell, a housing crisis quickly spread into other financial sectors. By late 2007, the Federal Reserve Bank began to cut interest rates and make anonymous loans to banks to keep them afloat. In 2008, major banks began to fail, culminating in Black September, during which the U.S. government nationalized two banks central to home loans – Freddie Mac and Fannie Mae – and stabilized the banking industry by purchasing "toxic assets" through the Troubled Assets Relief Program (TARP).

The costs associated with TARP were ultimately much greater than anticipated, with $2.5 trillion in direct costs, and $12 trillion more in additional guarantees. At the same time, banks did not loosen the strings on their own lending. The Fed attempted to encourage lending, but found its options limited as it had already cut interest rates to near zero. Instead, it turned to non-traditional monetary policies, notably quantitative easing, in which a central bank purchases financial assets from commercial banks, to raise asset prices as well as increase the money supply.

These efforts, while preventing economic collapse, were met with skepticism by the public. TARP, in particular, was widely unpopular and was considered by many to be a bailout of Wall Street (Chinn and Frieden, 2011: 116–117).[3] Public anger grew as banking executives were paid record bonuses in 2009, just one year after the government intervened to save the industry.

Stagnation of real income and increasing inequality

The American public also became increasingly skeptical about economic engagement with the rest of the world. In 2008, 65 percent of the public said globalization was bad for American workers, 58 percent thought globalization was bad for job creation, and 51 percent said globalization was bad for the U.S. economy. NAFTA was also increasingly viewed with skeptical eyes, with 64 percent saying that it was bad for American workers and 55 percent answering it was bad for the U.S. economy as a whole (The Chicago Council on Global Affairs, 2009).[4]

United States public opinion has shifted somewhat in recent years. In 2016, the public continued to question the utility of globalization in terms of its effect on workers (65 percent say "bad"), job creation (60 percent say "bad"), and the U.S. economy (41 percent say "bad"). There had emerged, however, dramatic partisan differences, with Republicans 10–15 percentage points more likely to answer in the negative to each question (Smeltz et al., 2016: 23).[5]

What has not changed is that U.S. wages continued to stagnate for the average worker. Even as the economy has improved and the stock market rose dramatically in 2017–2018, wages remained flat. Figure 15.1, reveals that, although weekly wages have risen slightly from 2008 to the present in current dollars, once inflation is accounted for, real weekly wages are largely unchanged.

At the same time, economic inequality has risen consistently since 1980. While the top one percent earned 11 percent of U.S. income and possessed 24 percent of American wealth in 1980, by 2014 those figures had increased to 20 percent of income and 39 percent of wealth. The share of income and wealth going to the bottom 50 percent, by contrast, dropped from 19.9 percent of income and one percent of wealth in 1980, to 13 percent of income and near zero percent of wealth in 2014 (Saez, 2016: 14–16).[6] The growing inequality in earnings and wealth has greatly exacerbated other societal cleavages in the United States. In this context, Candidate Trump's populist message found an audience.

FIGURE 15.1 United States median weekly earnings for full-time employees

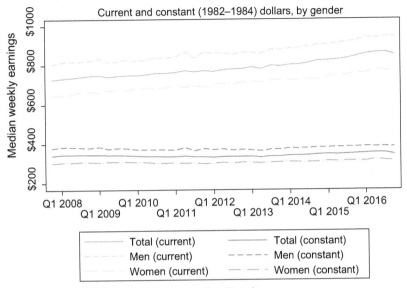

Source: U.S. Bureau of Labor Statistics. Salaries are seasonally adjusted

THE TRUMP ADMINISTRATION'S ECONOMIC AGENDA

The Trump economic agenda is a mix of populist rhetoric with some traditional Republican views. The Trump administration reduced regulations and passed a large tax cut as part of a broader effort to promote business-friendly policies, which contradicted Trump's claims that it was a "middle class tax cut" and threatened a massive tax deficit, but the administration also enacted protectionist policies and greater economic nationalism. As President-elect, Trump publicly shamed companies that moved production or invested abroad. At the same time, he threatened to levy tariffs on foreign companies, a policy that appears at odds with congressional views, especially those of Republicans (Werner et al., 2018).[7] Trump also promised to take a more aggressive stance toward China – a promise which he carried out – a policy that has harmed U.S. companies that use global supply chains, as well as increasing prices for U.S. consumers (Eavis, 2018).[8] Lastly, Trump criticized the value of multilateral trade accords and international economic institutions. The unifying thread of these policy positions is a sense that America has been taken advantage of economically and that Trump intended to put "America First."

ECONOMIC NATIONALISM

One of the central aspects of Trump's economic agenda is that the rules of international trade disadvantage the United States. While expressing support for free trade, the Trump administration has also demanded "fair trade." In order for trade to be "fair," according to the Trump administration, Washington must reduce bilateral trade deficits. Rather than viewing imports as a way to reduce opportunity costs – allowing resources to be spent on more efficient economic pursuits – as has been argued by liberal economists dating back to Adam Smith and David Ricardo, the Trump administration has adopted a neomercantilist perspective (Graceffo, 2017).[9] From this outdated perspective, trade deficits are viewed as incurring a cost to the debtor nation, making it a less powerful actor in the global arena (Appelbaum, 2016).[10] This perceived cost, it is argued, results in lower economic output and the loss of jobs.

While proponents of free trade accept that job losses may occur in industries in which a country lacks a comparative advantage, the net benefit of increased economic activity should produce greater economic opportunities, with employment reallocated to industries in which a country enjoys a comparative advantage. Standard economic theory suggests that employment depends more on demographic, technological, and social factors, and that trade has little, if any, impact on aggregate employment. Rather, trade has an impact on the price of goods, and, as trade restrictions decrease and additional trade occurs, goods can more easily move from countries where they are plentiful to those where they are scarce, resulting in lower prices for such goods.

Furthermore, modern global supply chains, especially for high-tech products, in which components of finished products are made in different countries, often heighten trade deficits from countries with a comparative advantage in human capital. For example, despite technological innovations originating in the U.S., Apple's iPhones are assembled exclusively in China. Following standard trade calculations, the *entire* total manufacturing cost of a product is included in trade figures, meaning that iPhones contributed $1.9 billion to the U.S.-China trade deficit in 2009 alone, despite China's contribution of only 3.6 percent of the product's value (Xing and Detert, 2010).[11]

That trade has had little impact on aggregate jobs is also supported by the available data. Figure 15.2 shows the number of nonfarm payroll jobs in the U.S. over the last thirty years.

FIGURE 15.2 United States employment, 1985–2017

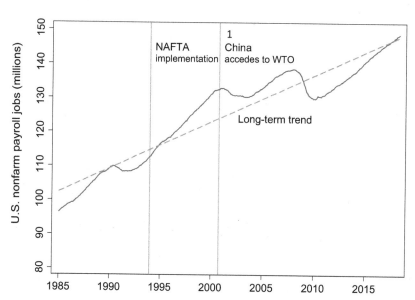

Source: FRED, U.S. Bureau of Labor Statistics. Employment is seasonally adjusted

The general trend has been an increase in employment. The figure also shows the timing of two large shocks to American trade – the implementation of NAFTA, which reduced trade barriers among the U.S., Canada, and Mexico, and the accession of China to the World Trade Organization, which normalized U.S.-Chinese trade relations. As the figure makes clear, neither of these events had a significant impact on overall U.S. employment. Indeed, by 2015, U.S. employment figures remained consistent with the long-term trend.

Standard economic theory also contends that employment will grow in the economic sectors in which a country has a comparative advantage, and will decline in those in which it lacks such an advantage. The United States is no exception. Thus, even as American employment increased in the financial, service, and creative sectors in which it enjoys a comparative advantage, employment decreased in the sectors in which its trade partners are comparatively stronger, notably manufacturing and agriculture. These sectors, which could charge a higher price and turn a profit when the goods they produced were scarce, are less competitive when facing cheaper foreign goods. In sum, while society as a whole gains from lower prices, losses are concentrated in a subset of industries.

Figure 15.3 shows the number of manufacturing jobs in the United States for the period from 1985 to 2016 during which the implementation of NAFTA and the normalization of trade with China took place. As is evident, *manufacturing* jobs decreased during that period, especially after the normalization of trade with China. While the increase in trade is a likely factor, it is also important to keep in mind that increases in productivity – primarily from automation – also reduced the need for employment in the manufacturing sector.

These changes are important from a political perspective because the portion of the U.S. electorate that experienced a loss in employment overlaps to a high degree with that of Trump's voting base, which shared Trump's long-standing skepticism of free trade and his focus on bilateral trade relations (McDermott, 2016; Porter, 2017).[12] Trump used this to his

FIGURE 15.3 United States employment in manufacturing, 1985–2017

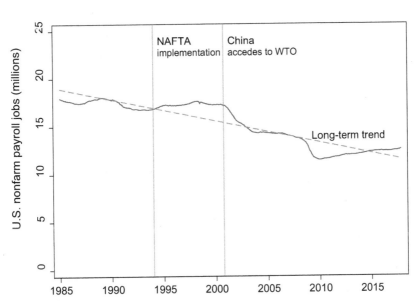

Source: FRED, U.S. Bureau of Labor Statistics. Employment is seasonally adjusted

advantage. From early in the presidential transition onwards, the Trump administration has focused on combating trade imbalances through the use of protectionist policies for specific industries and implementing retaliatory tariffs against economic rivals that are perceived to be taking advantage of America's free trade policies. For example, the president employed Section 201 of the 1974 Trade Act in the case of solar panels and washing machines after the U.S. International Trade Commission found that American companies were being harmed by imports. Trump's application of Section 201 was the first by a U.S. president since George W. Bush imposed trade barriers on steel imports in 2002, which the WTO declared was a violation of global trade rules. Trump also enacted tariffs on aluminum and steel imports from Canada and the EU on the grounds of "national security." Both the tariffs and the reason given to justify them angered these traditional allies. Finally, Trump imposed tariffs on $50 billion worth of goods from China, in retaliation for Chinese trade espionage and Beijing's requirement that foreign firms turn over proprietary technological information.

Applying tariffs is not without costs. Tariffs increase the cost of imports for U.S. consumers, and increase inflation. Tariffs also invite foreign retaliation, which harm export-oriented U.S. industries. In response to Trump's tariffs on solar panels and washing machines, for example, China launched its own investigation and threatened sanctions on imports of U.S. sorghum. This initial round of tariffs has resulted in retaliatory tariffs, creating a vicious cycle resulting in tariffs on goods to the tune of hundreds of millions of dollars. Tariffs also impose unintended costs, especially given the global nature of many firms' supply chains. Thus, the president of the national solar panel association warned that the 30 percent tariff on solar panels would cause the loss of 23,000 U.S. jobs (SEIA, 2018).[13] These losses will occur because the U.S. solar industry is focused primarily on *installation* rather than *manufacturing*. Thus, an increase in the price of parts harms the industry as a whole, even if the small group of solar manufacturers benefit temporarily from increased prices.

The solar panel and washing machine tariffs, as well as actions against "unfair" trade from the European Union – and, especially, Germany – as well as Canada, Mexico, Japan, and South Korea, highlight another difference in policy between the Trump administration and its predecessors, in that Trump emphasizes the use of sanctions and retaliation against *economic* rather than political or military rivals. While all U.S. administrations have "talked tough" to some degree on trade policies that disadvantage the United States, they also sought trade agreements and the reduction of trade barriers, especially with politically friendly countries and allies. By contrast, the Trump administration has levied accusations of unfair trade practices and currency manipulations at the same countries that Trump has sought to reassure or work with them in terms of military and political security. South Korea, for example, has been both the target of demands to renegotiate existing trade deals to meet Trump's economic goals while simultaneously being reassured that Washington will work with it to counter North Korean nuclear ambitions. Trump has also used strong rhetoric against Chinese trade practices as well as issuing threats to raise tariffs on Chinese imports, even as Washington seeks greater cooperation with China on the North Korean issue.

The Trump administration has also sought to change trade relationships with long-standing allies. In order to protect the U.S. airplane manufacturer, Boeing, Washington imposed a 220 percent tariff on Canadian airplanes, angering both Canada and the United Kingdom. While Washington ultimately backed down on the airplane tariff, it has maintained tariffs of up to 18 percent on Canadian lumber. In addition, the aforementioned use of tariffs against Canadian and EU steel, justified on national security grounds, resulted in retaliatory tariffs and generated ill-will among these traditional allies.

The potential consequences of uprooting trade relations with traditional allies pose several risks. First, there is the risk of reduced trade and investment placing a strain on their willingness to cooperate with Washington on other issues. Second, these countries may seek new strategic alliances, harming the U.S. politically while aiding rivals. Finally, America's traditional allies may become rivals for influence in their own right. Thus, Japan is seeking closer relations with India and Latin American countries, while France and Germany are seeking a more independent Europe, and the United Kingdom is flirting with China. A rejection of the liberal economic order by Trump, an order that Washington helped to establish and maintain, will undermine U.S. influence, because economic power has long been a tool that Washington has employed to encourage or coerce other states to follow its policy preferences (Lake, 2009: 80–81; Nieman, 2016).[14]

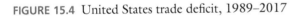

A FOCUS ON TRADE DEFICITS

In order to advance his America First agenda, as noted earlier, Trump has emphasized reducing the U.S. trade deficit. Trump views trade deficits as harmful to the U.S. economy and representing a sum of money that another state has taken from America. As noted earlier, Trump has a neomercantilist perspective on trade, conflating a negative trade balance with a cost to the United States, rather than a choice made by individuals to purchase more goods from firms in one country than the individuals in that country choose to purchase from American firms.

The U.S. trade deficit, from 1989 to 2017, is displayed in Figure 15.4. Although the trade deficit increased steadily from 1990 until 2006, this trend appears to stop during the Great Recession. In the years after the Great Recession, the trade deficit actually decreased.

FIGURE 15.4 United States trade deficit, 1989–2017

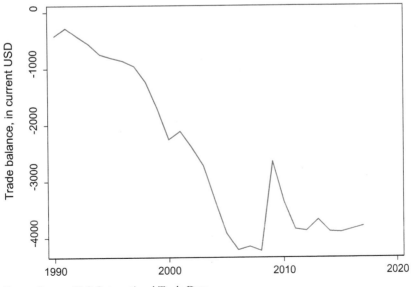

Source: U.S. Census Bureau, U.S. International Trade Data

Rather than reflecting an increase in U.S. competitiveness, the change in the trend of the trade deficit likely reflected a decrease in consumer purchases.

Figure 15.5 shows America's trade deficit with five countries that have often been named by Trump as taking advantage of the U.S. – China, Germany, Japan, Mexico, and South Korea – from 1989 to 2017. Thus Trump's use of Section 201 to place tariffs on solar panels and washing machines targeted China and South Korea, in addition to the broader use of tariffs against Chinese manufacturers. The Trump administration's economic policy specifically mentions South Korea and China, as well as Mexico, as threats to America's economy (Office of the United States Trade Representative, 2017: 5–6).[15] In the case of South Korea, the Trump administration specifically notes that there has been a trade deficit of $1.2 billion since the Obama administration negotiated a free trade deal. There is little evidence of a change or a new trend, however, in the data displayed in Figure 15.5. Instead, the trade deficit with South Korea has remained relatively small during the last ten years. The trade deficits with Germany and Japan are roughly the same as they were in the mid-to-late 2000s, while the trade deficit with Mexico has actually decreased in the same period. The only country with which the trade deficit has increased – and dramatically so – is China. It has grown more than $300 billion since 2000, more than the other four states combined that President Trump has highlighted, and was over $370 billion in 2017.

The trade deficit with China has caused concern for several U.S. administrations. A common charge that the George W. Bush, Obama, and Trump administrations have all leveled against China is that Beijing is a currency manipulator. Although estimates vary widely depending on the theoretical assumptions adopted, there is a broad consensus – shared by U.S. Treasury officials, legislators on Capitol Hill, the Group of 20 (G-20), the World Bank, and the International Monetary Fund (IMF) – that China was deliberately keeping

FIGURE 15.5 United States trade deficit with specific countries, 1989–2017

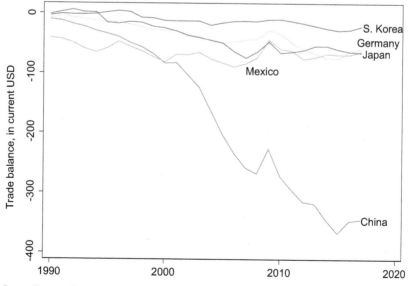

Source: U.S. Census Bureau, U.S. International Trade Data

its currency, the renminbi, substantially undervalued in order to increase exports. For the last decade, however, Beijing has actually been raising the value of its currency, and the president himself has rescinded his original claim (*The Economist*, 2017).[16]

It is also worth noting that currency manipulation is not the only potential cause of a trade deficit. The currencies of Germany, Japan, Mexico, and South Korea, for example, have either increased or stayed roughly the same in recent years. Consumer tastes are also an important factor, as it drives the demand half of the supply/demand equation. As an example, German automobiles have a reputation for quality and efficiency that has resulted in high U.S. demand. The sectors in which America is most competitive, meanwhile, are those in which Germany also has competitive domestic firms, lowering German consumers' demand for US products. Thus, the German trade surplus with America is more likely to reflect consumer preferences than unfair trading practices. Changing consumer preference would be difficult for any U.S. government to influence unilaterally, and to do so would be antithetical to America's free market ethos.

ECONOMIC BILATERALISM VERSUS MULTILATERALISM

Another feature of Trump's view of trade and investment is his emphasis on bilateralism. This also distinguishes it from all prior U.S. administrations since World War II, which had assumed leadership in establishing multilateral treaties or working in the context of international institutions. Thus, Trump withdrew from the Trans-Pacific Partnership on the first day of his presidency, has threatened to withdraw from NAFTA unless it was later renegotiated, and has frequently acted unilaterally outside of the World Trade Organization , which maintains the rules for the global trading system, and which the president seeks to undermine. While there has long been tension between a desire by Washington to pursue its own goals and the desire to uphold the international "rules of the game", which it helped create, America has largely adhered to and advocated those rules with a few exceptions, in the context of the liberal economic order (Wade, 2002).[17] An outright rejection of multilateralism and opposition to the institutions on which the liberal economic order is built would certainly constitute a major change in U.S. foreign policy.

Multilateral trade agreements

The Trump administration has justified this shift in policy by arguing that multilateral agreements limit America's bargaining position. Bilateral negotiations favor Washington, contends the administration, because the U.S. has a huge economy and an enormous market for which other countries should pay a premium to access. Moreover, with a highly educated population, technologically sophisticated production, and a strong financial infrastructure, foreign businesses would find a favorable environment for producing value-added products. By contrast, operating in a multilateral framework, the administration argues, only reduces the concessions that America could expect in bilateral trade and investment treaties.

The TPP and NAFTA both attracted Trump's scorn, with the former being called a "horrible deal" and the latter "the worst trade deal ever signed." Trump's opposition to the TPP stems from a belief that it would strengthen China, despite China not being part of the agreement, because he thinks China will join the TPP later. Trump maintains this view even though the TPP was designed with the goal of counterbalancing China's political and economic influence in Asia. His opposition to NAFTA reflects his view that it has cost manufacturing jobs in the U.S. and that Mexico has been the primary beneficiary at America's expense. Trump contends that he can negotiate a better deal with each of the eleven remaining members of the TPP in a bilateral setting, as well as negotiating improved terms with Canada and/or Mexico if he pulls the U.S. out of NAFTA.

International institutions

The argument that bilateral negotiations favor America's bargaining position is also offered to explain why Washington should resolve trade disputes outside of existing international institutions. Trump seeks to reduce the influence of the WTO over how the U.S. resolves trade disputes, even threatening to withdraw from the organization altogether (Swanson, 2017).[18] His criticisms of the WTO are somewhat puzzling because the U.S. has won nine-tenths of the trade disputes brought to the organization in which it was the complainant, including several major complaints against China, which has tended to obey WTO decisions (Chon, 2017).[19] Not only has the Trump administration sought to reduce the WTO's influence over U.S. cases, but it has acted to undermine the organization more broadly. Thus, Washington has blocked the appointment of new judges to the WTO's appellate body, limiting its ability to process cases, and has used "national security" as an excuse that had never been used before in the WTO. These actions are self-defeating inasmuch as Washington is the claimant in several cases involving its Chinese quotas on agricultural products.

GLOBAL RESPONSE: DECLINE OF MULTILATERALISM OR ABSENCE OF AMERICA?

As we have seen, the Trump administration believes that the use of bilateral negotiations improves America's leverage when negotiating trade deals and resolving trade disputes, and he believes that this justifies a reduced role for America in multilateral treaties and institutions. There are costs that the U.S. faces, however, that extend beyond the terms of any single agreement. Just because Washington is not a party to a treaty or active in an international organization, does not mean that these cease to exist. Instead, it means that there is a power vacuum that other states like China will fill. It also means that the remaining states will accrue benefits from their multilateral trade agreements and institutions that the U.S. will not share. In addition, firms in these countries will confront fewer trade barriers when interacting with one another than will U.S. firms, helping foreign firms increase their profits and employment prospects for their workers, while limiting benefits for U.S. firms and workers.

Thus, the remaining eleven member states to the TPP are forging ahead with what will still be the world's largest free trade agreements. One of the benefits of multilateral negotiation is that states can offer side payments or concessions that can justify potentially painful concessions on the part of other states. After years of tough negotiations, the TPP includes long-sought agreements involving agriculture, intellectual property rights, and labor standards. In addition, the treaty includes provisions to combat currency manipulation. Under the leadership of Japan and Canada, it is expected that free trade areas will make overtures to Washington in the future, but on tougher terms than before.

Not only has the U.S. failed to gain in absolute terms, it also has lost in relative terms in the Pacific region. The TPP was originally intended to deepen integration between America and its Asian allies, increasing their capabilities and serving as a bulwark against China. With the U.S. out of the picture, China has an opportunity to seize the leadership role that Washington has ceded. The communist government of China has already begun to position itself as the unlikely global defender of free trade. Similarly, the EU has begun to negotiate its own trade deals. Taking advantage of America's absence, the EU has reached deals with countries such as Canada and Japan that provide access and advantage its own agricultural sector at the expense of U.S. farmers (Behsudi, 2017).[20]

Much as withdrawing from the TPP has reduced America's influence in Asia, scrapping or revising NAFTA would harm several U.S. economic sectors. The primary goal of the Trump administration in the NAFTA negotiations is to reduce America's trade deficit with Canada and Mexico and to remove NAFTA's system of independent arbitration. While getting tough on trade may play well politically in areas hit hard by the loss of manufacturing jobs, any effort to withdraw or renegotiate NAFTA that serves to reduce the trade deficit will likely harm U.S. business, especially manufacturing and agriculture, and result in the loss of U.S. jobs. The automotive industry, for example, relies heavily on a global supply chain. Before NAFTA, vehicles imported from Mexico had only 5 percent U.S. content, whereas today they have 40 percent U.S. content. Repealing NAFTA and instituting a 35 percent tariff, as Trump has threatened, would result in a loss of at least 35,000 jobs (Muller, 2017).[21] In addition, the Farm Bureau notes that 30 percent of all U.S. agricultural exports are to NAFTA members and that ending the agreement would devastate the US farm economy (Farm Bureau, 2017).[22] Across the U.S. economy, some thirteen million jobs depend on NAFTA.

CONCLUSION

The Trump administration has embarked on a new path in U.S. international economic relations. By focusing on the trade deficit and viewing trade as a zero-sum game, using the tools of economic statecraft against U.S. allies, preferring bilateral trade agreements, and acting outside of international institutions, Trump has greatly changed America's role from that of free trade advocate to trade skeptic. Trump's increasing reliance on tariffs to reduce bilateral trade deficits, with the hope of gaining trade concessions, is evidence of an increasingly neomercantilist America. Moreover, each tariff Trump imposes meets with retaliation, and every threat he makes triggers retaliatory threats from those he threatens.

Yet, it is important to note that Trump's rhetoric on trade has somewhat differed from the actions of his administration. In many cases, Trump has failed to follow through on his campaign promises and threats while in office. He did not declare China a currency manipulator, nor has he implemented several of the tariffs that he threatened. Moreover, although its name was changed, NAFTA was successfully renegotiated in late 2018. Aside from withdrawing from TPP – a major event – and a handful of tariffs, the world continues to watch and wait for Trump to increase protectionism. Inasmuch as the performance of America's economy in 2017 and early 2018 has been the greatest source of Trump's self-congratulatory rhetoric, undertaking actions in trade that might worsen the economy may be a bridge too far, even for this president.

ESSAY QUESTIONS

1) Describe and discuss the causes of the 2008 Great Recession. What effect has the Great Recession had on real wages and public opinion?

2) What is "economic nationalism"? Specifically, how do trade deficits and tariffs relate to this idea?

3) What are the benefits of multilateralism in trade and investment? What are the costs? What are the costs of the U.S. leaving multilateral trade agreements and international institutions?

4) What is the relationship between trade and employment? Given this relationship, what explains public opinion about the net costs/benefits of trade?

5) How do trade deficits affect the U.S. economy? What are the causes for bilateral trade deficits?

SHORT ANSWER QUESTIONS

Define and describe the importance of the following:

Global supply chain
Multilateralism
Neomercantilism
Trade deficit
Trans-Pacific Partnership

NOTES

1 Piketty, T. and Saez, E. (2003). Income Inequality in the United States: 1913–1998. *Quarterly Journal of Economics*, 118:1, pp. 1–41. Wealth inequality figures from Saez, E. and Zucman, G. (2016). Wealth Inequality in the United States since 1913: Evidence from Capitalized Income Tax Data. *Quarterly Journal of Economics*, 131:2, pp. 519–578.

2 Saez, E. (2016). Striking it Richer: The evolution of top incomes in the United States. Available at: https://eml.berkeley.edu/~saez/saez-UStopincomes-2015.pdf [Accessed 3 Feb 2018].

3 Chinn, M.D. and Frieden, J.A. (2011). *Lost Decades: The making of America's debt crisis and the long recovery*. New York: W.W. Norton, pp. 3–4.

4 The Chicago Council on Global Affairs (2009). Anxious Americans Seek a New Direction in United States Foreign Policy. Available at: www.thechicagocouncil.org/sites/default/files/2008%20Public%20Opinion%202008_US%20Survey%20Results.pdf [Accessed 2 Feb 2018].

5 Smeltz, D., Daalder, I., Friedhoff, K., and Kafura, C. (2016). America in the Age of Uncertainty: American public opinion and US foreign policy. Chicago: The Chicago Council on

Global Affairs. Available at: www.thechicagocouncil.org/sites/default/files/ccgasurvey2016_america_age_uncertainty.pdf [Accessed 2 Feb 2018].

6   Saez, E. (2016). Income and Wealth Inequality: Evidence and policy implications. Available at: https://eml.berkeley.edu/~saez/SaezCEP2017.pdf [Accessed 3 Feb 2018].

7   Werner, E., Long, H., and Lynch, D. (2018). GOP Lawmakers Condemn Trump's Tariff Decision. *Washington Post* [online]. Available at: www.washingtonpost.com/business/economy/gop-lawmakers-condemn-trumps-tariff-decision/2018/01/24/e01ee876-0139-11e8-8acf-ad2991367d9d_story.html [Accessed 3 Feb 2019].

8   Eavis, P. (2018). How Companies Are Making Customers Pay for Trump's Trade War. *New York Times* [online]. Available at: www.nytimes.com/2018/07/30/business/dealbook/trade-war-customers-pay.html [Accessed 30 Jul 2018].

9   Graceffo, A. (2017). Trump's New Protectionism: Economic and strategic impact. *Foreign Policy Journal*. Available at: www.foreignpolicyjournal.com/2017/02/01/trumps-new-protectionism-economic-and-strategic-impact [Accessed 3 Feb 2018].

10   Appelbaum, B. (2016). On Trade, Donald Trump Breaks with 200 Years of Economic Orthodoxy. *New York Times* [online]. Available at: www.nytimes.com/2016/03/11/us/politics/-trade-donald-trump-breaks-200-years-economic-orthodoxy-mercantilism.html [Accessed: 3 Feb 2018].

11   Xing, Y. and Detert, N. (2010). How the iPhone Widens the United States Trade Deficit with the People's Republic of China. ABDI Working Paper (257). Available at: www.adb.org/sites/default/files/publication/156112/adbi-wp257.pdf [Accessed 3 Feb 2018].

12   McDermott, N. (2016). Trump in 1989: Tough Press Coverage Doesn't Bother Me Anymore. *CNN* [online]. Available at: http://money.cnn.com/2016/10/18/media/trump-on-morton-downey-jr/index.html [Accessed 4 Feb 2018]. See also Porter, E. (2017). Why the Trade Deficit Matters, and What Trump Can Do About It. *New York Times* [online]. Available at: www.nytimes.com/2017/10/17/business/economy/trade-deficits-nafta.html [Accessed 4 Feb 2018].

13   SEIA (2018). President's Decision on Solar Tariffs is a Loss for America. Solar Energy Industries Association Press Release. Available at: www.seia.org/news/presidents-decision-solar-tariffs-loss-america [Accessed 4 Feb 2018].

14   Lake, D. (2009). *Hierarchy in International Relations*. Ithaca, NY: Cornell University Press; Nieman, M. (2016). The return on social bonds: Social hierarchy and international conflict. *Journal of Peace Research*, 53:5, pp. 665–679.

15   Office of the United States Trade Representative (2017). The President's 2017 Trade Policy Agenda. Available at: https://ustr.gov/sites/default/files/files/reports/2017/Annual-Report/Chapter%20I%20-%20The%20President%27s%20Trade%20Policy%20Agenda.pdf [Accessed 3 Feb 2018].

16   *The Economist* (2017). China and Currency Manipulation [online]. Available at: www.economist.com/news/finance-and-economics/21717997-government-has-been-pushing-price-yuan-up-not-down-china-and [Accessed 2 Feb 2018].

17   Wade, R. (2002). U.S. Hegemony and the World Bank: The fight over people and ideas. *Review of International Political Economy* 9:2, pp. 201–229.

18   Swanson, A. (2017). Once the WTO's Biggest Supporter, U.S. Now Is Its Biggest Skeptic. *New York Times* [online]. Available at: www.nytimes.com/2017/12/10/business/wto-united-states-trade.html [Accessed 3 Jul 2018].

19   Chon, G. (2017). Trump's Criticism of W.T.O. Hurts America First. *New York Times* [online]. Available at: www.nytimes.com/2017/12/11/business/dealbook/wto-trump.html [Accessed 4 Feb 2018].

20   Behsudi, A. (2017). Trump's Trade Pullout Roils Rural America. *Politico Magazine*. Available at: www.politico.com/magazine/story/2017/08/07/trump-tpp-deal-withdrawal-trade-effects-215459 [Accessed 5 Feb 2018].

21   Muller, J. (2017). How Trump's Protectionism Would Destroy Auto Industry Jobs, Not Create Them. *Forbes Magazine* [online]. Available at: www.forbes.com/sites/joannmuller/2017/01/20/how-trumps-protectionism-would-destroy-auto-industry-jobs-not-create-them/#2182ee939b32 [Accessed 4 Feb 2018].

22   Farm Bureau (2017). Importance of NAFTA to Agriculture in Each State for 2016. Available at: www.fb.org/market-intel/importance-of-nafta-to-agriculture-in-each-state-for-2016 [Accessed 4 Feb 2018].

SUGGESTED READINGS

Chinn, M.D. and Frieden J.A. (2011). *Lost Decades: The making of America's debt crisis and the long recovery.* New York: W.W. Norton.
Wade, R. (2002). U.S. Hegemony and the World Bank: The fight over people and ideas. *Review of International Political Economy* 9:2, pp. 201–229.

Part IV

Conclusions

16 Prospects for America: An eroding global order and American decline?

Richard W. Mansbach and James M. McCormick

INTRODUCTION

Preceding chapters have noted how President Donald Trump's demagogic, transactional style have undermined America's leadership, and the liberal global order that Washington helped establish after World War II. Indeed, U.S. officials and legislators routinely advise allies not to pay attention to Trump's frequently contradictory tweets. As noted in the Munich Security Report: "Trump's 'transactionalist' understanding of world politics and promotion of 'America First'" contradicts America's former commitment to serve as a 'benign hegemon'" (Munich Security Conference, 2018: 8).[1] Trump endorses what Adam Posen calls the "widespread but misguided belief that the United States provides global public goods while others free-ride," and that "the global system has played American voters for fools" (Posen, 2018: 29–30).[2]

HEGEMONIC RETREAT AND THE LIBERAL GLOBAL ORDER

President Trump's withdrawal from the TTP, the Paris Climate Accord, and his criticism of multilateral trade agreements and U.S. allies have ceded leadership in these areas to "rising" China. America's absence from the negotiating table regarding Syria, along with Trump's reluctance to criticize Moscow, have facilitated Russian efforts to regain its great power status. "America first" fosters unilateralism and may produce an "illiberal global system." China and Russia "will try to promote their own order in what they see as their spheres of influence," producing a "'multi-order world'" (Munich Security Conference, 2018: 9).[1] Unlike his predecessors who viewed spreading democracy and human rights as U.S. obligations, Trump sees these as challenging the realization of America's interests that reflect heightened nationalism, itself a global trend. And, the president's preference for "strong" leaders have eroded Washington's opposition to dictators such as Xi Jinping, Vladimir Putin, Abdel Fattah el-Sisi, Recep Tayyip Erdoğan, and perhaps Kim Jong-un.

President Trump's foreign policies and his tweets insulting allied leaders including Germany's Chancellor Angela Merkel and the United Kingdom (UK)'s Prime Minister Theresa May have produced a dramatic reduction in U.S. popularity, diminishing its soft power and capacity to exercise leadership.

Just 30 percent of people interviewed in 134 countries last year [2017] approved of American leadership under Mr. Trump, a drop of nearly 20 percentage points since President Barack Obama's final year and the lowest finding since the Gallup polling organization began asking the question overseas more than a decade ago. The decline was especially steep in Latin America, Europe and Canada.

(Cited in Baker, 2018)[3]

As Gallup's Jon Clifton concludes, "It makes it more challenging to lead when people are this down on your leadership" (cited in Baker, 2018).[3]

Institutions and individuals

The foreign-policy institutions and the individuals filling them have also changed during the Trump administration. During its first year, the Trump administration lost more personnel than the five previous administrations – three times more than the Obama administration and twice that of the Reagan and George W. Bush administrations. Over half of the top White House advisers had left by May 2018, including Reince Priebus, chief of staff; economic adviser Gary Cohn; and Michael Flynn and H.R. McMaster, the first and second national security advisers.

John Bolton, whose bellicosity and attacks on the UN while America's UN ambassador earned widespread criticism, replaced McMaster in March 2018. Bolton replaced several national security officials with his supporters during his first weeks in office. After Trump withdrew from the Iran deal, Bolton, who had opposed it before joining the administration, declared: "It sends a very clear signal that the United States will not accept inadequate deals" (cited in Gearan, 2018).[4]

Further, after subjecting Secretary of State Tillerson to humiliating criticism, Trump replaced him with hawkish CIA Director Mike Pompeo. Many key foreign policy positions remained unfilled after eighteen months, and, in many cases, no one had been nominated to fill them. With Tillerson and McMaster gone, observers believe Trump "feels" that Bolton and Pompeo "will finally deliver the foreign policy the president wants" on Iran and North Korea (cited in Sargent, 2018).[5] These personnel changes doomed the Iran nuclear agreement, but Pompeo had two clandestine meetings with Kim Jong-un to arrange a meeting between Kim and Trump in in June 2018. In the off-and-on-again decisions about the meeting, Bolton apparently opposed Trump's decision to meet Kim, and Pompeo advised the president not to permit Bolton to attend a meeting with a North Korean emissary. Bolton, however, bypassed traditional policymaking processes advocated by John Kelly in not calling a National Security Council (NSC) meeting before Trump's summit with Kim.

President Trump has sought to shape the foreign-policy institutions to implement "America First," but he has not clarified the details of his policies. Recent policy statements by the NSC, the intelligence community, and the defense department, however, provide a window into the tasks and dangers ahead.

According to the administration's National Security Strategy (NSS), a yearly congressionally mandated statement about the direction of U.S. foreign policy, America faces "three main sets of challengers – the revisionist powers of China and Russia, the rogue states of Iran and North Korea, and the transnational threat organizations, particularly jihadist terrorist groups." Thus, "Inter-state strategic competition, not terrorism, is now the primary concern in U.S. national security" (Department of Defense, 2018: 1).[6] The reference to China and Russia, quickly brought objections from these states. A Chinese official described the National Security Strategy as "outdated, zero-sum thinking," and a Russian official declared that it reflected America's continuing "aversion to the multipolar world" (cited in Kramer, 2017).[7] However, U.S. protectionism is likely to push its allies into closer economic relations with China and Russia, identified by the NSS as America's leading rivals.

China

President Trump has sought a warm personal relationship with China's President Xi, and he sought Beijing's help in confronting North Korea's nuclear ambitions. However, Trump's efforts to reduce America's trade deficit with China is testing the relationship. China's economy will soon become the world's largest. Its military budget ranks second globally and is growing with an eye toward reducing U.S. influence in the Pacific. The NSS argues that Beijing "is using economic inducements and penalties, influence operations, and implied military threats to persuade other states to heed its political and security agenda" (White House, 2017: 46).[8] However, if China's economy shrinks Beijing may initiate risky foreign ventures to minimize domestic unrest, and the continued rise of China may produce the "Thucydides trap" between the U.S. and China with profound consequences for global politics (Allison, 2017).[9] The U.S. intelligence community also concludes that China poses a growing military threat owing to the modernization of its nuclear missile force, its development of an hypersonic glide vehicle, and its deployment of a new generation of submarines that give Beijing a long-range, sea-based nuclear capability (Coats, 2018: 7, 18).[10] China's vast "Belt and Road" investments will foster geopolitical objectives, and its neighbors contest its vast maritime territorial claims. Those claims also risk a confrontation with America.

In several respects, President Trump has ceded Washington's leadership to China, notably on promoting free trade and addressing climate change, and has allowed Beijing to surpass the U.S. in key technologies like quantum computing. The Trump administration threatened and then imposed steep tariffs on Chinese imports, especially its high-tech products, thereby emphasizing Beijing's theft of U.S. technology. In turn, China threatened to retaliate against U.S. imports including agricultural products from politically sensitive Midwest states. Whether the Trump administration will ultimately have success in halting the theft of intellectual property and technology, reducing the trade deficit, and regaining leadership in these other areas remain uncertain.

Russia

Russia, too, remains a central concern for America. Richard Haass notes that "Russia is no longer a superpower, but . . . it remains one of two major nuclear-weapons states, has a permanent seat on the UN Security Council and is willing to use its military, energy and cyber-capabilities to support friends and weaken neighbors and adversaries" (Haass, 2018).[11] Russian leaders seek to regain the status their country enjoyed during the Cold War and demand to be consulted on major issues.

Ukraine remains a contentious issue in U.S.-Russian relations. Ukraine has failed to end domestic corruption and may experience renewed domestic unrest as it approaches elections in 2019. On the ground, the current Russo-Ukrainian stalemate is likely to persist, even as Moscow seeks to destabilize Ukraine and prevent it from joining NATO or the EU, and Russia remains the target of Western sanctions owing to its intervention in Ukraine. One scholar concludes that Russia's "annexation of Crimea responded to people's dormant phantom pains for the lost empire . . . . Crimea is an imperial territory, both culturally and historically. That's precisely why most Russians see its annexation as the restoration of historical justice" (Kolesnikov, 2018).[12]

Russian ambitions extend beyond Europe. Its presence in the strategically important Arctic, its intervention in Syria, and its role in aiding the Assad regime reflect Moscow's growing global involvement. Moscow has established strong ties with China, and has blatantly violated UN sanctions on North Korea by providing banned materials, employing its workers, and exporting oil to Pyongyang. Moscow has also extended its reach to the Western Hemisphere by aiding the bankrupt Venezuelan regime.

Trump repeatedly ignores warnings from advisers regarding policy toward Russia. Notwithstanding Trump's infatuation with Putin, Moscow remains a dangerous rival, and Washington recognizes this. "Russia has violated the borders of nearby nations and pursues veto power over the economic, diplomatic, and security decisions of its neighbors" (White House, 2017: 1)[8]. According to one prediction (Coats, 2018: 23):[10]

> President Vladimir Putin will rely on assertive and opportunistic foreign policies to shape outcomes beyond Russia's borders. . . . Moscow will seek cooperation with the United States in areas that advance its interests. Simultaneously, Moscow will employ a variety of aggressive tactics to bolster its standing as a great power, secure a "sphere of influence" in the post-Soviet space, weaken the United States, and undermine Euro-Atlantic unity.

Russia will also continue trying to influence U.S. politics, and will employ cyberespionage and limited and deniable military force.

Owing to Russia's pro-Trump intrusion in America's 2016 elections and ensuing investigations, Congress has made it difficult for Trump to negotiate with Moscow. Trump views allegations of Russian interference in U.S. elections as efforts to delegitimize his electoral triumph. Instead of acting vigorously against Russian information warfare in U.S. politics, he called the Russian enquiry "a witch hunt," assailing the special counsel as well as the FBI and CIA, which have confirmed Russia's involvement. He describes suspicions of collusion between his campaign and Russia as a politically motivated "hit job" by Democrats to explain their electoral defeat. Perhaps most startling was Trump's claim after meeting Putin in Helsinki that he questions the well-documented findings of seven U.S. federal and congressional entities that Putin's Russia had interfered in America's 2016 election to foster Trump's election.

Nevertheless, Congress legislated sanctions on Russia in August 2017 over its electoral intervention that were subsequently implemented by the administration, albeit reluctantly. Nevertheless, negotiations are necessary, and after the Helsinki summit, Washington may open a dialogue with Moscow on issues of mutual concern like arms control, Syria, and Ukraine despite congressional opposition. At Helsinki, Trump and Putin may have agreed to negotiate the continuation (or revision) of the New START Treaty, which is supposed to expire in 2021, as well as the Intermediate Nuclear Force Treaty that Washington and Moscow accuse each other of violating. Thus, these may be additional new approaches to arms control with Russia, especially to avoid another nuclear arms race between the two countries. After the smoke clears, we may find out whether the Trump-Putin summit in Helsinki reduces Russo-American differences, was a disaster for Trump, or simply provided Putin with a photo opportunity to enhance his domestic support.

Europe

America's ties with its European allies have frayed, and the relationship will need repair in coming years. Trump's initial reluctance to commit himself to NATO's Article 5 and his criticisms of the EU frightened Europeans even though the president later endorsed America's commitment to NATO. At his urging, Europeans are increasing defense expenditures and have begun to make progress toward a goal for alliance members to spend at least two percent of gross domestic product on defense by 2024. Nevertheless, European publics remain skeptical of Trump's foreign policy. A poll of the German public, for example, revealed that they see Trump as a bigger foreign-policy challenge than the leaders of Russia, North Korea, or Turkey (Mischke, 2017).[13]

To reassure America's allies after Russia invaded Ukraine in 2014, the Obama administration introduced the European Reassurance Initiative (ERI), using funds that it originally intended to fight terrorism ("Overseas Contingency Operations"). To date, Washington has spent or planned to spend $10 billion on the ERI, and the Trump administration increased its budget by $1.5 billion for 2018 (Posen, 2018: 22).[2] ERI is part of a multiyear program, which will pay for military exercises in Eastern Europe, military infrastructure in that region, equipment for Ukraine, and equipment in Europe for a U.S. armored division if necessary.

Optimists point to the sweeping electoral triumph of EU-enthusiast and liberal President Emmanuel Macron over Marine Le Pen's populist followers. Macron declared: "Our relationship with the United States is absolutely critical, in fact. Fundamental. We need it" (cited in Rubin and Nossiter, 2018).[14] Reflecting unease about Trump's commitment to Europe's defense, Macron, however, sought to establish a European coalition for military cooperation outside NATO that would include post-Brexit UK, Germany, and Estonia, which abuts Russia (Taylor, 2018).[15]

European leaders, notably Macron and Merkel, have sought with little success to temper Trump's national populism. In a speech to Congress in April 2018, Macron took issue with several of Trump's policies, and spoke of the need to oppose "isolationism, withdrawal and nationalism," which "requires more than ever the United States' involvement. . . . The United States is the one who invented this multilateralism; you are the one who has to help to preserve and reinvent it." He opposed Trump's withdrawal from the Paris Climate Agreement, declaring, "we must find a transition to a low-carbon economy," and Trump's trade policy by emphasizing the need to use the World Trade Organization (WTO). Finally, he restated his support for the Iran nuclear deal. "There is an existing framework, the JCPOA [Joint Comprehensive Plan of Action] to control the activity of Iran. We signed it, at the initiative of the United States. We signed it, both the United States and France. That is why we cannot say we should get rid of it like that" (cited in DeYoung, 2018).[16]

However, Macron was unable to alter Trump's populist views, and Trump's decision to cancel the Iran nuclear deal, President Obama's most significant foreign-policy achievement, further divided America and its allies, which continued supporting it. With no evidence that Iran was violating its commitment, Trump declared: "We cannot prevent an Iranian nuclear bomb under the decaying and rotten structure of the current agreement" (cited in Tharoor, 2018).[17] Indeed, Trump's decision may facilitate Iranian secret development of nuclear weapons because it may end the International Atomic Energy Agency's access to Iranian nuclear sites. America's European allies along with Russia and China are seeking to negotiate changes to rescue the Iran agreement despite Trump's stance.

The emergence of European populism also exacerbates divisions in the European Union. Although Macron's electoral victory in France suggested that the populist wave had ebbed, the Brexit referendum in the UK and elections in Germany and Italy suggested otherwise. The Brexit majority attracted voters similar to those who had elected Trump. In Germany, elections in September 2017 saw dramatic losses by Merkel's Christian Democratic Party and the Social Democratic Party, which subsequently formed a coalition government. The election witnessed the emergence of the right-wing Alternative for Germany as the leading parliamentary opposition. In Italy in March 2018 two right-wing populist parties, the Five Star Movement and the League triumphed, and in May 2018, this coalition, which opposes the euro, formed the new government.

Latin America

The most visible and disturbing aspect of the Trump administration's policy toward Latin America were his denunciation of Mexican immigrants as "drug dealers, criminal and rapists." His heated rhetoric, demands for a wall, dispatch of troops to the border, and efforts to deport "dreamers" who had entered the U.S. as children have soured relations with Mexico and much of Latin America.

As had been the case for past administrations, the Trump administration has taken Latin America for granted and has not paid sufficient attention to the region. Nevertheless, America's NSS (White House, 2017: 51)[8] suggests that serious challenges exist in the region, including transnational criminal groups that "perpetuate violence and corruption, and threaten the stability of Central American states," and "the Venezuelan and Cuban governments that cling to anachronistic leftist authoritarian models." Moreover, major U.S. rivals are now involved in the region. "China seeks to pull the region into its orbit through state-led investments and loans . . . . Both China and Russia support the dictatorship in Venezuela and are seeking to expand military linkages and arms sales across the region." Although the administration has imposed sanctions on Venezuela and downgraded ties with Cuba initiated by the Obama administration, its policy has remained largely directed at reducing immigration from the region. Hence, a broader and more inclusive strategy toward this historically important region needs to be developed.

The Middle East

One analyst calls the Middle East "the most unstable part of the world," and points to "local realities, along with a mixture of American acts of commission and omission, of action and reaction," as the source (Haass, 2017: 175).[18] Although America remains the most powerful actor in the region, the Trump administration's policies and actions have eroded Washington's moral authority and reduced the prospect for resolving lingering conflicts. Regarding the Palestinian-Israeli imbroglio, Trump tilted toward Israel's hard-line right-wingers, notably in its decision to recognize Jerusalem as Israel's capital. Key allies in Europe and the Middle East including the UK, France, and Germany criticized Trump's decision as "dangerous" and "irresponsible" (Noack, 2017).[19] American policies have also exacerbated differences among Sunni and Shia Arabs and deepened differences between Iran and its Sunni adversaries. Trump's decision to withdraw from the 2015 Iran nuclear deal met united opposition from all the other parties to the agreement ranging from Germany to Russia, albeit cheered by Israel and Saudi Arabia. The administration's sole achievement in the region to date was the eviction of IS from Iraq and Syria, albeit aided by Russian and Iranian intervention in Syria and Iraq.

The Trump administration has lacked a clear strategy in the Middle East. The president has focused on keeping his campaign promises of supporting Israel, defeating IS, and withdrawing from the Iran agreement. The lack of an overall strategy was evident when President Trump announced his decision in April 2018 to withdraw U.S. troops from Syria "very soon," and then reversed this within days. This was a retreat from Trump's efforts to minimize America's foreign entanglements. Indeed, he dispatched additional troops to Afghanistan to fight a war he had said he would end. Even when the administration launched a missile attack on Syria after its use of chemical weapons in April 2018, there was little follow-up except to warn against future use of such weapons. Commenting on the rapid changes in policy, one scholar noted, "Trump seems to think that if he accepts what his advisers recommend on even days of the month and rejects their recommendations on odd days, the result will be a strategy" (cited in Baker, 2018).[20] Moscow and Tehran have achieved their objective of keeping Bashar al-Assad in power, while Washington was not involved in negotiations to bring peace to Syria.

The NSS identifies Iran as a rogue state that threatens America. Its regime, the strategy notes, "sponsors terrorism around the world. It is developing more capable ballistic missiles and has the potential to resume its work on nuclear weapons that could threat the United States and our partners" (White House, 2017: 26).[8] The Worldwide Threat Assessment (Coats, 2018: 19)[10] echoes this, albeit with greater specificity. "Iran will seek to expand its influence in Iraq, Syria, and Yemen, where it sees conflicts generally trending in Tehran's favor, and it will exploit the fight against IS to solidify partnerships and translate its battlefield gains into political, security, and economic agreements," and "will develop military capabilities that threaten US forces and US allies in the region." Its ballistic missiles constitute a threat to U.S. installations and allies throughout the region, which could become more dangerous if it resumes developing nuclear weapons in response to American withdrawal from the nuclear deal. Moreover, its naval capabilities in the Red Sea threaten America's ability to protect the oil-rich Arab states in that area.

Tehran's support for Shia militias threatens U.S. forces in Syria and Iraq, and Iran is working to force American forces to leave the region. The Iranian presence in Syria also threaten Israel and may trigger a serious Israeli-Iranian military confrontation, similar to the military incidents in the Golan Heights in May 2018. While supporting Assad, Iran also seeks economic benefits from rebuilding Syria. Iranian support of the Houthis in Yemen's civil war also threatens U.S. access to the Red Sea and East Africa, while challenging Saudi Arabia's regional influence.

Nuclear proliferation and arms races

The Trump administration seeks modernization of the nuclear triad – land-based, sea-based, and long-range bombers (Posen, 2018: 25).[2] This policy directive, while more extensive than Obama's, builds on the proposal announced by the previous administration in 2014. The Trump administration also sought a significant increase in defense spending (about $700 billion for FY2018). The request includes production of low-yield nuclear weapons that critics fear Washington might use in a conventional or cyber-conflict.

Nuclear weapons are so destructive that decision-makers are unlikely to resort to them except in retaliation for an enemy's nuclear first strike. Trump's policy was announced shortly after the Obama-era Russo-American New START Treaty went into effect. The Trump administration has shown some interest in extending the agreement beyond 2021, and "remains willing to engage in a prudent arms control agenda," according to the administration's Nuclear Posture Review (Office of the Secretary of Defense, 2018).[21]

> Risking a new nuclear arms race, as is now likely and would be even more so should New START be allowed to expire without a replacement in hand, would divert American resources away from our conventional advantage, and bring us no additional security. It would also repeat the great mistakes of the Cold War when we learned that arms races and nuclear wars cannot be won, and are better left unfought.
>
> (Wolfsthal, 2018)[22]

The Worldwide Threat Assessment (Coats, 2018: 7)[10] concludes: "State efforts to modernize, develop, or acquire weapons of mass destruction (WMD), their delivery systems, or their underlying technologies constitute a major threat to the security of the United States, its deployed troops, and its allies." It notes the use of chemical weapons in Syria and the dissemination of knowledge about chemical and biological weapons to other states as well as terrorists. It also cites the threat posed by Russia's military modernization that Washington claims violates the INF Treaty: "Russia has developed a ground-launched cruise missile (GLCM) that the United States has declared is in violation of the Intermediate-Range Nuclear Forces (INF) Treaty. . . . Moscow probably believes that the new GLCM provides sufficient military advantages to make it worth risking the political repercussions of violating the INF Treaty" (Coats 2018: 7).[10]

North Korea's nuclear weapons and intercontinental missiles remains the world's most dangerous WMD proliferation. America's NSS calls for a global response to North Korea's provocations, which it regards as a global threat. It concludes that North Korea's retention of nuclear weapons could trigger additional proliferation in "the Indo-Pacific region."

A meeting between Kim Jong-un and South Korean President Moon Jae-in led to Kim's offer to meet with Trump. The two Korean leaders declared that they sought "denuclearization" of the Korean peninsula (without clearly defining the term). Kim's comments about allowing U.S. troops to remain in South Korea and his willingness to end nuclear tests and possibly surrender nuclear weapon if the U.S. signs a formal peace treaty to end the Korean War and assures Pyongyang that it will not seek regime change were hopeful. However, Kim later denied he was willing to give up his country's nuclear weapons.

However, in a sudden shift, Trump canceled the meeting with Kim, "based on the tremendous anger and open hostility displayed in your most recent statement." Trump was apparently referring to a comment of a North Korean official who called Vice President

Mike Pence "ignorant and stupid." Pence had declared that relations with North Korea "will only end like the Libyan model ended if Kim Jong-un doesn't make a deal," that is, regime change. A day later, however, Trump said that the U.S. had received a positive note from the North Koreans, and the meeting would take place, and the White House announced that the Singapore meeting of June 12 was back on schedule.

The meeting itself was cordial and President Trump declared that the two leaders had signed a "comprehensive agreement" in which Kim would act to end its nuclear-weapons program and Washington would halt joint military exercises with South Korea. In reality, the agreement was short on detail, and U.S.-North Korean negotiations will be lengthy, and a war caused by misperception remains possible. One potentially negative consequence of the Trump-Kim meeting may be divisions between the U.S. and its East Asian allies. Japan is geographically close to North Korea and fears that a deal which eliminated Pyongyang's ICBM threat to America and/or a U.S. retreat from East Asia would leave Japan and South Korea alone to face shorter-range North Korean nuclear-armed missiles.

America's threat assessment also notes that Tehran wants to retain the Iran deal in order to get sanctions removed. However, it "recognizes that the U.S. Administration has concerns about the deal" but claims that the agreement "has extended the amount of time Iran would need to produce enough fissile material for a nuclear weapon from a few months to about one year." The deal "has also enhanced the transparency of Iran's nuclear activities, mainly by fostering improved access to Iranian nuclear facilities for the IAEA and its investigative authorities under the Additional Protocol to its Comprehensive Safeguards Agreement" (Coats, 2018: 8).[10] Nevertheless, as noted above, Trump abrogated the agreement and announced that it will reinstate sanctions and impose new ones on Iran's Central Bank to pressure Tehran to revise the agreement.

Climate change

Despite Trump's description of global warming as a hoax, and removal of America from the Paris Climate Accord, the Worldwide Threat Assessment predicted: "The impacts of the long-term trends toward a warming climate, more air pollution, biodiversity loss, and water scarcity are likely to fuel economic and social discontent – and possibly upheaval – through 2018" (Coats, 2018: 16).[10] The Navy's chief civil engineer identified rising oceans as a security threat. In 2009, the Department of Defense (DOD) identified 128 U.S. coastal installations including 56 naval sites valued at $100 billion that would be at risk by rising sea levels, as would numerous overseas naval facilities. The Arctic, too, is becoming a source of U.S.-Russian competition owing to melting ice and growing Russian military and commercial presence there. Defense Secretary Mattis called climate change "a driver of instability" and continued the policy begun in the Obama years of reporting which of its military assets were threatened by global warming.

The U.S. Climate Assessment describes the threats of climate change to all aspects of American life (Mooney, 2018),[23] and the Munich Security Report (Munich Security Conference, 2018: 46)[1] vividly outlined the issue:

> The year 2017 was one of the three hottest on record . . . . Critics warn that political progress toward a more sustainable future is far too slow as many parts of the world are already suffering from the devastating consequences of climate change

and environmental degradation. . . . Since the United States had pledged emission cuts amounting to some 20 percent of all cuts agreed upon in the Paris Agreement, President Trump's decision [to withdraw] has major consequences. . . . As the Trump administration embarked on its lonely path . . . it seems that the leadership gap might be filled by unexpected actors: China, the world's number one polluter, announced plans for an ambitious carbon emissions trading scheme . . . numerous US states, cities, and corporations pledged their continued support for efforts to combat climate change.

Terrorism

The intelligence community's Worldwide Threat Assessment declares that "Sunni violent extremism – most notably IS and al-Qa'ida – pose continuing terrorist threats to US interests and partners worldwide, while US-based homegrown violent extremists (HVEs) will remain the most prevalent Sunni violent extremist threat in the United States." It also contends that Iran and Hezbollah pose a "persistent threat" to America and its friends worldwide (Coats, 2018, 9).[10] The NSS notes that "the United States continues to wage a long war against jihadist terrorist groups," but "the threat from jihadist terrorists will persist, even as we intensify efforts to prevent attacks on Americans, our allies, and our partners" (White House, 2017: 26).[8] The challenge will be to deny these groups safe havens in failed states and counter their propaganda in cyberspace (Monaco, 2017).[24]

Failed states

America's intelligence agencies believe that in Africa Nigeria and its neighbors including countries in the Sahel region continue to face Islamic terrorism and domestic secessionist movements (Coats, 2018: 26).[10] In East Africa, human-rights violations continue in South Sudan and Somalia as tribal and terrorist militias compete for control, and elsewhere the Democratic Republic of the Congo confronts ongoing civil strife and untold human-rights abuses. In South Asia, attacks by government forces on the Rohingya Muslim minority in Myanmar, and their resulting flight to Bangladesh reflect the dangers to human dignity that are prevalent on that subcontinent. In the Western Hemisphere, political instability, civil unrest, drug trafficking, and economic hardship in some Central American countries (e.g., Honduras and Guatemala) have resulted in mass migration northward.

Cyber threats

Since taking office, cyber threats have challenged the Trump's administration. Trump's cyber-agenda is dominated by Russian interference in America's 2016 elections that aimed to aid Trump, undermine democratic institutions, and exploit America's racial and religious divisions – thereby reinforcing Trump's nationalist populism. According to former NSA Director, Mike Rogers, Washington has done little to respond to Moscow's cyberwarfare, and has eliminated the position of cybersecurity coordinator on the NSC, a position crucial to developing policy to prevent cyberattacks. The indictment of thirteen Russians, including a close associate of President Putin and Director of the Internet Research Agency

(IRA), by the special counsel investigating Russian cyber-interference in U.S. elections revealed the extent Russia's cyber-campaign. The IRA established "bots," especially in social media like Facebook and Twitter, to spread misinformation.

The administration also confronts aggressive hacking, cyberattacks and cyberespionage by North Korea, Iran, and China, which pose significant threats to Americans and U.S. companies. North Korea's "WannaCry," cyberattack involved a ransomware cryptoworm that infected computers worldwide and Russia's "NotPetya" ransomware attacked Microsoft Windows-based systems, preventing Windows from booting, thereby freezing infected computers.

Other issues are linked to cyber threats. "Cybersecurity issues," declared the Munich Security Report (Munich Security Conference, 2018: 50)[1]

> have immediate ramifications for classic security topics, such as nuclear deterrence. If cyberattacks on nuclear capabilities materialize, uncertainty and poor decision-making might bring instability to an already fragile nuclear arms regime. . . . The past years have been marked by the emergence of a group of countries with superior cyber-capabilities, fundamental disagreements over norms governing cyberspace, and previously unseen levels of cybercrime activity.

The initial foremost challenge for the Trump administration in responding to cyber threats has been disorganization in the White House. Infighting among appointees and the administration's failure to fill key positions and retain qualified personnel have precluded a coherent effort to limit cyberattacks. Trump's preoccupation with investigation of alleged collusion of his campaign with Russia and his attacks on the credibility of the FBI, NSA, CIA, and Justice Department have intensified this problem. These attacks have resulted in a lack of clarity of mission and failure to coordinate cyberdefense and cyberdeterrence among these agencies. In August 2018, however, National Intelligence Director Coats and the Secretary of Homeland Security Nielsen forcefully acknowledged the continuous efforts of Russia to interfere in the American electoral process and the commitment to address them.

Looking ahead, the Worldwide Threat Assessment predicted:

> Influence operations, especially through cyber means, will remain a significant threat to US interests as they are low-cost, relatively low-risk, and deniable ways to retaliate against adversaries, to shape foreign perceptions, and to influence populations. . . . We assess that the Russian intelligence services will continue their efforts to disseminate false information . . . about US activities to encourage anti-US political views. Moscow seeks to create wedges that reduce trust and confidence in democratic processes, degrade democratization efforts, weaken US partnerships with European allies, undermine Western sanctions, encourage anti-US political views, and counter efforts to bring Ukraine and other former Soviet states into European institutions.
>
> (Coats, 2018: 11)[10]

In sum:

> The potential for surprise in the cyber realm will increase in the next year and beyond as billions more digital devices are connected – with relatively little built-in security – and both nation states and malign actors become more emboldened and better equipped

in the use of increasingly widespread cyber toolkits. . . . [However, w]e assess that concerns about US retaliation and still developing adversary capabilities will mitigate the probability of attacks aimed at causing major disruptions of US critical infrastructure, but we remain concerned by the increasingly damaging effects of cyber operations and the apparent acceptance by adversaries of collateral damage.

(Coats, 2018: 5–6)[10]

International trade

As noted earlier, President Trump knows little about economics, believing America's loss of manufacturing jobs and trade deficit are the result of "unfair" policies of trading partners rather than automation and American spending habits. As in other issues, he views trade as a zero-sum relationship.

Trump raised tariffs on washing machines and solar panels in January 2018 and dismayed free-trade advocates by placing tariffs on aluminum and steel imports in March. Steel is largely imported from U.S. allies such as the EU, Canada, South Korea, and Mexico, and there is a global surplus owing to China's subsidized overcapacity. Moreover, Washington invoked Section 232 of the 1962 Trade Expansion Act, which permits imposing trade limits if imports pose a threat to national security. The latter was questionable, especially inasmuch as U.S. allies were the sources of those imports but made it impossible for the WTO to oppose because Article 21 of the WTO Treaty permits tariffs for to be raised for "essential security interests."

Trump also threatened to impose tariffs on Chinese imports and raise tariffs on European automobiles if the EU retaliated and exempted Canada and Mexico in order to increase pressure on them to capitulate to his demands regarding NAFTA. In late May, the administration imposed 25 percent tariffs on steel imports and 10 percent tariffs on aluminum imported from the EU, Canada, and Mexico and subsequently imposed a tariffs on a series of Chinese products. These actions challenge the WTO, an institutional pillar of the liberal order and its dependence on multilateral rules and norms that benefit *all* countries. A trade war may ensue, as others retaliate and/or invoke Article 21.

CONCLUSION

Owing to President Trump's economic nationalism, his rejection of U.S. foreign-policy commitments, and his divisive style and impetuosity, America faces a difficult future in foreign affairs. As one observer put it:

Being a real estate mogul is, in a lot of ways, like being a gambler. You do your best due diligence on properties and investments, but at the end of the day you are betting on markets, the future desirability of locations and other things that are out of your control. And, you need to bet big to win big. So it's probably no surprise that Trump is taking this same approach to his presidency. But it *is* notable how increasingly big the stakes are on Trump's foreign policy – and how big the risk is that one of his gambles will shake out the wrong way.

(Blake, 2018)[25]

America is growing weaker as revisionist states challenge its leadership and the liberal order's norms and practices. America's president is largely uninformed about foreign affairs; its bureaucracies remain short of experienced foreign-policy experts; and the administration lacks a coherent strategy to cope with different regions and issues. Thus, the coming years will be dangerous.

ESSAY QUESTIONS

1) To what extent is there evidence that the Trump administration has engaged in "hegemonic retreat" from the liberal global order? Use examples from this chapter to make your argument.

2) What has been the approach of the Trump administration in dealing with China and Russia, and the challenges that each pose for American foreign policy? Are the approaches similar or different with these two states?

3) How would you characterize the current state of relations between the U.S. and its traditional allies in Europe? What are two or three issues that divide the U.S. and Europe under the Trump administration?

4) Discuss the major foreign policy actions by the Trump administration in dealing with Latin America and the Middle East. Provide at least three specific actions by the administration to support your response.

5) Select one of the functional issues discussed in the chapter (e.g., cybersecurity, terrorism, nuclear proliferation, etc.), and outline the policy response of the Trump administration to that issue.

SHORT ANSWER QUESTIONS

Define and describe the importance of the following:

National Security Strategy (NSS)
Kim Jong-un
Iran nuclear deal
Failed states
Climate change

NOTES

1   Munich Security Conference (2018). Munich Security Report: To the brink – and back? Available at: www.securityconference.de/en/discussion/munich-security-report/munich-security-report-2018 [Accessed 22 Feb 2018].
2   Posen, A. (2018). The Post-American World Economy. *Foreign Affairs* 97:2, pp. 28–38.

3   Baker, P. (2018). Souring World Views of Trump Open Doors for China and Russia, *New York Times* [online]. Available at: www.nytimes.com/2018/01/18/us/politics/global-survey-trump.html [Accessed 18 Jan 2018].

4   Gearan, A, (2018). Trump's Trust in His Gut-Driven, Out-of-the-Box Approach to International Relations Grows. *Washington Post* [online]. Available at: www.washingtonpost.com/politics/trumps-trust-grows-in-his-gut-driven-out-of-the-box-approach-to-international-relations/2018/05/09/e8c3f252-4fc0-11e8-84a0-458a1aa9ac0a_story.html [Accessed 10 May 2018].

5   Sargent, G. (2018). The Real Reason Trump's choice of John Bolton Should Terrify You. *Washington Post* [online]. Available at: www.washingtonpost.com/blogs/plum-line/wp/2018/03/23/the-real-reason-trumps-choice-of-john-bolton-should-terrify-you [accessed: 23 Mar 2018].

6   Department of Defense (2018). Summary of the 2018 National Defense Strategy of The United States of America. Available at: www.defense.gov/Portals/1/Documents/pubs/2018-National-Defense-Strategy-Summary.pdf [Accessed 27 Feb 2018].

7   Kramer, A. (2017). Russia and China Object to New 'America First' Security Doctrine. *New York Times* [online]. Available at: www.nytimes.com/2017/12/19/world/europe/russia-china-america-first-doctrine.html [Accessed 25 Apr 2018]

8   White House (2017). National Security Strategy. Available at: www.whitehouse.gov/wp-content/uploads/2017/12/NSS-Final-12-18-2017-0905.pdf [Accessed 27 Apr 2018].

9   Allison, G. (2017). China vs. America: Managing the next clash of civilization, *Foreign Affairs* 96:5, pp. 80–89.

10 Coats, D. (2018). Worldwide Threat Assessment of the US Intelligence Community. Available at: www.dni.gov/files/documents/Newsroom/Testimonies/2018-ATA–Unclassified-SSCI.pdf [Accessed 3 Mar 2018].

11 Haass, R. (2018). Cold War II. Project Syndicate. Available at: www.project-syndicate.org/commentary/new-cold-war-mainly-russia-s-fault-by-richard-n-haass-2018-02 [Accessed 27 Feb 2018].

12 Kolesnikov, A. (2018). History Is the Future: Russia in search of the lost empire. Carnegie Moscow Center. Available at: http://carnegie.ru/commentary/75544 [Accessed 30 Apr 2018].

13 Mischke, J. (2017) Germans See Trump as Bigger Challenge than Turkey or Russia. *Politico*. Available at: www.politico.eu/article/trump-germans-bigger-challenge-than-turkey-or-russia [Accessed 5 May 2018].

14 Rubin, A. and Nossiter, A. (2018). Macron Takes a Risk in Courting Trump but Has Little to Show for It. *New York Times* [online]. Available at: www.nytimes.com/2018/04/22/world/europe/donald-trump-emmanuel-macron.html [Accessed 4 May 2018].

15 Taylor, P. (2018). Emmanuel Macron's Coalition of the Willing. *Politico*. Available at: www.politico.eu/article/emmanuel-macrons-eu-defense-army-coalition-of-the-willing-military-cooperation [Accessed 4 Apr 2018].

16 DeYoung, K. (2018). French President Macron Charms Both Parties in an Impassioned Speech to Congress. *Washington Post* [online]. Available at: www.washingtonpost.com/world/national-security/french-president-macron-charms-both-parties-in-an-impassioned-speech-to-congress/2018/04/25/bbd600ba-4894-11e8-827e-190efaf1f1ee_story.html [Accessed 27 Apr 2018].

17 Tharoor, I. (2018). Trump Axes the Iran Deal and Creates a New Crisis. *Washington Post* [online]. Available at: www.washingtonpost.com/news/worldviews/wp/2018/05/09/trump-axes-the-iran-deal-and-creates-a-new-crisis [Accessed 10 May 2018].

18 Haass, R. (2017). *A World in Disarray*. New York: Penguin Books.

19 Noack, R. (2017). U.S. Allies Reject Trump's Jerusalem Pronouncement as 'Very Dangerous' and 'Catastrophic'. *Washington Post* [online]. Available at: www.washingtonpost.com/news/worldviews/wp/2017/12/06/its-catastrophic-u-s-allies-reject-trumps-expected-jerusalem-pronouncement; see also Barkin, N. and Lawson, H. (2017). Germans see Trump as Bigger Problem than North Korea or Russia. *Reuters*. Available at: www.reuters.com/article/us-usa-germany-survey/germans-see-trump-as-bigger-problem-than-north-korea-or-russia-idUSKBN1DZ0GY [Accessed 30 Apr 2018].

20 Baker, P. (2018). Trump Scraps New Sanctions Against Russia, Overruling Advisers. *New York Times* [online]. Available at: www.nytimes.com/2018/04/16/us/politics/trump-rejects-sanctions-russia-syria.html [Accessed 17 Apr 2018].

21 Office of the Secretary of Defense (2018). Nuclear Posture Review, February. Available at: https://media.defense.gov/2018/Feb/02/2001872886/-1/-1/1/2018-NUCLEAR-POSTURE-REVIEW-FINAL-REPORT.PDF (Accessed 18 Nov 2018).

22 Wolfsthal, J. (2018). Does Trump Want a Nuclear Arms Race Because Obama Didn't? *Foreign Policy* [online]. Available at: http://foreignpolicy.com/2018/02/02/does-trump-want-a-nuclear-arms-race-because-obama-didnt [Accessed 6 Feb 2018].

23 Mooney, C. (2018). The Government is Nearly Done with a Major Report on Climate Change. Trump isn't going to like it. *Washington Post* [online]. Available at: https://s2.washingtonpost.com/4c57ec/5aa7c521fe1ff62bafaa308e/bWFuc2JhY2hAaWFzdGF0ZS 5lZHU%3D/66/130/a929b82a974b52692a00653799eaa482 [Accessed 1 May 2018].

24 Monaco, L. (2017). Preventing the Next Attack. *Foreign Affairs* 96:6, pp. 23–29.

25 Blake, A. (2018). Trump's Withdrawal From the Iran Deal is Yet Another Major Foreign Policy Gamble. *Washington Post* [online]. Available at: www.washingtonpost.com/news/the-fix/wp/2018/05/08/trump-flirts-with-potential-disaster-on-the-world-stage-again [Accessed 10 May 2018].

SUGGESTED READINGS

Allison, G. (2017). China vs. America: Managing the next clash of civilization. *Foreign Affairs* 96:5, pp. 80–89.

Kagan, R. (2018). *The Jungle Grows Back*. New York: Knopf.

Posen, A.S. (2018). The Post-American World Economy. *Foreign Affairs* 97:2, pp. 28–38.

The White House (2017). *The National Security Strategy of the United States of America*. December. Washington, D.C.

Index

Note: Information in figures and tables is indicated by page numbers in *italics* and **bold**.